Lectures on Ancient Philosophy

Manly P. Hall

Must Have Books
503 Deerfield Place
Victoria, BC
V9B 6G5
Canada

ISBN: 9781773236926

Copyright 2021 – Must Have Books

All rights reserved in accordance with international law. No part of this book may be reproduced or transmitted in any form or by any means, electronic or mechanical, including photocopying, recording, or by any information storage or retrieval system, except in the case of excerpts by a reviewer who may quote brief passages in an article or review, without written permission from the publisher.

THERE IS NOTHING BETTER THAN *THOSE MYS-TERIES* BY WHICH, FROM A ROUGH AND FIERCE LIFE, WE ARE POLISHED TO GENTLENESS AND SOFTENED. AND *INITIA,* AS THEY ARE CALLED, WE HAVE THUS KNOWN AS THE *BEGINNINGS OF LIFE* IN TRUTH; NOT ONLY HAVE WE RECEIVED FROM THEM THE DOCTRINE OF LIVING WITH HAPPINESS, BUT EVEN OF *DYING WITH A BETTER HOPE.*

—CICERO

PREFACE TO THE FIRST EDITION

Although complete in itself, this book is primarily designed to complement and amplify the larger volume on *Symbolical Philosophy* published last year. During the spring and fall of 1928 I delivered two series of lectures on Symbolism and the Ancient Mysteries—one in San Francisco and the other in Los Angeles—to groups largely composed of subscribers to *An Encyclopedic Outline of Masonic, Qabbalistic and Rosicrucian Symbolical Philosophy*. These lectures were carefully taken down in shorthand, and form the basis of the present work.

A considerable portion of my larger book is devoted to the rituals and figures of the Greek Mysteries, and this treatise is an effort to clarify the subject of classical pagan metaphysics. In his *Miscellanies,* published at the beginning of the last century, Thomas Taylor, the eminent Platonist, predicted that the "sublime theology which was first obscurely promulgated by Orpheus, Pythagoras and Plato, and was afterwards perspicuously unfolded by their legitimate disciples; a theology which, though it may be involved in oblivion in *barbarous,* and derided in *impious* ages, will again flourish for very extended periods, through all the infinite revolutions of time."

Our civilization has not yet learned to value appreciation for the beautiful as the very foundation of an enduring culture. Unless we respond to the harmonious, the elegant, the symmetrical, and the rhythmic, we are recreant to past good, a menace to present integrity, and an obstacle to future effort. This truth is well made in the *Merchant of Venice*:

"The man that hath no music in himself
Nor is not moved with concord of sweet sounds,
Is fit for treasons, stratagems and spoils."

For lack of aesthetics man lives the life of a Caliban, and in death receives the reward of a Thersites. It is not enough that our codes be true; they must also be beautiful. If learning does not teach us to love, we learn without understanding. We have shackled the Titans and bound the elements to our service. Like proud Bellerophon we have bridled Pegasus, but already the gadfly of Zeus is at work. By concentrating all our energies upon temporal concerns we have builded an empire, moving each stone into place at terrific cost. We have heaped up institutions as the Pharaohs piled up pyramids, yet our monuments, like those along the Nile, shall become the tombs of their own builders. We have paid a frightful price for our boasted success, for our strength has taught us to hate, our power to kill, and our thought to reason away our souls.

We must seek for that sufficient code which guided the wise through every generation. We must again establish those perfect Mysteries through which alone, as Plato declared in the *Phaedrus*, man becomes truly perfect. Ares was burned up by his own flame, and his host of evil spirits consumed with him. Man, tired of vain wrangling and contending for power, longs for those quiet groves where olden sages communed with their familiars.

Neoplatonism forms the basis for this exposition. Never in the history of metaphysics, since that great Alexandrian day, has the mind of man contemplated so rationally and lucidly the riddle of Abiding Destiny. The fruitage of noble endeavor can never die, nor is truth to be lightly cast aside. Unmoved by the calumny of ungrateful ages and the anathemas of a bigoted theology, the Platonic philosophers sit upon their golden thrones, awaiting with philosophic patience the day when an unbelieving world shall comprehend.

MANLY PALMER HALL

Los Angeles, California, June 1, 1929.

CONTENTS

CHAPTER ONE.
    THE NATURE OF THE ABSOLUTE 1

CHAPTER TWO.
    GOD, THE DIVINE FOUNDATION 25

CHAPTER THREE.
    ILLUMINED MIND, THE UNIVERSAL SAVIOR 49

CHAPTER FOUR.
    THE INFERIOR CREATION AND ITS REGENT 73

CHAPTER FIVE.
    THE ANNIHILATION OF THE SENSE OF DIVERSITY 97

CHAPTER SIX.
    THE DISCIPLINES OF SALVATION 121

CHAPTER SEVEN.
    THE DOCTRINE OF REDEMPTION THROUGH GRACE 145

CHAPTER EIGHT.
    THE MISSION OF AESTHETICS 169

CHAPTER NINE.
    THE CYCLE OF NECESSITY 193

CHAPTER TEN.
    PAGAN THEOGONY AND COSMOGONY 217

CHAPTER ELEVEN.
    MATHEMATICS, THE MASTER SCIENCE 241

CHAPTER TWELVE.
    DEMIGODS AND SUPERMEN 265

CHAPTER THIRTEEN.
    EMERSON'S CONCEPT OF THE OVERSOUL 289

CHAPTER FOURTEEN.
    EXOTERIC AND ESOTERIC KNOWLEDGE 313

CHAPTER FIFTEEN
    SYMBOLISM, THE UNIVERSAL LANGUAGE 337

CHAPTER SIXTEEN.
    ANCIENT MYSTERY RITUALS 361

CHAPTER SEVENTEEN.
    A PHILOSOPHIC CONSIDERATION OF MAN 385

CHAPTER EIGHTEEN.
    THE LADDER OF THE GODS 409

CHAPTER NINETEEN.
    ROSICRUCIAN AND MASONIC ORIGINS 433

CHAPTER TWENTY.
    THE GOAL OF PHILOSOPHY 457

INDEX 480

About the Author 514

Books by Manly P. Hall 515

THE VOICE OF THE WORLD

"But since the generated world is a collective whole, if we apply the ears of our intellect to the world we shall, perhaps, hear it thus addressing us:

"'There is no doubt but I was produced by divinity, from whence I am formed perfect, composed from all animals, entirely sufficient to myself, and destitute of nothing; because all things are contained in my ample bosom, the nature of all generated beings, gods visible and invisible, the illustrious race of dæmons, the noble army of virtuous souls, and men rendered happy by wisdom and virtue. Nor is earth alone adorned with an endless variety of plants and animals, nor does the power of universal soul alone diffuse itself to the sea and become bounded by its circumfluent waters, while the wide expanse of air and æther is destitute of life and soul; but the celestial spaces are filled with illustrious souls, supplying life to the stars and directing their revolutions in everlasting order. Add too, that the celestial orbs, in imitation of intellect which seeks after nothing external, are wisely agitated in a perpetual circuit round the central sun. Besides, whatever I contain desires good, all things collectively considered, and particulars according to their peculiar ability; for that general soul by which I am enlivened, and the heavens, the most illustrious of my parts, continually depend on *good* for support, together with the gods which reign in my parts, every animal and plant, and whatever I contain which appears destitute of life. While some things are seen participating of being alone, others of life, and others besides this are indeed with sentient powers, some possess the still higher faculty of reason, and lastly others are all life and intelligence; for it is not proper to require every where equal things among such as are unequal, nor to expect that the finger should see, but to assign this as the province of the eye, while another purpose is desired in the finger, which can, I think, be no other than that it remains as a finger and performs its peculiar office.'" —(Plotinus *On Providence.*)

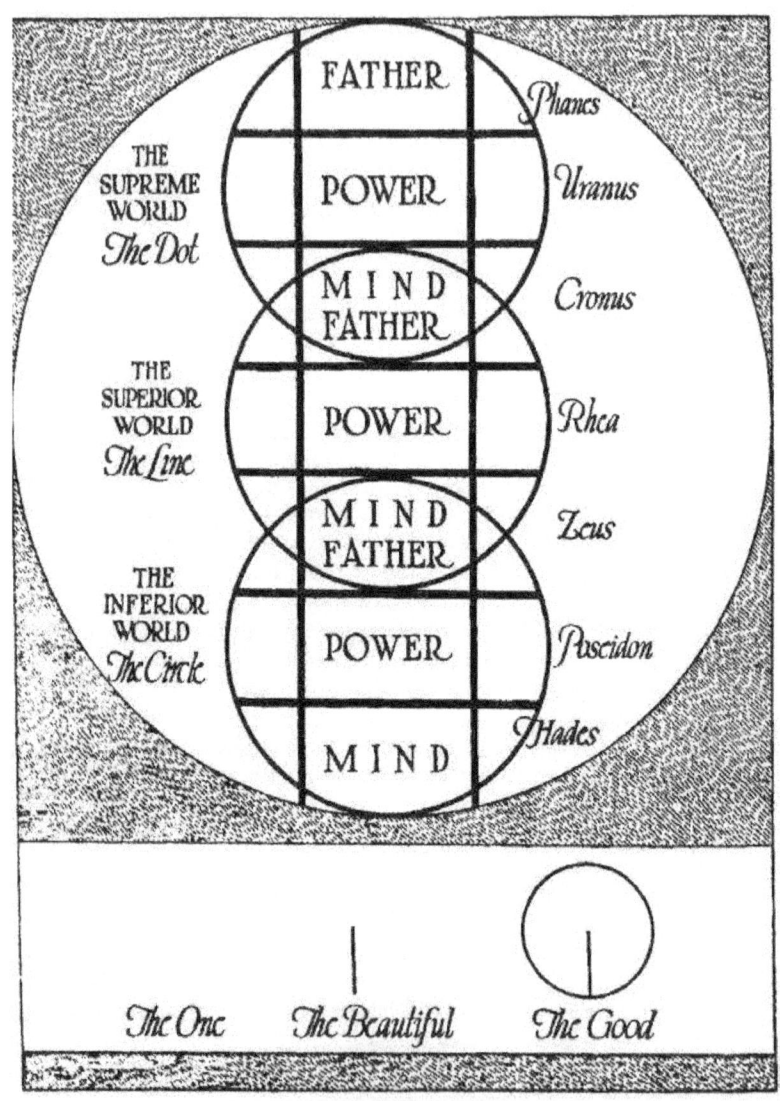

THE HOMERIC CHAIN

The order of the gods of the three worlds, grouped in Chaldean triads, is here set forth according to the doctrines of Orpheus. This mystery was concealed by the first symbolists under the figures of the dot, the line, and the circle. To the mystic, the fables of the ancients are indeed resplendent with unsuspected truths.

Lectures on Ancient Philosophy

CHAPTER ONE

THE NATURE OF THE ABSOLUTE

TO define adequately the nature of the Absolute is impossible, for it is everything in its eternal, undivided, and unconditioned state. In ancient writings it is referred to as the NOTHING and the ALL. No mind is capable of visualizing an appropriate symbolic figure of the Absolute. Of all the symbols devised to represent its eternal and unknowable state, a clean, blank sheet of paper is the least erroneous. The paper, being blank, represents all that cannot be thought of, all that cannot be seen, all that cannot be felt, and all that cannot be limited by any tangible function of consciousness. The blank paper represents measureless, eternal, unlimited SPACE. No created intelligence has ever plumbed its depths; no God has ever scaled its heights, nor shall mortal or immortal being ever discover the true nature of its substance. From it all things come, to it all things return, but it neither comes nor goes.

Figures and symbols are pollutions drawn upon the unblemished surface of the paper. The symbols, therefore, signify the conditions that exist upon the face of SPACE or, more correctly, which are produced out of the substance of SPACE. The blank sheet, being emblematic of the ALL, each of the diagrams drawn upon it signifies some fractional phase of the ALL. The moment the symbol is drawn upon the paper, the paper loses its perfect and unlimited blankness. As the symbols represent the creative agencies and substances, the philosophers have declared that when the parts of existence come into manifestation the perfect wholeness of Absolute Being is destroyed. In other words, the forms destroy the perfection of the formlessness that preceded them. Symbolism deals with universal forces and agencies. Each of these forces and agencies is an expression of SPACE, because SPACE is the ultimate of substance, the ultimate of force, and the sum of them both. Nothing exists except it exists in SPACE; nothing is made except it is made of SPACE. In Egypt Space is called TAT.

SPACE is the perfect origin of everything. It is not God; it is not Nature; it is not man; it is not the universe. All these exist in SPACE and are fashioned out of it, but SPACE is supreme. SPACE and Absolute Spirit are one; SPACE and Absolute Matter are one. Therefore SPACE, Spirit, and Matter are one. Spirit is the positive manifestation of SPACE; Matter is the negative manifestation of SPACE. Spirit and Matter exist together in SPACE. SPACE, Spirit, and Matter are the first Trinity, with SPACE the Father, Spirit the Son, and Matter the Holy Ghost. SPACE, though actually undivided, becomes through hypothetical division Absolute (or Ultimate) Spirit, Absolute (or Ultimate) Intelligence, and Absolute (or Ultimate) Matter.

The most primitive and fundamental of all symbols is the dot. Place a dot in the center of the sheet and what does it signify? Simply the ALL considered as the ONE, or first point. Unable to understand the Absolute, man gathers its incomprehensibility mentally to a focal point—the dot. The dot is the first illusion because it is the first departure from things as they eternally are—the blank sheet of paper. There is nothing immortal but SPACE, nothing eternal but SPACE, nothing without beginning or end but SPACE, nothing unchangeable but SPACE. Everything but SPACE either grows or decays, because everything that grows grows out of SPACE and everything that decays decays into SPACE. SPACE alone remains. Philosophically, SPACE is synonymous with Self (spelled with a capital S), because it is not the inferior, or more familiar, self. It is the Self which man through all eternity struggles to attain. Therefore the true Self is as abstract as the blank sheet of paper, and only he who can fathom the nature of the blank paper can discover Self.

The dot may be likened to Spirit. The Spirit is Self with the loss of limitlessness, because the dot is bound by certain limitations. *The dot is the first illusion of the Self, the first limitation of SPACE, even as Spirit is the first limitation of Self.* The dot is life localized as a center of power; the blank paper is life unlimited. According to philosophy the dot must sometime be erased, because nothing but the blank paper is eternal. The dot represents a limitation, for the life that is everywhere becomes the life that is somewhere; universal life becomes individualized life and ceases to recognize its kinship with all Being.

After the dot is placed on the paper it can be rubbed out and the white paper restored to its virgin state. Thus the white paper represents eternity, and the dot, time; and when the dot is erased time is dissolved back into eternity, for time is dependent upon eternity. Therefore in ancient philosophy there are two symbols: the NOTHING and the ONE—the white paper and the dot. Creation traces its origin from the dot—the *Primitive Sea,* the Egg laid by the White Swan in the field of SPACE.

If existence be viewed from the Self downward into the illusion of creation, the dot is the first or least degree of illusion. On the other hand, if existence be viewed from the lower, or illusionary universe, upward toward Reality, the dot is the greatest conceivable Reality. *The least degree of physical impermanence is the greatest degree of spiritual permanence.* That which is most divine is least mortal. Thus, in the moral sense, the greatest degree of good is the least degree of evil. The dot, being most proximate to perfection, is the simplest, and therefore the least imperfect of all symbols.

From the dot issues forth a multitude of other illusions ever less permanent. The dot, or Sacred Island, is the beginning of existence, whether that of a universe or a man. The dot is the germ raised upon the surface of infinite duration. The potentialities signified by the blank paper are manifested as active potencies through the dot. Thus the limitless Absolute is manifested in a limited way.

When considering his own divine nature, man always thinks of his spirit as the first and greatest part of himself. He feels that his spirit is his real and permanent part. To the ancients, however, the individualized spirit (to which is applied the term *I*) was itself a little germ floating upon the surface of Absolute Life. This idea is beautifully brought out in the teachings of the Brahmans, Buddhists, and Vedantists. The Nirvana of atheistic Buddhism is achieved through the reabsorption of the individualized self into the Universal Self. In Sir Edwin Arnold's *Light of Asia*, the thought is summed up thus: "Om, mani padme, hum! the daybreak comes and the dewdrop slips back into the shining sea." The "dewdrop" is the dot; the "sea" the blank paper. The "dewdrop" is the individualized spirit, or I; the blank paper that Self which is ALL, and at the achievement of Nirvana the lesser mingles with the greater. Immortality is achieved, for that which is impermanent returns to the condition of absolute permanence.

The dot, the line, and the circle are the supreme and primary symbols. The dot is Spirit and its symbol in the Chaldaic Hebrew—the *Yod*—is actually a seed or spermatozoon, a little comma with a twisting tail representing the germ of the notself. In its first manifestation the dot elongates to form the line. The line is a string of dots made up of germ lives—the monadic lives of Leibnitz. From the seed growing in the earth comes the sprig—the line. The line, therefore, is the symbol of the dot in growth or motion. The sun is a great dot, a monad of life, and each of its rays a line—its own active principle in manifestation. The key thought is: *The line is the motion of the dot.*

In the process of creation all motion is away from self. Therefore there is only one direction in which the dot can move. In the process of return to the perfect state all motion is toward self, and through self to the Universal Self. Involution is activity outward from self; evolution is activity inward toward self. Motion away from self brings a decrease in consciousness and power; motion toward self brings a corresponding increase in consciousness and power. The farther the light ray travels from its source the weaker the ray. The line is the outpouring or natural impulse of life to expand. It may seem difficult at first to imagine the line as a symbol of general expansion, but it is simply emblematic of motion away from self—the dot. The dot, moving away from self, projects the line; the line becomes the radius of an imaginary circle, and this circle is the circumference of the powers of the central dot. Hypothetically, every sun has a periphery where its rays end, every human life a periphery where its influence ceases, every human mind a periphery beyond which it cannot function, and every human heart a periphery beyond which it cannot feel. Somewhere there is a limit to the scope of awareness. The circle is the symbol of this limit. It is the symbol of the vanishing point of central energy. The dot symbolizes the *cause;* the line, the *means;* and the circle, the *end*.

The AIN SOPH of the Hebrew Cabalists is equivalent to the Absolute. The Jewish mystics employed the *closed eye* to suggest the same symbolism as that of the blank sheet of paper. The inscrutable NOTHING conveyed to the mind by the closing of the eyes suggests the eternal, unknowable, and indefinable nature of Perfect Being. These same Cabalists called spirit the dot, the *opened eye,* because looking away from itself the Ego (or I AM) beholds the vast panorama of *things* which together compose the illusionary sphere. However, when this same objective eye is turned inward to the contemplation of its own cause, it is confronted by a blankness which defies penetration.

Only that thing which is permanent is absolutely real; hence that unmoved, eternal condition so inadequately symbolized by the blank sheet of paper is the only absolute Reality. In comparison to this eternal state, forms are an ever-changing phantasmagoria, not in the sense that forms do not exist but rather that they are of minor significance when compared to their ever-enduring source.

While through lack of adequate terminology it is necessary to approach a definition of the Absolute from a negative point of view, the blank sheet of paper signifies not emptiness but an utter and incomprehensible fullness when an attempt is made to define the indefinable. Therefore the blank paper represents that SPACE which contains all existence in a potential state. When the material universe—whether the zodiac, the stars, or the multitude of suns dotting the firmament—comes into manifestation, all of its parts are subject to the law of change. Sometime every sun will grow cold; sometime every grain of cosmic dust will blossom forth as a universe, and sometime vanish again. With the phenomenal creation comes birth, growth, decay, and the multifarious laws which have dominion over and measure the span of ephemerality. Omar Khayyam, with characteristic Oriental fatalism, writes:

"One thing is certain and the rest is Lies;
The Flower that once has blown forever dies."

The illusions of diversity—form, place, and time—are classed by the Orientals under the general term *Maya*. The word *Maya* signifies the great sea of shadows—the sphere of things as they seem to be as distinguished from the blank piece of paper which represents the one and only THING as it eternally is. The mothers of the various World Saviors generally bear names derived from the word *Maya*, as for example, *Mary*, for the reason that the various redeeming deities signify realization born out of illusion, or wisdom rising triumphant from the tomb of ignorance. Philosophic realization must be born out of the realization of illusion. Consequently the Savior-Gods are born out of *Maya* and rise through many tribulations into the light of eternity.

The keys to all knowledge are contained in the dot, the line, and the circle. The dot is universal consciousness, the line is universal intelligence, and the circle is universal force—the threefold, unknowable Cause of all knowable existence (the three hypostases of Atma). In man the spirit is represented by the dot and conscious activity or intelligence by the line. Conscious activity is the key to intelligence, because consciousness belongs to the sphere of the dot and activity to the sphere of the circle. The center and the circumference are thus blended in the connecting line—conscious activity or intelligence. The circle is the symbol of body and *body is the limit of the radius of the activity of mind power pouring out of the substance of consciousness.*

The Nature of the Absolute

In ancient philosophy the dot signifies Truth, Reality, in whatever form it may take. The line is the motion of the fact and the circle is the symbol of the form or figure established in the inferior or material sphere by these superphysical activities. Take, for example, a blade of grass. Its form is simply the *effect* of certain active agents upon certain passive substances. The physical blade of grass is really a symbol of a degree of consciousness or a combination of cosmic activities. All forms are but geometric patterns, being the reactions set up in matter by mysterious forces working in the causal spheres. Conscious activity, working upon or brooding over matter, creates form. Matter is not form, because matter (like SPACE, of which it is the negative expression) is universally disseminated but, as stated in the ancient doctrine, the activity of life upon and through its substances curdles (organizes) matter so that it assumes certain definite forms or bodies. These organisms thus caused by bringing the elements of matter into intelligent and definite relationships are held together by the conscious agent manipulating them. The moment this agent is withdrawn the process of disintegration sets in. Disintegration is the inevitable process of returning artificial compounds to their first simple state. *Disintegration may be further defined as the urge of heterogeneous parts to return to their primitive homogeneity;* in other words, the desire of creation to return to SPACE. When the forms have been reabsorbed into the vast sea of matter, they are then ready to be picked up by some other phase of the Creative Agencies and molded afresh into vehicles for the material expression of divine potentialities.

In its application to the divisions of human learning, the dot is the proper symbol of philosophy in that philosophy is the least degree of intellectual illusion. It is not to be inferred that philosophy is absolute truth but rather that it is the least degree of mental error, since all other forms of learning contain a greater percentage of fallacy. Nothing that is sufficiently tangible to be susceptible of accurate definition is true in the absolute sense, but philosophy, transcending the limitations of the form world, achieves more in its investigation of the nature of Being than does any other man-conceived discipline. The more complex the form, the farther removed it is from its source. As more marks are placed upon the white sheet of paper a picture is gradually created which may become so complicated that the white paper itself is entirely obscured. Thus the more diversified the creations, the less the Creator is discernible. Taking up the least possible space upon the paper, the dot detracts the least from the perfect expanse of the white sheet.

Philosophy *per se* is the least confusing method of approaching Reality. When less accurate systems are employed, a cobweb of contending and confusing complexities is spread over the entire surface of the blank paper, hopelessly entangling the thinker in the maze of illusion. As the dot cannot retire behind itself to explore the nature of the paper upon which it is placed, so no philosophy can entirely free itself from the involvements of mind. As man, however, must have some code by which to live, some system of thought which will give him at least an intellectual concept of ultimates, the wisest of all ages have contributed the fruitage of their transcendent genius to this great human need. Thus philosophy came into being.

Like the dot, philosophy is an immovable body. Its essential nature never changes. When the element of change is introduced into philosophy it descends to the level of theology, or rather, it is involved and distorted by the disciplines of theology. Theology is a motion, a mystical gesture as it were; it is the dot moving away from itself to form the line. Theology is not a fixed element like philosophy; it is a mutable element subject to numberless vicissitudes. Theology is emotional, changeable, violent, and at periodic intervals bursts forth in many forms of irrational excess. Theology occupies a middle ground between materiality and true illumined spirituality which, transcending theology, becomes a comprehension, in part at least, of divine concerns.

As has already been suggested, the line is the radius of an imaginary circle, and when this circle is traced upon the paper we have the proper symbol of science. Science occupies the circumference of the sphere of self. The savant gropes in that twilight where life is lost in form. He is therefore unfitted to cope with any phase of life or knowledge which transcends the plane of material things. The scientist has no comprehension of an activity independent of and dissociated from matter; hence his sphere of usefulness is limited to the lower world and its phenomena. The physical body of what man calls knowledge is science; the emotional body, theology; and the mental and supermental bodies, natural and mystical philosophy respectively. The human mind ascends sequentially from science through theology to philosophy, as in ancient days it descended from divine philosophy through spiritual theology to the condition of material science which it now occupies.

Consider the great number of people who are now leaving the church at the behest of science. Most of these individuals declare their reason for dissenting to the dictates of theology is that the dogma of the church has proved to be philosophically and scientifically unsound. The belief is quite prevalent that nearly all scientists are agnostics, if not atheists, because they refuse to subscribe to the findings of early theologians. Thus the mind must descend from credulity to absolute incredulity before it is prepared to assume the onus of individual thinking. On the other hand, the scientist who has really entered into the spirit of his labors has found God. Science has revealed to him a supertheology. It has discovered the God of the swirling atoms; not a personal Deity but an all-permeating, all-powerful, impersonal Creative Agent akin to the Absolute Being of occult philosophy. Thus the little tin god on his golden throne falls to make way for an infinite Creative Principle which science vaguely senses and which philosophy can reveal in fuller splendor.

The primitive symbols now under discussion bring to mind the subject of alphabets. The ancient *Alphabet of Wisdom* is symbolism, and all the figures used in this supreme alphabet are taken out of the dot, the line, and the circle; in other words, they are made up of various combinations of these elementary forms. Even the Arabic numerical systems and the letters of the English alphabet are compounded from these first three figures. In Oriental mysticism there are certain objects considered peculiarly appropriate for subjects of meditation. One of the most important of the native drawings is that of a lotus bud carrying in its heart the first letter of the Sanskrit alphabet, the letter usually made resplendent by gold leaf. This letter, as the first of the alphabet, is employed to direct the mind of the devotee toward all things which are first, especially Universal Self which is the first of all Being and from which all Nature emerged, as all the letters are presumed to have come forth from the first letter of the alphabet. Thus from one letter issue all letters, and from a comparatively small number of letters an infinite diversity of words, these words being the sound symbols which man has employed to designate the diversified genera of the mundane creation. The words were originally designed as sound-names, and were so closely related to the objects upon which they were conferred that by an analysis of the word the mystical nature of the object could be determined.

St. Irenaeus describes the Greek cosmological man as bearing upon his body the letters of the Greek alphabet. The sacredness of the letters is also emphasized in the New Testament where Christ is referred to as the Alpha and the Omega, the first and the last, the beginning and the end. The letters of the alphabet are those sacred symbols through the combinations of which is created an emblem for every thought, every form, every element, and every condition of material existence. Like the very illusional world whose phenomena they catalog, words are slayers of the Real, and the more words used the less of the nature of Reality remains. In the introduction to *The Secret Doctrine*, H. P. Blavatsky gives several examples of the ancient symbolic alphabets in which the Mystery teachings are preserved. Writing was originally reserved for the perpetuation of the Ancient Wisdom. Today the Mysteries still have their own language undefiled by involvement in the commercial and prosaic life of the unillumined. The language of the initiates is called the Senzar, and consists of certain magical hieroglyphical figures by which the wise men of all lands communicated with each other.

In the primordial symbols of the dot, the line, and the circle, are also set forth the mysteries of the three worlds. The dot is symbolic of heaven, the line of earth, and the circle of hell—the three spheres of Christian theology. Heaven is represented by the dot because it is the first world or foundation of the universe. In its mystical interpretation the word *heaven* signifies a "heaved up" or convoluted area, and may be interpreted to mean that which is raised above or elevated to a state of first dignity. In a similar manner the origin of the word *salvation* may be traced to *saliva*, though the kinship of the two words has long been ignored. Thus salvation signifies the process of mixing gross substance with a spiritual fluidic essence which renders it cosmically digestible and assimilable. Heaven is a figure of the superior state or condition of power, and consequently is the proper symbol of the supreme part of the Deity out of whose substances (or, more correctly, essences) the lesser universe is composed. Heaven is the plane of the spiritual nature of God, earth the plane of the material nature of God, and hell that part of existence in which the nature of God (or good) is least powerful; the outer circumference of Deity. The Scandinavian *hel-heim*—the land of the dead—is a dark and cold sphere where the fires of life burned so low that it seemed as though they might at any moment flicker out. Thus hell may be defined as the place where the light fails, or in which divine intelligence is so diluted by matter as to be incapable of controlling the manifestations of force. In the ancient Greek system of thought Hades, or the underworld, simply signifies the physical universe in contradistinction to the spiritualized and illumined superior worlds. The Greeks conceived the physical universe to be that part of creation in which the light of God is most obscured, and darkness not as primordial Reality but rather the absence of divine light. Darkness in this sense represents the *privative* darkness as distinguished from the darkness of the Absolute which includes the nature of light within its own being.

So-called physical life begins at the point where matter dominates and inhibits the manifestations of energy and intelligence.

Spirit, so-called, is only one-fifth as active in the physical world as it is in its own plane of unobstructed expression. Therefore the physical plane is simply a sphere in Nature wherein are blended four-fifths of inertia and one-fifth of activity. This does not mean that the inhabitants of this sphere are composed four-fifths of material substances but rather that the greater part of their spiritual natures can find no medium of expression, and consequently are latent. Thus the spiritual nature signified by the dot is inclosed or imprisoned within matter signified by the circle, the result being the various ensouled forms evolving through the material sphere.

It may be well to summarize in the simple terminology of the Alexandrian Neoplatonists, to whom the modern world is indebted for nearly all the great fundamentals of philosophy. If you will turn to the diagram at the beginning of this chapter you will note three circles in a vertical column and each horizontally trisected and overlapped. The upper circle signifies the power of the dot, the central circle the power of the line, and the lower circle the power of the circumference. Each of these circles contains its own trinity of potencies, which were called by the Chaldeans the Father, the Power, and the Mind. The three circles each trisected give nine hypothetical panels or levels which signify the months of the prenatal epoch and also the philosophical epoch as given in the nine degrees of the Eleusinian Mysteries. By this symbolism is revealed much of the sacredness attached to the number 9. By the method of overlapping, however, the 9 is reduced to 7, the latter number constituting the rungs of the Mithraic or philosophic ladder of the gods—the links of the golden chain connecting Absolute Unity above (or within) with Absolute Diversity below (or without).

The first trinity (the upper circle) consists of God the Father and the nature of his triple profundity; the second trinity (the middle circle), God the Son in his triple sphere of intellection; the third trinity (the lower circle), God the Holy Spirit, the Formator with his formative triad which is the foundation of the world. God the Holy Spirit, the third person of the Christian triad, is synonymous with Jehovah, the racial god of the Jews; Shiva, the destroyer-creator of the Hindus; and Osiris, the Egyptian god of the underworld. A study of the form and symbols of Osiris reveals that the lower portion of his body is swathed in mummy wrappings, leaving only his head and shoulders free. In his helmet Osiris wears the plumes of the law and in one hand clasps the three scepters of the underworld—the Anubis-headed staff, the shepherd's crook, and the flail. As the god of the underworld, Osiris has a body composed of death (the material sphere) and a living head rising out of it into a more permanent sphere. This is Jehovah, the Lord of Form, whose body is a material sphere ruled over by death but who himself, as a living being, rises out of the dead not-self which surrounds him. In India Shiva is often shown with his body a peculiar bluish white color. This is the result of smearing his person with ashes and soot, ashes being the symbol of death. Shiva is not only a destroyer in that he breaks up old forms and orders, but he is a creator in that, having dissolved an organism, he rearranges its parts and thus forms a new creature. As the bull was sacred to Osiris, was offered in sacrifice to Jehovah, and was also a favorite form assumed by the god Jupiter (consider the legend of Europa), so *Nandi* is the chosen *vahan* of Shiva. Shiva riding the bull signifies death enthroned upon, supported by, and moving in harmony with law; for the bull is the proper symbol of the immutability of divine procedure.

It is now in order to consider the subject of recapitulation. The vision of Ezekiel intimates that creation consists of wheels within wheels, the lesser recapitulating in miniature the activities of the greater. In the diagram under consideration it is evident that by trisecting each of the smaller worlds or circles they are capable of division according to the same principle that holds good in connection with the three major circles. Thus as the first large circle itself is synonymous with the dot, so the upper panel of each of the trisected circles is also symbolic of the dot. Hence the upper panel of each circle is its spiritual part, the center panel its intellective or mediatory part, and the lower panel its material or inferior part. The entire lower circle ruled over by Zeus was designated by the Greeks as the world, because it was wholly concerned with the establishment and generation of substances. The upper panel of the inferior world, partaking of the same analogy as the first world or upper circle (which it recapitulates in part) is termed the spirit of the world. The central panel, likewise recapitulating the central circle, becomes the mind or soul of the world, and the lower panel, recapitulating the lower circle, the body or form of the world. Thus spirit consists of a trinity of spirit, mind, and body in a spiritual state; mind of a spirit, mind, and body in a mental state; and form or body of a spirit, mind, and body in a material state. While Zeus is the God of Form, he manifests as a trinity, his spiritual nature bearing the name Zeus. The intellective nature, soul or mediatory nature of Zeus is termed Poseidon, and his lowest or objective material manifestation, Hades. As each of the Hindu gods possessed a *Shakti* (or a feminine counterpart signifying their energies), so Zeus manifests his potentialities through certain attributes. To these attributes were assigned personalities, and they became companion gods with him over his world.

The Zeus, Poseidon, and Hades triad of the Greeks is the Jupiter, Neptune, and Pluto triad of the Romans. Jupiter may be considered synonymous with the spiritual nature of the sun which, according to the ancients, had a threefold nature symbolic of the threefold Creator of the world. The vital energy pouring from the sun and one of its manifestations becomes Neptune, the lord of the hypothetical sea of subsolar space. In Neptune we have a parallel with the hypothetical ether of science, the super-atmospheric air which is the vehicle of solar energy. Pluto becomes the actual gross chemical earth, and his abode is presumed to be in dark, subterranean caverns where he sits upon his ancient throne in impenetrable and interminable gloom. The analogy to the dot, the line, and the circle again appears. Jupiter is the dot, Neptune the line, and Pluto the circle. Thus the life body of the sun is Jupiter; the light body of the sun, Neptune; and the fire body of the sun, Pluto ruling his inferno. It should be continually borne in mind that we are not referring to great universal realities, but simply to those phases of cosmogony directly concerned with matter, which is the lowest and most impermanent part of creation. Over this inferior world with its form and its formative agents sits Jupiter, lord of death, generator of evil, the Demiurgus and world Formator, who with his twelve Titanic Monads (the Olympic pantheon) builds, preserves, and ultimately annihilates those things which he fashions in the outer sea of divine privation.

It is noteworthy that the astronomical symbol of the sun should be the dot in a circle, for as can be deduced from the subject matter of this lecture the dot, the circle, and the hypothetical connecting line give a complete key to the actual nature of the solar orb. When Jupiter, or Jehovah, is called the lord of the sun, it does not necessarily mean the sun which is the ruler of this solar system; it means any one of the millions of universal suns which are functioning upon the plane or level of a solar orb. Jupiter manifests himself as a mystical energy which gives crops, perpetuates life, and bestows all the blessings of physical existence, only to ultimately deprive mankind and his world of all these bounties. Jupiter is the sun of illusion, the light which lights the inferior creation but has nothing in common with that great spiritual light which is the life of man and the light of the world.

According to the Gnostics, the Demiurgus and his angels represented the false light which lured souls to their destruction by causing them to believe in the permanence of matter and that life within the veil of tears was the true existence. According to philosophy, only those who rise above the light of the inferior universe to that great and glorious spiritual luminescence belonging to the superphysical spheres, can hope to discover everlasting life. The physical universe is therefore the body of Jupiter, Jehovah, Osiris, or Shiva. The sun is the pulsating heart of each of these deities, and sun spots are caused (as H. P. Blavatsky notes) by the expansion and contraction of the solar heart at intervals of eleven years. In the Greek and Roman mythologies, Zeus, or Jupiter, is the chief of the twelve gods of Olympus. Olympus was a mythical mountain rising in the midst of the world. It is the dot or sun itself, for it is written that the tabernacle of the gods is in the skies. From the face of this sun shines a golden corona whose numberless fiery points are the countless gods who transmit the life of their sovereign lord and who are his ministers to the farthest corners of his empire. In the Hebrew philosophy the rays of the sun are the hairs of the head and beard of the Great Face. Each hair is the radius of a mystical circle, with the sun as the center, and outer darkness as the circumference. It is curious that in Egypt the name of the second person of the triad—the manifester—should be *Ray* or *Ra,* and his title, "the lord of light." Ra bears witness, however, to his invisible and eternal Father, for the light of the sun is not the true sun but bears witness to the invisible source of the effulgence. Thus, as the beams of the physical sun become the light of the physical body of existence, so the rays of the intellectual sun are the light of the mind, and all power, all vitality, and all increase come as the result of attunement to the fiery streamers of those divine beings to whom has been given the appellation of "the gods."

A few words at this time concerning the symbolism of Neptune. While Neptune is popularly associated with the sea, occultly he signifies the albuminous part of the great egg of Jupiter. In certain schools of Orphic mysticism, the inferior universe (like the supreme, all-inclosing sphere) is symbolized by an egg. This lesser egg has Jupiter for a yolk, Neptune for the albumen, and Pluto for the shell. It is therefore evident that Neptune is not associated with the physical element of water, but rather with the electrical fluids permeating the entire solar system. He is also associated with the astral world, a sphere of fluidic essences and part of the mirror of Maya, the illusion. As the connective between Jupiter and Pluto, Neptune represents a certain phase of material intellect which, like the element of water, is very changeable and inconstant. Like water, Neptune is recognized as a vitalizer and life-giver, and in the ancient Mysteries was associated with the germinal agents. The fish, or spermatozoon, previous to its period of germination, was under his dominion.

Descending from the sphere of cosmology to the life of the individual, it is important that certain analogies be made between Jupiter as the lord of the world and the microcosmic Jupiter who is the lord of each individual life. That which in our own nature we call *I* is, according to mysticism, not the real I or Self but the Jupiterian or inferior I—the demiurgic self; it may even be said to be the false self which, by accepting as real, we elevate to a position greater than it is capable of occupying. A very good name for Jupiter is the *human* spirit as differentiated from the *divine* spirit which belongs to the supermaterial spheres. In man Jupiter has his abiding place in the human heart, while Neptune dwells in the brain, and Pluto in the generative system. Thus is established the formative triad in the physical nature of man. As the physical universe is the lowest and least permanent part of existence, so the physical body is the lowest and least permanent part of man. Above the lord of the body with his Aeons or angels is the divine mind and all-pervading consciousness. The body of man is mortal, though his divine parts partake, to a certain degree, of immortality. Over the mortal nature of man rules an incarnating ego which organizes matter into bodies, and by this organization foredooms them to be redistributed to the primordial elements. As Jupiter had his palace on the summit of Mount Olympus, so from his glorious cardiac throne on the top of the diaphragm muscle he rules the body as lord of the human world. Jupiter in us is the thing we have accepted as our true Self, but meditation upon the subject matter of this lecture will disclose the true relationship between the human self and the Universal ALL of which it is a fragmentary yet all-potential part.

Recognizing Jupiter to be the lord of the world, or the incarnating ego which invests itself in universal matter, it then becomes evident that the two higher spheres of trinities of divine powers constitute the Hermetic *anthropos*, or nonincarnating overman. This majestic and superior part, consisting of the threefold darkness of Absolute Cause and the threefold light or celestial splendor, hovers above the third triad consisting of the threefold world form, or triune cosmic activity.

The highest expression of matter is mind, which occupies the middle distance between activity on the one hand and inertia on the other. The mind of man is hypothetically considered to consist of two parts: the lower mind, which is linked to the demiurgic sphere of Jupiter, and the higher mind, which ascends toward and is akin to the substance of the divine power of Kronos. These two phases of mind are the mortal and immortal minds of Eastern philosophy. Mortal mind is hopelessly involved in the illusions of sense and substance, but immortal or divine mind transcending these unrealities is one with truth and light. Here we have a definite key to several misunderstood concepts as now promulgated through the doctrines of Christian Science.

Since intelligence is the highest manifestation of matter, it is logically the lowest manifestation of consciousness, or spirit, and Jupiter (or the personal *I*) is enshrined in the substances of mortal mind where he controls his world through what man is pleased to term *intellect*. The Jupiterian intellect, however, is that which sees outward or toward the illusions of manifested existence, whereas the higher or spiritual mind (which is latent in most individuals) is that superior faculty which is capable of thinking inward or toward the profundities of Self; in other words, is capable of facing toward and gazing upon the substance of Reality. Thus the mind may be likened to the two-faced Roman god Janus. With one face this god gazes outward upon the world and with the other inward toward the sanctuary in which it is enshrined. The two-faced mind is an excellent subject for meditation. The objective or mortal mind continually emphasizes to the individual the paramount importance of physical phenomena; the subjective, or immortal mind, if given opportunity for expression, combats this material instinct by intensifying the regard for that which transcends the limitations of the physical perceptions.

Subservient to Jupiter who, bearing his thunderbolt and accompanied by his royal eagle is indeed the king of this world, are Neptune and Pluto. The god Neptune, of course, is not to be regarded as either the planet or as an influence derived from the planet, but as the lord of the middle sphere of the inferior world. In man the middle sphere between mind and matter is occupied by emotion or feeling. The instability of human emotion is well symbolized by the element of water which is continually in motion, the peaceful surface of which can be transformed into a destroying fury by forces moving above its broad expanse. The emotional nature of man is closely associated with the astral light or magical sphere of the ancient and mediaeval magicians. In this plane illusion is particularly powerful. As one writer has wisely observed, "It is a land of beauty, a garden of flowers, but a serpent is entwined about the stem of each." Among the Oriental mystics this sphere of the astral light is considered particularly dangerous, for those who are aspiring to an understanding of spiritual mysteries are often enmeshed in this garden of Kundry, and believing they have found the truth are carried to their destruction by the flow of this astral fluid.

Riding in his chariot drawn by sea-horses and surrounded by Nereids riding upon sporting dolphins, Neptune carries in his hand the trident, a symbol common to both the lord of the illusion and the red-robed tempter. Neptune is the lord of dreams, and all mortal creatures are dreamers; all that mankind has accomplished in the countless ages of its struggle upward toward the light is the result of dreaming. Yet if dreams are not backed up by action and controlled by reason they become a snare and a delusion, and the dreamer drifts onward into oblivion in a mystic ecstasy. You will remember that according to Greek mythology there was a river called the Styx which divided the sphere of the living from that of the dead. This river is the mysterious sea of Neptune which all men must cross if they would rise from material ignorance into philosophic illumination. This Neptunian sea may be likened to the ethers which permeate and bind together the material elements of Nature. The sphere of Neptune is a world of ever-moving fantasy without beginning and without end, a mystical maze through which souls wander for uncounted ages if once caught in the substances of this shadowy dreamland.

The lowest division of the Jupiterian sphere is under the dominion of Pluto, the regent of death. Pluto is the personification of the mass physical attitude of all things toward objective life. Pluto may be termed the principle of the mortal code, in accordance with which Nature lives and moves and has her being. Pluto may also be likened to an intangible atmosphere permeated with definite terrestrial instincts. Unconsciously inhaling this atmosphere, man is enthused by it and accepts it as the basis of living. The individual who is controlled by the Plutonic miasma contracts a peculiar mental and spiritual malaria which destroys all transcendental instinct and spiritual initiative, leaving him a psychical invalid already two-thirds a victim of the Plutonic plague. As Plato so admirably says, "The body is the sepulcher of the soul," and whereas Neptune is symbolic of the astral or elemental soul (which is a mysterious emanation from elementary Nature) Pluto is the god of the underworld, the deity ruling the spheres of the mysterious circle of being and therefore represents the lowest degree of Jupiterian light, which is physical matter. Hades, or the land of the dead, is simply an environment resulting from crystallization. Everything that exists in a crystallized state furnishes the environment of Hades for whatever life is evolving through it. Thus the lower universe is ruled over by three apparently heartless gods—birth, growth, and decay. From their palaces in space these deities hurl the instruments of their wrath upon hapless humanity and elementary Nature. But he who is fortunate enough to escape the thunderbolts of Jove will yet fall beneath the trident of Neptune or be torn to pieces by the dogs of Father Dis (Pluto). The ancient Greeks occasionally employed a centaur to represent man, thus indicating that out of the body of the beast which feels upon its back the lash of outrageous destiny rises a nobler creature possessed of God-given reason, who through sheer force of innate divinity shall become master of those who seek to bind him to a mediocre end.

While on the subject of the dot, the line, and the circle, there is one very simple application of the principle which we insert in order to emphasize the analogies existing through the entire structure of human thought. Take a simple problem in grammar. The noun, which is the subject of the sentence, is analogous to the dot; the verb, which is the action of the subject, is analogous to the line; and the object, which is the thing acted upon, is analogous to the circle. These analogies may also be traced through music and color and through the progression of chemical elements. Always the trinity of the dot, the line, and the circle has some correspondent, for it is the basis upon which the entire structure of existence and function—both universal and individual—has been raised. Consider this fundamental symbolism, philosophize upon it, dream about it, for an understanding of these symbols is the beginning of wisdom. There is no problem, whether involved with the simple mechanism of an earthworm or the inconceivable complex mechanism of a universe, that has not been constructed upon the triangular foundation of the dot, the line, and the circle. These are the proper symbols of the creative, preservative, and disintegrative agencies which manifest the incomprehensible Absolute before temporary creation.

The three worlds we have outlined are the supreme, the superior and the inferior worlds of the Orphic theology as revealed by Pythagoras and Plato. The supreme world is the sphere of the one indivisible and ever-enduring Father; the superior world is the sphere of the gods, the progeny of the Father; and the inferior world is the sphere of mortal creatures who are the progeny of the gods. "Therefore," says Pythagoras, "men live in the inferior world, God in the supreme world, and the men who are gods and the gods who are men in the intermediate plane." You will recall that it was said of Pythagoras by his disciples that there were of two-footed creatures three kinds: gods, men, and Pythagoras. It should be inferred that the dot represents the gods, the circle men, and the line connecting them Pythagoras, or the personification of that superhuman wisdom which binds cause and effect inextricably together, and which is the hope of salvation for the lesser. The Deity dwelling in the supreme world and which the Platonists termed the One, was, according to the Scandinavians, All-Father, the sure foundation of being. In India it was Brahma and in Egypt, Ammon. The line always represented the Savior-Gods, they being the eldest sons or first-born of intangible Deity. The line bears witness of the dot as the light bears witness of the life. All this gives a clue to the statement in the New Testament, "Whoso hath seen the Son, hath seen the Father, for the Son is in the Father and the Father in the Son." In other words, whoso hath seen the line, hath seen the dot, for the dot is in the line and the line is in the dot. In the ancient Jewish rites the line was Michael, the archangel of the sun; in Scandinavia, Balder the Beautiful.

It is to the lower world of men that the light (the dot pouring into the line), personified as the Universal Savior, descends to redeem consciousness from the darkness of a living grave (the circumference of the circle). The Mystery God who lifted souls to salvation through his own nature thus represents the line, the divine symbol of the way of achievement, for it is written that none shall come unto the Father save by the Son and none of those creatures dwelling in the circumference can reach the center or dot save by ascending the hypothetical line of the radius. The line is the bridge connecting cause with effect. In Immanuel Kant's philosophy we find the dot designated the *noumenon* and the circumference the *phenomenon;* the former the Reality, the later the unreality. The line (the human mind) must ever be the agency that bridges the void between them.

In the Platonic philosophy there are three manners of being: (1) gods, or those most proximate to the Absolute, who dwell within the nature of the dot; (2) men, or those who are most distant from the Absolute, who dwell in the circumference of the circle; (3) the heroes and the demigods, who are suspended between Divinity and humanity and who dwell in the sphere of the line. So, according to philosophy, the line is a ladder up which man ascends to light from his infernal state and down which he descends in his involution. The *fall of man* is the descent down the ladder from the dot to the circumference; the *resurrection* or *redemption* of man is his return from the circumference to the dot. Of such importance are these primary symbols that we have felt it absolutely necessary to devote the introductory lectures of this series to the subject of the dot, the line, and the circle. It should ever be borne in mind that the veneration for symbols is not idolatry, for symbols are formulated to clarify truths which in their abstract form are incomprehensible. Idolatry consists in the inability of the mind to differentiate between the symbol and the abstract principle for which it stands. If this definition be accepted, it can be proved that there are very few truly idolatrous peoples. Philosophically, the literalist is always an idolater. He who worships the letter of the law bows down to wood and stone, but he who comprehends the spirit of the law is a true worshiper before the measureless altar of eternal Nature upon which continually burns the Spirit Fire of the world.

THE VEDIC TRIMURTI

It is proper that the Leader of Universals should be regarded as the head of the world and that its three complexions should be symbolized by faces. Speaking its word of power, each face causes to issue from its mouth a sacred syllable, by which the surfaces of the three worlds are agitated and caused to assume the semblance of creation.

CHAPTER TWO

God, the Divine Foundation

FROM the preceding lecture it is evident that any description or definition of unknowable ultimates is possible only in the terms of negation. In other words, every definition so-called must be eliminative, and that which remains when all else is taken away must necessarily be the only thing incapable of removal. When considering the nature of primordial substance, the average school of philosophy postulates an active First Cause; otherwise it is wholly at a loss to explain how creation can be the product of a passive power. Activity is accordingly postulated as a fundamental attribute of Being. To me, however it is inconceivable that the First Cause (or more correctly the Causeless Cause) should be either positive or negative. Rather it seems more fitting to posit a permanent condition which is neither positive in an "active" sense nor negative in a "passive" sense, but which is *power in absolute suspension*. For lack of a better defining term we might conceive of Eternal Being as an enduring neitherness, partaking of neither the presence nor the absence of any tangible force or condition. The condition of the Absolute can only be suggested by a suspended neitherness of both activity and inertia.

To attempt an analysis of the fabric of even the groundwork of SPACE far exceeds the capacity of any human intellect. Never in the history of philosophy has there been evolved a mind capable of grasping all the multitudinous elements of Being. The world is filled with people who foolishly try to teach or seek to be taught the length, breadth, and thickness of ultimates, when but a moment's true thinking would demonstrate the fallacy and futility of such effort. Since the groundwork of SPACE—the ultimate abstraction—transcends every faculty and every dimension, it can never be comprehended by a reasoning organism that must necessarily arrive at its conclusions on the basis of faculty and dimension. For the human mind to understand that which is greater than itself is as impossible as for a mere man to swallow the ocean. The effort of the human mind to circumscribe the entirety of manifestation is comparable to a mollusk trying to enclose the sea within its shell. Realizing, therefore, how apropos is the ancient statement that to define Deity is to defile it, we are forced to accept the inevitable conclusion of the ages: namely, that the ultimates of beginning and end are alike unknowable. These conclusions are in harmony with the deductions of both Socrates and Buddha.

The gods may be conceived of in either the singular or the plural sense; in the singular if we consider the deities as fractional parts of one Creative Agent; in the plural if we look upon the various parts as separate vehicles of cosmic intelligence. Thus in many ancient doctrines we have evidence of a fundamental monotheism manifesting through a complex polytheism. For example, the Elohim, or secondary gods of the ancient Jews who, as the Creative Demiurgi, moved upon the face of the deep and together constitute a single cosmic deity. In the same way the elaborate pantheon of the Hindus is a mosaic of gods, who in combination form the nature of the supreme and all-powerful Brahma. The gods may be considered as symbolic of the individual states of consciousness continually unfolding within the nature of Absolute Being. The concept of a single personal Deity who was prudent enough to fashion himself without eyelids lest he fall asleep from that exhaustion which must necessarily result from an eternal vigil is hardly adequate to meet the evident needs of existence. Up to the present time the advocates of monotheism have advanced no concept of Deity adequate to control creation without the assistance of a privy council or celestial parliament. A few moments of serious consideration will reveal that a fundamental monotheism manifesting through an elaborate polytheism is by far the most noble concept of cosmic government, and is the basis of all the successful governments maintained by man upon earth.

The modern world is inclined to look askance at the elaborate pantheons of the Greeks, Egyptians, and Hindus, and rather prides itself that it has outgrown such theological crudities. Even now, however, there is a definite reversion to the pantheistic cults of antiquity, and when properly understood the Orphic theogony will enjoy a glorious renaissance.

The subject of philosophic polytheism deserves further attention. Polytheism must not be considered synonymous with the blind adoration of an infinitude of imaginary superhuman beings, but rather as the recognition of a concatenated progression of evolving creatures, each influencing and to a certain degree controlling those inferior to itself, and in turn controlled by those superior to itself. The gods should not be considered as personally directing the destiny of individuals. Rather they are vast centers of radiant force consciously or unconsciously influencing anything that exists or subsists upon their sphere of manifestation. For example, a city does not wilfully mold the character of its inhabitants; nevertheless it is an active factor in determining the character of each individual unit of its population. This simile, while possibly not apparent at first thought, is particularly apt, for as cells exist in the human body, so man is but a cell in a larger organism which he pleases to term a god. The cells of the human body may feel a similar veneration for man, who in the light of cell intelligence must be a boundless and infinitely powerful deity.

Polytheism therefore may be best defined as a veneration for causal agencies. Obedience to the will of the gods was regarded as the basis of human happiness and simply meant that only those who lived in harmony with natural law could hope for a tranquil existence. To the ancients it seemed essential that intelligence should manifest from an intelligent Creator; in other words, the manifesting thought proved the existence of the unmanifested Thinker. Intelligence exists in every department of creation. The entire universe is controlled by definite laws that evidence the omniscience of the Eternal Thinker. From the fountainhead of immeasurable Mind the cogitations of Deity stream forth to make fertile with thought the whole area of Being. Broken up by creations as upon a prism, the Mind-Light of Deity becomes manifest as an infinite order of separate and specialized intelligences. Thus upon the surface of the sea of Universal Mind appear numberless foci, each controlling a definite phase of cosmic activity. The gods are such foci; so are men, but to a more limited degree. The sum of all these individual minds is the one Universal Mind, so that in the last analysis gods, men, and worlds are each fragments of the whole. The philosophers of all ages have realized that the achievement of perfect wisdom lies in the elevation of the power of comprehension to that state where it is able to grasp the relation of the parts of existence to the sum of existence, which the Buddhists designate the *Self*.

All great systems of religious philosophy agree that anterior to the gods is the One and Undivided, who is the very foundation of manifested existence or the first limitation of Absolute Being, and who may properly be designated the Father of gods and men. We shall now turn our attention to a consideration of the powers and attributes of this first of all mortals, the chief of those who die, the first-born of Absolute Self. In seventy-two languages men call this first power God, the first and most perfect of creations, the eldest of the old, and the Most Ancient of the Most Ancient. God is best defined as the first manifestation of Infinite Existence, the limitation of Limitlessness. In his adoration of Deity man is prone to consider God as synonymous with ALL in that God is synonymous with all that man can hope to comprehend. But behind comprehension is that which is incomprehensible, the thrice-black darkness which exists unhonored and unsung through the unmeasured duration of eternity, and upon whose placid surface time comes and goes, and beginnings and ends are but incidental. To return to the symbolism of the preceding lecture, God is the dot, the first island floating in and upon the permanent depths of Unlimited Existence. God is therefore capable of definition in the terms of the Dervish, by whom as chief of beings he is denominated the *Axis of the world*, or that immovable center about which all revolves.

Before it is possible to approach Deity through philosophy, it is necessary to nullify the traditional practice prevalent throughout Christendom of referring to Deity as a masculine potency and ascribing to him most human vices, which, however, become virtues by reason of his unquestioned position as despotic arbiter of right and wrong. The modern religious thinker is no longer inclined to venerate a deity who is simply a highly glorified King George III. In that now vanishing picturesque period of absolute monarchies when fretful and senile princes, arrayed in ridiculous periwigs, ruled by "divine right", God was invested with all the propensities of the "blood royal", and the celestial hierarchies were metamorphosed into landed gentry.

In spite of the repeated emphasis upon our age of enlightenment, the majority of people still continue the age-honored practice of molding God into a likeness of themselves. The reason for this probably lies in the fact that man, possessing a spark of Divinity within himself, feels his kinship with God and believes himself privileged to rush in where angels fear to tread, and give definition to the undefinable. God being, as Ingersoll so well expressed it, "the noblest work of man," we find in the attributes of the God people worship, a definite key to their own ethical and philosophic status. It is noticeable that people with puerile intelligences and petty concerns conceive God to be localized as a neighborhood sprite who spends most of his time eavesdropping, and who can afford to ignore universal concerns while he heaps maledictions upon some poor, benighted wretch who did not keep his eyes closed during grace! On the other hand, those who have learned to know something of the greater verities of life worship a *growing* God. This does not presuppose that God is necessarily increasing, but rather that man's increasing capacity to comprehend ever reveals more of the stupendous nature of Divinity. As a person approaches a physical object, the object apparently increases in size. The same is true of the mind as it approaches the subject of its consideration. Hence, to the philosopher God extends through the infinitude of time, distance, and thought, and to him it is inconceivable that even for a second Deity should descend into a state less dignified than the all-inclusiveness of its intrinsic nature.

Among many ancient peoples God was considered as being androgynous, and referred to as the Great Father-Mother. When the Creator was represented by an image, various subtle devices were employed to indicate its hermaphroditic nature. The *Iswara* of the Hindus is depicted with one side of his body male and the other female. In Greek and Roman statuary frequent examples are found of a masculine divinity wearing feminine garments and vice versa, or a heavily-bearded god may have his hair arranged in a distinctly feminine coiffure. Again, the structure of the face of such deities as Bacchus and Dionysus often shows a sensitive, feminine countenance disguised by a beard or some article of masculine adornment. In other cases the feminine counterpart of the deity is considered as a separate individuality. For this reason each of the gods was declared to have had his consort or feminine aspect of his own being. Thus *Mithras*, the Persian Light-Savior, is considered to be masculine, but a certain portion of himself divided from the rest becomes *Mithra*, a feminine and maternal potency. As previously noted, in India each god has his *shakti*, or feminine part.

Among some peoples Diety has been considered for ages as primarily feminine, as the Brahmans who refer to God as "the Great Mother." In Roman Catholicism there is also a definite tendency to idealize the feminine principle of God through the person of the Virgin Mary, who is elevated to a most exalted position as *"Queen of Heaven."* The custom of depicting God either as male or female is the outgrowth of man's oldest form of worship: phallicism. Masculine and feminine properties are presumed to be positive and negative respectively. Hence God, being an active or positive agent, was conceived to be masculine; nature, being a passive or negative body, was regarded as feminine in that it received into itself and nurtured to maturity the germinal essences of Divine Life. The proponents of a masculine God declare that in the beginning was activity, the positive cause of existence. On the other hand, the proponents of the pre-eminence of the feminine principle declare that activity first issued from a universal matrix; consequently that which comes forth from the matrix is subordinate to its own origin. To a certain degree the Madonna expresses this concept, for the man child is creation born out of the womb of SPACE—the Holy Mother of Ages.

To the philosopher, God, as the first manifestation of unmanifested and incomprehensible ALL-ness, contains both the potencies of the mother and the father in equilibrium. Material existence is the result of the hypothetical division taking place within the nature of this androgynous Deity, from whose higher (or masculine) nature is created the superphysical universe, and from whose inferior (or feminine) nature is divided the world of form. From this point of view God does not act upon an extraneous body, but action and reaction are simply the interaction of the parts of one universal Deity. The English language lacks a proper term with which to designate Deity. The word *God* is comparatively meaningless, as it gives no hint of the gender or dignity of Divinity other than merely signifying "good." Since either a masculine or a feminine term is inappropriate and obviously incomplete, and a neuter term entirely too negative, a word is needed which will express the undivided potencies of both positive and negative in equilibrium.

When the terms *masculine* and *feminine* were used in philosophic symbolism the ancients gave a certain supremacy to the masculine principle for two reasons: (1) as the male was endowed with greater physical endurance, among primitive peoples physical strength was considered the most necessary attribute of Divinity; (2) as the tribal or state government was a patriarchate, it necessarily followed that God as the Supreme Ruler became dignified as a masculine entity. Those races, however, which elevated woman to a high social status were more prone to endow Deity with distinctive feminine characteristics than were those peoples where woman was regarded as little better than a slave. As time went on man thus became the personification of the positive principle and woman of the negative. This viewpoint, however, will not bear close philosophic scrutiny. The so-called inferiority of the female is simply a symbolic figure, having no reference whatever to either the political or ecclesiastical status of woman. It is surprising, however, the extent to which the stigma of this little-understood symbolism has influenced both the racial and individual life of woman. It is still not uncommon to meet people who, while they can give no definite explanation for their feelings, are convinced that the feminine organism lacks some peculiar psychical or soul quality which has been reserved exclusively for masculine expression. The popular misconception (presumably promulgated by the Moslems) that heaven was a place accessible to woman as the result of special intercession on the part of her husband, while not publicly taught in Christendom, is nevertheless painfully evident to those able to analyze accurately the mental and emotional reactions of the average man. Woman's responsibilities as the mother of humanity afford ample evidence to the profound thinker that she is far from being a "negative" creature. The maternal principle was elevated by the Greeks to first place, and the *Mater Deorum* (Mother of the Gods) was esteemed worthy of universal veneration.

The relative superiority or inferiority of either the positive or negative principles leads to one inevitable conclusion: namely, that all manifestation being ordered by Divine Providence, it is impossible to determine intelligently the ultimate importance of conditions, each of which is essential to all. God as the Father impregnates SPACE with his seed; God as the Mother receives this seed into herself and protects it through the ages necessary for its unfoldment; and God as the Child is himself the very seed which as God the Father he sowed. Thus is explained the ancient Rosicrucian adage: "All is in All; All is All."

The commentaries of the Cabalists upon the early Hebrew Scriptures contain lengthy dissertations upon the nature of God as the first being or power to manifest itself upon the surface of AIN SOPH, the limitless and boundless Sea of Eternal Potentiality. According to the Cabalistic version, there appeared upon and in AIN SOPH a great, gleaming, jewel-encrusted crown.

God, the Divine Foundation

This John Heydon calls the wise man's crown set with suns, moons, and stars and ornamented with archangels. Ten sparkling sapphires sent streamers of celestial splendor from their faceted surfaces, and the great crown, Kether, which was the foundation of the world, rested upon the intangible but immovable foundation of the Absolute Divinity. From the crown issued forth the multitudes of divine and elementary beings who people the forty spheres comprising the Cabalistic universe. Thus, to a certain degree, the crown is an ark which, resting upon the hypothetical Ararat of Limitless Being—the Mount of Eternity—caused to issue from itself by twos and by sevens all that pageantry of life which had been preserved within it through the *pralaya,* or deluge of cosmic oblivion. Kether, the Ancient of Ancients, the Long Face, the Opened Eye, the Holy One, and the Father Foundation, enthroned in the midst of Being, wills creation and it is. Kether has neither shape nor form imaginable to us, but in an effort to conceive in part its dignity we ascribe to it the noblest forms within the vista of our comprehension. The sphere is the most perfect of all bodies and was therefore chosen by both Pythagoras and Plato as the most perfect symbol of "Him who shall remain." It is evident, however, that this Being does not actually resemble a crown, an opened eye or, as the Cabalists affirm, a bald head. These figures of speech in no way limit or change the enduring nature of this first power. Whether we call It Father or Mother or Son; whether we consider It as androgynous or sexless, human or composite, personal or impersonal, It remains forever itself, the first manifestation of unmanifested power. It was in the beginning, for Its appearance marks the term of beginning and end, and Time has its inception with the establishment of this first Divinity. God is as enduring as Time, but Time and God are both servants of Infinity.

The meditation of the mystics upon the nature of the first God revealed to them that Deity occupies a position somewhat analogous to a focal point. In God the unknowable potentialities of Absolute Existence were concentrated, and through the nature of Deity pass downward and are distributed as active potencies throughout the negative sphere or field of manifestation. Infinite Being thus flows through God into creation, and existence ascends through God to its Infinite Source. God is therefore the least material and the most spiritual of all created things; of all beings the eldest; of all things the newest. Yet, being differentiated from Immortal Being, Deity is mortal and subject to ultimate reabsorption into Universal SPACE. In the most abstract sense, God is a hypothetical point established in the midst of Absolute Self through which It (Absolute Self) manifests forth into tangibility and consequent impermanent existence. God is the All made One; the universe is the One made All.

Of all the terms with which Deity has been invested there is none more simple and yet more consistent with the nature of ALL than that used by Plato, who defines God as the unmoved, self-moving Mover. God is unmoved in the sense that It is the sure foundation which will remain as long as time. God is self-moving in that activity is its innate quality. God is the all-mover in that it is the life-giving principle animating all the structures which combine to form the inferior universe. God is the seed in the field of SPACE. From the dark philosophic earth of Infinite Being it draws all that it manifests. In the symbolism of the Far East, God comes as a lotus bud upon the surface of the Great Sea which, after living its appointed span, dies back into the infinite Ocean of Chaos. God is the first-born, the infinite Monad so well described by Democritus in his development of the atomic theory.

Now comes the legitimate question: If Absolute Being is unlimited and unconditioned with all its forces in a state of suspension, what causes these periodic centers or deities to come into being and what law governs their continuance and ultimate dissolution? In other words, if the Absolute possesses neither will nor activity in a centralized or manifesting state, how is the genesis of gods and worlds to be explained? Why does not the Absolute remain throughout duration in the same unknowing and all-pervading state?

It is difficult to conceive of a perfect state giving birth to an imperfect state, and yet, according to philosophy, this is exactly what occurs when Universal Being supports ephemeral creation upon the surface of itself, or, as the Hindu mythologist would say, Varaha (the boar incarnation of Vishnu) elevates cosmos upon its tusks. The answer to the problem of First Cause has confounded several otherwise excellent systems of theology, and the solution advanced by mystical philosophy is one of the most daring postulates of the human mind. Yet for man with his limited intelligence to ponder too deeply upon such abstract mysteries is highly dangerous, for the solidarity of thought itself is jeopardized.

Sir Francis Bacon, one of the greatest thinkers of the modern world, realized how fatal to the success of the seeker after truth is the assumption of knowledge. Knowledge he declared to be the end, not the beginning, of the rational quest after facts. Much of the body of truth, however, is ascertained by the aid of certain fundamental postulations which must then run the gauntlet of observation and experimentation. Unable to delineate the boundaries or profiles of Universal Cause, the mind must necessarily reduce cosmic phenomena to terms apprehensible to human reason. To cope with the problems of the abstract the mind must first discover in the concrete the analogy of the abstract. Having found a simple natural analogy, the philosopher employs the most basic of all the Hermetic axioms: namely, that which is below is like unto that which is above. The *law of analogy* is the most powerful weapon ever placed in the hands of man with which to solve the riddle of the Unknown, for by analogy he is able to classify the orders of invisible life, and chart that vast interval between the limitation of human nature and the limitlessness of Divine nature

With the assistance of the law of analogy, let us then approach the problem of First Cause. Sleep is a state somewhat resembling death; in fact St. Paul definitely relates them to each other. Death, moreover, is analogous to the state of the Absolute in that it is the cessation of that activity which destroys the tranquillity of infinite duration. Again, no sense of time, place, or condition is apparent during sleep. A few seconds of a distorted dream may represent a lifetime in which persons and places come and go with kaleidoscopic speed. Speed also partakes of the nature of the Absolute in that the objective world disappears; the sleeper rests in an unknowing state and an almost Nirvanic trance-like condition controls the functioning parts. During sleep there is neither will nor rational activity in the objective world; oblivious to the entire panorama of existence, the objective soul lies in a state which is neither light nor darkness and which defies intelligent definition.

Sleep, however, does not override the claims of habit. If a person is accustomed to awake at a certain hour, when that hour arrives consciousness seemingly rises out of unconsciousness with no apparent motivation other than the subtle, innate urge of habit. The individual wakes, and grasping with drowsy fingers the sense perceptions, assumes the labors of the day. The mind was never told to rouse the sleeper, nor did he have any realization that some intangible agent would at a certain time dissipate the state of dreaming and force the life back into wakeful activity. The sleeper suddenly opens his eyes and discovers it to be the usual rising hour. Habit is seemingly stronger than the state of sleep, for it is something that awakens the sleeper even when he cannot wake himself. Therefore, says th Ancient Doctrine, the comings and goings of creation upon the surface of infinite expanse are the impulses of the *law of periodicity*. Thus periodicity may be defined as the *habit of Infinite SPACE*. Habit causes the unknown elements and agencies comprising the Absolute periodically to spawn forth worlds and to draw them back again into itself periodically. Habit causes the sleeping universe to awaken after the Seven Nights of Rest, and after its Seven Days of Labor habit and necessity again cause the tired creation to sink back into the arms of SPACE.

Though not a thinking substance, SPACE contains the potentiality of thought. Thought is simply one of the numerous limited expressions of SPACE and does not come into manifestation until the creative processes have limited the ALL to that condition known as intelligence. That is the reason why the law of periodicity, or the spontaneous awakening of life, is necessary, in that SPACE possesses no tangible urge or force other than habit, which is itself a purely hypothetical term. It is the supreme and eternal habit of Absolute Being to create and also to take creation back again into itself. Thus the outpouring and the inflowing may be likened to the ebb and flow of an eternal sea. Creation sinking into SPACE is no better able to conceive of the Absolute than is man to conceive of the substance of sleep. Nor do the Seven Sleepers upon awakening from their ages of slumber have any more concept of the condition from which they have emerged than has man when he rises from his slumbers. It is a daring thought to define cosmic law as the habit of SPACE, but the urges which immutably direct all things to their predestined end are thus explained. Periodically upon the face of Not-Being (which is ALL Being) there appear centers of life—the *chakras* or seeds of future worlds. The swastika is their proper symbol, for it is the whirling across that represents the centralizing motion of the Eternal ALL. This first all-inclusive bubble, a magnificent iridescent sphere floating gracefully through eternity, is called *God*, and within its transparent shell creation lives and moves and has its being. Its purpose finally fulfilled, the bubble bursts and disappears, its parts are reabsorbed into the surrounding apparent nothingness.

All that man is or can ever hope to be depends upon his concept of God. No individual is greater than the God he worships, nor is he capable of worshipping a concept of God greater than himself. Thus is established a vicious circle. The noble concept of Baron von Leibnitz that the universe is made up of monads or metaphysical germs all contained within one great Monad may be contrasted with the theological concept of the last century which conceived the Deity to be a married man who took strange delight (as Voltaire has noted) in watching his creation eat the body of his beloved Son at the sacrament. Man's concept of God must pass through three definite states symbolized by the dot, the line, and the circle, which received so much consideration in the preceding lecture. The lowest concept of God is as a personality, a physical entity, whose symbol is the circumference of the circle. Superior to this concept is that of God as an individuality, a mental entity, whose symbol is the line. The third and highest definable concept is that of God as a spiritual entity, a permeating and diffusing life-giving principle, whose symbol is the dot. But above all these concepts and superior to God even as a spiritual entity is that concept of Absolute SPACE—formless and definitionless—whose only symbol is the blank sheet of paper.

In every philosophic system God is either the beginning or the end of the chain of thought. We may invest our concept of Deity with certain qualities and conditions and, accepting that as a starting point, seek to grasp the necessary process involved in the creation of the phenomenal sphere. Or we may posit as our working formula certain divine manifestation in the material universe, and by induction seek to understand the nature of a Deity capable of producing such phenomena out of its own nature. Thus in our investigation we either begin with the dot and travel toward the circumference, or we begin with the circumference and travel toward the dot. On the one hand we posit a Deity and then, imagining ourselves to be that Deity, construct a universe; on the other hand we posit a minute atom and through an infinite series of combinations and unfoldments trace manifesting life back to its spiritual source. Antiquity posited Divinity and then constructed the universe; the twentieth century first posits the universe and then looks for God. As God, however, is not obvious to the crass materialist, he is often entirely eliminated in the findings of that particular type of scientist. You will remember that upon reading Laplace's great work upon astronomy Napoleon made the remark, "But you make no mention of God," to which the great scientist haughtily replied, "Sire, I have no need for that hypothesis."

Generaly speaking, the elimination of God by the scientist is only a passing symptom. It occurs at that stage where the scientist, like the precocious child, upon reaching the summit of Fool's Mountain decides that he himself is sufficient to postulate a cause for the universe and is qualified to manipulate it according to his own whims. Upon essaying the role of general manager of cosmos, man invariably discovers that the task is far too arduous, and so eventually returns to God his universe. Modern thought, which is basically skeptical, declares God to exist only when discovered. As yet, however, none has discovered Deity. The only discovery thus far made is the absolute *necessity* of a First Cause, and this paramount need for such a Supreme Activity is conclusive proof of the existence of such a force or being.

To summarize, the modern world bases its entire philosophy of life upon the reality of the visible, whereas the ancient world conceived the invisible to be the real. Thus we have two diametrically opposing viewpoints. In the final analysis it is evident that the viewpoint of antiquity is correct. In the first place, the visible is actually such a small part of existing Nature, it is inconceivable that it should be accorded a position of first importance. All bodies float in a vast sea of SPACE, forming but a fractional part of the contents of this great sphere of Being. The invisible life must be superior to its vehicle of manifestation. Therefore the great Reality—life—cannot actually be considered a part of the phenomenal universe. It is a strange but fundamental truth that the least permanent thing in the universe is a rock, and the most permanent is so-called empty space; for the time will come when the rock will cease to be, but space will never pass away. Form can be destroyed and is ever changing, but space, by its very nature, is indestructible and forever the same.

We now come to the nature of *emptiness*. Emptiness merely implies the absence of form; but the formless active agent, being all-permeating, fills all existence. You may pour the water out of a glass and then declare the glass to be empty because apparently it contains nothing. Any scientist, however, will assure you that the empty glass contains a sufficient number of atoms to blow the earth out of its orbit if their combined energy could be properly directionalized. Emptiness, therefore, is paradoxically an incomprehensible fullness. Philosophically considered, the absence of form means impossibility of destruction. That which has no form cannot have the form taken away. Emptiness, so-called, is consequently more permanent than fullness. In its conventional sense, fullness means that the container is filled to capacity with physical elements. The true fullness, however, is that area which is completely filled with spiritual and eternal agencies. Of such a nature is SPACE which, far from being empty, may be likened to a spiritual solid, whereas the physical world may be best described as a spiritual vacuum.

According to the Platonists, all the creations manifesting outward from the nature of God are arranged in the order of their proximity to First Cause. Those nearer the source of life partake more of the celestial effulgence than those more distant; in other words, the light radiating from a flame more closely resembles the flame at the source than at the extremity of its rays. The order of the gods is therefore determined by their proximity to the central creative fire of the universe, which is termed the Altar of Vesta or the Tower of the All-Wise Father. The gods are not to be considered as independent entities or forces, but rather as monads with numerous subordinate powers and intelligences dependent upon them. Each deity is, in turn, a dependency of a superior being, until at last all unite in a common dependency upon the benevolence of First Cause. Thus each individual deity may be symbolized by the dot, the line, and the circle. As a dot, each god is the central monad of a host of inferior dependencies; as a line, each god is a streaming radiance nourishing its subordinate parts; and as a circle or circumference each god is a fractional part of a still greater monadic entity. The majesty of these divinities is therefore established by the law of relativity. Each god is the father of a multitudinous progeny which exists within its own nature and which must unquestioningly obey its dictates. Each deity is, in turn, part of the progeny of a still higher and more exalted power to which it renders homage. Thus each deity is both a creator and a creation in one. As man ascends the ladder uniting effect with cause, he approaches ever closer to conscious realization of Source. He therefore passes through the angelic choirs described by Dante in his *Paradisio*. These choirs in concatenated circles about the flaming throne of the Eternal Father represent the orders of divine emanations. Thus the central flame is ever surrounded by a many-ringed nimbus of subordinate lights supporting all creation.

Let us approach the problem of macrocosmic interdependency through a consideration of certain microcosmic realities. The human body may be considered either as a single unit or as a host of minute living organisms combining in accordance with certain definite laws. Each individual cell is a living and immortal creature and it also has been definitely established that various organs of the human body possess at least a selective intelligence. Yet all these separate, living parts are suspended, as it were, from the single monad of the human heart. The heart is to the body what the sun is to the solar system and First Cause to existence. If one of the cells within the body dies, the body still lives, but if the chief governing monad ceases to function, then all the cells or dependent parts partake of the general dissolution. As the life of the body is centralized in the heart even though a general life is diffused throughout the body, so, while life may be discovered in every creature existing in the manifested sphere, all these subordinate lives are swept to a common destruction if the Great Monad upon which they depend be removed. The lesser lives have their origin in the greater and must always remain its dependents. Deity as the first Monad of the world is the foundation of the universe, the Sacred Island, sometimes analogous to Shamballah, the City of the Gods. Upon this Monad is erected all creation; with its dissolution the far-reaching and diversified phenomena collapse like a house of cards. Therefore God may be defined as that upon which a lesser part depends; our God is the Monad from whose nature we as lesser monads hang by hypothetical threads. Hence there are many gods, for all beings, both great and small, hang as dependencies upon the natures of superior forms of life.

Next we must consider the philosophic principle of priority. Of a number of things related to each other, that which is fundamental is primary or first, and the rest are dependencies.

For example, a ship may carry a large and diversified cargo. If any part of the cargo be thrown overboard, the safety of the ship is not necessarily endangered. If, however, the ship should sink, all its cargo goes down too. Thus the cargo depends upon the ship for its preservation, but the ship does not depend upon the cargo. The priority of either a science or a living organism is established by the degree of its fundamental importance to all other sciences and organisms. The destruction of priority automatically annihilates all its dependencies. If you destroy that which is first, that which is secondary also ceases. If you destroy that which is secondary you in no way injure that which is first; you simply limit some phase of its manifestation. Pythagoras used the science of mathematics to illustrate the principle of priority. Remove mathematics and you destroy every form of human knowledge which is in any way dependent upon numbers or the theory of mathematics. For example, consider the relationship between mathematics and music. The science of harmonics is wholly dependent upon mathematics. If you remove the knowledge of music from the world, you destroy a certain phase of mathematics, but the body of numbers is left uninjured. On the other hand, if you remove mathematics from the world, the entire theory of harmonics perishes. Of the two, mathematics is primary and music secondary. Another simple illustration: The tree has one trunk and many branches. The branches are dependencies of the trunk, for if one of the branches be removed the life of the tree is not seriously impaired and the other branches remain unaffected. Destroy the trunk, however, and all the branches die together. In the search for knowledge the highest wisdom is first to learn those things which have priority. To learn mathematics, for example, is to possess already a certain knowledge of all sciences, because it is the first among the sciences. For this reason the Greeks and Egyptians demanded of all disciples seeking initiation into the Mysteries an understanding of mathematics.

The identity of first things can be determined by applying the principle of priority. Things are considered of greater or lesser importance according to what they depend upon and what is dependent upon them. Man is master over those forms of life dependent upon him, but a slave to that infinity of forces which he depends upon for every expression and manifestation. The gods are merely symbolic representations of states of relative dependency. The gods are greater than man because they represent the members of existence upon which man depends. Such a chain of dependency is well represented by the institution of feudalism. A country was divided among a group of nobles whose relative importance depended upon the extent of their individual domains. A certain number of baronies constituted an earldom, and a group of earldoms, in turn, formed a dukedom. Above the dukedom was the principality, and over all the king, who on a smaller scale was the god of his nation. Greatness depends upon constructive and destructive power—destructive in the sense of changing rather than annihilating.

A further thought concerning the term *dependency*. Our hands and feet are dependent upon us for their animating principle; we are dependent upon them for the expression of certain innate desires and attitudes. Our hands and feet protect us, but they are obviously less than that which they protect. They may be likened to vassals or stewards. In the days of knighthood, when knights went into battle they were attended by esquires or stewards who rode behind their masters to free them from their heavy armor in the event they were unhorsed, or to arrange for a ransom with their conqueror. In ancient philosophy the gods represent the hands and feet and vital members of the cosmic body. Like the cherubim of the Jews, they run back and forth in the whirlwinds, executing the orders of the Most High even as our busy fingers carry out the dictates of our brain. The one Supreme Power manifesting throughout the cosmic organism should be considered as manifesting throughout all created things, each of which is a faculty or member of minor or major importance.

An interesting story came to our attention of an East Indian pundit who was trying to explain to a rather bigoted Christian missionary the reason for the great number of heads appearing upon the shoulders of certain Hindu divinities. "My dear sir," exclaimed the missionary, "yonder many-headed image is a ghastly caricature of a god, and how can any people who have risen above an aboriginal state worship such a grotesque and unnatural concept of God?" the pundit smilingly replied: "You do not understand our method of symbolizing divine agencies. In your own scriptures it is plainly implied that God is all there is and that in him we live and move and have our being. God is the heavens and the earth and all the creatures that inhabit them. You have a head, I have a head, all human beings have heads. Has God, therefore, not as many heads as there are heads, as many hands as there are hands, and as many feet as there are feet? Are not all minds his mind, all thoughts his thoughts, and all works accomplished for him done by him through his manifested parts? Therefore, my dear sir, our failure is not for lack of comprehension but because no artist alive is able to carve enough heads to adequately represent the nature of the Creator."

Philosophy is not solely an intellectual reasoning process whereby certain definite conclusions are reached concerning macrocosmic and microcosmic realities. Philosophy utterly fails in its mission unless that mystical elixir—understanding—tinctures the whole. Understanding is the rarest of all faculties. It is a subtle power which adds to the intellectual concept a definite stimulating realization or intuitive grasp of the fundamental elements involved in any problem and their relationship to each other. Understanding is the ultimate stage of knowledge; it is the perfect realization of the purpose and meaning of things. For two thousand years the men of the church have been studying Christianity; orators have shouted its precepts from the housetops; the Crusaders carried the message with the sword, the monk with the crucifix, and the Holy Inquisition with the firebrand. For nearly two thousand years men and women of devout spirit have prayed and fasted and meditated; they have even died as martyrs that the spirit of their faith might go on. Of this host of propagandists of Christianity, most had either an intellectual or an emotional concept of the Master Jesus and his mission. Only here and there was one who understood, and too often his fate was to fall before the mob of enthusiastic but misunderstanding zealots. Today there are innumerable truths which remain unrevealed to the seeker after knowledge because he does not possess the philosophic *open-sesame*. To the understanding mind all doors open; to those without understanding life must ever remain a tormenting enigma.

At the beginning of this chapter is a diagram showing the god Brahma as the creator of the universe. From his three heads, representative of the triune nature of First Cause, extend three streamers of force outward to form the foundations of the three worlds. In modern Hindu mysticism Brahma is generally represented with four heads and occasionally with five, one of which is supposed to have been cut of by Shiva. The four-headed Brahma is a demiurgic god, being the foundation of the four elements. The three-headed Brahma here referred to signifies the abstract Creative Logos, or the dot, manifesting as primitive potencies the threefold darkness of the Absolute, from whose incomprehensibility Brahma is but one degree removed. The three mouths of Brahma breathe forth the sacred whirlwinds of cosmic breath, which become incarnate in the universe as the creative Trimurti of Brahma, Vishnu, and Shiva, and which correspond to the first trinity of all peoples. From one mouth issues the breath which is to become spirit, which, after passing through numerous modifications, manifests as the causal agent throughout the worlds. From the second mouth streams that force which is to be the intermediary state throughout the universe. This state is most tangible as mind or that mysterious thinking air which, permeating the objective thinking structure, manifests as continuity of reason, perception, and ultimately apperception. The third head breathes forth the Maker of worlds and his angels, and from these outpouring essences are fashioned the objective spheres and their diversified genera.

In mystical philosophy the dot, or first emanation, is presumed to have three faces. The key to their meaning is at once apparent if the word *phases* is substituted for *faces*. The dot contains three phases of one power, yet in an undifferentiated state. Thus God in mystic Christianity is the dot, while the Father, Son, and Holy Ghost are his phases, or the first manifested Trimurti. The three phases or faces are sometimes referred to as the three modes of Being. From these primary modes manifests an infinitude of complex organisms. Between this cosmological mystery and the allegory of Noah's ark there is a certain analogy. Noah is the dot, his three sons are the faces, and their wives are the shakti, or negative expressions of these faces. As from the positive pole of Being there is manifested this triad of agencies, so from the negative pole of Being is manifested the quaternary of demiurgic forces. The two combine to form the sacred septenary so appropriately symbolized in the Masonic apron with its triangle rising out of or falling into (according to the degree) the square. The descent of the 3 into the 4 properly symbolizes the ensoulment of the world by its spiritual cause; the ascent of the 3 out of the 4, the resurrection of life from its sepulcher of form.

The process by which the entire objective universe is caused to issue forth from the first monadic dot can be likened to that process by which the oak tree emerges from the acorn. It is unreasonable to assume that the oak tree manifests any qualities that were not originally in its seed, yet that so much should have come from apparently so little is indeed a mystery. The oak tree is in the acorn in potentiality, yet when these potentialities come into objective existence they seem vastly greater than their source. According to the Oriental mystics, the universe is an inverted tree. The seed is the dot from which springs forth the World Tree whose branches are the gods and whose leaves are creation. This is the great tree of the Cabalists and also the illusional banyan of the Hindus, for it exists but a moment upon the substances of Eternity and then falls back again into SPACE.

From the three mouths of the first Trimurti issue powers: spiritual, intellectual, and material; divine, human, and animal; also the creative elements of air, fire, and water, air being symbolic of the intangible Father, fire of the radiant Son, and water of the Demiurgus who seeks with material impulses to quench the fire of spiritual light. These three are personified as the Builders of the world. The Father is King Solomon, the Son is Hiram Abiff, and the Holy Spirit is Hiram of Tyre, who furnishes the materials.

Having thus established the fundamental nature of the dot, we now pass to the constitution of the line wherein is revealed the mystery of the Savior-God of all ages and the second Principle of existence.

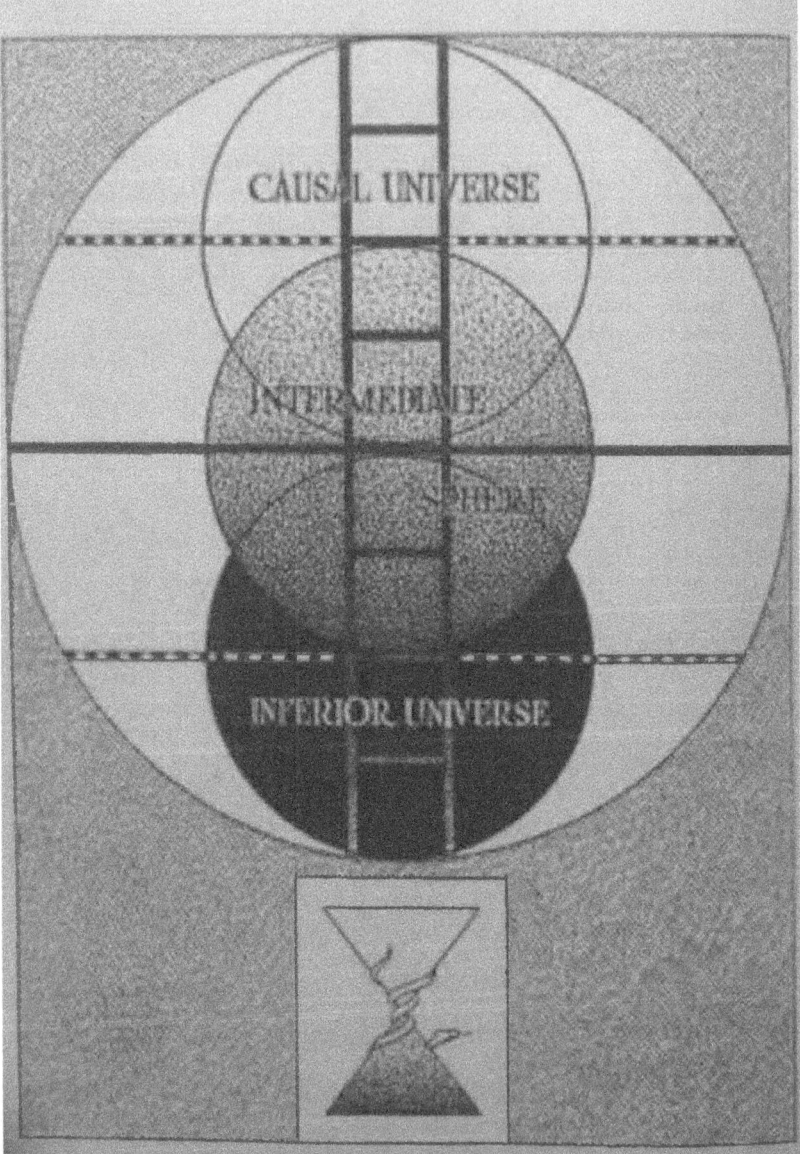

THE INTERPLAY OF THE WORLDS

In this figure is set forth the constitution of the Intermediate Sphere, by which the extremes of Spirit and Matter are reconciled and the harmony of the universe preserved. The ancients unite in the recognition of three worlds existing within one vast and unlimited state. Philosophy is the science of the relationships of these worlds.

CHAPTER THREE

Illumined Mind, the Universal Savior

LIGHT is the most appropriate symbol of manifesting spirit because it is the inherent nature of light to radiate, and this outpouring is represented by a simple vertical line drawn downward from the dot, or heart of existence. An analysis of the flame reveals its threefold constitution and their correspondence to the three phases of the dot considered in the preceding lecture. The blue (or nearly colorless) heart of the candle flame signifies the dark, hidden Father; the golden radiance surrounding this area is the bright, flaming Son who bears witness before the worlds of his unknowable Father; and at the circumference is a reddish, smoky flame representative of the Demiurgus, or Lord of the World. Because of its triune nature, fire for ages has been employed as the symbol of the threefold God. Pyrolatry is one of the oldest forms of religious expression.

Light can also be symbolized by a globe, the outer surface of which is the hypothetical point where the rays of light terminate. In reality, light is a rate of vibration pouring off, or outward, from the heart of the vibratory ray or cause of vibration, which must be symbolized by the flame. For the sake of the analogy, the heart of the flame can be compared to the dot; the radiant light pouring from the flame to the line; and the outer darkness which absorbs the light, to the circumference or outer limit of manifestation. Consider for a moment the relationship of the ray to its source. The true flame is invisible and superphysical, but it is made discernible to the eye through a rate of vibration called light, and to other sense perceptions through a rate of vibration called heat. Life, light, and heat are the trinity, with life as the Father, light as the Son, and heat as the Demiurgus. It may well be said, therefore, that no man hath seen the Father, for the transcendency of Being is concealed behind a flaming ring which blinds all who gaze upon it.

Radiance is the ceaseless effort of a central force to expand; it is the continual pouring off of sparks from an endless supply. The dot may be likened to a tube through which a mysterious spiritual fluid ever pours. The moment this fluid is free from the restraining pressure of the tube it has a tendency, like water, to expand and spread out in the form of a huge fan. Activity is continually manifesting throughout the universe. There is a never-ending battle between the effort of all life to expand and the effort of substance to resist expansion. A concrete example of this particular point may be helpful. By means of experimental balloons it is possible to estimate atmospheric conditions above the earth's surface. As the toy balloon ascends it expands until at an altitude of approximately eleven and one-half miles it will explode, in spite of every precaution that may be taken. The reason for this is that the outside pressure decreases as the atmosphere grows less dense, until finally the expanding quality of the gas inside the ballon meets with so little outside resistance that the walls of the ballon are unable to support the pressure. We have present in Nature, therefore, a continual expansion from within which is offset by a continual pressure from without. Thus the physical nature of every organism is particularly adapted to the pressure of its environment. Man's entire evolutionary progress has fitted him to sustain the atmospheric pressure at the earth's surface. The moment he leaves this atmospheric environment he must readjust himself, and beyond a certain point he cannot exist. The aviator has felt every part of his body racked with this effort to meet the ever decreasing pressure of higher altitudes. For similar reasons explorers climbing lofty mountains frequently suffer from bursting blood vessels. The pressure at the earth's surface is not as great, however, as that beneath the ocean, where the most powerful apparatus is required to withstand the pressure of the water. As man's physical existence is confined to a certain stratum of air pressure, so spiritually he is likewise limited to a definite plane of cosmic activity.

The denser the substances surrounding the individual, the greater the pressure from without. Hence materiality continually checks the natural expansion of the spiritual and intellectual self. The less material the environment, the greater the opportunity for the spiritual nature to expand, until finally at the gate of the Absolute the little globe of individual consciousness—like the toy balloon—reaches the point where there is no outward pressure whatsoever. The shell itself is symbolic of a degree of external pressure, but when all pressure has been removed, consciousness now freed from limitation is diffused again throughout the nature of existence. Hence the Absolute represents the vanishing point of external pressure. The circumference of the sphere of being is the plane established by the inward pressure of substance and the outward pressure of consciousness. As the scope of consciousness is enlarged the power of expansion increases and the walls of substance are pushed farther back. Conversely, as consciousness is denied expression and its impulses become weaker, the circle of substance approaches ever closer to the center of consciousness.

Philosophically defined, growth is the struggle of life to control its environment or, rather, to include more and more of its environment within the area of its own self-knowing. Perfect freedom of expression is the goal of all life. All things, both animate and inanimate, are striving for that freedom which lies in perfect expression. It naturally follows that there is but one freedom—perfection. Every creature is a slave to those parts of itself as yet unresponsive to the impulses of its internal life principle. Every individual consequently is a slave to his own material constitution; he is a prisoner held in by walls of unresponsive substance. Thus the natural expression of the inner life principle is to refine and improve the qualities of its outer vehicles that it may the more easily control and direct them. It is evident that the more refined the substance, the more easily it is influenced by subtle forces. By a certain definite organization, consciousness equips its outer nature with organs of responsiveness, so that the lower self comes ever more nearly *en rapport* with its own Cause. A common example is the radio, which is a mechanical contrivance constructed according to definite scientific principles which enable it to pick up vibratory rates of sound inaudible to even the delicate mechanism of the human ear.

Returning to the symbolism of the line, the line is a potential cosmic nerve ray designed to confer consciousness upon the area covered by its tiny threadlike fingers. Man is slowly acquiring control over his physical body by ever increasing the acuteness of his nervous organism, for by his nerves the various parts of his body are tied together. The nerve is an impulse carrier which gives man consciousness over a certain area of otherwise unresponsive substance. Man's nerves function far more acutely now than in ages past; they are becoming much more sensitive and bring to man much knowledge concerning the nature of the substance composing his world. As the result of this increasing sensitiveness, nervous disorders are increasing, for the finer the mechanism the greater the likelihood of derangement. The Romans termed the line Mercury, the messenger of the gods. Like the lines of the telegraph and telephone, the nerves bring the distant parts of the organism into direct contact with the central station of the brain. The nerves do not necessarily end at the outer circumference of the physical body, but in the form of etheric streamers extend outward into the aura, or intangible atmosphere surrounding the physical body. Here they continue to function in a limited degree as impulse carriers. These etheric nerve ends are continually contacting forces and forms both visible and invisible, and conveying certain indefinite impulses back to the brain. Many of our so-called "hunches" and unaccountable antipathies or affinities are the result of curious reactions set up by these etheric nerve threads which bind every part of the lower organism of man, visible and invisible, into one solid body.

The line or ray coming out of the dot may be likened to a primitive nerve giving to the dot a consciousness of the nature of its environment. It thus becomes the messenger between the center and the circumference of life. *The line is the outpouring of cause into effect.* The line permeates its environment with the qualities of the first innate life principle of the central dot; it is the effort of the center to include the circumference within itself. The phenomena of growth represent the gradual effort of life, which is innately perfect, to objectify its perfection and blend itself with the perfection of all. In this manner the subjective potentialities of life gradually become objective potencies or powers. Growth is really the bringing of the inside of life to the outside; a gesture from within outward; the unceasing effort of the active agent to communicate its conscious qualities to its unconscious environment. The ultimate of growth is the bringing into conscious expression all of the seed germs of power lying latent in every atom of existence. The dot contains within itself all potentialities as the symbolic acorn contains the oak tree. Every leaf that in the future will grow upon the oak tree exists as a potential power in the germinal essences of the acorn. Growth merely brings these latent potentialities into active manifestation by building into them material elements which make them apparent to physical sense perceptions. The fundamental reason for this growth is the active urge to express the potencies of self and escape the imprisonment of limited vehicles.

Pythagoras said that when the triangle is once established any problem is already two-thirds solved. The foundation of all existence is triangular. We are a threefold creation; the triangle of man consists of his spirit, his body, and the link connecting them. In its macrocosmic sense there is a divine creation, an elemental creation, and the link connecting them. Life is a divine, eternal principle; matter (except in its absolute sense) is a temporal and transitory thing. These two are separated by the whole interval of being. They are the opposites, and between them is a neutral field where one acts upon the other, for in their self-sufficient states the two have little in common. Divine nature is essentially a part of the divine creation; physical nature a part of the material creation. In ancient symbolism it was declared that the two seas—the ocean of

Divinity above and the ocean of Nature below—were divided, "the waters which were under the firmament from the waters which were above the firmament."

The universe of divine energy above and the universe of material energy below are the substances from which are extracted respectively the spirit and the body of man. The spirit is an atom of divine substance, the body an atom of material substance, and the higher vests itself in the lower and the product is a living thing. Presuming spirit to be the actuating part and matter the part worked upon, it will be evident that the spirit cannot control the body without the assistance of a connecting tissue wherein the irreconcilable opposites are blended. Thus in order that the abstractly spiritual may affect the concretely material, a great hierarchy of mediatory agencies must be established. In certain of the ancient Mystery schools it was taught that there were eighty thousand degrees of intelligence intervening between absolute consciousness and absolute unconsciousness, each degree representing a mediatory element or condition. Considered as a unit, these degrees represent the middle or neutral field. In alchemy mercury, or quicksilver, is used to symbolize this blending element, because mercury accepts into its own nature other metals. In mythology the god Mercury was the mediator or neutral power serving as the messenger between the gods above and mortal man below.

Still another pair of opposites must be considered: divine truth and human ignorance. Above (in the sense of proximate to cause) is divine Reality, the one great need of all creation; below (in the sense of distant from Source) is man, who may achieve salvation only through the attainment of Reality. Here are both the living water and the empty bowl waiting to receive it. But absolute truth and ignorant humanity are divided by a vast interval of understanding. *Truth knows no man; man knows no truth.* Truth is that mysterious, infinite, boundless Reality; man a mere worm existing in minutes, hours, and days, and spending most of them foolishly. Here the sum of the knowable is the dot, gross ignorance the circumference of the circle. That which is necessary to unite these two and thus blend them into the perfection of type is the line, the mediator between cause and effect.

A simple analogy of the dot, the line, and the circle with the processes of knowledge may be traced in the following manner. In the center of the circle is the dot representing a fact; at the circumference of the circle stands a student desirous of learning this fact; between these two is an interval filled with a number of agencies, any one of which (in many cases the sense perceptions) may become the mediator between the knowable and the one capable of knowing. In order to gain a more extensive understanding of existence with its vast number of physically apparent facts, the interval is occupied by an elaborate educational system, and thus between knowledge and the student body stands the professor who acts as mediator and assists in the dissemination of the subject matter.

Everywhere in Nature is to be found a mediating principle which is capable of contacting both extremes simultaneously, or at least intermittently. It is most difficult to unite the abstract and the concrete in a single nature, consequently you may hear such remarks as "Genius is eccentric," "A wonderful man, but—", etc. Those who possess abstract knowledge can seldom clothe it in words understandable to others. As man attempts to elevate himself spiritually he gradually separates himself from his material environment. To have a stature great enough to raise its head to heaven and still keep its feet upon the earth is the proof of true enlightenment. If wisdom is to instruct ignorance, it must be capable of appreciating the state of ignorance as truly as the state of knowledge. If the mind has raised itself above the consciousness of ignorance, it will never be able to impart wisdom to the ignorant. To instruct the minds of others it is necessary to approach them along the lines of the familiar; they must be reached on a thought level commensurate with their own, otherwise they cannot grasp the problems presented.

Since in the universal scheme the divine mediator must have the consciousness of both the upper and the lower, philosophy postulates three manners of beings: gods, who are great centers of intelligent power; men, who are little centers with marvelous potentialities; and god-men or man-gods who act as mediators between the superior and the inferior. Thus is revealed the meaning of that enigmatic statement of the Pythagoreans that there were three kinds of creatures: gods, men, and Pythagoras, the latter being representative of the mediator who was able to bind together the superior and the inferior creations. In a similar manner the identity of Jesus (according to the Gnostic traditions) is clarified, for in some places he is referred to as the Son of God and in others as the Son of man. As the Son of man he ascended out of the earth to the inheritance of a heavenly state (heaven in the sense of accomplishment); as the Son of God he veiled his sense of knowing in a mortal vehicle and descended from the mysteries of the higher aeons into the state of human ignorance, and was thus able to converse with mortals upon the level of their own understanding. In the words of an ancient philosopher: "He who has not even a knowledge of common things is a brute among men. He who has an accurate knowledge of human concerns alone, is a man among brutes. But he who knows all that can be known by intellectual energy is a God among men."

Man's status in cosmos is determined, therefore, by the *quality* of his thinking. Quality, as applied to mental processes, is not necessarily intensity but rather refinement and delicacy. The trained scientist may reach a very high degree of intellectuality and yet lack that beautifying element which is indispensable to true understanding. Unless the inner nature transcends the limitations of both the flesh and the mind, the self can never attain to a full measure of expression. Whether a man be a beast or a god does not depend upon his outward appearance but rather upon the clarity of his inner perceptions. Many of the most respected citizens of every community are actually ravaging beasts concealing their primitive instincts under a thin veneer of culture. On the other hand, some whom the world regards as failures possess an innate beauty which elevates them far above the level of their fellows.

The gods may be defined as those in whom the state of knowing has reached a degree of relative perfection, and beasts those creatures in whom the state of knowing is asleep. Between these two extremes is man, who wanders about in a state of partial knowing, united to the bestial creation by his ignorance and to the higher orders of divinities by his dawning rationality. Between the states of knowing and not-knowing the Greeks postulated the *middle distance*, a point where consciousness and unconsciousness are blended in semiconsciousness. Between the light of spirit above and the darkness of matter below there is the twilight zone which is the proper sphere of mind and where creatures endowed with minds seek to read the book of their destiny by the all-too-insufficient light. This central twilight zone is divided by a hypothetical median line into two hemispheres. The upper hemisphere, partaking most directly of the supreme effulgence which is proximate to it, is the dwelling place of the Sons of God—the Ben Elohim of the Hebrews—or those beings fundamentally divine but who partake somewhat of the qualities of the *middle distance* and therefore descend to the hypothetical median line dividing the upper and lower hemispheres of the *middle distance*. The lower hemisphere is proximate to the dark sphere of ignorance, but partaking, to a certain degree, of the superior light, becomes the abode of the redeemed souls—the Ishim of the Hebrews. Inferior creatures rising out of the darkness of their mortal night, though they be of the earth earthy, may ascend into the *middle distance* and at this hypothetical median line contact the demigods who descend from the superior spheres. Thus in the *middle distance* are to be found both the demigods who have descended from above as instructors of mankind, and the supermen who, rising from the insufficiency of matter, converse with the demigods through the hypothetical median line.

It follows that the ancients conceived the instructors of humanity to be of two kinds: (1) those who descended from the light aeons of the internal causal world, and, brooding over humanity, spoke through oracles and oracular souls or prophets; (2) those who through the peculiar culture of the Mysteries were elevated to a state of sensitiveness wherein they became ready pens in the hands of the heavenly writers. Knowledge likewise is twofold: that knowledge which, having its origin among the celestial beings of the light world, is communicated to man and constitutes the *revealed* or sacred writing; and that knowledge which is evolved by man himself during his ages of struggle in the inhibiting environment of the mortal world. The wisdom imparted by the demigods partakes of that higher knowledge which belongs to the sphere of consciousness and causation, while that wisdom imparted by the superhuman (or illumined human) souls, being further removed from cause, lacks the definiteness and authority of the divinely-given code. The demigods teach the celestial or inner body of knowledge; the superman, the terrestrial or outer body of knowledge. Therefore, the initiates and the prophets bear witness of the light, though not directly partaking of its power to the extent of the demigods.

According to the esoteric doctrines of Platonism, the demigods can never become men or descend to the level of mortality because they are of a different and higher order of creation. On the other hand, though man through discipline and enlightenment rises to a state approaching deification, he can never actually become one with the gods, for he must continue in the life stream of which he is a part. This does not mean that man will not ultimately attain to the state of Divinity but rather that he will create his own genus of gods, for the life of one creation can never become identical with the life of any other creation but must evolve its own vehicles of manifestation. The same law that prohibits man from becoming like the gods also prohibits the gods from becoming like man, even though they control and direct his destiny. In spite of its magnificent power and divine abundance of wisdom and understanding, the demigod is unable to build a physical body and hence must borrow one already prepared for its use. Such a body then becomes its oracle or shrine, and through it the demigod reaches the dwellers in the dark sphere of matter. Thus when one of the demigods, or great Devas, desires to communicate with mankind it descends to the median line where, working through the plane of mind (the mediating principle), it overshadows a mortal who has raised himself to this exalted state, and through the higher vehicles of such a mortal contacts humanity. By thus overshadowing the mind of the mortal initiate, the Deva causes him to think, speak, and act according to the celestial will.

The demigods must not be considered as personalities but rather as individualities, in that they function in substances too rarefied (free of gross physical elements) to permit the existence of personal organisms. The demigods are units of knowing, relatively superior to mortal men but incapable of molding physical matter except through the medium of mind. Supermen are personal beings who are gradually outgrowing personality. Though still limited by mortal bodies, they have learned to separate consciousness from form and function (temporarily at least) in the same substances that constitute the attenuated organisms of the demigods. Various Greek philosophers are said to have been overshadowed by gods or *daemons*. Thus Pythagoras was declared to be overshadowed always by the spirit of the Pythian Apollo, and Socrates likewise by a mysterious creature which he referred to as his "god." Bringing with it certain great truths otherwise inaccessible to man, such a deity elevates the one so overshadowed to a position of unusual philosophic dignity.

At this point it is necessary to remind the reader that the demigods, since they are part of the causal agencies which together constitute the spiritual world, are themselves in and of the spiritual natures of all creatures. Thus man's own spirit is a demigod hovering over his lower organisms, which are as disciples receiving the instruction necessary to right living from the god within. In Oriental art Arjuna is frequently shown receiving instruction from Krishna on the battlefield of Kurushetra. Arjuna, the son of Kunti, the mortal man, is often represented as a diminutive figure while above him in all the splendor of his azure radiance stands the blue Krishna. Here Arjuna represents the personal or mortal *I* and Krishna the demigod or oversoul upon whose instruction the mortal man depends for his inspiration to right action.

Occasionally the spiritual and the material worlds are symbolized by two pyramids, one inverted with its base in the heavens and the other upright with its base upon the earth. The two pyramids meet at their apexes. The pyramid with its foundation in heaven decreases in size as it descends, and is the proper symbol of the decreasing choirs of celestial beings (forces and intelligences) that descend in concatenated order from the effulgence of the Twenty-fourth Mystery which is the First Mystery from above. The upright pyramid with its foundation in matter indicates by its converging sides the gradual decrease of materiality until at its apex materiality vanishes. Occasionally a serpent is wound about the point where the two apexes meet, thus indicating the mystery of mind and the astral light which is the blending of the superior and the inferior Aeons.

This concatenated order of decreasing materiality and increasing spirituality forms the many-runged ladder rising from the darkness of oblivion below and the perfect light of celestial splendor above, and was the ladder that the angels ascended and descended in Jacob's vision. Man painfully climbs the many steps leading to the summit of the pyramid of material attainment, and upon reaching the apex finds himself at the foot of an incalculable flight of steps that leads upward to the very source of Being. Upon this upper flight of steps stand the demigods, above them the gods, and around about the winged spirits who dwell in the *middle distance* and are the divine messengers. This entire picture must be considered, however, as a symbolic representation of the states and conditions of consciousness, intelligence, and force, which by their orderly combinations bring all phenomena into manifestation.

The figure accompanying this chapter sets forth in a diagrammatic manner the interplay of the three worlds forming the basis of Greek and Hindu philosophy. Once this point is comprehended, the entire structure of ancient thought is revealed. The circles, of course, merely represent vast areas of spiritual activity occupying the same place at the same time but separated from each other by the vibratory rates of their atomic particles. The white sphere represents the causal nature, the black sphere the material universe. It will be noted that the third, or intermediate sphere consists of a dotted area, the dots increasing in number below and decreasing in number above the horizontal line. The entire diagram is divided horizontally by a heavy line which represents the definite point of separation between the causal universe and the universe of effects. This diagram should be considered as applicable not only to cosmos but to every organism in the universe, which by its very existence demonstrates that it is composed of spiritual and material agencies combined as shown in the drawing. The ladder rising through the three worlds signifies the path of attainment that leads from darkness into light. That part of the ladder occupying the space below the central dividing line represents the mystery of water, which is purification; that part of the ladder above the central dividing line represents the mystery of fire, which is the baptism of the spirit. Here is the key to the two baptisms of the Christian Gnostics, for John the Baptist is made to say, "I indeed baptize you with water unto repentance: but he that cometh after me * * * shall baptize you with the Holy Ghost, and with fire." In this figure is thus set forth the entire purpose of the ancient Mysteries and the processes of human regeneration. Here also is set forth a still greater mystery—the mystery of the *dying god*—with which we must now concern ourselves.

The Augustinian, or outer, interpretation of the dying god *mythos* declares the martyr Savior to be the line descending from the dot to the circle which, falling into the darkness of the circumference, is swallowed up (or allegorically *dies*) by becoming immersed in the irrational sphere of matter. Man is declared to have two souls, or rather, two hypothetical phases of one soul consciousness. The first and superior is the rational soul; the second and inferior, the irrational soul. The rational soul is that part of man which is ever in awareness of divine and eternal self. The irrational soul is that part which, being incapable of retiring into the mysteries of self, mistakes the outer nature for the inner and assumes the objective man to be the real. The qualities of the rational soul are apperception, realization, comprehension, and other higher mental and supermental faculties. The qualities of the irrational soul are external perception, ignorance, selfishness, lust, greed, and kindred vices. The rational soul is necessarily unselfish because it conceives self to be distributed throughout the entire substance of Being. Glimpsing the universal ultimates of life, the rational soul is not hypnotized by the illusion of a personal self and therefore does not urge toward personal aggrandizement and accumulation. The irrational soul is fundamentally selfish because it conceives self to be isolated, and the service and preservation of self therefore becomes an all-important consideration. Sin and death are the masters of the irrational soul. Realizing the kinship of one with the All, the rational soul, however, attains immortality and omnipotence. Socrates defines man as a self-knowing being immersed in a not-knowing body. This is the outer mystery of the dying god slain for the sin of the world or, more correctly, *by* the sin of the world.

Descending from the spiritual Aeons and dying by reason of immersion in the unknowing nature of the inferior creation, the self-knower becomes the motif of many allegories. A well-known example is that of Jonah being thrown overboard and swallowed by the *hippocampus* or mythological whale. Jonah (the knower) is immersed in the sea of illusion (life) and swallowed by *cetus* (the leviathan or monster of mortality). St. Augustine explains the allegory differently, declaring the whale to symbolize God who, when the prophet was cast by men into the sea of tribulation, was accepted into the body of God and carried safely to shore. The three days that Jonah remained in the whale's belly, however, links the allegory definitely to the dying-god myth, for according to the Mysteries the rational soul is immersed for three days in the nature of the inferior sphere. Again, the irrational universe (the not-knowing part) is divided into twelve sections which are symbolized by the signs of the zodiac and called the Twelve Holy Animals. These are the twelve parts of unreality. In the Greek Mysteries they are called the Titans or primordial giants who took the body of Bacchus (the rational soul) and tearing it to pieces devoured the flesh. This signifies, in the terms of the Pythagoceans, that the *one* knower—the real part of every creature and the rational soul of the universe—is destroyed and its integrity dissipated by *multitude*, representing by the Titans.

Paracelsus calls man a *composita*, or a being composed of man and beast, a concept symbolized in the Mysteries by the centaur who had the head and shoulders of a man and the body of a horse. Man is twofold: a rational nature rising out of an irrational nature—hence, the mystery of the dying god. The rational soul is the eternal martyr who awaits the day of his liberation, which can only be accomplished when man elevates himself above the level of material impulse. Bacchus torn to pieces by the Titans, Atys gored by the wild boar, Adonis dead at the foot of the pine tree, Orpheus slain by the Ciconian women—all these ancient martyrs represent the rationality of man falling a victim to the inconstancies of his inferior nature. Chiron, the centaur instructor of Achilles, has a different significance however, for here the centaur represents the god-man with its head in the supreme world and its body in Nature. The centaur is therefore one of the demigods overshadowing a highly evolved human soul. The irrational nature of man is well symbolized by the Cretan labyrinth where rules the Minotaur, the bull-headed lord of matter, the creature which most mistake for their own true self. Into this irrational sphere descends Theseus, who prevents himself from being lost in the tortuous passageways by unraveling behind him Ariadne's thread. The rational soul thus slays the beast-man and becomes king of the country of its own life. So much for the exoteric significance of the dying-god allegory.

In the secret teachings it is written that mind itself is the Savior-God. Mind is the martyr of the ages, the eternal and universal Prometheus sacrificed upon the altar of human necessity. Mind is the willing sufferer upon the tree. Mind must destroy itself that that which is greater than mind may endure. According to the Mysteries, there comes that time in the quest of consciousness when man discovers the mind to be the slayer of the Real. Then as he sloughs off his evil nature, he must slough off his mind that his consciousness may be disentangled from the infinite complex of the mental web. The mind is incapable of ascending to the state of consciousness. The mind can never completely annihilate the sense of separateness, for it depends upon comparison for its function and differentiation for its very existence. Consequently, though the mind is ever the link between consciousness and unconsciousness, it too must be ultimately sacrificed in order that the Great Work be accomplished. By the death of the mind consciousness is released to complete perfection, but woe unto him who slays the mind without that understanding which must be given out of the Mysteries.

The mind must not die until its own work has been completed and its function has reached the highest possible degree of perfection. As the mind increases in power and rationality, it grows gradually to realize that there is something beyond thought. The mind is capable of realizing this power but is never able actually to contact it. There is a supermental state which is synonymous to a certain extent with the causal sphere. The Buddhist sees consciousness as a universal sea. Consciousness is therefore something that is moved only by a divine ebb and flow, by a realization of itself. This universal, all penetrating sea is the true substance of everything, for consciousness (or Self) was before the beginning and consciousness (or Self) is after the end. Beginning and end are illusions, but Self is eternal. Consciousness is therefore union with Self. Consciousness knows no separateness. As long as *me* and *thee* exist, consciousness is not perfected. Life and death, good and evil, light and shadow—these are the illusions of mind. But in consciousness diversity is totally annihilated and all things are one in reality and in essence. The bond of brotherhood is proved by the mind to be good, but the realization of brotherhood is not consciousness. The bond of friendship is demonstrated by the intellect to be necessary, but frendship is less than consciousness. There is no consciousness until the *I* in each is one and indivisible from the *I* in All. Until we are everything that we in our ignorance believe surrounds us, there is no complete consciousness. We may study the star intellectually, but we have never attained consciousness until we are the star, the stone, the heavens, and the earth. When our consciousness is perfect we extend from the heights of height to the depths of depth; we permeate the whole nature of existence; we are in everything, we are through everything, we are the whole nature of everything.

The difference between intellect and consciousness is therefore the difference between a mental concept of an object and an actual mingling of our consciousness with the consciousness of the object itelf. This latter state is realization. The intellectual concept, however, must to a certain degree precede the consciousness. As the mind is higher than the body, and the body must ultimately accept the thinking organism as its master, so consciousness is higher than mind, and the mind must ultimately give way to it. The mind is a bridge connecting consciousness and unconsciousness, but having crossed the bridge, it is left behind, its usefulness past. As a bridge, however, the mind is a vital necessity, and he who depreciates it is as false as he who permits himself to become the servant of its whims.

The Buddhist priest entering into Nirvana, and the Brahman bridging the chasm between mortal consciousness and *samadhi*, both cast aside mind as a snare and a delusion; yet without it the very principles upon which they work would be incomprehensible to them. The Eastern mind, endeavoring to annihilate the unreal and mingle itself with the Real, depends first upon the intellect to reveal the processes of illumination and the reasonableness of their abstract conceptions. The Western schools of philosophy differ from the Eastern in that they teach the perfection of the mind before its rejection, whereas the Eastern schools are prone to regard the mind as a hindrance, to be discarded at the very beginning of spiritual growth. Thus the Eastern mystic with his own nature slays the mind, while the Western philosopher, by elevating the mind to a realization of its own insufficiency, causes the intellect voluntarily to offer itself as a willing sacrifice upon the altar of spirit.

The ability to feel *with* rather than *for* is the essential difference between consciousness and emotion. When we feel *for* things we are emotionally moved. Pity, sympathy, and kindred feelings stir us, and yet they seldom give any definite impulse that is of value in the adjustment of any chain of circumstances. When we feel *with* things we are so much a part of them that we understand the innermost elements of their being. Thus understanding comes with consciousness, and knowledge with intellectual comprehension. According to the ancient doctrines, perfect consciousness—the ability to feel with everything as part of everything—was regarded as the ultimate state of so-called human unfoldment, and he who had achieved this had attained to godhood in his own right. The gods are simply emblematic of varying degrees of consciousness in that vast interval between ignorance and realization. At present humanity is semiconscious—conscious over the area of the known and unconscious over the area of the unknown. We have reached a degree of consciousness that enables us to study the exoteric, or outer constitution of things. We will never know the urges, however, that cause the diversified phenomena of existence until we are united with the inner nature that animates the outer body. Consciousness is gauged, therefore, by our ability to unite ourselves with the soul urges of those creatures that surround us, and true greatness is measured by the power to come *en rapport* with the causes of objective manifestation.

Many centuries ago there was founded in Korea a group of Eastern thinkers of Buddhist persuasion who developed the science of realization to a higher degree than any group since Gautama himself. The story is told that to one of the monasteries of this order in Japan there came a disciple who dedicated his life to the attainment of this inner consciousness. Year after year he struggled to master the illusions of his outer nature and find the infinite and all-pervading self within. His patience was tireless, his devotion unwavering. Yet the passing years found no apparent improvement in his spiritual condition; he was never able to be one with all the life that surrounded him. After having spent the best part of a lifetime in wandering and meditation without reward, he finally returned to the little monastery, having decided that if he could not attain to consciousness life was useless and he would destroy himself. Just inside the monastery grounds was a tall tower, and climbing to the top the monk cast himself off with a silent hope that his search would end in the peace of death. While in the act of falling, consciousness came to him, and with it the realization that the earth below was so surely a part of himself that it would not injure him when he fell upon it. The result of this realization was that he landed on his feet uninjured after a fall which would have killed the ordinary man. His face radiant with the inner conviction that had come upon him, he rushed to the abbot of the monastery who had been his friend for many years, and bowing before the aged man exclaimed, "At last I know, Master; at last I know!" Seeing the look of divine understanding upon the face of the mendicant, the abbot smilingly asked, "What do you know?" "I cannot tell you what I know, Master. There are no words, no thoughts that can express it. If you know, you must know as I know. I can make no revelation of it to any man." The abbot looked at him for a moment and then replied, "It is evident, my son, that you know. The fact that you cannot tell it is the proof that you possess it. Nothing of which we may speak can transcend the world of illusion, for words themselves were created to describe unrealities. Therefore the unutterable is the real and the unthinkable is the true; the utterable is the false and the thinkable is the phantom of a dream."

In this renaissance of the metaphysical we hear much of consciousness and understanding and spiritual realization. But one thing is certain and to be depended upon he who possesses consciousness will make no effort to reveal it, for the very achievement brings with it a realization of the hopelessness of attempting to communicate the wonders of the Self to a world that knows nothing of the contemplative life. People talk glibly of cosmic consciousness and unity with Absolute Being, but their very words belie the fact. A great Buddhist monk was once brought into the presence of the Emperor of China, and the Emperor addressed him thus: "Anwser me, O servant of the enlightened, one question." And the saffron-robed sage replied, "Noble sire, what is your question?" The Son of Heaven answered, "I would know the end of things, the ultimate state."

Daruma gazed upon him for a moment with a strange expression of mingled sadness and amusement—amused that any man should dare to ask in words that which no words can explain, sad that anyone should know so little as to ask so much. Finally the sage answered, "O Emperor, bring me a potted plant." A servant brought one in and the monk, looking at it for a second said, "This is a rare porcelain, is it not?" "It is worth a fortune," replied the Emperor. Thereupon the sage dashed the potted plant to the hard floor where it was shattered to bits. Filled with wrath the Emperor cried out, "Foolish one, what have you done?" "I have answered your question concerning the ultimate of things," the sage rejoined. "Words fail, thoughts fail, but in this way I can give you evidence of that which must be evidenced by the self alone." For a time the Emperor was buried in thought, and then shook his head. "I do not understand," he said. "Alas," replied the sage, "alas, sire, I can do no more!"

During the progress of our lectures we have been asked again and again to describe those spiritual processes by which the mystery of the Self is to be revealed. If those who asked knew or realized the nature of their question they would know that it is unanswerable by mortal man, and that he who even attempts to give an answer thrice proves his unfitness to possess the answer. Many are the paths of Dharma by which the law is revealed, and more than this of the law cannot be said: He who would know and comprehend must learn to think and dream and feel in the rhythm of universal concerns, leaving behind him the pettiness of personal affairs. To achieve to the end of Tao he must exchange the rhythm of the senses for that vast ebb and flow of measureless eternity, for only when man ceases to be man is he not man. When he ceases to be a creature; when he ceases to think or to feel or to know; when he ceases to feel his kinship with the earth or the sky; when he is no longer mortal or immortal; when he is neither one with the grain of dust nor with the gods; when all conditions have passed away; when dimension and time have disappeared; when nothing remains except the all-pervading Universal Self, unthinkable, unknowable, transcendent, and perfect; when the interval between the self and the Self in all has been annihilated—when all these things are one and I-am-that-one and yet *I* am not, then the soul has ceased to be a soul and is Self. Nirvana is reached when each finds himself to be all and rests forever in the state of Not-Being, which is All-Being, indivisible and perfect.

In Japan the Tango no Sekku, or Festival of the Boys, is a very important one, and is celebrated annually early in May. Among the important symbols in evidence at this time is the paper flag or kite cut in the shape of a great fish. This banner is hollow and the wind blowing into it causes the carp to become inflated and swim about in the air in a very lifelike manner. The ceremony of flying the carp had its origin in the ancient Chinese legend of the dragon carp. This fish, which swims with great resolution against the current, is considered in the Orient to be a fitting emblem of the soul of man swimming against the stream of illusion and striving to reach perfection despite the opposition of time and circumstance. The dragon carp, according to the legend, desired to swim against the Dragon Gate rapids, and again and again threw its body into the air, only to be beaten back by the strength of the angry current. The gods, beholding the struggle of the carp, marveled at its patience and endurance, for it returned from each new defeat with fresh courage and determination to conquer the rapids. At last, with a supreme effort the carp achieved its end, and when it reached the haven of the placid waters above the rapids, the body of the great fish glowed with a celestial splendor and became the symbol of the accomplishment of perfection. The gods gave the fish the life span of a thousand years, and at the end of this period it was transfigured. Surrounded by streamers of divine radiance, it ascended into the heavens and became one of the immortals. In Buddhist symbolism, the achievement of the dragon carp, fittingly symbolizes the attainment of Nirvana. Again and again the human soul seeks to stem the tide of mortal fate. Heedless of wordly ridicule and misunderstanding, the mystic patiently continues his effort to clear the rapids of his own lower nature. At last, passing through the maelstrom of the lower self he finds peace, and being transfigured ascends into the heavens to be united in Nirvana with all creatures and all ages.

The difference between the intellectual concept and consciousness lies in certain indescribable realities too deeply imbedded in the nature of Being to permit description. In the East, consciousness is likened to the lotus bud which, gradually opening, reveals more and more of itself to a wondering world until at last the golden heart in all its splendor is disclosed. Perfect consciousness to man is perfect realization of the nature and relationship of parts to the fundamental unity in which they exist. The ability to understand the actual order of Being, and to see everything correctly, is to be conscious. To see things as they seem to be is to be subject to the illusions of the lower mind.

An example of consciousness may be briefly summed up in the statement that to know the nature of all things is to realize that all things are good. To intellectually achieve this attitude is very simple, for it is only necessary to affirm continually that the thing is good, and after a while the mind, following the line of least resistance, accepts the affirmation as a fact and no longer questions the reality of that good. But there is a vast difference between convincing oneself intellectually of the goodness of things, and becoming really conscious of the goodness of things. *Consciousness is not the result of the mind convincing the Self; consciousness is the result of the Self convincing the mind.* The mind incarnated in the *Christos* speaks of consciousness personified in the Father in these words: "The Father is greater than I." Consciousness is greater than mind, which is born out of and is a limited expression of the Supreme Parent.

What then did the Emperor Julian infer when he spoke of the sacred Mysteries of the Seven-Rayed God who lifted souls to salvation through his own nature? Simply this: No more can Reality descend to the level of ignorance than can the lesser of anything contain the greater. If man would grasp the Infinite, it is therefore necessary for him to raise himself to the level of the Infinite, and as he ascends the mystery becomes ever more clear. Universal Mind is the Seven-Rayed Savior-God through which man must ascend from the primitive state of darkened mindlessness to the perfect state of all-knowing mindlessness. Thus mind is indeed the Savior-God who leads the soul to the comprehension of Self. But, as was true of Moses, the Lawgiver of Israel, it is not written that mind shall enter into the Promised Land. Having led the children of Israel (the parts of the inferior nature) through the Wilderness of Sin to the portals of the Gates of Peace, the mind lies down among the bleak hills of Moab, its work accomplished, and rests in the Law. His face illumined by the celestial radiance reflected from the sphere he can never fully understand, mind, the Universal Savior, dies at the gate of Nirvana while the souls he has redeemed pass on to perfection.

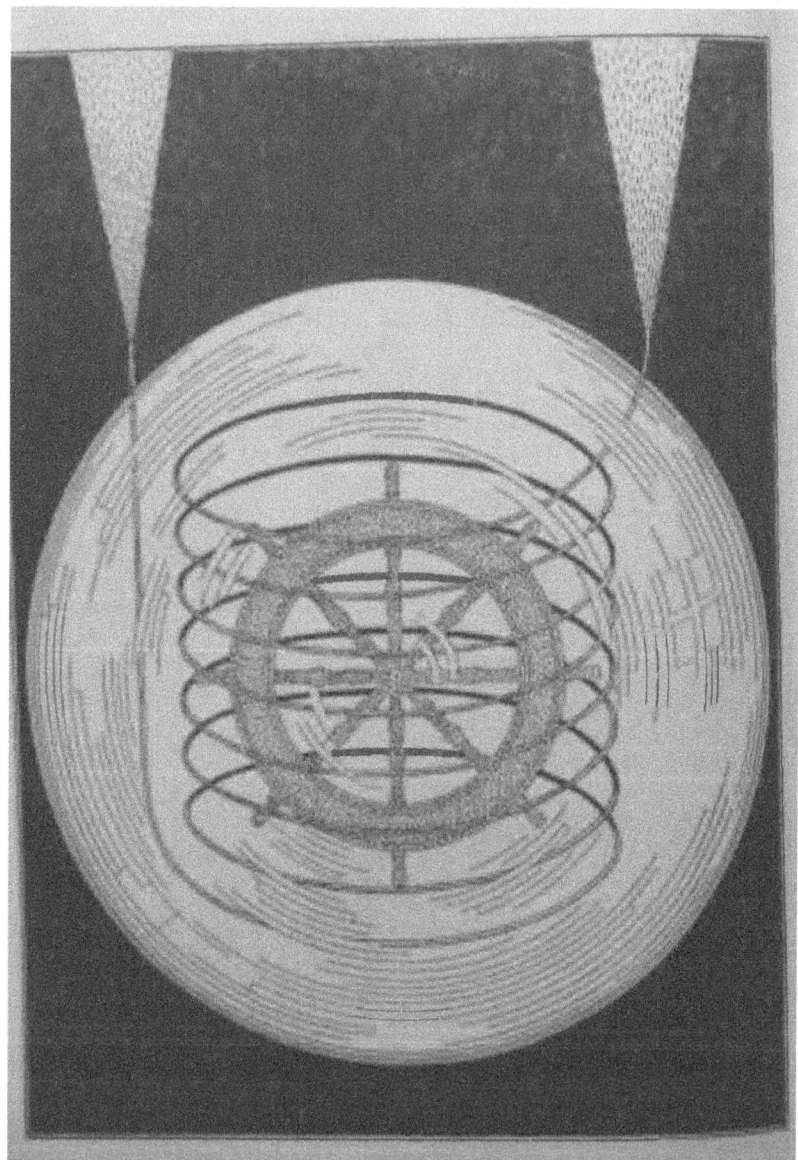

THE WHEEL OF THE LAW

The pathway of the generating soul is here represented by a converging line of force which, piercing the wall of the Auric Egg, descends, as is shown on the left, into the Demiurgic sphere. The soul then begins the ascent of the seven spirals, by which it is ultimately liberated and diffused back again into First Cause, as shown on the right.

CHAPTER FOUR

The Inferior Creation and its Regent

IN THE Platonic system of philosophy the dot is called the One. The early mystics held that Being should be considered the first, in that One is a being. Plato, however, maintained that the One is All-Being, because being is a condition of the One and consequently dependent upon it. The fallacy of terms is again apparent. Being in this sense has no connection with the thought of *to be* or *exist*, but signifies that which is without existence in that it has neither a positive nor a negative state. Thus while Plato assails the term, he still maintains in his philosophic writings the existence of a universal state preceding the One but denies that this universal state should be called Being, intimating that it should always be assumed by the mind but no effort ever made to denominate it. The moment denomination is given, this abstract quality becomes the One, in that definition cannot possibly be applied to the Absolute, the One being the highest definable state. The line out of the dot, or the One, is called the *Beautiful*: the circle, or radius of the line, the *Good*. In this manner is established the great Platonic triad: the One, the Beautiful, and the Good.

The Pythagoreans conceived the number 1 to be before all numbers. It is called the capstone of the pyramid of numbers. All other numbers are simply aggregations of 1's. Two is two 1's; three, three 1's; a million, a million 1's. Remove the 1 and you destroy all numbers. Therefore it is the first and has absolute priority. The power and dignity of the number 1 are expressed in permanence, stability, immovability. In philosophy beauty is a form of motion or emotion. The Beautiful is an eternal flow; it is the One in motion. The Good, which is the third and lowest aspect, contains or accepts into itself the nature of the Beautiful; it is the manifestation of the Beautiful in the sphere of creation. For example, he who has the Beautiful within his own soul radiates the Good and is called the Good. It may be said that to be beautiful is good; also that to be good is beautiful. Consquently that is good which contains beauty.

From this Platonic definition it is apparent why the Savior-Gods of all nations have been symbolized as Beautiful. Aesthetically considered, Beauty is the redeeming power. When the human soul opens itself to the reception of Beauty it is then transmuted. Beauty is a force into the presence of which none can come and remain unmoved. Beauty is an internal force symbolic of supersubstantial harmony manifesting through goodness. In its final analysis Good is symmetry, or the harmonious coordination of parts. In other words, that is good in which the parts work together. That individual is good in whom the natural forces function naturally. It also follows that a symmetry of parts is harmonious and harmony of parts produces a concord which is termed beautiful. According to the ancients, the world is the receptacle for the Beautiful, which in turn manifests the all-knowing of the One. This lecture is to be devoted to a consideration of the world that is called Good, and how, through the continual Adversary, it ultimately effects the perfection and liberation of the rational nature.

The world is a form, and forms are molded from matter. Matter ranges from an unrecognizable state of crystallization to an unrecognizable state of vitalization, both extremes alike intangible because of the inability of our sense perceptions to cognize any ultimate. Form exists not only in things that can be seen but in such as can be perceived through the senses of hearing, touch, taste, and smell. Form therefore is not merely a physical body that can be seen; it may be a subtle emanation as light or sound. A word cannot be seen and yet a word is a form. Under certain conditions drug addicts can see words coming out of people's mouths, their supersensitiveness being the result of a low form of drug-invoked psychism. A thought is not visible nor can it be held between the fingers, and yet a thought is as truly a form as is a piece of stone. The inferior universe therefore includes every conceivable state or condition of form. Form is the inferior nature of everything manifesting being. Form includes not only every part of the universe from the mental level downward but, ultimately, up through the higher spiritual spheres; in fact every plane upon which differentiation exists. But the planes of consciousness above that of thought, and the entities dwelling therein, have a term other than form applied to them. The circle, or circumference, is therefore the symbol of feelings, thoughts, and bodies in all their infinite ramifications.

The ancients symbolized form and the laws controlling the organization of matter into bodies by a reaping skeleton, the emblem of death. Form has ever been regarded as the parent of ignorance. Throughout the inferior creation consciousness lies buried in form. Form is the confusing, resisting, limiting, inhibiting, and imprisoning part of existence. Nothing in whose nature even a trace of form remains is capable of absolute consciousness. Form is the graveyard of consciousness. Since all life is thus inhibited by form, no creature controlled by the form part is rational.

Philosophically speaking, absolute form—that is, the ultimate degree of form—is ultimate negation, because it is the absence of all that is necessary to the greatest good. In its most enmeshed state life is at its lowest ebb. Therefore, in philosophy form is termed the *Eternal Adversary*. In Egypt form was called Typhon, and as a symbol of his disrepute he was pictured with the head of a crocodile and the body of a hog—sometimes the wings of a bat were added. Form is always the destroyer. In India form is known as Shiva, or Rudra, the lord of destruction, or rather, the principle behind the form is so defined. In the realm of philosophy form is one of the unsolved problems of the ages, for it is in reality simply an inferior life inhibiting the manifestation of a superior life. In this sea of confusing form elements men live and move and have their being, and out of the ever-changing substances of form all mortal creatures build their bodies, which are thus destined to return to the elemental spheres from which they were derived.

The universe of matter that extends throughout the infinite vistas of unmeasured space and includes within itself the heavenly bodies functioning through space and bearing with them an indescribable diversity of flora and fauna, is all part of what the ancients termed the *underworld*. Even the apparent vacuum in which these mighty bodies exist, and the host of invisible agencies that order sidereal dynamics, form part of a vast but inferior creation manifesting through the realm of form. This world of form—suns, moons, and stars—is called *hades*, or the land of death. It is the world of darkness. It is called dark because in it the light of spirit is swallowed up and creatures move in the haze of uncertainty. Darkness, however, does not imply evil, but simply the lack of light. In the sphere of form all creatures lack the full brilliance of consciousness or awareness. In this dark world, which is the circumference of the circle of existence, man is at his greatest degree of separateness from spiritual Source, and the sphere in which he functions is the lowest degree of divine agency. All through mythology the gods of light and life fight the demons of darkness and death. In the Babylonian mythology Merodach slays the dragon, and in the Christianized version of the myth St. George is the hero. The dragon of matter, a foul, flame-breathing monster, must be slain by Siegfried in order that the treasure of the Nibelung may be recovered.

Every creature struggles against the inertia of its immediate personal environment. Inertia is the characteristic attribute of form. It must be realized that this is inertia in a relative sense, for if matter be reduced to its ultimate it will be found to consist of life particles vibrating at incredible rates of speed. In comparison to the consciousness of man, however, matter is unconscious; in comparison to the active principles of the universe, matter is negative. On the other hand, in comparison to orders of life undoubtedly existing, but unknown to us, matter may very well be considered positive. Matter, or form, simply represents the unconquered environment that surrounds every life struggling for existence. As the world of life and consciousness represents the spiritual nature of Deity, so the vast ocean of matter, continually changing and manifesting an infinitude of forms, is the inferior part or body of Deity. As all creatures are made in the image of their Universal Creator, it follows that each has a spiritual nature which is part of and harmonious with the spiritual nature of the universe, and also a material nature which is part of and harmonious with the cosmic body. When the emphasis of the life is upon its spiritual part we term the individual *idealistic*, but when the emphasis is upon the material part we term him *materialistic*. Character is determined by the plane of his own nature upon which the emphasis of the individual's life is placed. Every human being has moments when he rises above his own level; also moments when he sinks below that level. This level may be termed in music the keynote of the individual, with the sharp as its higher and the flat as its lower phase.

In Chaldean philosophy there is the wonderful legend of Ishtar and Tammuz. The story deals particularly with the descent of Ishtar through the seven worlds into hades, the inferior sphere. The allegory simply signifies the incarnation of the rational soul in the substances of the irrational world. The irrational world is divided into seven strata by the rings of the planets upon which sit, according to the Mysteries, the Seven Governors of the World, each of whom bestows upon the incarnating soul one of the seven limitations of matter called *veils* by Hermes. However, in the myth of Ishtar, instead of the soul being veiled or having certain adornments given to it, the allegory sets forth the limitation of spiritual power through the removal of certain divine attributes. These attributes signify the functioning of certain spiritual forces, which functioning is rendered impossible by the involvements of the soul in matter. The spiritual properties of the rational self are symbolized by a crown, jewels, breast and body adornments, and sandals. As Ishtar descends through the seven gates of the seven Governors, each takes from her one of her spiritual qualities until, deprived of all the evidence of her royal birth (spiritual origin), she arrives in the "house of no return," the dark and gloomy precincts of death.

Each human soul entering into mortal incarnation has thus been robbed, by the seven worlds of matter, of the manifesting proofs of its divinity until, helpless and impotent, the all-knowing spiritual man appears in the physical world as a wide-eyed babe incapable even of self-preservation. Thus the immortal assumes the dream of mortality, and clouded by the veils of the seven planets takes up the humdrum of mortal existence, all oblivious to the godhood within. Robbed of her adornments, Ishtar must patiently accept the infirmities heaped upon her by the irate goddess of death. After many tribulations Ishtar is at last rescued from her infernal prison through the intercession of the deities, and ascending once more through the heavenly gates receives back the symbols of her royal rank and dignity. Then, speading her wings, she soars upward to the spheres of light.

Philosophically considered, the descent of the rational nature of man into its irrational body is *involution*; the resurrection of the rational nature from this condition of immersion, *evolution*. The physical universe is the sphere of ignorance where each creature is at its worst in that it has forgotten the best within itself. So thick and numerous are the veils of the rings that the light of spirit is obscured until but a dim haze bears witness of its effulgence.

It naturally follows that accomplishment in the physical world is the greatest of all accomplishments, for it is under the most difficult of all situations. Here is a key to the story of the prodigal son, who represents the incarnating soul. The pigsty where he must eat and sleep with the hogs represents one ancient patriarch's concept of the physical universe. When at last the prodigal, having repented of his iniquities and having seen the folly of material existence, returned to the house of his Father (the light-world), the fatted calf was killed in his honor, for his accomplishment was great. Jealous of the attention bestowed upon the improvident youth, the elder brother made his dissatisfaction known to his Father, who replied that there was ample cause for rejoicing in that the lost had been found and the dead lived again.

The story carries the same thought permeating Egyptian philosophy: namely, that life in the mortal sphere without a realization of the Divine Plan is the true death; that resurrection from this state is the most desired of all attainments. Yet to rise victorious from the dark world of hopeless involvement is an accomplishment so noble that it elevates the conquering soul to a dignity exceeding that of the angels who are never confronted with this problem.

The stupefying effect of matter (rather its organizations into form) is appropriately symbolized by cold. Those of you who have been out when it was sixty degrees below zero know what it means when the mercury freezes and the air is filled with a continuous crackling sound. Huge logs split from end to end with a sound like the report of a great gun, and even the nails seem to ooze out of the wood. It is hard to fight cold because it discourages the effort to resist its influence. Over the nature gradually comes a feeling of comfort and peace accompanied by an overwhelming desire to rest. No prospect seems so pleasant as to go to sleep in the snow; no effort seems so unnecessary as to fight against the innate urge to drift off into the sleep of death. Cold fights you by taking away your desire to resist. This is the most insidious of all foes, and is comparable to the way in which form destroys spiritual initiative.

Materiality does not attack the body or the conscious functioning of the mind; it assails the will power and destroys the morale. As long as there is the desire to fight ignorance and degeneracy, as long as there is the inner urge to resist evil and the illusions of matter, it is possible to attain liberation with reasonable effort. Form, however, fights in an underhanded way by taking away the desire to master its elements, and substituting therefore the lethargy of indifference which prefers to leave things just as they are and go along with the rest of the world, enjoying its momentary pleasures and suffering as resolutely as possible the concurrent ills of life. When the material urge of physical environment has so benumbed the inner nature that every spiritual aspiration is anesthetized, the individual is reduced to the level of that mediocre throng who are content to struggle along in the age-old ruts. Such have hypnotized themselves into the false belief that existing conditions are inevitable and unchangeable.

When the desire to do right for the sake of right is smothered by matter, there is left but one power capable of dealing with the problem of inertia: namely, pain, either mental, physical or emotional. Through suffering, the insufficiency of material accomplishments is demonstrated. The desire to do good for the sake of good is an urge far too subtle to survive the stifling influence of matter. Hence to counteract man's incessant effort to forget his own spiritual needs is his continual proclivity to hurt himself. Man's effort to control his own life without intelligence invariably demonstrates its futility. He strives to live without the help of consciousness, with the result that he exists in pain and tribulation. Because of his suffering he acquires a great incentive toward knowledge for its own sake in order to save himself from the pain resulting from ignorance. Thus the law of self-preservation is ever forcing the wayward feet back into the path that leads to light. Physical suffering first led man to ponder the mysteries of his own being. In the last analysis, however, the pain of the body is the least poignant.

Then came emotional suffering—the pain in the heart—much more desperate and difficult to endure. Lastly came mental suffering, in which the entire constitution is torn and racked by that gargantuan conflict when the faculties of the mind hurl thought missiles at each other. Looking at the average individual, we see a consciousness that is impotent in the grasp of form which, like cold, has benumbed its sensibilities. Cold is the proper symbol of the circumference of the sphere of Being.

The word *hell*, derived from the Scandinavian *hel*, means cold, though its has long been associated with its opposite term, heat. This discloses a certain consistent inconsistency characteristic of the works of man. Some missionaries visiting the Far North described in "glowing" terms the sulphurous nature of hell. As a result the Eskimos were immediately interested, for the underworld was thereby made particularly inviting to a race that found extreme difficulty in keeping heat in their chilled organisms. Obviously, any intimate description of hell depends for its effectiveness upon the equation of longitude and latitude. Just as life, light, and heat are associated with the quality of expansion, since the natural impulse of life is to expand, so death, darkness, and cold are related to the quality of contraction, since the natural impulse of death is to contract.

Realizing (according to the ancient Mysteries) that the physical universe was the sphere of death and that there was no death so real as immersion in form, let us now consider the nature and structure of this great dark sphere as it was taught to the philosophers of ancient days, and is still preserved among those groups who are perpetuating the Ancient Wisdom. The material universe considered as a unit is the body of the Lord of Form or the Master of the World. This World Lord, whose consciousness is of the nature of mind, is the Jehovah or IHVH of the Jews, the Zeus of the Greeks, and the Jupiter of the Romans. In the philosophy of the Gnostics and the Neoplatonists he was called the Demiurgus. The original interpretation of this word is difficult to ascertain, but it may be rendered in its philosophic sense as the *false urge*. The Demiurgus is therefore to be defined as the composite material universe considered as a personal being or power.

The emanations from this Lord are called his powers, and are sometimes referred to as the princes of the world. You will remember that Jesus warned his disciples that the princes of this world would never understand him, and that they had nothing in common with him. The princes of the world are the divisions of the forces controlling the form universe, these forces being considered as gods. Philosophically, the Lord of the World is the great autocrat, for autonomy is a principle nonexistent in the universal sense. This despot, who is conceived as using the earth for his footstool and the heavens for his throne, is presumed to control his universe through the inexorable justice of law, which because of man's ignorance breeds fear, hate, and death. When you think of the philosophic trinity, remember that the third person of this triad is the Lord of the World, called the Heartless One because he is the slave-driver of the Cycle of Necessity. He is the terrible ogre or giant of hate, so-called, who grinds our bones to make his bread.

The ancients were divided in their opinions concerning the real nature of the Demiurgus. Some affirmed him to be a devil because he is an agency that is ever destroying, but does he not wreak destruction in order that reconstruction may follow upon a higher level of manifestation? He is the Lord of Death because he controls birth and death, for these phenomena exist nowhere except in the world of forms. Again, some have attributed to him the diabolical genius of a madman who created a nightmare universe where everything is as it should not be. He is the power that binds man to the world of illusion, and in the terms of the early Church Fathers is the enemy of the eternal God (Good).

Paraphrasing, however, the statements of Omar, the question may be asked: If he be evil, who placed him there? In Faust, Mephistopheles—the agent of the Demiurgus—is made to say, "I am the spirit of negation, part of the power that still works for good while ever scheming ill." Accordingly, the second group of ancient philosophers declared the Demiurgus to be ever adding to the glory of God by demonstrating the insufficiency of the form-world. He is therefore not the enemy of good but the eternal contrast to good necessary that man may realize the perfection of right. Who would know or appreciate good if he had not experienced the lack of it? The Lord of the World is therefore the master who whips man until, unable longer to bear the lashes of unkind destiny, the sufferer revolts against his own insufficiency and thus is directed into the way of light. In antiquity the Lord of the World was well symbolized as the master of the whip and the wielder of the flail. The Egyptian Pharaohs carried three scepters symbolic of their authority from the Demiurgus: The Anubis-headed staff, symbolic of the sagacity of the World Lord; the shepherd's crook, symbolic of the priesthood and the authority of the World Lord over the souls of men; and the flail, symbolic of the mastery which the Demiurgus exercises over the bodies of all creatures.

Returning to our primitive symbolism, the Anubis-headed staff is symbolized by the dot, the shepherd's crook by the line, and the flail by the circle. These are representative respectively of rulership through wisdom, rulership through faith, and rulership through force. Thus the dot is now termed government. It was once the crown, but now so large a part of government is administered by the people that the crown can only be used in its abstract sense. The dot, however, signifies government by the state. The line is the tiara, or government by the church, and the circumference is the people who are the beneficiaries of government. Thus we find three tremendous forces continually focussed upon the objective life of man, and the perversion of these forces constitutes the threefold fountain-head of evil as opposed to the threefold fountain-head of light. Through the perversion of government we have ignorance; through the perversion of the church, superstition; and through the perversion of the people, fear. Thus come into existence the great Masonic trio of evils: ignorance, superstition, and fear, the murderers of human liberty and the destroyers of understanding.

Although we conceive ourselves to exist in a world amply lighted physically by the sun, and adequately illumined mentally and ethically by philosophy, religion, and science, we actually dwell in a sphere as dark as Egypt's night. There is but one true light in the universe: namely, the light of understanding, a trait in which humanity is woefully deficient. The presence of hope, belief, and fear is definite proof that the world lacks knowledge and adequate spiritual perceptions. The darkness of this underworld is so dense that we cannot perceive the hearts of our fellowmen. We cannot sense the motives that inspire our neighbor to action, nor can we pierce the surrounding gloom and see that which lies but a few steps ahead. While humanity sojourns in this underworld of mortal light and spiritual darkness, it is actually passing through an embryonic state. Within the womb of matter fetal man is being prepared for birth into the greater universe of divine realities. The physical universe may therefore be termed the antechamber of Cosmos, the little room with the hole in the floor referred to in the Mysteries. As infant man must be carried for the nine months of the prenatal epoch before his organisms are able to bear exposure to external conditions, so the world must carry within the darkness of its own nature for nine philosophic months that mortal who is to be born into life and unfoldment through the substance of higher spheres.

In ancient philosophy this physical universe is referred to as a great egg wherein all manners of creatures are passing through prenatal epochs. People have the mistaken idea that when they come into physical existence they are born. In their egotism they have forgotten that all mortal things are embryo gods who cannot achieve to Divinity until they have transcended every vestige of mortality. Every living thing is an embryo. In some previous embryonic state we lost our gills and caudal appendage. The webs of our fingers and toes were also cut, and our tongues loosened, but even with these evidences of progress we come into this world imperfect and incomplete; or, as the theologian would say, "we are conceived in sin and born in iniquity." This statement has no reference to indiscretions of our ancestors but to the philosophic fact that the mortal universe, when compared to the transcendency of the higher worlds, is a sphere of sin and death. By physical birth we have merely exchanged the amniotic fluids of the womb for the somewhat less dense atmospheric fluids of the world. We are still bound to the earth by an umbilical cord of sense, interest, and desire, and not until through the development of our discerning faculties we acquire the power to sever this bondage to the inferior nature can it be said that we are really born.

This great egg surrounding the material sphere has for its inner surface that canopy of the heavens which man vainly seeks to explore with high-powered telescopes. With each improvement in equipment he is enabled to penetrate a little farther into the blue haze of SPACE. He always reaches a point, however, where vision fails and impenetrable SPACE goes on. The moment man arrives at the limit of his own faculties, he reaches the walls of a hypothetical sphere that hems him in and isolate him from the rest of Being.

The Hermetist likened the physical universe to a glass globe in which were contained numberless vapors and seething forces.

As the agonies of chemical change may be viewed through the walls of the test tube, so, like the Bunsen burner, that mysterious power called cosmic urge unceasingly agitates the chemicals contained within the globe of physical existence. While enclosed within this impenetrable shell man cannot conceive of a universe beyond; of a state nobler or more enduring than his present state.

Life is thus composed of a host of creatures, seemingly like atoms in SPACE whirling round and round forever within this crystalline shell of the Universal Egg. At last, however, comes the great day, "Be With Us," when the Egg of the Universe is broken and the substances therein imprisoned flow back once more into their first and primitive Absoluteness. Thus, floating upon the face of Absolute Being is a finite globe destined to remain for a little while. This globe is the vast material universe of countless worlds and suns which overwhelms us with its immensity but which, when compared with the absolute limitlessness of SPACE, is of pigmy proportions. Though but an atom within the tortured body of this globe, humanity cherishes its dream of existence, striving with the feeble fingers of its mind to grasp the threads of Universal Wisdom by which the globe is held suspended from its unknown source.

Although this globe filled with the contents of material existence is being hurled through space to ultimate destruction, the secret philosophy of the ancients taught that it was possible for the individual to free himself from the swirling mass and by right of his own divinity break through the shell of the World Egg and thereby achieve individual liberation. Upon this hypothesis nearly all the Mysteries of antiquity were established, a notable exception being the Jewish which taught that there was no liberation for one apart from all. Alchemy offers an excellent symbolic description of the processes of spiritual liberation. At this point it is apropos to consider the philosophical definition of the word *spirit*. This has nothing in common with its accepted theological meaning. In philosophy spirit is not the divine part of every nature considered as an individuality, but rather this divine part considered as one undivided causal nature permeating all life. In the Buddhist philosophy spirit and soul are considered part of the illusion of matter in the sense that an individual who speaks of *his* spirit or *his* soul speaks without realization of the fact that there is but one spirit in the universe and all so-called divisions of it are purely hypothetical. Hence, though there may be an infinity of bodies existing in the sphere of *maya* there is but one consciousness, which the Oriental mystic pleases to term the *Self*. Of not-selves there are myriads; of Self, but one.

To think of spirit as divided into a host of individual units, each embodied in a separate form, is to think in terms of error. To the mystic the idea of the growth of his own spirit apart from the growth of the spirit of all is inconceivable. That which grows to the point where it bursts through the Egg of Existence is consequently not the spirit but what the Greeks termed the *rational soul*, or the *mental knower*, which represents the highest form of individuality. It therefore follows that it is as impossible for one individual to have a spirit more highly evolved than another as for one area of the sea to be wetter than another. The degree of development is thus measured first by the extent to which the parts of the lower nature have been synchronized, and secondly by the *interval of quality* between them and their spiritual cause. No one has a consciousness higher than another, for there is but one consciousness in the universe. He who is presumed to have a higher consciousness is simply one whose organisms are fine enough to manifest more completely the potentialities of this single consciousness. Mankind may be considered as a vast organism with one Spirit or Self manifesting through an infinite number of intellectual and physical organisms, the latter deluded into the belief that they are free and independent. On a still higher level this composite Spirit of all mankind, which is merely an expression of the Universal Spirit of all things, is deluded, in turn, by the concept that mankind is different and separate from the rest of Universal Being. Such terms as old and young, highly evolved and less evolved, spiritual and material, should be applied only to personalities and individualities, for in the sphere of consciousness they do not exist. As the Absolute is ageless, being all age, no part can technically be older than another. Hence difference is an illusion of the mind, but necessary however to the present evolution of life, yet without foundation in Divine Reality.

To return to alchemy, Self or Spirit is the universal gold, the king of the metals. Gold exists in every element of the universe; even the sunlight and the atmosphere contain minute quantities of this precious metal. The base substances surrounding this universal or spiritual gold, are referred to as the lesser metals. The purpose of alchemical experimentation was to germinate that seed of universal gold, which when properly nurtured would take unto itself and tincture the base metals, absorbing them all into its own glory. Ultimately Self, the only enduring state, thus absorbs into its own Being all the phases of the not-self. Touching them with its transmuting power it causes them to become one with its own effulgence.

According to the Greek terminology the gold is the rational soul, and the transmutation process that of distilling the golden elixir from the base substances of ignorance and perversion. When you have gathered your proper elements, says the alchemist, you place them in a retort and hermetically seal it. You then begin the cycles of distillation, causing the chemicals to pass through an orderly sequence of increasing intensity until finally a point is reached where the elixir thus distilled seeps through the glass without injuring it and passes off like a hot oil, there being no container in the world sufficiently strong to hold it. The allegory is evident. The hermetically sealed vessel is the lower world, the way in and out stopped by the mysteries of birth and death. The chemicals are the heterogeneous mass of created things thrown together in a mysterious fashion. The cycles of distillation are the processes of evolution, so-called, by which the life is given ever fuller expression through regenerated vehicles and gradually released from irrationality. When the cycles of intensification have reached a certain stage, those beings who have attained to this point can no longer be held within the globe of the inferior creation, and the soul seeps through the wall of the Egg of Existence or, as the Buddhist might say, enters Nirvana. This is the rebirth out of the Womb of Necessity; this is the time when man releases himself from the bonds that bind him to the Wheel of Birth and Death. He who has attained this end is rightly termed no longer a man but the *Philosophers' Stone.*

According to the concept of mystical philosophy, every individual passes through two births and two deaths. At the time of the first, or lesser birth, man is born into the irrational sphere where he becomes an objective manifesting creature but loses contact with the subjective spiritual spheres. Technically, therefore, this birth into the outer universe results in the death of the higher self which must remain asleep in the tomb of material organisms until the Great Day of Liberation.

The second birth is, in reality, the death of the lower nature. When it occurs the rational part reawakens, and rising triumphant from its rational sheath, mingles itself with the victorious and illumined Aeons. At the first birth the self dies out of Eternity and enters into the illusion of Time; at the second birth, the self ascends out of the illusion of Time and diffuses its being throughout the substances of Eternity. Everything that is born into material existence passes from a greater to a lesser state.

After the elementary birth, which is the immersion of the rational soul into the irrational universe, the soul enters upon what is called the Cycle of Necessity. The Cycle of Necessity is simply the Wheel of Births and Deaths. During this cycle the temporarily individualized soul passes from one condition of unreality to another. The intervals between these conditions are the lesser births and deaths which take place within the World Egg. There is first the birth into the great egg, then the cycles of birth and death within the egg (referred to as reincarnation or metempsychosis), and finally the philosophic death out of the irrational nature forever. At the time of the philosophic death, which is also the second birth, the soul escapes from matter forever, and having pierced through the hypothetical wall of existence returns to the ever-enduring state of the Absolute.

By way of disgression, let us consider a little more in detail the subject of reincarnation. There is a popular misconception concerning the continuity of identity throughout the cycle of incarnations. People are heard to say, "I wish I knew who I was in my last incarnation," or "I think I must have been a Hindu in my last life." According to the most profound systems of thought, the so-called personalities which come forth out of the "Silent Watcher" are all pendent from this single cause but are not directly related to each other. Among the potentialities of the self is the power of projecting a host of individualities into temporary existence. After existing their appointed span, these individualities are reabsorbed into the Self from whose essences they were originally differentiated. Thus the spiritual causal nature of man is capable of objectifying periodically a chain of personalities, each a separate and individual creation endowed with separate and individual faculties.

For example, John Doe is a personality, being objectified from an impersonal and transcendental nature, itself neither personal nor individual. When John Doe has finished the span of his physical existence, he is absorbed back into his own spiritual causal nature, which is not John Doe nor does it know John Doe, but which is an all-pervading superphysical life. When John Doe has been returned to this universal state, he simply ceases to exist. He will never reincarnate again, nor will his characteristics and traits be perpetuated. The universe will never again know of John Doe. After a period of inaction, however, the spiritual causal nature which gave John Doe being will create a new personality. This personality will neither remember John Doe nor associate its life in any way with that of John Doe, and yet certain qualities will be manifested in the new personality which could not have come into expression had they not passed through certain definite stages of growth while in the personality of John Doe. Therefore, the incarnating individuality of one incarnation never incarnates again, but out of the spiritual origin in which this incarnating life was individualized new individualized lives will be formed which will come into manifestation, and then in turn vanish. Thus the Self gives birth to an infinite number of personalities, but it is the Self—not the personalities—that endures. This Self does not actually incarnate or reincarnate, but from itself it individualizes incarnating organisms.

Consider for a moment the diagram at the beginning of this chapter. The large circle represents the Egg of Existence—the cosmic sphere, or aura, of the Demiurgus,—whose outer circumference is termed the "Ring Pass Not," or the extremity of manifestation. The line descending and piercing the wall of the great Egg is consciousness emerging from the Self and merging into the substances of the Egg. The point where the descending line breaks the wall of the circle and enters into the limitation of existence is the first birth—the true philosophic death,—for the Egg is the sepulcher in which consciousness is buried. Having penetrated the wall of the Egg, the line of consciousness begins the spiral path of the Wheel of Necessity. This spiral path is made up of lives and deaths, which are termed *incarnations*. At last, having through philosophy learned of the true mystery of existence, the consciousness breaks through the wall in the second death, or philosophic birth, and reascends to the sphere of Universal Consciousness which is its true dwelling place. It will thus be seen that while the Buddhist theory differs in minor details from the philosophic atheism of the Greeks, its essential nature is the same.

In Buddhism (which, as you know, considers Deity only in the form of Self, or Absolute Existence, and has no concept of a personal God) reincarnations occur within the lower spheres of the Egg of Being, those spheres being considered as the ground wherein is set up the Wheel of Necessity. Accordingly, one great Buddhist philosopher is declared to have said: "Of births and deaths there are a countless number, but one Great Death and one Great Birth is the measure of accomplishment." Thus are differentiated the greater and the lesser cycles.

By divine prerogative, by the impulses controlled by law— which is the habit of SPACE—life is periodically immersed in creation, where it continues its spiral progress in the smaller cycle until finally it escapes through the wall of being and finds

The Inferior Creator and its Regent 91

perfection in its own source. Thus we have physical existence contrasted with divine existence. The physical birth and death of man is a minor mystery. As sleep is a little death, so birth and death are miniature cycles of existence, but the Great Death and the Great Birth are the supreme cycle of existence and the grand mystery of life.

Although its physical nature is alone susceptible of analysis, there is within each so-called material creature a spiritual, or superphysical, part. Whether we term it spirit, soul, higher mind, or consciousness it is that something within the shell of matter which is superior to and must eventually become master of the irrational universe. The only reason that this higher part is confined within the lower world is that man as an individual neither appreciates this inner strength nor understands how to directionalize it in order that it may achieve liberation and carry with it to perfection the lesser parts which are under its domination. The rational soul, or spiritual life of man, has a higher origin, and is predestined to attain a far more noble end than is appreciable to the mortal mind with its limited comprehension.

Now comes a legitimate question: "Just how can man escape from the crystal ball of matter with its limiting materializing agencies and return to the Dawn Land from which he originally came?"

Liberation is to be attained most simply (according to the Eastern school) through the projection of consciousness. We have already intimated that man lives upon the level of his thoughts; the universe that is real to him is simply that world with which his thinking has attuned him. When man causes his consciousness to accept the reality of the illusionary universe, he is swallowed up in the illusions he has thus affirmed. The moment consciousness rises above the level of illusion man is freed from its limiting influences.

Man is composed of three major parts: a divine part which may be correlated to the dot of primitive symbolism; a superhuman part correlated to the line; and a human or natural part correlated to the circle. When he lives upon the level of the physical plane and is controlled by his physical propensities, man is necessarily *en rapport* with the physical universe and subject to the inconsistencies and incongruities of matter. When he lifts his consciousness above material things and lives in the world of his higher mind, man then dwells in the intellectual sphere. This is a much broader vista but still is limited to certain fallacies of thinking, for even the higher mind with its magnificent grasp of the problems of lower existence is necessarily imperfect and to a great degree immersed in the *maya* of physical existence. When ultimately he lifts his consciousness above mind and thought to spiritual realization, man then lifts his entire nature from the intellectual to the spiritual world. The consummation of this elevation is the goal of human effort, and here and there among the elect of the earth one, like the great Buddha, achieves to perfect realization and absolute liberation. The path of liberation, however, is too difficult for the majority to travel, for few will give up the lesser self with its likes and dislikes in exchange for an abstract Reality which has neither desire nor feeling but which dwells in unbroken contemplation throughout eternity.

The world in which we live is simply the sphere wherein we have centered our activities. The higher our ideals, the higher are our activities, and consequently the higher is our world. Selfishness is the key to the inferno, for the inferno, or inferior universe, is ruled by selfishness. The physical world is that sphere controlled and directionalized by selfish urges, and every soul that is selfish is bound to the physical universe. Qualities within us bind us to forces outside which are like those qualities. As long as selfishness endures within our own souls it holds us to the sphere of selfishness without. As we transmute qualities within our own natures we ascend into new worlds of corresponding consciousness outside.

Man is held by his materiality to the material sphere, by his intellectuality to the intellectual sphere, by his ideality to the ideal sphere. But regardless of his own viewpoints or activities, man is eternally bound by his innate Reality to the Absolute, which is the fullness of Reality. When he has extricated himself from the instincts and impulses of materiality, man is philosophically free from the material world. When the intellect within him is transmuted into idealism, man passes from the world of thought to that supermental sphere for which there is no adequate name. *The philosophic ascension of the soul is simply the process of raising motives and activities to ever higher levels of idealism.*

Having lifted his mind to the contemplation of cosmic realities, the philosopher is no longer moved by the considerations of immature materialistic intellects. Having mastered material ambition, the philosopher is incapable of stooping to the petty accomplishments of physically-minded people. Having lifted himself out of the physical life, he no longer lives to gratify the whims of his physical nature. The true philosopher is free from material bondage because he ceases to desire material power or material possession. Incapable of desire, he is incapable of the sense of loss; having outgrown unimportant things, he is not disappointed if he does not possess them. He has learned with the Buddha that possession is a curse, desire a snare, and selfishness an illusion. Of such a sage it may be said that he has climbed up from the valleys of worldliness to the high mountains of clear thinking where the panorama of the greater life spreads out before him. Dwelling in his world of thought, the philosopher gradually achieves to the realization that the mind which lifted him out of matter has also been outgrown. The mind which made him a man will prevent him from becoming a god; the stone upon which he raised himself thus far has now become a millstone about his neck. Thus as the philosopher first casts off worldliness to dwell in the broader vista of the mind, so ultimately he casts off *mind*fulness that he may enter into the newer and greater vision—the rulership of intellect by spirit. He casts aside the thinker as he would a worn-out body, and rises from the mountain tops into the free air of SPACE to vanish gradually as an inconceivable speck in the vast expanse of ALL.

As the sage sits upon his mountain about to cast aside mind and rise into the Nirvanic reaches of Eternity, the world passes in panoramic review before his enlightened vision. He sees the great inferno spread out below him; about him on the mountain tops the gods of the world—the Keepers of the Vale of Tears. The illumined sage beholds the ways and byways of the earth, a great crisscrossed labyrinth of complexities wherein immortal creatures mistakenly struggle not to prove their own immortality but rather to establish the evidence of mortality. He sees life as a vast chamber with two doors, with birth as the entrance to and death the exit from this mortal span. He then understands the allegorical rituals through which he passed as a neophyte in that day when he himself was "raised" to light. He realizes that the world of mortal man is a gloomy subterranean sphere peopled with distorted imps who, like the Nibelungen, hoard up treasures in ancient crypts in obedience to the dictates of their crafty king. The philosopher then grasps the import of the mystical allegory of the rope that is lowered into the pit that those who can cling to it may be drawn up to life. The rope is the secret doctrine and those who catch hold of the swinging cable may be drawn up into the light of Reality and Truth. In the life of every struggling creature there comes a time when the insufficiency of life within the narrow confines of matter is apparent. By the disciplines of illumination the soul learns how to cast aside the inadequate coil of mortal limitation and ascend into the sphere of reason, there to dwell in the luminosity of divine proximity. The words of Milton concerning the fall of Satan then become profoundly significant:

> Him the Almighty Power
> Hurled headlong flaming from the ethereal sky,
> With hideous ruin and combustion, down
> To bottomless perdition, there to dwell
> In adamantine chains and penal fire,
> Who durst defy the Omnipotent to arms.

Satan, who signifies worldliness and self-sufficiency, is rewarded for his effort to establish a kingdom in opposition to the kingdom of good by being forced to dwell in the state of separateness which he himself conceived. In the East the illusion of separateness is looked upon as the cause of all suffering and sorrow. The great work of primitive Buddhism was to emphasize the fundamental unity of life through the doctrine of the one Universal Self. In the Western world where competition is held to be the only sound basis of commercial progress there is a continual wrong emphasis, for the parts are then arrayed against each other and no effort made to emphasize the common ground of Being in which all exists as parts of a tremendous whole.

The next chapter will be devoted to a consideration of the Eastern philosophy of perfection as accomplished by conscious reunion with Absolute Being through the *Dharma* of realization. The mortal sphere of competitive endeavor is hell indeed, wherein creatures exist in servitude to their own desires, while over them the Regent of the World, grim and unrelenting, sits with folded wings upon His throne raised on the dais of the Seven Heavens.

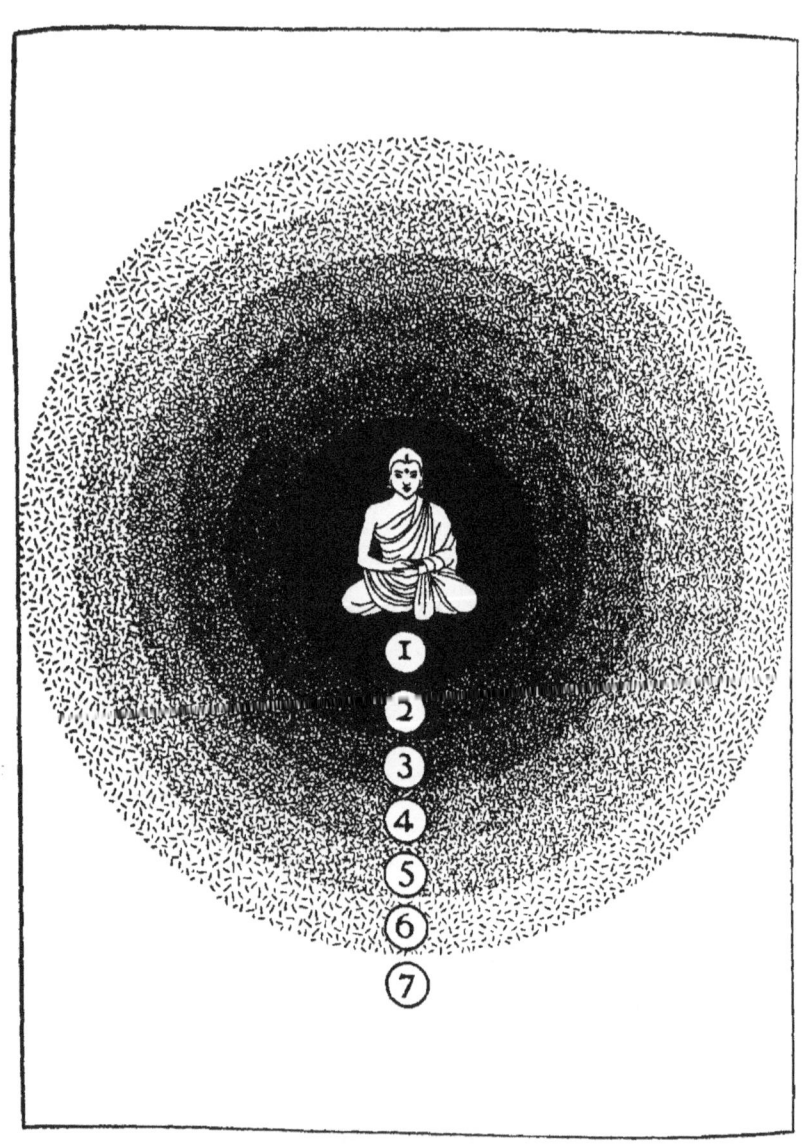

THE MYSTERY OF REALIZATION

The Oriental mystic is here diagrammatically shown seated in the midst of his own area of consciousness. Through the disciplines of his order he is enabled to so withdraw himself from the concerns of the outer life as to dwell in a *samadhic* felicity. Thus the aspiring soul seeks Self in the selflessness of the Great Law.

CHAPTER FIVE

THE ANNIHILATION OF THE SENSE OF DIVERSITY

THE gods have already been defined as personifications of divine attributes, that is, they signify conditions of Universal Consciousness. Whereas the Absolute signifies All Consciousness in suspension, the gods are differentiated phases of Universal Consciousness. While the ignorant venerate the gods either as personalities or divine beings, the philosopher recognizes them as cosmic planes or modes of realization. Thus Buddha is to be regarded primarily as the condition of perfect illumination rather than as a personality.

A subtle point is contained in the fact that he who attains to Buddhahood is not *a* Buddha but *the* Buddha. In other words Buddha, like light, is an all-pervading state, and he who becomes luminous shines not with a separate light but rather is merged with the one light whose radiance is diffused throughout all worlds. In its ascent to source, consciousness is merged sequentially with ever higher universal aspects of itself, becoming one with each level or plane with which it is temporarily blended. These planes or levels, representing the various phases of expanding consciousness, form the concatenated order of the gods. Hades, for example, was the Greek god of death or, more explicitly, materiality. Accordingly, Hades represents the consciousness of materiality.

Whoever moves and feels in terms of materiality is materiality, for we are what our consciousness is. The modern thinker would term the material-minded person a materialist. The esoterist, however, would say that *the material-minded person is materiality*. Again, the western scholar considers a lawbreaker a criminal, whereas the Oriental thinks of the lawbreaker as crime. If, therefore, the Eastern sage conceives of crime as an individualized monster, then each criminal becomes not an individual expression of that monster but the actual monster itself. Hate, for example, can hardly be thought of as an individual, and yet it is definitely a state of consciousness (more correctly, unconsciousness). The Eastern mind cannot conceive of a number of entities each a separate condition of hatred, because the moment hatred is born in the human heart the person who permits this condition to exist within himself becomes the embodiment of the plane of universal hatred. In other words, a universal condition is made manifest in that individual. Several men may hate at the same time in different parts of the world, yet there is but one consciousness of hatred with which they all hate. Hence this demon of hate may exist in more than one person simultaneously. During a great war millions may hate at the same time, yet each is neither a fraction of hatred nor simply manifesting hatred. Each is himself hate, and all who indulge this passion are identical with the nature of hatred.

The multiform images of the Buddhists all signify extensions and modes of consciousness. As realization increases and the unfolding self grasps more and more of the infinite span, the symbols become ever more complex while the principles for which they stand become ever more simple. Frequently a number of arms are used to represent the metaphysical potencies. Thus the consciousness of right judgment may be depicted as a hand holding some legal instrument. Similarly, the consciousness of priestly protection by another arm sustaining some implement of the priestcraft; the consciousness of rulership by still another arm elevating a crown or scepter; the consciousness of the good and just physician by a hand holding some instrument of surgery or healing herb; the consciousness of all-knowing by a hand holding a short staff or a scroll; and the consciousness of the divine avenger by a closed fist shaking a thunderbolt. A plurality of arms and heads thus becomes a method highly appropriate to symbolize the invisible but all-powerful qualities which the *chela* during his development expresses through the depth of his own being.

The Annihilation of the Sense of Diversity

Whenever through self-unfoldment an individual attains to the state of consciousness symbolized by a certain god, then that god is declared to be incarnate in that personality and to actually walk the earth. Thus the god of joy is incarnate in the joyful man, the god of mercy in the merciful, the god of truth in the truthful, and the god of war in those who fight. Being divine attributes, the gods thus become flesh in those mortal creatures who have unfolded and given expression within themselves to those godlike attributes.

In the Temple of Ten Thousand Buddhas at Kyoto, Japan, are to be found numberless images of the Buddha and the attendant Bodhisattvas, or disciples of the Lord of Enlightenment. Perfection is represented in the form of the Buddha, and the disciplines or ways of perfection in the forms of Bodhisattvas. The latter are the stages of enlightenment, the symbols of the sure and eternal path which winds through the illusion and leads ultimately to the attainment of perfect good.

Dear to the heart of the East is the beloved Kwan-Yin, or Kwannon, the great Bodhisattva Avalokiteswara, the Oriental Madonna, commonly called the Goddess of Mercy. For centuries the Buddhist monks have striven in their meditations to blend their consciousness with this divinity of compassion—the Merciful, Enduring One. The artists-priests have loved to depict upon silk or carve in stone, wood, or ivory the form of this compassionate "Consciousness of Protection."

Kwan-Yin was originally a masculine figure, probably based upon an historical Buddha (presumably the second of the great line), but through the centuries the compassionate nature of Avalokiteswara is responsible for the gradual metamorphosis of the figure into a feminine divinity. In China and Japan Kwan-Yin is usually a standing figure robed in graceful flowing garments with the face set in compassionate repose. Often the figure has only two arms, although a favorite number is six. When shown with six arms, Kwan-Yin is generally seated with her head resting upon the palm of her hand. In Japan there are figures of the Kwan-Yin with as many as a thousand arms to symbolize the universal scope of the Kwan-Yin consciousness. In Tibet the figure is often shown with eleven heads. Certain late Buddhist writings give definite philosophical meaning to numbers, so the multiplicity of members is of particular import.

The poses of the various hands give a key to the exalted nature of Eastern mysticism. The *mudras*, or hand postures of the Buddha, constitute a secret science of which little is known to those not initiated into the Buddhist Mysteries. The hand may be extended in an attitude of giving, which then signifies the consciousness of giving, and which, when free from all terrestrial taint, gives an exquisite pleasure to the inner self. The joy of giving is a commendable state of consciousness, as is also the joy of receiving. All these joys are finally discarded, however, until but one remains: namely, the perfect bliss of contemplation of Self.

In Japan there is a lovable Buddhist divinity usually shown with a bald head and a benign countenance. This is Jizo, the god of little children. Because of his great love for helpless child souls, Jizo has become their patron and protector. When a baby dies, according to the Japanese legend, it wanders in a gloomy cavern awaiting rebirth, where it has for its only task the heaping up of little piles of stones. In his *Glimpses of Unfamiliar Japan* Lafcadio Hearn describes the cave of the children's souls where flows the legendary fountain of milk from which the dead children drink and where in the gloom sits the smiling Jizo. When the evil spirits frighten them the loving Jizo extends his arms and the children's souls all run and hide in the sleeves of his kimono.

It is evident that Jizo signifies not only the consciousness of the love of children but also, in a more lofty sense, that consciousness which, having elevated itself to the heights of realization and gazing down upon unknowing humanity, realizes all creatures to be but little children piling up heaps of stones. Whether these piles be in the distant Japanese cave of Kaka or the stone heaps of a great city, Jizo gazes with boundless compassion upon infant humanity. When the monsters of war, greed, and lust frighten the ignorant and immature, he then extends his arms, and like the Master Jesus brooding over Jerusalem longs to gather the weak and helpless under the protection of his flowing robes. The god Jizo is incarnate in those in whom love for the weak and desire to serve the helpless springs from a true realization of that which must be accomplished. Jizo is a principle, and those possessing and manifesting this principle are one with him in his labor of love.

In the Tushita heaven of the Lamas dwells the radiant consciousness of Maitreya, the loving one, the desired of all nations—the Buddhist Messiah who is yet to come. This Bodhisattva is the personification of man's hope of ultimate achievement. He signifies the eternal tomorrow, the time of all accomplishment. Robed in futurity, he is the consciousness of noble destiny. At the Lama temple in Peking is to be seen a gigantic figure of Jam-pa (Maitreya), whose gilt lacquered body dazzles the beholder with its brilliance and whose expressionless face gazes down upon the altar seventy feet below. Maitreya gives a definite key to the world-wide belief in a coming Savior whose advent will be marked by miracles and who shall lead his people to spiritual and temporal victory. Maitreya is the consciousness of hope and he comes to those who can sense, even abstractly, the existence of a nobler and more illumined state. According to popular superstition, the advent of Maitreya, like the tenth avatar of Vishnu, will be a particular and definite occurrence. In reality, however, Maitreya is continually manifesting as the circumstances that lead worlds, nations, and individuals up along the path of the law to final absorption with the Absolute. Maitreya saves the world by revealing to the world that it is capable of salvation; for out of the realization of possible perfection is born the hope and strength to persevere. Maitreya is therefore the embodimnt of Dharma, and he who accepts the Law shall be saved by the Law. Jesus, another personification of the Law, assured his followers that those who believed in him should not perish. Maitreya is the way, the truth, and the life which, coming to every life, redeems all who accept it.

In dealing with the subject of consciousness, it is possible to conceive of Reality as permeating the entire area of space and gradually contracting itself toward the center, thereby limiting itself in the establishment of unreality. Or, on the other hand, consciousness may be regarded as occupying a central point from which it radiates itself throughout all Being, pouring its effulgence into the Abyss of the not-self, which is thereby redeemed. The Cabalists reconciled both these viewpoints by affirming that AIN SOPH (the Absolute) first retired from the circumference to the center to establish the illusion and then diffused itself over the area privated by its first withdrawal, thus re-establishing Reality.

The Ptolemaic system of astronomy, though untrue from a scientific point of view, clarifies one of the esoteric teachings of ancient learning so long misconstrued by modern scholars. By placing the earth in the center of the solar system and dividing the interval between the earth and the inner wall of the heavens by a number of planes corresponding to the orbits of the planetary bodies, a diagrammatic figure of consciousness and its extensions is created. Outside the orbit of the earth were the spheres of the Moon, Mercury, Venus, Sun, Mars, Jupiter, and Saturn in the order noted. Beyond the sphere of Saturn was the plane of the constellations which formed the inner surface of the zodiacal globe. Outside this globe was the Empyrean, or dwelling place of the gods. The Mysteries taught that man must ascend in realization from the earth through the rings (or planes) of the planets to the circle of the zodiac. Having reached the wall of heaven, he was then to break through and enter the supreme universe. After realization has pierced the crystalline shell of Being, it then ceases to be under the jurisdiction of the Governors of the seven planets and the vast body of cosmic agencies controlling all mundane creations. The student, however, should not conceive of his consciousness as rising but rather of his inferior self ascending through various levels of consciousness to ultimate union with the All-Knowing.

This idea requires further amplification. What man pleases to call his spirit is, in reality, the level of Self to which he is attuned by the quality and completeness of his realization. The Oriental symbolizes Universal Self as an immense sunburst, its inconceivably magnificent center surrounded by innumerable rings of petal-like emanations, which decrease in brilliancy as they recede from the center. This sunburst fills all conceivable space, extending from *up* to *down* and from *in* to *out*, and each of its petals, or rays, supports (in the sense of being the causal nature of) a definite genus of so-called evolving life. Thus the infinite diversity of manifestation reflects the infinite potentialities of the causal nature. The question may properly be asked how the Self, though an absolute unity and hence incapable of diversity, can still exist in a number of apparently different states. To employ a simple analogy, let us take two goblets, one containing wine and the other water. The wine will symbolize Self; the water, the illusionary universe of privation of the Self (the *Abyss* of the German mystics). If a small quantity of the wine be poured into the water, the wine will undergo no actual change, yet it will be so diluted as to be apparently different from its original state. Then imagine all the wine to be divided into single drops which are allowed to fall into the water one at a time. Each drop will cause a minute but definite difference in the degree of dilution and, consequently, the wine will exist in as many conditions as there are degrees of dilution. Yet the wine will actually undergo no change, and regardless of how much water is added it will still remain a single substance. Thus the infinite diversity of manifestation has its origin not in separate spiritual agencies but in the conditions which the Self is capable of assuming in relation to its own absence.

In East Indian philosophy the human figure is substituted for the earth; otherwise the Ptolemaic system of the planets is preserved, the outermost orbit becoming the boundary of limitation that separates the individual from the universal state. Sitting in meditation in the midst of his little universe, the philosopher by definite projection of the faculties of realization annihilates one by one the walls that enclose him until finally with one supreme effort he shatters the globe of his individuality and achieves Nirvana.

Let us try to conceive the process whereby the mystic transcends all environment and becomes *en rapport* with universal principles. Recognizing in the orbits of the planets certain major levels of realization, it soon becomes evident that the mind *per se* in unable to cope with the situation, for in spiritual concerns the intellect is well-nigh powerless. In an effort to explain simply the theory, let us presume that the earth in the center of the Ptolemaic chart represents the state of absolute ignorance, and the Empyrean beyond the circle of the zodiac, absolute wisdom or consciousness.

Humanity numbers in its ranks many so-called worldly-wise men—powerful intellects thickly encrusted with the catalogued notions and superstitions of others. Since all material knowledge is added on from without, under the stress of desperate need the inner nature is discovered to be incapable of sustaining the intellectual conceits thus foisted upon it. On the other hand, realization is a power which has its source within the inner nature itself. Like the balm of Gilead it brings with it peace, courage, and understanding. It tinctures the outer nature with a spiritual comprehension, giving an intuitive grasp of facts and the power to discern Reality. It may therefore be stated that the fundamental difference between knowledge and understanding lies in the direction of the flow of power, knowledge flowing in from without and undesrtanding flowing out from within. Realization is consequently a problem of the inner life and can receive little assistance from the outer nature. The mind creates elaborate theologies and intricate systems of reasoning which are without other than intellectual foundation, and in moments of dire need it is all too apparent that these adumbrations lack the substance of sufficiency. Hence, to convert an individual by outer means is useless, for true conversion can only come through the inner realization of certain divine or natural facts. To *affirm* oneself to occupy a certain position in the universe means nothing, but to realize the nature of a certain position or condition is to be one with that condition or to occupy that position.

While Ptolemy knew that the earth was not the center of the solar system, he also knew that earthiness was the beginning point of all achievement and that each struggling creature rising from its own earthiness must ascend through the circles of realization to eventually achieve complete liberation from the grossness of inferior nature. Seated in the midst of the circles and separated from the Universal Self by seven great walls of limitation of consciousness, the unillumined nature dwells in a state of isolation, accepting in its ignorance the illusion of diversity and regarding all creation as conspiring to bring about its destruction. Man must attain the realization necessary for his liberation by one of two paths: (1) He must follow the apparently endless spiral of life which leads in and through creation and eventually brings him to realization through experience. This experience is largely the essence of the reactions of joy and sorrow together with the recognition of the sequence of cause and effect in all the incidents of life. (2) By the Dharma of Realization the disciple may so intensify his attitudes through philosophic discipline as to achieve in a comparatively brief period of time that which the mass of humanity must attain by the slower and more circuitous route of natural processes.

Through realization alone can the Great Work be consummated. Only he who possesses realization is able to dispel the illusion of diversity. The true magnitude of an individual is measured by both the intensiveness and extensiveness of his realization, for the individual extends in every direction as far as his realization is capable of penetrating. For example, in his least illumined state man is but a mere speck in the midst of universal expanse. In his most illumined state, however, man has so increased in rational magnitude that universal expanse becomes a mere speck within his realization. In his ignorance man conceives the universe as including him, only to ultimately discover that his divine potentialities are so boundless that, when adequately manifested, the universe and countless vistas unmeasured are but infinitesimal parts of his own being. In Pythagorean terminology, man in his relapsed states conceives himself to be one of many, only to find upon arrival at the fullness of understanding that he has encircled the many and resolved them into his own unity.

The figure seated in the rings represents the mystic directionalizing his realization upon the Eternal. By this process he recapitulates the entire scheme of universal unfoldment, and reveals the causal urge behind all racial and individual development. In the diagram the rings are numbered from 1 to 7. The first ring immediately surrounds the seated form of the sage, and the area thus enclosed by it, being the smallest division, signifies the most limited state of realization. Those whose poverty of realization restricts them to this level of consciousness may be considered ignorant to the degree of the savage. Here the life is ruled by fear and hatred—fear of the unknown and hatred for that which possesses superior knowledge. With crude implements and cruder instincts these unknowing ones seek to fulfill Nature's first law, self-preservation. The finer emotions and sentiments are entirely absent, and the organic quality of the body is so low that the capacity for physical pain is thereby reduced to a minimum. Understanding is totally lacking, but in its place is a certain primitive cunning which warns of danger and instructs in the rudiments of physical survival. Little or no effort is made by this type to communicate its attitudes or feeling to others. It does not establish any definite communal life, but lives by itself and for itself alone, and finally creeps away to die leaving its unburied bones to bleach upon some wind-blown crag.

Though civilization has reached practically every corner of the earth and savage tribes are fast vanishing before its advance, it is possible to veneer the exterior and still leave the interior nature as primitive as ever. The addition of a Prince Albert coat or a pair of spats does not necessarily result in a highly advanced degree of culture, for many people suspected of considerable refinement are still innately barbaric. In fact, all who advocate isolated individualism are reverting to aboriginal type. Whenever the activities of life are centered exclusively upon the aggrandizement of the lesser self, such an attitude is unfailing evidence of the survival of Crookbone traits. Where the individual is completely wrapped up in himself, feels himself sufficient for himself, and regards all humanity as legitimate prey for exploitation, we have definite proof that his consciousness is still limited to the narrow confines of the first ring. The universe beyond means nothing to him, for beyond his realization it has no existence.

When the meditating sage elevates his realization until it recognizes the insufficiency of such a code and can no longer live in this sense of utter separateness, then the first ring is said to be annihilated and the realization sweeps outward to meet the limiting confines of the second ring. The circle of realization has thus been considerably enlarged and the self has taken the first step to escape from the not-self. As growth is synonymous with increasing inclusiveness, the individual functioning upon the level of consciousness of the second ring accepts into himself a limited number of external objects. In the dawn of civilization the family was lifted to a certain degree of equality with the individual who constituted himself its head. Such an individual still viewed the world as hostile, but out of it he chose a few and these he accepted on a parity with himself. His sense of protection included them; his love of self regarded them as part of himself and consequently legitimate objects for his affection. To a certain degree he viewed the members of his family as possessions, but psychologically he possessed them because his realization included them; for nothing can be actually possessed unless it is enclosed by the realization of possession.

There is to be found in human nature an inherent trait which causes each individual to feel himself to be different from any other living thing and consequently superior to and free from the laws governing the body of creation. In this ring the individual rises to that state of consciousness where he decides that those of his immediate circle upon whom he confers his affections are likewise composed of this superior substance and, like himself, differ from the rest of society. However, the fact that even one or two are included with self demonstrates that the annihilation of the sense of diversity has begun, for as the self accepts into itself that which was previously a stranger to it, the cosmic march toward unity begins and continues until all existence has thus been absorbed.

Today there are millions of people whose spiritual natures are the substance of the second ring. They will cheat the world that they may lavish their ill-gotten gains upon their own family circle. Humanity at large is still a stranger to them; their realization fails to recognize in all mankind the common heritage of similar loves, hopes, fears, and aspirations. This particular thought brings to mind the plea of Shylock in the third act of the Merchant of Venice for scattered and downtrodden Israel. By taking a few liberties with Shylock's speech, a truth is established beyond the conception of those whose realization limits them to the consciousness of the second ring. "Have not all men eyes; have not all men hands, organs, dimensions, senses, affections, passions; are not all men fed with the same food, hurt with the same weapons, subject to the same diseases, healed by the same means, warmed and cooled by the same summer and winter as you are? If you prick them, do they not bleed; if you tickle them, do they not laugh; if you poison them, do they not die?"

To summarize, the consciousness of the second ring covers blood relations and those upon whom particular affections are lavished: the mother, father, husband, wife, and child. These are accepted as parts of self and the work of unification has been inaugurated; for while in the first ring these are five separate people, in the second ring they are included as members of the one in whom the realization of their proximity has been established.

When realization increases to the point where it includes the stranger without the gate, the spirit of friendship is born. A friend is one to whom we are related by consciousness rather than by blood. Pythagoras declared his friend to be his *alter ego* —his other self. At another time he stated friendship to be that condition in which one soul existed in two bodies, thereby elevating this relationship far above that of the ties of blood. Until realization reaches the third plane friendship is impossible because up to that point egotism is so dominant a motive that man's love for himself precludes all other affections. When realization annihilates the substances of the second ring and flows through into its enlarged field of expression, the tribal (later the national) spirit is evolved. A certain clannishness is manifested, for though the great world without is still excluded, nevertheless the sense of inclusiveness has been increased to take in those having a similar origin or living in close proximity. Having one leader, the tribe is simply an enlarged family, the chief or head symbolizing the father; for nearly all tribal forms of government are patriarchies.

Eventually the tribe grows into the nation and there is born a curious mental attitude termed *patriotism*. Patriotism is merely an accentuated egotism which embraces the members of the tribe or nation to which the egotist himself belongs. Fundamentally it is based upon the belief that that of which the individual is a part, is, like himself, incapable of wrong. Consequently all examination of motive is regarded as superflous, and the attitude that "I and mine are right and you and yours are wrong" is an attitude to be assumed and maintained at all costs. Long regarded as a virtue, patriotism will yet demonstrate itself to be a most pernicious attitude, for it can be and has been controlled and directionalized by personal interest, frequently to tragic ends.

To affirm that an individual can do no wrong merely because he is of the same blood or clan as oneself, and to defend him because of such relationship is a fault, and contributes to his own moral delinquency and the destruction of the nation. There can be but one true patriotism: namely, patriotism to principle. But those dwelling in the consciousness of the third ring are as yet unaware of principle, and to them their tribe or nation is elevated to a position approximating Deity. Yet with all his faults and blindness, the one who has attained to this degree of consciousness has gone far in the mastery of diversity, for his realization has increased until in part, at least, it has included an entire nation within the range of common interest. True, it has not yet learned to understand the structure and consciousness of nations, but this comes later. Here is the man who will die for his friend but cannot possibly understand his friend; for he serves not the consciousness of his friend but rather his own preconceived standard of friendship. It may therefore be said, regardless of the actual integrity of the friend himself, that he dies not for his friend but for his own concept of friendship. Man creates standards and later serves them as though they were divine creations, only to discover ultimately that Deity had no hand in their fashioning.

When the sage, seated in the midst of his rings of consciousness, elevates his realization to the sphere of the fourth ring, he passes from national to racial concerns. His ever increasing vista of understanding has revealed to him that the inhabitants of earth are not merely isolated individuals nor even families and tribes, but rather can be classified under a few racial headings. It naturally follows that the mind establishes comparisons between the relative superiority of these races; also that the unillumined man should upon some pretext or other elevate the particular race of which he is a part to the position of superiority. If at the time of making the comparison his own nation occupies a position that is evidently inferior, he will philosophize upon their past glory or dream of their future ascendancy. Such an individual, however, continues to annihilate diversity, for in his analysis of peoples he no longer conceives of a billion and a half separate units but rather of a score of major segments, each composed of a vast number of lesser parts.

From this attitude is born the racial spirit: we have "chosen" peoples and "rejected" peoples, racial gods, racial attitudes, and racial prejudices. Practically all civilized humanity is now in the throes of racial upheaval. The white man regards the black man as his inferior. Throughout the Southern States there is a definite color line drawn which in some cases is incalculably unjust. There are schools in the United States where the pupils, encouraged by parents of puerile intelligence, have risen in a body and refused to admit the enrollment of colored children in their classes. While the white man views with contempt the black man, he considers with ever increasing alarm the machinations of the yellow man and the brown man. The lot of the red man apparently gives his white brother little concern, for the latter feels that the work of extermination goes on apace. It is interesting to note at this stage the effort man makes not to be inclusive; for he seems to fear lest he should learn to love everything so much that he would have nothing left to hate.

The question of sex equality becomes an issue during this period and man has undertaken to determine whether woman really has the consciousness of a human being or whether she must depend upon man for rational intelligence. We see people everywhere who function upon this level of the fourth ring. They are called broad-minded, charitable citizens with progressive ideas. In many instances they foster foreign missions and believe in spreading the white man's light throughout the dark and gloomy areas where the benighted non-Aryans reside. As Charles Erskine Scott Wood has noted, they discuss the holy war of Christendom and the unholy wars of the barbarians! They are more or less patronizing and condescending in their attitudes, feeling that by reason of their exalted status they can well afford to be "nice" to their less fortunate younger brothers. Such people do not compare favorably with those few outstanding examples of intelligence produced by the world. If contrasted, however, with the primitive attitudes of the first ring, their progress is apparent. These people are trying to be big, but are bound to their littleness by precedent, environment, education, and fear. They dread to be on the unpopular side of any issue, yet sincerely wish that the popular side might occasionally be the right side.

In ancient astrology the fourth plane—that of the sun— was regarded as a middle point dividing the inferior or subsolar planets from the superior orbs moving outside the solar orbit. It naturally follows that when the realization has been lifted to the consciousness of the fifth circle it should concern itself with greater verities. He who has reached this stage is capable of understanding the immortal words of Thomas Paine: "The world is my country, and to do good is my religion." The only defect in the slogan is the lack of definite understanding regarding the word *good*. The ideal is an excellent one but its fulfillment is very difficult, for good can never be discovered as long as the individual considers himself its true criterion.

Having thus pierced all the rings of consciousness to the fifth, realization has now reached that point where it begins to recognize the magnitude of the plan behind manifesting life. The concerns of nations and the politics of men then recede into insignificance; for from this comparatively exalted level of realization humanity is viewed as a single unit.

At this stage there also comes the realization that human life is not the only rational manifestation of Deity. Consciousness and intelligence are recognized in the lower kingdoms, and brotherhood extends to all corners of the earth, including all races and species without distinction. The vastness of the whole and the infinitesimal smallness of the part we call the world begins to be apparent. Upon this level philosophy begins,—that is, philosophy as apart from the individualistic codes established by primitive man with no thought for that which was beyond the vista of his own comprehension. The principles of justice emerge from the codes of primitive retribution. Power becomes thoughtful of weakness and might considerate of that which is less than itself. From the code of the survival of the fittest comes the realization that it is possible to make fit the unfit that all may survive. The subtler virtues are elevated above the grosser propensities and grace and beauty are regarded as superior to strength.

Although truth is still but a concept, the increasing realization gives the sense of magnitude which overawes and causes the half awakened faculties to glimpse the immeasurable that lies beyond. The sage within is coming into himself; the sky wanderer is casting off the bonds which bind him to earth; the voices of the Seven Spheres are calling and something far down in the depths of man's nature is tugging at its fetters, crying out for freedom to join in the ecstatic dance of life. Having raised himself to the contemplation of the world and its mystery, the sage finds himself one with the world and its mystery, his heart merged with the heart of the world, his mind teeming with the thoughts of the world, his whole being filled with the longings of the world. He ultimately reaches the state where he may truthfully say that he understands the world, for man understands what he is and is what he understands.

When realization pierces the sixth ring and blends itself with the consciousness of that plane, it is declared that the individual transcends individual concerns and becomes a citizen of the universe. His kinship with the sun, the moon, and the stars is established; for the consciousness that was formerly individual discovers individuality to be a limiting and binding illusion. Of such souls as have attained to this exalted state are the Bodhisattvas,—those who stand at the very gateway of liberation. These exalted ones may still turn back and as Elder Brothers walk the dusty roads of the lower worlds; but before them the swinging veils of Eternity are very thin and the voice of the great sea of Reality calls to them to immerse their lesser selves in its limitless expanse. To describe the consciousness of those so proximate to Reality is a futile undertaking for any one not so illumined. It can only be said that such as these brood over mortality, and leaning from the casements of heaven regard with solicitude divine this mundane sphere. These are the Great Ones who walk from star to star, whose souls are so vast that the whirling bodies of the firmament are encircled by them. These are the ones who gaze straight into the face of the sun unblinded.

The Oriental mind conceives these illumined and perfected ones to be vast beings whose statures extend from earth to heaven, whose feet rest upon pink lotus buds, and whose flowing draperies reveal in their grace the innate perfection of the wearer. Nowhere in all the mighty figure is a single incongruity to be found. The long, slender fingers either assume the *mudras* with perfect rhythm or hold the symbols of divine accomplishment. Surrounded by its blazing nimbus, the noble head is set in absolute repose, yet in the awesomeness of its grandeur there is nothing to inspire fear, for the perfected ones are not terrible in power but rather beautiful in humility. Though the great face of the Bodhisattva blazes like burnished gold, there is in it that sweet repose which makes all who behold it cease their strivings and enter into meditation. The jewels in the crown gleam and glisten with a holy light, and the clanking rings upon the mendicant's staff sound the music of the spheres. With his feet rising from the earth in lotus cups and his head blended with the heavens, the Bodhisattva thus stands as the embodiment of those redeeming graces which, latent in most men, have been awakened and brought to full expression through the aeons of preparation. The lips of the illumined are as lotus buds, for they have been perfected through ages of perfect speech and from them issue the words of perfect wisdom. The half-closed eyes contemplate the measureless vistas in whose depths resides the perfect Buddha, and toward this ultimate that lies beyond the seventh ring the Great One thus directs the ageless chant of the Law:

> I take my refuge in Thy Name and Thee!
> I take my refuge in Thy Law of Good!
> I take my refuge in Thy Order! *OM!*

It is not written that the lesser shall include the greater in its scope of awareness. It is impossible, therefore, to trace the magnitude of that illumination which, standing at the threshold of Reality, already glimpses the Endless. Of this consciousness all that can be said is that, robed in its own exaltedness, it awaits the day when it shall be merged with the All.

At last for the aspiring soul there comes the Great Day "Be With Us," which is indeed the end of all beginnings. This day, that has a dawn but no sunset, begins in time and lasts throughout eternity. Diversity has been completely absorbed and naught remains save the meditating saint and the Absolute. The iridescent bubble of being now floats upon the great Ocean from whose primordial spray it was fashioned. For one breathless, unmeasurable second of time the bubble hangs suspended, an opalescent sphere. Against its confining walls the imprisoned sage hurls the blazing thunderbolt of his will. The bubble bursts and instantly disappears except for a fine mist that settles back into the endless sea.

Thus is accomplished the annihilation of the last ring of illusion, when realization becomes so exalted as to be incapable of further qualification; when nothing but All is sufficient and the multitude of illusions—including the dream of existence—have been dissipated. The leering Yama (the god of illusion) who sought to grasp the bubble and its holy contents, retires discomfited, for the perfected one has escaped into the Refuge that endures. No more will the illumined one walk with man; his last discourse has been given; for the last time he has taken upon himself the veil of sorrow, for he has now merged himself with the Law that is his Refuge. Those who seek the perfected one must search for him in perfection, for he has become one with all the good which he sought. He is identical with the beauty that he served; he is the truth whose actuality he conceived; he is the sure foundation that is the absolute necessity.

To the disciples left behind, the Master who passes into Nirvana is one who has passed out of the world which shall cease, into the world which ceases not. He has become one with all the permanence that is and through all the manifestations of Infinite Law he is revealed. He has become one with the finger that traces the sunsets upon the western sky; one with the god of morning who, parting the curtains of night, ushers in the day; one with the winds and the rains. He gazes down from the blue mists of heaven and up from the dark mystery of the earth; his voice is heard in the mantra and his eloquence in the booming of the temple gong; his strength is made manifest in the Law and his meekness in the humility of the mendicant.

The one gone has ceased to be *somewhere* but has grown to be *everywhere*, for he has found Reality and is himself one with that which all men seek. One by one the aspiring soul has discarded the limiting rings of consciousness. From the least to the greatest he has risen, and this he has accomplished by becoming the least among the least. With one supreme effort of realization he has renounced death and become deathless; he has willingly surrendered life and become lifeless. So, lifeless and deathless, he remains immovable in Eternity.

Climbing up the ladder of the stars he has followed the path to perfection; he has walked the Middle Road which has been established since the beginning of the world; he has followed in the footsteps of the sages gone before, and after him will come myriads yet unborn, until sometime the way to Nirvana shall be the royal road by which all humanity passes from the ephemerality of mortal existence to the unchangeableness of divine existence.

He who attains the Absolute is himself the Absolute; for while all men contemplate some world to which their consciousness has attuned them, he who has attained the Absolute contemplates only the inconceivable perfection of the Absolute itself. United with that which eternally endures, the perfected soul is freed forever from the illusion of change, of difference, of time, and of distance.

It is useless, however, to attempt an analysis of the consciousness of the one in whom consciousness has thus been merged with Reality. While we struggle impotently with the tangled skein of life, such a one has gathered all its strands together and rewound the line of life to its own beginning. While we are borne upon its surface, powerless to stem its currents, such a one has reversed the waters of the river of life and caused them to flow back to their own source.

Having revealed to all men through his life the fulfillment of the Law and having preached his farewell sermon that all might understand, the great Buddha entered Nirvana. Having by his resurrection demonstrated to all mankind the illusion of death, the Master Jesus ascended into the aeons to be united with his heavenly Father. Having demonstrated that justice alone shall survive, Socrates drank the hemlock and with perfect realization exchanged the death of life for the life of death. Certain of the Reality that lies beyond, and given courage by ever increasing vistas of consciousness, the aspiring soul proceeds to the annihilation of the unreal by hurling himself voluntarily through the wall of his prison into the embrace of the Law which is his Refuge and his End.

The Annihilation of the Sense of Diversity

Having thus considered, in diagrammatic fashion at least, the principle involved in the unfoldment of realization, let us view the subject from the standpoint of the philosopher. If asked to describe the sensations through which he passes as he projects his realization inward toward the Self, the Oriental mystic would reply that he first seats himself in the midst of the bustle and confusion of the world. Then, having established his physical body in the posture and state prescribed by the Law, he begins the conscious withdrawal of himself from his outer life. Gradually the turmoil around him ceases until the physical world seems to sink away into space, leaving him alone immersed in a quasi emptiness which is permeated, however, by the sense of protection and well-being.

In its ascent realization passes through various states or conditions where, if right-mindfulness is not employed, the mystic wanders off into a phantasmal world which the European magicians of the Middle Ages chose to call the sphere of the astral light. Here the sense of emptiness is no longer present, for space seems filled with strange and exotic perfumes, and the one in meditation beholds flowers falling from space upon him until he is literally buried beneath a mass of sweet-smelling blossoms. Over him then steals a bliss unalloyed and the compelling urge to drift off into the astral gardens which have thus suddenly materialized into being. As Eliphas Levi says, however, the serpent of evil is entwined about each flower, and he who tarries here will never find the Real. But, resolute in his defiance of the phantasms thus conjured up by Mara, the realization of the mystic rises above all these through spheres of light and color, through planes where endless music peals as from a heavenly organ. At length all phenomena cease; light and darkness cease; the realization of the personal self ceases. Slowly over the entire being descends an absolute peace and the mystic is swept into infinite realization. At this point the sage will end his description, for here description fails.

Realization is the power by which the great achievement is rendered possible. Realization, as previously stated, must not be confused with intellectual acquiescence in, or concept of an idea. Realization is the measure of accomplishment. Realization is the product of right-thinking, right-feeling, and right-acting. Realization is not attainable except as the reaction of right-doing; only experience, renunciation, compassion, love, service, and ideality can build realization, and only realization is capable of elevating man through the various spheres of consciousness. Thus are definitely set forth the way, the means, and the end; but no man can take this path for another.

Diversity is the paramount illusion. Only realization can overcome the concept of diversity. A great soul is obvious from his instinctive effort to synthesize the elements of life. Take, for example, the so-called body of knowledge. That which man believes he knows he has divided into a host of subdivisions, each of which is served by intellects naturally segregative and separative. The physicist, the biologist, and the anthropologist all live in worlds apart, each seeking with his own particular fragment of the body of knowledge to solve the riddle of it all. However, as consciousness reveals more and more of Reality to man, all these man made divisions disappear and the multitude of streamlets converge to form the three great rivers of science, philosophy, and religion. These, in turn, eventually empty into the one great ocean of Truth. Never will knowledge be possible, however, until we realize that each part is helpless without all the others; that all branches of learning are useless until merged in a single science representing the sum of human thought, feeling, and belief.

It is sad but true that with few exceptions what man thinks he knows actually stands between him and knowledge, for he who is rich in beliefs is usually a pauper in facts. The theorist is too involved in his own irrational complexities to recognize rational simplicity. Barring the individual from the path of attainment are not only the unrecognized absurdities of his own life, but also the cumulative prejudice, bigotry, and false emphasis of generations. The theology of his fathers, the philosophy of his ancestors, and the stupendous scientific institutions of his contemporaries all tend to overawe the individual into acceptance of the unreal. The gods are so silent and man so bombastic that ignorant mortals may well be excused if they regard the dogmatic utterances of man as more authoritative than the silence of the gods. Only after much experience with the pyrotechnics of discordant isms is the eloquence of divine silence discernible. The world is largely composed of people whose smugness is impervious—people who are orthodox in their orthodoxy and orthodox in their heterodoxy. With equal facility they defend both their plethora of beliefs and their paucity of them. Exhibiting the keenest pleasure, they conduct one through the many chambers of their minds, woefully unaware that all this vast mental establishment represents a prison and not a palace. He who would tread the path that leads to light and liberation must first cast aside not physical possessions —which, at best, are but gew-gaws—but the so-called treasures of the mind, which are actually a hodgepodge of notions. Divorced from all bias and assumption, stripped of the garments of pomp and ceremony, and exchanging the robes of self-satisfaction for the simple saffron garment of humility, the mendicant soul achieves by the Middle Road. His reliance is neither upon God nor man but upon the Law. In full realization that the Law of all things is ultimate perfection, the seeker after Reality takes his stand upon that eternal urge which moves all to this ennobled end.

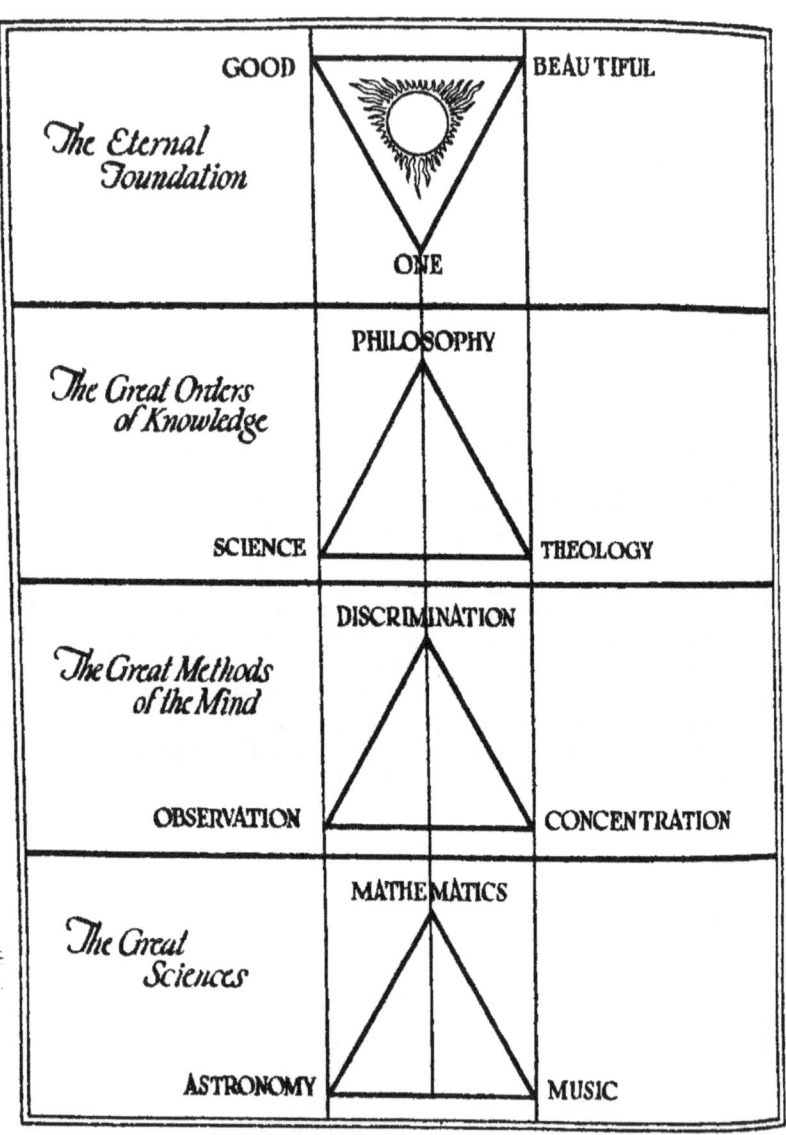

THE PYTHAGOREAN THEORY OF TRIADS

The fundamental motion of the One toward the Two and from their sum the triad is established. The triangle is the skeleton of the universe, the whole diversity of life being erected upon a threefold foundation. The complicated order of manifestation may cause the uninformed to lose sight of the unchanging Three, which is indeed the God of the wise.

CHAPTER SIX

The Disciplines of Salvation

ASSUMING realization to be the product of definite philosophic disciplines, we now turn to a consideration of the sciences and procedures which are most valuable in the unfoldment of the rational intellect and the directionalization of the conscious Knower. Initiated into the mysteries of contemplative philosophy by the Brahman initiates of Ellora and Elephanta, Pythagoras set forth three disciplines as essential to salvation through unity with Universal Cause. Supreme in his contemplative genius, Pythagoras differs from his Eastern mentors in that he conceived the universal state to be attained through elevation of the mind rather than annihilation of thought procedure. As the first step toward realization, he accordingly taught the training of the mind so as to make it capable of sustained logical activity. The misconception is quite general that a common school education equips the mind for the profession of living, and, if supplemented by university training the individual is thereby qualified to question and debate intelligently the dictums of eternity. Modern education, is not founded upon strict rational procedure; hence the mass of humanity is not educated but rather supports its notions by the vain mumblings of archaic dogma. Unless first subjected to definite disciplines, the mind is incapable of rational functioning. There are few, alas, who, like the young Dalai Lama of Tibet, are able to rise in their cribs on their natal day and recite the *Sutras* in a convincing manner! If a man should approach us and say, "I am a human being and a biologist simply because I am a born biologist," we would consider him ridiculous, knowing that many years of definite application must be spent in equipping the reason to cope with the issues of biology. Yet if someone else equally lacking in fitness comes along and says, "I am free, white, and twenty one; my thoughts, consequently, are as good and my conclusions concerning life as sound as those of any other man," we would smile benignly and exclaim, "Ah, vive la democratie!"

Since few people regard thinking as an exact science, an intellect such as Socrates' could in a few moments literally rip to shreds the entire fabric of human notions. To learn to think intelligently requires more time and effort than any other profession known to man, and is only to be realized through the most exacting disciplines. Most wordly-wise men are in the same position as the young patrician, Alcibiades, who because he wrestled well and played the lyre not too badly considered himself qualified to sit in the Athenian Senate. But all are not fortunate enough to have Socrates, the plebeian, barking at their heels, continually reminding them in no uncertain terms that not on a single count could they qualify. With the same delightful inconsistency characteristic of human procedure, when Socrates revealed to the Athenians their ignorance they corrected the condition by poisoning the man who had the audacity to confront them with it.

Pythagoras invariably demanded of his disciples a familiarity with the principles of three sciences: mathematics, music, and astronomy. These sciences are today capable of filling the same ends which they served in ancient days, for they not only reveal to those familiar with their principles certain cosmic verities, but also instill the principles of order, rationality, and comparative values. The curse of the twentieth century is the superficiality of its thought and the resultant insufficiency of the foundation upon which the structure of life is erected. What does it mean to become proficient in mathematics, music, and astronomy? Remember, we do not refer to the utilitarian aspect of these sciences which too frequently realizes its ideal in the creation of the bookkeeper, the jazz pianist, and the elderly prognosticator who determines the annual precipitation from observation of the size of the sun-spots.

Those who approach life with the Oriental attitude—namely, that matter is a vast sea of illusion—may rightly question the advisability of devoting years to the mastery of sciences wholly concerned with the substances of the illusion. Such individuals, however, must learn to regard a certain rational grasp of the tangible as prerequisite to a conception of the intangible. It is not what man actually learns that is of value to him, but rather the mental and spiritual activities within his own nature that necessarily precede and follow learning. Like the carpenter building a chair, the accomplishment is not the production of the chair but the ability to build chairs. Thus thought in itself should not be regarded as an accomplishment or necessarily valuable, for only the ability to think represents a definite degree of unfoldment within the nature of the thinker himself.

When the student realizes that the entire fabric of creation is permeated by certain exact elements and principles, he unconsciously begins to figure and think in terms of exactness. The philosophy of salvation is nothing if not exact. According to both Pythagoras and Plato, mathematics is the father of the sciences—the first and greatest of the mystical disciplines of exactness. Without mathematics as a foundation, nothing can endure; upon its exactitude is raised the entire structure of order and sequence. All other arts and sciences are dependencies of mathematics, for into each enters the element of precision that manifests the unchangeable nature of number.

Referring to our fundamental symbolic triad, mathematics is the dot, music the line, and astronomy the circle. The mysteries of the invisible causal sphere are to be approached by the principles of mathematics; the mysteries of the intermediate sphere are revealed by the profundities of aesthetics and harmonics; the mysteries of the inferior sphere are disclosed by the study of astronomy. Thus these sciences are the first triad of knowing and he who masters them is equipped to face the universe with a definite assurance that he is part of a scheme whose principles are inflexible, whose agencies are beautiful, and whose results are exact.

Many people with whom we have discussed these Pythagoric disciplines complain that life is so short and its problems so numerous that time does not permit the mastery of such complicated studies. The inconsistency of such an attitude is primarily one of wrong emphasis. He who does not start because he fears he will not live to finish will never live to start. A certain friend approaching his eightieth year is on the verge of commencing the study of Spanish because he feels that it will be an important language during his next incarnation. An individual with such an attitude has surmounted a great obstacle. Too many live in the past and as the years roll by consider the future as an ever-diminishing quantity. The realization of infinite futurity is indispensable to accomplishment, but it is useless unless accompanied by a definite impulse to make *now* the starting-point of achievement.

Pythagoras was well aware that inconstancy and inconsistency render valueless the greater part of human rumination,—hence he regarded the quality of exactness as essential to true mental functioning. He knew that a mind trained to recognize but one right answer to any problem in mathematics would likewise recognize that there is but one right solution to any problem in life. Yet Pythagoras was not fundamentally a mathematician; he was a philosopher, but mathematics was the first and sharpest of his tools. Mathematics is the supreme discipline in the science of knowing. More mystics have come into an understanding of the unseen side of life and realized the unfoldment of their inner perceptions through mathematics than through any other science known to man.

Mathematics is the Pythagorean symbol of what the Buddhist terms the Law—the procedure of Being. Through numbers the intricate mechanism of divine will is disclosed, for nothing else reveals so patently the exactness of cosmic method and the immutability of cosmic ends. The vast field of manifestation is shown to be an orderly chain of emanations issuing from the incomprehensibility of First Cause, and after passing through definite phases of change returning to that from which they were temporarily separated. Through mathematics a hypothetical framework is established by means of which the natures of all manifestations are analyzed and the modes of their directionalization determined. He who understands mathematics can never conceive of himself as existing in an unorganized universe nor regard himself as an exception to the immutable laws of Being. Thus is established the realization of participation in all the activities of Cosmos, and the glory of the whole is augmented as mathematics unveils the magnificence of the Eternal Plan.

In music the Real and the ideal are blended. The mathematical basis upon which the science of harmonics is founded insures preservation of the principle of exactness. At the same time music stimulates lofty emotional reactions and thus ameliorates the austerity of numbers. While mathematics emphasizes the exactness of Deity, music reveals the moods of the Causal Nature. Like a flowering vine twining itself about the harsher outlines of mathematical procedure, music softens and beautifies the angles of cosmic discipline. Many dream of the beauty of things as they could be, but only the philosopher can recognize the beauty of things as they are. To such as are able to lift themselves above the personal concerns of life, the concord of the All is apparent.

When Pythagoras taught that men should depend not upon their ears but upon mathematics for the determination of harmony, he emphasized a subtle verity: namely, that the exactness of divine procedure is the absolute standard of harmony, and the order of universal flow is the perfect pattern of all rhythm. These are also the salient points of the philosophy of Taoism, and the ascetics of every age have striven to unite their own lesser natures with the harmonic procedures of divinity. Worlds, like atoms, are in a state of ceaseless vibration, and this vibration shared by all manifestations is the mysterious dance of life. From the inner nature the study of music causes to issue forth a love for life in all its diversity. While mathematics inspires awe for the immutability of divine jurisprudence, music reveals the all-knowing Lawmaker as tempering justice with mercy.

Astronomy strangely supplements both mathematics and music, and in turn is completed by them. The author of the *Merchant of Venice* causes one of his players to say:

> There's not the smallest orb which thou beholdst,
> But in his motion like an angel sings,
> Still choiring to the young-eyed cherubims.

By the science of astronomy the magnitude of Reality is established, for if the unreal stretches from time to timelessness, how much greater must that perfection be of which creation is the inferior past? Gazing out into the infinite from the anthill he calls the earth, man comes to realize the insignificance of his personality; but as the eyes of his inner reason open he beholds the Reality within through the transcendency of which he is made to partake of the glory of both the manifested and the unmanifested.

In an effort to catch a possible glimpse of any stray gods who might be prowling about the fringe of creation, astronomers are fashioning ever larger and more efficient equipment with which to scan the heavens. A new telescope is now under construction by which stars of the twenty-fifth magnitude will be brought within the range of human vision. Thus, of all forms of human learning none possesses the power of astronomy to impress the individual with the realization of cosmic magnitudes. The contribution of astronomy to the attitude of toleration is incalculable; for from the time when Giordano Bruno gave his life that the heavens might be saved for astronomers, the insufficient god of theology was doomed. Equipped with the realization awakened by contemplation of the profundities of mathematics, music, and astronomy, the candidate after spiritual understanding may fearlessly knock at the portals of the House of Wisdom and demand admission to the hidden house of the Mysteries.

To those just beginning to awaken to the immensities of life, philosophy is a very hard religion. At first philosophy seems to be faith without sentiment, for it is not concerned with emotion in the ordinary acceptance of the term. Having no time for the petty interests which constitute the life of the average individual, philosophy, because of its concern over infinities and ultimates, seems distant and austere. Most individuals live in a universe of trivialities, spending their entire appointed span in the struggle for worthless trinkets. Such naturally desire and create a God concerned with trivialities, for their Deity is presumed to be interested in the effect of early frosts upon the crops or the probability of the leghorns escaping the roup; He must also be invoked at conferences and haled willy-nilly into court to act as sponsor for the integrity of those who testify. On Sunday he is likewise obligated to be in attendance at all the churches, not to mention the Wednesday evening prayer-meeting.

When philosophy attempts to dissipate this puerile conception of the Causal Agent, a great hue and cry goes up and those who never had a God other than themselves, cry out, "You have destroyed our faith; you have blasphemed our Creator and you strive to take away our God!" To such mediocre minds philosophy is assuredly a monster who demands a degree of intelligence requisite for attainment which would require time and application far beyond their willingness to sacrifice for such an end. In reality, however, philosophy has a heart greater than all the hearts of the world, and it is most loving and most kind because it is most just. Philosophy, like a wise parent, occasionally finds it necessary to chastize its children, not in anger but in the realization that man himself has no enemy like his own uncorrected vice. The truly great philosophers have been men and women whose hearts overflowed with love and understanding; but also they have been strong, and their strength lay in their recognition of that which was necessary for the good of all.

Out of philosophy is born the camaraderie of the spirit. Philosophy does not grind the masses down to a state of bondage in order that it may elevate a few. On the contrary, philosophy is a mental democracy. Thought is not turned to the disqualification of one another, but directed by all to the common end of wisdom. The humanity of today opposes the mind that generalizes, for we live in an age of specialization. The fact that philosophers think in terms of cosmic immensity causes the conservative intellect to view them askance. While minds of small caliber are concerned with the issues of ward politics, the philosopher contemplates that camaraderie which he has discovered among the sparks of infinite Being that fill the endless vista of beginnings and ends. The philosopher is a wanderer through the fields of space; to him the earth is a tiny oasis in a vast wilderness. Two or three palm trees, a little fountain, and a winding road—these constitute the caravansery where he rests between his daily journeys.

To people who are selfish; who seek prestige and demand attention; who are superior to others; who feel that in their veins courses a noble blood; who believe that when God molded them he breathed upon them twice while upon less fortunate mortals he breathed but once—to these and all other varieties of hypocrites philosophy is not pleasing, for it is the creed of honest men and can never come into its own until there are honest men.

Philosophy stands for something infinitely superior to physical honesty; something far more difficult of attainment: it stands for mental honesty. It is the fellowship of those who understand; a brotherhood of as many orders as there are degrees of understanding. It is strange that in modern times those who espouse philosophy are prone to grow either unfeeling or eccentric. They are inclined to become mentally lazy. Trusting themselves to the laws of which they have but an insufficient concept, they cease that individual struggle which, after all, is the only measure of true greatness. They have not discovered that while law governs the universe, love is its administrator in the hearts of men. Hence, the knowledge of law is not sufficient. To such knowledge must be added the realization that we are the administrators of that which we know, and that within ourselves we have the privilege of tempering the blast of eternal glory so that the shorn lamb may not be destroyed thereby.

Observation, discrimination, and concentration are prerequisites of knowing. It is first necessary to observe the infinite diversity of phenomenal being; then to discriminate between that which is primary in importance and that which is secondary. Having determined that which is most worthy of consideration, it is then necessary to concentrate the attention upon the task of discovering the recondite truths therein contained. When these three faculties are properly combined they result in a very high degree of rational penetration. Only such individuals as have learned to observe, discriminate, and concentrate are qualified to occupy executive positions in any walk of life. If, for example, these faculties had been possessed to even a reasonable degree by the early translators and editors of the Bible, what a different aspect would be taken on by the Scriptures; for instead of words, words, words, the spirit of Holy Writ would have been preserved.

In what particular does observation differ from seeing? We prefer to think of observation as the perfection of seeing, and the perfection of seeing is not the mere beholding of an object but rather the instant discernment of its inner constitution. Observation is not the mere seeing of things but rather the ability to see *through* things, making transparent, as it were, their outer nature so that the causal agencies precipitating them may be estimated. Observation, therefore, not only envisages the inherent nature of an object but also its relationship to that which precedes it as cause and follows it as consequence. Readers of the works of Sir Arthur Conan Doyle are familiar with the fascinating deductions of Sherlock Holmes which he was forced to explain in all their detail to the ever bewildered Dr. Watson. Into the mouth of Sherlock Holmes his creator puts an excellent description of the powers of observation, for it is true that a man's shoes, the manner in which he holds his hands, his air and carriage all reveal to the trained observer the characteristics of the inner nature which must manifest through these physical peculiarities. The range of human vision is able to take in a comparatively immense area of manifestation, and yet comparatively little of that which is seen is recorded in such a way that it can be evoked by the reasoning processes. Only when the consciousness itself is focused upon the organs of sight is their record preserved. We are most likely to behold and preserve the memory of that which is related to some major interest of life. Thus, a plumber will instinctively turn his attention to water pipes, while the artist will scrutinize the lower corner of the canvas for the painter's signature.

In great measure, therefore, observation is directionalized by interest, for man sees first that which interests him. Only after ages of mental unfoldment does man learn that in the last analysis all things are of equal interest. Interest is generally unjust in that it focuses the attention upon some fractional part before the panorama of the whole has been taken into consideration. At this point the problem of philosophic indifference should be considered. The philosopher is indifferent not in the sense that he ignores or refuses to concern himself with the diversity of being, but rather that he refuses to become biased by directionalizing his interest primarily upon any single phase of life to the exclusion of the remainder.

We study observation first because of its generalizing effect. If particularity precedes generality, the result will be mental intolerance and injustice. If however, specialization follows generalization, then the mind—familiar with all—may justly choose one phase of existence and develop it with rationality. But when the individual, having first conceived generality and estimated its profundity, chooses to continue dealing with and thinking in terms of generality, he truly remains a philosopher.

In his introduction to *An Essay on the Beautiful* by Plotinus, Thomas Taylor writes: "But surely the energies of intellect are more worthy our concern than the operation of sense; and the science of universals, permanent and fixed, must be superior to the knowledge of particulars, fleeting and frail. Where is a sensible object to be found which abides for a moment the same; which is not either rising to perfection, or verging to decay; which is not mixed and confused with its contrary; whose flowing nature no resistance can stop, or any art confine? * * * Since then there is no portion of matter which may not be the subject of experiments without end, let us betake ourselves to the regions of mind, where all things are bounded in intellectual measure; where every thing is permanent and beautiful, eternal and divine. Let us quit the study of particulars for that which is general and comprehensive, and through this learn to see and recognize whatever exists."

Observation may be considered as the process of seeing with the mind rather than with the eye. It involves an analysis of the object beheld and the effort to sense or conceive its intrinsic nature. The end of observation is the ability to cognize the life behind the form, the fact behind the fancy, the truth behind the symbol, and the Self behind the not-self. Through observation one is able to discover wisdom in the words of fools and foolishness in the words of most wise men. Observation, furthermore, is the ability to comprehend the pervading wholeness. He who sees may see the parts, but he who observes closely may glimpse the divine cement that binds the fractions together. We live in a world of men who see in part and are seen in part; who think in part, hope in part, fear in part. The universe is regarded as fragmentary or partitive because we lack the faculty of seeing the *wholeness* of things. Observation is that transcendent faculty which is able to grasp the wholeness of things in its span of comprehension, whereas ordinary sight is simply the ability to analyze the fragments. Thus sight differs from observation as widely as analysis differs from synthesis.

The inherent danger of observation is that when the man of ordinary vision begins to observe the vastness surrounding him and to realize that even the most minute particle of that vastness is itself immeasurably great, bewilderment ensues. There is an overwhelming sense of inadequacy to cope with the enormousness of the scheme. Then it is that the faculty of discrimination comes to the rescue, emphasizing the fact that if man is not capable of knowing all now he must compromise by devoting himself to a consideration of only the best. We all realize that in one short span of physical life we cannot do everything, we cannot know everything, we cannot have everything, we cannot be everything—the major part of accomplishment must be left in the keeping of futurity. So, contemplating the heterogeneous mass of phenomena, the rational soul establishes itself upon the surface of phenomena and directs its attention to the specific task of choosing from all that which is next and most necessary to the unfoldment of the faculty of realization.

He who possesses discrimination is master of the science of values. Discrimination is the value sense; it is the ability to look upon a number of objects apparently equally important, and instantly, instinctively, unerringly recognize that which is chief among them. Recognizing the whole to be of paramount value, it is then necessary to determine the nature of those parts which contribute most to the whole, or that part of the tangible proximate to the intangible.

According to the Greek philosophers discrimination is that faculty which organizes things into their value sequence, placing that which is primary first, that which is secondary second, and so on *ad infinitum*. Discrimination is one of the most valued possessions of the inferior man, for it enables him to conserve energy and thus evade the illusions of time, distance, and quality that he himself has established. Discrimination reveals to man that he has what he saves and loses what he wastes in the realm of the physical. By concentrating the energy upon that which is primary, and hence superior, discrimination results in the proper conservation of life. The length of life is not to be estimated by the number of years that we plow blindly through the mire of matter. Not time but accomplishment is the true measure of existence. The attainment of true wisdom in all its phases—spiritual, aesthetic, and ethical—is the supreme accomplishment. By directionalizing all the energies upon these more important matters, discrimination liberates the mind from the hopeless drudgery of the mediocre.

There are three forms of discrimination. The first has for its goal the discovery of that part of visible and sensible things which is primary. It is limited to the form sphere and deals with the problems of multitude and magnitude. For example, in the human body this form of discrimination determines the heart to be the chief part of the body. The second form of discrimination is that concerned with the relative integrity or excellence of innate characteristics. It is limited to the comparison of mental and moral excellences. This type of discrimination would elevate the idealist above the realist, the generous above the penurious, the unselfish above the selfish, the beautiful above the so-called practical; for it conceives the greatest good to occupy always the highest place. The third and highest form of discrimination is the power to differentiate between permanence and impermanence, Reality and unreality. It is limited to an estimation of the degrees of spiritual permanence. Through this type of discrimination is established the philosophic fact that the spiritual, or invisible man is the real man. Only the one in whom the faculty of discrimination is highly evolved is brave enough to elevate to the position of first importance and greatest solidarity that which to most men is an intangible mystery.

Discrimination is essential to success in every department of life—spiritual, mental, and physical. Men and women in the physical world must choose means and methods of solving the problems of livelihood, and through the use of right discrimination the material activities can be chosen so as to produce definite benefit in the superphysical nature. Discrimination differentiates between people and what they do; between the thinker and his thought; between the spirit and its body; between the innate Divinity within and the objective materiality without. Discrimination gradually elevates the consciousness of the individual until it is prone to seek out the good as that which is most worth-while. The height of discrimination is the recognition of the best. Evil is recognized as the least degree of good; matter, the least degree of spirit; the notself (which is the personality), the least degree of the real Self (which is the principle).

Discrimination has for its arch-enemy human selfishness. Because of its innate dishonesty, humanity deprives itself of the right to know good and evil. Justice is symbolized as blindfolded so that its personal attitudes may not influence its decisions. If discrimination is to be of value, it must also be applied with a strictly impersonal attitude; for the instant the mind is personally involved in its problem, the sense of true perspective and relationship is lost. Most people sit in one end of the scales when they weigh a problem. We are prone to live not according to our knowledge of right and wrong but according to our prejudices and whims. Things have an unpleasant way of looking not as they actually are but as we want them to, all because we cannot divorce the personal equation from our problem. Thus we make the decision fit our own desire and try to resolve the universe into a facsimile of our own notions. Many people who would scorn to be dishonest in the physical sense are dishonest mentally. The one who possesses true discrimination realizes only too well that he can never be just while he is personally involved in the question on which he must pass judgment.

A slight digression may not be out of order for the purpose of considering two terms which modern psychology has popularized: namely, the *inferiority* and *superiority* complexes. In reality, these two types are each twofold in character. The inferiority-inferiority complex is that mental attitude which causes the individual to picture himself as a groveling, squirming worm of the dust, predestined to be blind, to live in darkness, and eternally to be trodden under foot. This attitude paralyzes initiative and is a never-ending blasphemy against the Divinity innate in every creature.

The inferiority-superiority complex is the index of the hopeless egotist. Its victims have full confidence in their own integrity and excellence and in every act evince the realization of their self-importance. They make themselves heartily obnoxious, however, by assuming airs of modesty and inferiority in order to adduce evidence that they are not what they know they are. They have heard that great people are invariably distinguished by their modesty,—hence their assumption of the virtue!

The superiority-superiority complex manifests itself as boundless self-assurance. Such an individual, like the character of the story book, "can achieve the impossible, do the un-do-able, and unscrew the inscrutable!" The pages of history teem with the exploits of these colossal egotists who, however, backed their egotism up with achievement. Such achievements, though, are almost invariably of a temporal nature. Several philosophers also exhibited this moral obliquity, but are remembered chiefly for more worthy accomplishments.

The superiority-inferiority complex is usually borne by an individual who is an inveterate but unconscious liar. Such a person gives an external exhibition of consummate nerve while internally recognizing himself unable to cope with the situation. In other words, he is the high-pressure bluffer, the "personality plus" product of modern pseudo-psychology. If it were possible for such a person to be honest with himself but for a single instant, his courage would ooze out like a cold sweat and leave him a moral bankrupt.

Discrimination is not only the ability to choose wisely from the mass of mental and physical phenomena around us, but is also the ability to analyze the elements of our own thinking, feeling, and acting for the purpose of unfolding that which is good and eliminating that which is unnecessary. A very good way to approach this particular problem is to make an inventory of our assets and liabilities—mental, emotional, and physical. While so engaged we might choose as our motto: What is man that the Lord should be mindful of him? What do we know that our opinions should be of vast pith and moment? By what right do we sit in judgment upon the world and its Maker? During such self-examination we are lost without honesty or, more correctly, integrity. It is well that we differentiate between honesty and integrity. Honesty gives sixteen ounces to the pound because of law, while integrity gives sixteen ounces to the pound because sixteen ounces make a pound.

Having decided to judge yourself with absolute integrity, make a list of the virtues you possess, together with the degree of their opposites which manifest in your nature. If you are kind, to what degree are you unkind? If you are generous, to what degree are you penurious? If you are just, to what degree are you unjust? Perfections are determined by the degree of imperfections. Thus truthfulness is determined by the degree of untruthfulness. This is doubtless the reason one is so prone to see faults in others, for faults are the basis upon which the degree of faultlessness is to be estimated. Possibly for the same reason few people are congratulated for their virtues with either the fervor or the frequency that they are criticized for their vices. Having arrived at a reasonable estimate of the proportions of ignorance intervening between your present state and the desired state, next list the arts, sciences, and crafts with whose principles you have some degree of familiarity. Then ask yourself what is the percentage of your understanding of them as compared to that which is knowable concerning them. Discrimination will assist you to judge accurately the relation occupied by what you know to that which can be known. It logically follows also that your capacity to understand is measured by that which you understand, and by the understanding with which you understand you are most likely to be understood.

Since it reveals man's incompleteness, discrimination is therefore a continual urge toward completion. Man is not perfect until he knows all and is united in consciousness with all. Until this state is reached there can be no cessation of activity without disaster. We all have mental faculties that are weak; sense perceptions uncertain in the quality of their acuteness. Discrimination assists us to develop rationality by balancing the faculties until all the parts involved in the process of knowing are equilibrated. The result is a balanced and rational attitude toward the various conditions of life. Discrimination inspires tolerance in that it reveals the relationship which man as a spiritual condition bears to the body which he occupies. Discrimination proves that while the spirit is willing, the flesh is weak. Criticism should therefore be directed against these inconsistencies existing in the relationship of the parts. In this way the sting of personality is removed.

The spirit of man is ever composing beautiful melodies, but by the time they reach physical expression they are mostly reduced to discords. Such was the dilemma of the young man learning to play the cornet, who, turning to his teacher, exclaimed: "Why is it that when I blow the music in it is so sweet, but when it comes out it is so sour?" Discrimination helps man to recognize the melodies of the spirit and ignore the inharmonies of the flesh. Hence, discrimination is a forgiving faculty, not in the general acceptation of the word but in the sense of understanding; for the moment we fully understand people we have forgiven them.

Spirit is intrinsically beautiful, and those who raise their consciousness to the recognition of universal life dwell in the sense of beauty. Discrimination reveals the beautiful in that it chooses to gaze upon the face of Reality and to ignore the seething ocean of illusion. The realization of Self is synonymous with the recognition of Divinity, and he who beholds with his inner perception the radiant face of the One has reached the vanishing point of enmity and animosity. Discrimination also dispels the illusion of relationships. Relationship is a man made concept of proximities; it is an effort to give expression to the interval—mental or physical—by which things are separated, for relationship is not estimated by the proximity of one part to another but rather by the distance one part is away from another. Through believing that by the concept of relationship he unites life, man's efforts in this respect all too often contain only the sense of increasing separateness; for when we take that which is already synonymous with ourselves and relate it to ourselves we are really dividing it from ourselves.

Discrimination finally reveals to us that relationships are illusions of the mortal mind and that since all things are one in essence they are consequently indivisible and incapable of existing in any relationship of proximity one to the other. Even the ideal of friendship, though the loftiest of man's illusional attitudes, is thus revealed as insufficient. But even as wisdom is merely the vanishing point of ignorance, so illusion exists in a state of orderly concatenation, with friendship as the last, and consequently the least degree of the illusion of relationship.

Having through discrimination attained to a state of right-mindfulness, it is necessary to maintain such state and project it to perfection through the aid of concentration. Having discovered the purpose of life through observation and discrimination, man consummates that purpose through concentration of his faculties upon that single end. To concentrate means simply to focalize all the energies upon an appointed task. The mental activities of most people are scattered like spray when they are confronted by the solid wall of that which is to be known. Individuals read books while their minds are concerned with other interests. When the intellect is laden with responsibilities which it cannot cast off, it ceases to function with the acuteness necessary for philosophic perception. The true thinker realizes that his mind is capable of fatigue, and while this fatigue may not be apparent in the grosser activities it precludes the possibility of exactness in fine thinking. The normal mind works on the union basis of an eight-hour day with time and a half off for over-time. *For every period of intense effort the mind must be compensated by a similar period of relaxation.* The immature intellect of the average person must work slowly and orderly if it is to accomplish, for only a genius such as Julius Cæsar can do a dozen things at once with any degree of success.

It may truthfully be said that half an hour of profound mental activity is a day's work for the mind and he who accomplishes this is entitled to be termed industrious in things of the intellect. We presume ourselves to be mentally active during the entire period of wakefulness, but in reality we wander in a sort of mental delirium in which the elements of conception and reflection tumble over each other in hopeless disorder. Only when confronted by some actual crisis does the mind rise to organized activity, and after the crisis is past the resultant mental exhaustion is far greater than the average person realizes. About fifteen minutes of unremitting mental concentration will exhaust the ordinary man. Only by special training can the intellectual faculties be elevated to the stage of prolonged, orderly functioning. As exercise scientifically chosen will strengthen an otherwise deficient physical member, so definite and proper mental exercise will increase mental capacity. In the field of mental culture the Greeks enjoyed a supremacy never approached by any other race. They built gymnasiums not only for the culture of the body but also for the mind, the result being their overwhelming superiority in the realm of creative thought.

In its philosophic aspect concentration implies that all the life activities are centered upon the noblest goal and held in this state of fixation until the goal is achieved. Consecration of life to definite purpose is indispensable to accomplishment. Philosophy assures its disciples that when man, through discrimination, has discovered the desired end and is willing to sacrifice every other interest to the attainment of that end, he will ultimately arrive at indissoluble union with the object of his desire. This is, of course, a superphysical truth. If a man devotes a lifetime of effort to amassing a million dollars, he will not ultimately take upon himself the actual appearance of money. He will, however, gradually deteriorate until his life is susceptible of complete expression in terms of money. Through concentration the life energies are co-ordinated upon the path of achievement, and success is in direct proportion to the power or degree of concentration. As the sun's rays concentrated by a burning glass are able to generate a high degree of heat, so man's mental and physical energies when properly focussed give expression to potencies never dreamed of.

In order to find the solitude considered essential to concentration, the hermits of old retired from the world of men and immured themselves in the depth of the forest or in caves high upon the mountain side. Surrounded by the tranquillity of Nature they dreamed their lives away, finding in their solitary retirement a certain measure of peace. Of course, such an environment made the act of concentration comparatively easy, but for the same reason also made its efficacy less potent. By thus isolating himself from the social body—though never able to sever the physical bonds which still related him to it— the ascetic sought to approach Divinity by retiring from a world which he mistakenly assumed to be the antipode of Deity.

He overlooked the obvious fact that he who finds not God among men will find him nowhere else.

Rabindranath Tagore once expressed his aversion for the life of the ascetic by declaring that without love and companionship the path of perfection was not worth walking at all. Concentration is not necessarily promoted by isolation; in fact, the acid test of concentration is to be found in the environment of confusion. If the mind can be deflected from its goal by the phantasm of surroundings, it is incapable of concentration; for when concentration is perfected all the faculties are united in the performance of a definite task and no sense perceptions are left unoccupied with which to register external impressions.

While concentration seems a herculean effort to the mind that has not learned to co-ordinate its own parts, it is accomplished without effort by the trained thinker; in fact, many possess the faculty without the slightest knowledge of its existence. The musician lost in some rhapsody, the artist spellbound before his unfolding creation, the philosopher oblivious to the world as he ponders the immensity of space, the tragedian buried in his part, the financier frenziedly watching the blackboard of the stock exchange—all these not only exemplify the power of concentration but also its application to various ends, worthy or unworthy, according to the clarity of discrimination present.

Regardless, however, of the factor of worthiness, wherever we find true concentration we find excellence. The faculty of concentration also manifests through continuity, the least developed faculty of the American people. Continuity means the sequential unfoldment of a project from germinal beginning to final consummation, or the resolution not to relinquish the task until it is completed. This faculty is frequently lacking in children and seriously interferes with their efficiency in later life. When work seems arduous we quickly tire of it; or because we are not sure whether we really want the thing for which we strive we soon doubt our desire to gain it. When we are certain of our own minds, and carry labor to its legitimate end, our undertaking will be crowned with success.

THE DISCIPLINES OF SALVATION 141

We are then confronted with the problem of whether the finished product is an aid or a hindrance to us in our quest for Reality. We should never concentrate upon any desired end until discrimination has revealed it to be the supreme ideal; for the universe avenges itself for the misuse of its agencies by forcing us to abide by our own decisions. The ultimate ideal of concentration is attained when all the external parts are turned inward toward the contemplation of Self. When all the forces of the outer nature are thus united, then is generated the strength with which to achieve perfection.

The diagram at the beginning of this chapter sets forth in the figurative terms of Platonism the relationship of the elements under discussion The threefold Divinity—the One, the Beautiful, and the Good—manifests out of itself an inconceivable number of secondary triads. The secondary triad pertaining to absolute knowledge is composed of the rational principles now incorporated in the all-too-inadequate vehicles of philosophy, religion, and science. Thus it is demonstrated that philosophy partakes of the indivisible nature of the One and hence serves as the reconciling, unifying agent, being symbolic of the point of absolute intellectual convergence.

Theology likewise reflects to an imperfect degree the nature of the Beautiful, a postulate substantiated by the emphasis placed upon the fine arts by nearly all religious systems. Science, in turn, imperfectly manifests the nature of the Good, and those who minister at its altars lay special stress upon utilitarianism. Descending to the level of method we find a new triad established: namely, discrimination, concentration, and observation. Discrimination may be conceived to be the goal of philosophy, concentration the goal of theology, and observation the goal of science. On the mental plane these three may also be considered as indispensable factors in the acquisition of knowledge. Observation is the sharpest tool of science; concentration is essential to the esoteric doctrines of theology; discrimination is the secret of philosophic insight. In the world of physical arts and sciences, the One becomes mathematics, the first and most exact of all the sciences, which partakes of the powers of the One through the succession of philosophy and discrimination. The Beautiful becomes music, which partakes of the primal Beauty through the succession of theology and concentration. The Good becomes astronomy, which partakes of the original Good through the succession of science and observation. Thus is demonstrated the soundness of the ancient Pythagorean doctrine that the establishment and relationship of triads is the true basis of philosophic procedure.

If the diagram be considered from the standpoint of the Socratic school, we have an invaluable key to the unfoldment of the inner nature. Socrates affirmed the possibility of stimulating the superphysical nature by familiarizing the objective nature with those tangible arts and sciences that had their correspondences in the superphysical. For example, the study of astronomy increased the power of observation. Through its development observation in turn produced the scientist, and the scientist plying his scientific pursuits ultimately achieved to a knowledge of the Good. Thus unfoldment of the inferior stimulated unfoldment of its analogy in the superior, and step by step in such indirect fashion the highest was ultimately attained.

A question frequently asked by metaphysical students is how it is possible to stimulate the spiritual nature, and herein will be found the answer. Each part of the objective nature manifests some potentiality of the subjective life principle. The refinement and perfection of any part of the objective nature is a direct stimulus to its correspondence in the causal nature from which it was originally objectified. Thus the physical activity of thinking, when properly directionalized, develops the entire mental nature or body. Similarly, the proper directionalization of physical emotion results in the unfoldment of the emotional body which, being invisible and intangible, can only be contacted through its pole in the outer nature. Eventually man will be able to definitely relate all his physical parts and members with their incorporeal causal agencies. He can then at will stimulate his superphysical organisms through right directionalization of their corresponding physical organisms.

The purpose of this chapter is to give a brief outline of what constitutes a rational beginning of the philosophic life. He who would achieve to the highest must realize that without the systematic culture of the entire organism, even a relative degree of perfection is unattainable. The general metaphysical practice of platitudes, affirmations, and denials is unsound in theory and barren of results; for the organization of the life is only possible through certain definite, exact, and unchanging disciplines that have been preserved to the present generation as the priceless heritage of antiquity.

Many people possess to varying degrees so-called psychic powers. Such powers may be considered as natural to them; in other words, they have not been acquired by any definite effort. But regardless of how remarkable these natural endowments may seem to both their possessor and the world at large, they are a liability rather than an asset unless they are reduced to order through philosophic discipline. Nearly all so-called natural mystics have missed the goal for which they strove because they were satisfied to accept intangibles and indefinite attitudes as the lodestar of life. With few exceptions such natural psychics conceive themselves to be very highly evolved souls, unmindful of the fact that the lowliest canine possesses psychic powers far exceeding their own; but incapable of rationally directing its powers the animal must live and move and have its being in bondage to man. The psychic who has not through rational discipline become master of these psychic endowments is in no way superior spiritually to the brute, and will ultimately suffer some brutish end for his irrationality. The fond illusion that perfection comes "naturally" to such people must go if true consciousness is to be attained.

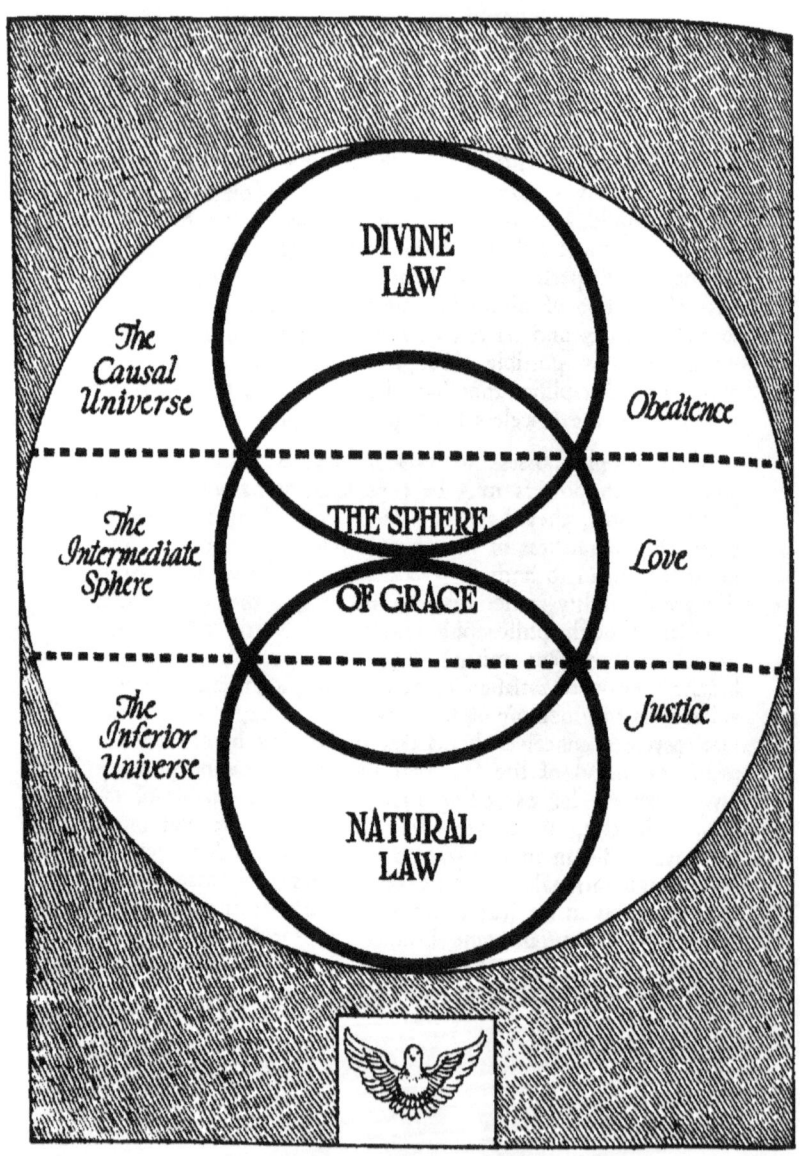

THE SPHERE OF GRACE

Herein is revealed the mystery of the Universal Soul and the redemption of man through the doctrine of grace. When atonement is understood in its Platonic interpretation as an at-one-ment, or reconciliation of the not-self and the Self through the disciplines of philosophy, we come to sense the magnitude of spiritual redemption.

CHAPTER SEVEN

The Doctrine of Redemption Through Grace

THE Christian theory of redemption is unique in that it emphasizes salvation as attainable in spite of vice rather than because of virtue; in fact, the prime saving virtue for the Christian is acceptance of the divinity of Jesus Christ. That a viewpoint so philosophically unsound could have gained so firm a foothold in the number and power of its adherents is more than passing strange.

The early Christian theologians condemned nearly every normal attitude of mankind, advocating extreme practices and austerities that have produced a full measure of religious neurotics and worse. Regarded as sanctified souls, these abnormals engrafted upon the main body of their faith attitudes and disciplines which, being the products of irrationality, only added to the general confusion. It is philosophically inconceivable, for example, that Deity should advocate flagellation as a means by which the flesh could be mortified into a state of piety. Nor has any utilitarian value, divine or human, yet been demonstrated to result from sitting like St. Simeon Stylites for thirty years upon the top of a pillar sixty feet in the air. It is a theory, ingenious but unconvincing, that to be born was a disaster because of the indiscretions of our first parents; that to live was a crime to be expiated only by living miserably; and that to die was simply a transition by which the members of the church militant were reborn into the choirs of the church triumphant.

For the individual living in the cosmopolitan religious atmosphere of North America it is difficult to realize the influence wielded by theology over the devout in those countries where religion still dominates almost every phase of individual and community life. Out of such a theological autocracy have risen organizations differing widely in attitudes and standards. On the one hand we find the Misericordia, whose hooded members—often men of distinction and culture—unhesitatingly served the needy of every class in the hour of plague or disaster. On the other hand we find the Ignorantine Friars—men of sincere motive but benighted vision—who boast of their illiteracy and consider a knowledge of even the fundamental principles of life as detrimental to the plan of salvation. While not actually requiring austerity of some kind, several great world religions openly encourage the practice among the members of their various orders. Even today most people view with a marked reverence one who has made of his physical body a broken and emaciated sacrifice in the effort to atone for his participation in humanity's heritage of sin.

The God of joy is dead, and in his stead rules the God of tears. Man, unillumined, cannot achieve tranquillity. He struggles impotently against a universe which, to his myopic vision, seems bent on his annihilation but which is really molding him into a future god. In his ignorance of the plan the suffering human creature conceives all being to be ruled by the scepter of sorrow.

In that supreme dramatic achievement, *Lazarus Laughed*, Eugene O'Neil enunciates the gospel of joy, a gospel which must some day supplant grief-stricken theology and lead man from the worship of death to the worship of life. Lazarus is made to say: "Man's loneliness is but his fear of life! Lonely no more! Millions of laughing stars there are around me! And laughing dust, born once of woman on this earth, now freed to dance! New stars are born of dust eternally! The old, grown mellow with God, burst into flaming seed! The fields of infinite space are sown—and grass for sheep springs up on the hills of earth! But there is no death, nor fear, nor loneliness! There is only God's Eternal Laughter! His Laughter flows into the lonely heart!"

Springing up during the decline of classical pagandom, Christianity felt itself divinely called to save the world from the insufficiency of previous doctrines. Witnessing with holy horror what it termed the perversions of the barbarians, the church finally arrogated to itself the office of sole mediator between the spirit of righteousness on the one hand and a wayward world on the other. Arbitrarily seating itself in the chief place, with one imperious gesture it dissolved the body religious, consigning all previous knowledge and beliefs of man into the limbo of decadent cults. Discovering that, like man, no faith can live by itself alone, Christianity was later forced to borrow from the pagans the very fundamental principles upon which its own philosophy is erected. It accordingly accepted the concept of heaven and hell as disseminated by the Egyptians and Greeks, but changed the personnel of the doorkeepers. The angelic hierarchies with which the Jews populated the celestial spheres were appropriated *en masse* and thereupon ceased their Hebrew chants to sing hymns in ecclesiastical Latin. With one fell swoop Christendom thus became master of all the spheres which the enraptured vision of pagan cosmologists had perceived. The church not only sought to stamp out heathenism from the earth but, invading even the uttermost parts of the invisible universe, drove the illustrious souls of pagandom from their own heavens and hells to make room for the proselytes of Christianity.

In its religious philosophy Christianity was thus truly eclectic, placing its mark of approval on isolated fragments of thought in such a haphazard manner that it is now impossible to find any thread of consistency which will bind the whole together. Hence, its articles of faith must be considered individually except in the few isolated cases where a common denominator is present. According to the churchmen, this weight of disagreement is not to be regarded as detracting from the sanctity or validity of the articles, since each is the direct revelation of a Deity who revealed what he wanted to when it pleased him, and whose reasons therefor transcended human estimation. Whatever profundity is found in Christian philosophy is due primarily to this infusion of pagan ideas. Conversely, the shallowness of Christianity is the direct result of the clumsy efforts made to improve upon the ancient doctrines.

The integrity of the individual was the keystone of pagan idealistic philosophy. The unfoldment of the triune nature of man—spiritual, mental, and physical—was based upon the foundation of personal integrity. Even the most bigoted church historian must admit that the magnificent edifices of pagan learning were raised upon the solid rock of personal virtue. Their philosophy emphasized to both the Egyptians and the Greeks the indispensability of right-thinking and right-living as prerequisites of right-being. Though the standards of ancient integrity may appear curious and obscure to this generation, they unquestionably produced an ethical type surpassing in many ways the products of what we conceive to be our more enlightened code. While the pagans are now regarded as a superstition-ridden people because of their offerings to their Lares and Penates, it remained for Christianity to present the human race with the most indefensible and at the same time the most vicious of all superstitions, namely, the doctrine of *vicarious atonement*—the redemption of a sinful world by the supreme sacrifice of one just man. While the myth of the dying god is to be found in many religious systems, Christianity was the first and only cult to construe the mythical incident as a literal atonement. Christ becomes, so to speak, a scapegoat, the sacrifice offered up that the people might go free.

According to the church, the Passion abolished the old order of approach to Divinity and supplanted it with a brand-new *modus operandi* of salvation. Heaven, earth, and hell were all dislodged from their time-honored foundation lines, and the sins of all creation were wiped out by the blood of the Lamb. Even the impassive sternness of Deity relaxed at the spectacle of this sublime and supreme ordeal. The incident of the crucifixion monopolized the stage in the drama of Christianity, for it speedily overshadowed any and all other dogmas to such a degree that mere admission of the universal import of Christ's incarnation and death became the sole prerequisite of spiritual redemption.

Thus a new standard of integrity was created which, however, still conveyed to the enlightened few its cryptic message of mystical ideality, but which could not fail to be interpreted by the unenlightened masses as evidence of the supremacy of words over works, of affirmation over action. Whereas the criers of the pagan Mysteries, according to Celsus, declared the superior worlds to be attainable only by men and women of outstanding intellect and lives consecrated to individual regeneration, the criers of the Christian Mysteries offered heaven with its eternal bliss to anyone who would confess his sins and affirm the divinity of Jesus Christ.

Twenty centuries of application have demonstrated the danger of the doctrine of vicarious atonement. Undermining the morale of Christendom, this concept has resulted in a philosophy of special privileges and exceptions which has infected church and state alike. This doctrine has caused the history of Christendom to be written in letters of blood. Nearly all who have enjoyed its privileges have donned the garments of sorrow, and kneeling in sackcloth and ashes cried for liberation from the bondage of its dogma. An emperor of China once said: "Wherever Christians go they whiten the soil with human bones; and I will not have Christianity in my empire."

How can anyone who has sensed the dignity of the Universal Plan reconcile the eternal justice of divine procedure with the right of excommunication in which the body religious ejects into outer darkness some offending hand or foot, enjoining such a soul forever from further participation in the goodness of God? How insignificant must be the power of that heaven or that hell which mortal man so easily manipulates at will! Where in the realm of all that is noble and just is there place for the concept that the souls of millions of babes are doomed to wander in the black vistas of the lost because they died in infancy without baptism? A faith cruel enough to espouse such doctrines inevitably inspires cruelty in its followers; for if it will damn its own with such unfeeling malignancy, how can it be expected to show mercy to the stranger without the gate?

The survival of the church, therefore, is contingent upon its own realization of how it has misinterpreted both the real mission of its founder and the symbolism of the pagan cults from which it derived the subject matter of its creed. Christianity will never be a great religion until its adherents recognize that it is merely a new body serving as the vehicle of an old idea; that when it departs from the original concepts to wander in the maze of theological absurdities, it defeats the primary purpose for which it was conceived. These unnatural attitudes of theologians toward life have resulted in the establishment of an unnatural faith wherein the lofty principles of the ancient philosophers have been distorted out of all semblance to their true import.

Christianity as the only true religion is worthless. If the faith, however, be regarded as a definite step in religious evolution, it is then possible to estimate its importance with a reasonable degree of accuracy. Christianity is not the sole revelation of God to man. It is but a fractional part of the body religious. It is simply a crutch upon which the *genus homo* leans until he learns to stand and walk alone. It is something he believes in before he is capable of believing in himself with understanding. Like all external things it will finally pass away and be remembered only for that which it contributed to the inner realization of its devotees.

The three major doctrines concerning the plan of redemption are: (1) redemption through mass effort; (2) redemption through individual effort; and (3) redemption through the vicarious atonement. The Jews, as a "chosen" people, are an example of the first concept; Platonic philosophy, with its repeated emphasis upon individual achievement, is an example of the second; and Christianity, with its World Martyr, is the outstanding example of the third.

Throughout the entire structure of Western thought there is a definite emphasis upon the factor of individuality. In the Orient, however, perfection is considered possible only through the annihilation of individuality. Without much careful examination of their underlying principles, these divergent systems of philosophy are apparently irreconcilable.

To the trained thinker the attainment of perfection as the result of individual effort is by far the most rational viewpoint toward the problem of redemption; for it is natural to presume that in an orderly universe each element must diligently work out its own salvation. In things spiritual, humanity in general realizes all too well the insufficiency of its own knowledge, and only because of its fatuous belief that it can reap where it has not sown is the situation rendered bearable.

The doctrine of the vicarious atonement opens the gates of heaven to millions who in their own right are not entitled to admission. It is surprising the tenacity with which this idea retains its hold upon the public mind, even after modern educational facilities have dissipated the theory of a personal God. The palpable inadequacy of the literal interpretation of the vicarious atonement is almost conclusive proof that it has a more subtle significance only to be discovered by the most searching analysis of the philosophic elements involved.

The doctrine of the vicarious atonement is based upon the debatable question of the precedence of love over law. It is written, "For God so *loved* the world that he gave his only begotten Son, that whosoever believeth in him should not perish, but have everlasting life." (John iii:16). If the postulate of a personal Deity is accepted, then it is not unreasonable that a just Creator should send his representative into the world to make known his will to man. It is not philosophically sound, however, that God should love the world more because that selfsame world had crucified his only begotten! In the early writings of the Church Fathers it is declared that Christ, by virtue of having died for mankind, appeared before the throne of his Father to intercede for the world for which he had sacrificed his life. Like his prototypes Bacchus and Dionysus, Christ was a personification of Divine Love—the inexplicable emotion. Since the dawning of his rational faculties, man has striven to understand the position occupied by spiritualized emotion in the Universal Plan. He is able to classify the entire procedure of life and postulate the laws by which the universe is governed, but the riddle of love has proved more elusive than even the riddle of life itself.

Since man invests Deity with feelings akin to his own, so God was considered to be not only the Lord of judgment and order, but also the Lord of love. Since man loved those who were close to him in the world, so he visualized the Deity as likewise bestowing his affections upon those "chosen" peoples who obeyed his laws and made proper sacrifice. As the outgrowth of this man-made concept, the God of antiquity was ever swayed by caprice. At one time he would exalt his people and prosper their efforts; at another time he would scourge them with his wrath and wreak his vengeance upon them. Like Zeus on Olympus, the Creator was subject to inconstant moods, at one moment minded to scatter with his divine lightnings all his fashionings and the next to elevate them to a parity with himself.

Since God had created man, it was assumed by theologians that he must also to some degree remember and love these imperfect products of his handiwork. Hence, to redeem an inconstant creation from its own inconstancy, the Word took upon itself flesh, and being fashioned in the image of man dwelt among men, preaching the law and giving those who accepted the law an opportunity to survive the Armageddon which would sweep away the unbelieving. After that event the earth, it was presumed, would then become once more an Edenic garden where the elect would dwell in unbroken felicity throughout the uncounted eternities of futurity. The inner realization of the truth of this concept was redemption, and insured membership in the body of the redeemed.

To the scientist and the philosopher, however, it is evident that God is not a man nor in any way limited in his manifestation by the laws governing the inferior creation. In spite of all theological argument to the contrary, it is unthinkable that the Universal Spirit—whose dwelling is immeasurable space and in whose vast nature suns, moons, and stars are infinitesimal atoms—could have localized itself in a little Syrian town and been born in the image of a man. In our search for fundamental truths we must discard the notion that the various elements in this mysterious drama are personalities, and thus restore them to their true dignity as universal principles.

For many centuries it has been believed that to destroy the personality of God was to detract from his magnificence, when in reality to invest him with a personality is to degrade him to the estate of man. Impersonality is a divine attribute; it is a state inherent in the nature of God, and a condition to which man must attain in the quest of his own divinity. If the personality—yes, even the individuality—of God is discarded as an illusion of the human mind, Deity is thereby elevated to its true philosophic estate, namely, an all-pervading, universalized essence. It naturally follows that this essence is without either footstool or throne; it does not hover over either communities or individuals but is distributed without partiality throughout the entire substance of space.

But, the orthodox Christian will exclaim, how did the prophets and saviors of old have face-to-face interviews with such a Deity? The answer is simple: They didn't. Wherever such conversations are recorded they are symbolic references to the inner experiences of the spiritual life. They come under the same general heading of what psychologists now term the "mystical experience," and are concerned solely with extensions of consciousness and degrees of realization. The phenomena accompanying these experiences are simply allegorical descriptions of mystical conditions couched in language suitable for the moral instruction of those in whom this inner nature is still dormant.

The impersonalizing of all the host of spiritual agencies introduces an entirely new aspect into the problem of the vicarious atonement, for it is quite evident that the cause of humanity could not be pleaded before a tribunal composed merely of symbolic figures of universal agencies. Archangels could scarcely be present when archangels are emblems of spiritual forces. And that God should appear in wig and robe is as inconceivable as that the Holy Ghost is actually a dove. At first glance the whole idea may savor of sacrilege, but upon sober reflection the reader will realize that it is the first step toward the elevation of Deity to an estate worthy of the Universal Parent.

A consideration of the problem of the vicarious atonement, if confined purely to the present superficial and conventional lines of treatment, must inevitably subject the doctrine to honest doubt and ridicule. Hence, the student of theology must cast about for the fountainhead in which the doctrine had its real inception. Christianity borrowed so much from the Orphic philosophy that the student should not be criticized but rather commended if he turns in that direction. Nor will he be disappointed. The Neoplatonism of Alexandria also furnishes a clue, and Gnosticism (especially the Alexandrian branch) is permeated with valuable suggestions.

The diagram at the beginning of this chapter should be studied carefully in connection with this subject. The three intersecting globes—designated the *Causal Universe*, the *Intermediate Sphere*, and the *Inferior Universe*—are representative of the threefold universe. The Causal Universe is the universe of spirit and is ruled over by the law of the spirit, which is absolute and unchanging. The Intermediate Sphere—which signifies the World Soul—is governed by its own laws, which laws are inconceivable to mortal man but whose mysterious synchronizing urge man defines as *love*. The dark Inferior Universe below also has its own laws by which it was created, is maintained, and will ultimately be dissolved. These are called the natural laws of life, but have been elevated by theology to the dignity of divine laws. Consequently, when we speak of those natural laws which we regard as the manifestations of God, we refer to those causal agencies governing the Inferior Universe, which in their entirety are termed in ancient philosophy the will of the Demiurgus, or Lord of the World.

The keynote of the Inferior Universe is law. Those whose consciousness does not elevate them above its limitations have not learned as yet to temper justice with mercy; they still live in the concept of an eye for an eye and a tooth for a tooth, and boast of the inexorable quality of these universal laws.

The keynote of the Intermediate Sphere is love, which is also a law moving in perfect concord with the principles of the soul, its true vehicle. The apparent inconsistencies of physical affection are referable to two sources: (1) the principle of love is often confused with animal emotion, a physical propensity; (2) where love does manifest in its true nature, its manifestation—like all spiritual functions in man—is intermittent; for meeting with the obstacle of matter it is distorted and its consistency usually broken up.

The keynote of the Causal Universe is divine law as opposed to the natural law of the Inferior Universe. Divine law is not comparable with natural law in that it is the power directionalizing consciousness. It never manifests in the physical universe in a manner sufficiently detached to be susceptible of analysis. In the famous play by that name, "Mr. Wu," the Chinese mandarin, is made to say when describing the customs of his people: "The law by which we live is the law by which we die." Tersely stated, such are the laws or forces manipulating the Inferior Universe. In the Causal Universe, however, are found only the laws by which things endure, for there neither life nor death exists.

By some eminent authorities Christianity is maintained to be an Oriental cult in that it emphasizes the necessity of the contemplative life and regards the visible universe as an illusional sphere from which man cannot escape save through the spiritual nature of Jesus Christ. Christ here is regarded as the channel or mediatory power by means of which it is possible to emerge from the dark underworld and become one with the sphere of Reality. St. Paul lays special emphasis upon the *effectiveness of belief* and, conversely, the *ineffectiveness of accomplishment*. He says: "For by grace are ye saved through faith; and that not of yourselves: it is the gift of God: Not of works, lest any man should boast." (Eph. ii:8-9).

The "works" here mentioned signify outward activities, regardless of the degree of their constructiveness. According to this view it is—strictly speaking—useless to engage even in virtuous endeavor, for all endeavor (virtuous or otherwise) is simply an illusion. The outward nature of the individual is regarded as incapable of good in that it is a part of the world and stained with the sin common to mortality. All of the outer life with its endless diversity of interest must consequently be cast aside and sole emphasis be placed upon the spiritual nature, which alone is capable of approach to Reality. This viewpoint (in which the best life is a failure unless accompanied by an unquestioning faith in the infallibility of the church) was the natural outgrowth of, and became most powerful in, an age of physical insecurity where life and property were in constant jeopardy. Investment in things physical had slight appeal where an entire community might be swept away to gratify a besotted emperor's whim, or where tens of thousands might perish to furnish sport for a Roman holiday.

With the twentieth century, however, new attitudes and new scenes occupy the world stage. Chief emphasis is now placed upon physical existence. Every effort of inventive and legislative genius is concentrated upon the improvement and security of this existence in order that at least a relative degree of comfort (if not happiness) may be enjoyed by the masses. When defeat in war or the distemper of his superiors brought to man no alternative other than that of slavery, he had but one hope: namely, that he might speedily die. Where social inequity thus decreed unhesitating obedience to the dictates of tyrants, there inevitably resulted a philosophy which emphasized as the only conceivable freedom the state beyond the grave. But the modern man and woman do not regard this earth as such a forbidding place that immediate escape therefrom is a pleasing prospect. Science is ever devising conveniences which, while they may ultimately result in deterioration of our more rugged racial virtues, are fast becoming the common enjoyment of nearly every stratum of society. Man's chief struggle is now for leisure in which to improve himself, and in the mechanical trend of his civilization he visualizes a world which will some day be maintained by *automata* so that the present slaves of industry may have opportunity to acquire the cultural benefits of art, science, and philosophy.

In every walk of life the necessity for finer mental functioning is keenly recognized. The world of St. Paul has disappeared forever, and with the passing of the old regime has gone that concept of the world as merely a highly magnified Roman Empire, with the Demiurgus, or fabricator of it, as a dissipated Caesar served by a degenerate court. The spirit of democracy prevalent in the realm of government has even invaded the domain of spirit, and in a certain sense the Lord of the world is now elected by the popular vote of the citizenry. Little by little the universe has assumed so many of the features of democracy that it begins to display the inconsistencies of a democratic system. Not many centuries ago man bowed stolidly before the doctrine of the divine right of kings, and if deep in his heart he resented the intolerance of his rulers he dared not breathe that criticism. It has been but a similar short time since man first dared to speak the name of God; when those few who had the temerity to discuss matters of religion hid themselves in attic or cellar lest the world should learn of their *lese-majeste*.

Today, however, if we do not like our magistrates we summarily impeach them; if our kings annoy us we dethrone them, while to ridicule and caricature their slightest eccentricity is an open-field diversion. In his unfoldment of self-expression man finally grew bold enough to question the dictates of theology; nay even to debate publicly the infallibility of dogma and challenge the God of antiquity to destroy him with his ire. Today man no more hesitates to dispute so-called divine mandates than he does to find fault with the conclusions of petty politicians.

To deal with such a complete reversal of attitudes requires an entirely new interpretation of divine law. Man no longer kneels when he worships; he stands up and faces his Creator unafraid. While at first this may savor of rank heresy, it will yet prove to be the solid foundation of a newer and truer criterion of conduct. By almost imperceptible degrees the Creator has come to be regarded as synonymous with the agencies controlling creation. He no longer makes laws and later breaks them; he is now an integral part of the great scheme itself, bowing before the same immutable principles that sway the whole of Being. The philosophic code for this age will emphasize obedience to Nature's laws, for he who follows most closely Nature's example will become the most virtuous and estimable member of society.

Primitive man innately worshipped that of which he was most afraid. The Demiurgus, or Lord of the Inferior Universe, was an imminent autocrat by whose thunderbolts all the achievements of man were shattered. This wielder of destiny, who arbitrarily dictated the end of things and who even molded the act of Providence according to his fancy, was regarded as part God, part demon. He was a God of every imaginable wrath and horror, whose voice was heard in the thunderclap, whose throne was the tempest, and who rocked the earth with his displeasure. According to this view laws were but divine whims to be changed at divine pleasure, and as diversified as divine moods. None dared to question the right of Deity to elevate one man an debase another for the same deed. The universe was run at the pleasure of an erratic agent who moved individual and nations like pawns upon a chess-board, and when he tired of the game simply brushed them all away with a gesture of his hand. While entire races languished in the benighted state of savagery, this God concerned himself particularly (as Voltaire has noted) with the number of bells on the petticoats of his high priest! In terms of modern psychology, this Demiurgus functioned in the "detail" mind.

While the Demiurgus was an important figure in all ancient philosophy, it remained for Christianity to elevate him to chief position among the gods of the universe. To the Greeks he was known as Zeus, who, though father of the gods and lord of the world according to popular concept, was in the enlightened eyes of the sage a subordinate deity who might thunder at his pleasure without ruffling the disposition of the wise; for only such as accepted the reality of ignorance, fear, and death could be controlled by the Demiurgus. As philosophy annihilated these three superstitions and liberated man from bondage to his own terror, those who drank of its life-giving waters escaped from the sway of the Demiurgus and became citizens of a greater and nobler world.

It is not difficult to understand the misconception that elevated the Regent of the physical universe to chief place among the gods. We understand best that which is most like ourselves,

THE DOCTRINE OF REDEMPTION THROUGH GRACE 159

and the Demiurgus partakes so abundantly of human frailties that we can almost truthfully declare that we understand him. When he casts down a rebellious people who insist on making altars round in form when he desires them square, he is simply treating us to that arbitrary exhibition of power which most men would like to exhibit if they possessed it. This God is therefore very close to the human heart; as close in fact as human concepts of hate, revenge, and destructiveness.

The Divine Spirit, superior to all this petty bargaining for favors; in whose nature virtue is supreme, and who with infinite "mildness" and perfect compassion broods over the destiny of Cosmos, is so unlike benighted humanity that man cannot estimate its qualities other than by intellectual means. Hence, the first person of the ancient triad of gods was the recipient of little veneration. Ammon is said to have had but one temple in Egypt, whereas Ra and Osiris (the lesser members of the Creative Triad) had sanctuaries to the number of many thousands. In India the shrines of Vishnu and Shiva dot the landscape on every hand, but where are the temples of Brahma? Throughout Christendom where are the altars of God the Father? His Son has churches unnumbered and even the Virgin and the saints all have niches in conspicuous places, but God, the sole Creator, is apparently forgotten, or rather absorbed in the glory of his own emanations. God the Father will thus remain without place of worship until men become capable of comprehending the principle for which Divinity stands. When the spirit of God the Father takes up its abode in their lives, then will his symbols representative of understandable principles be present in the world. The new religion to come will worship God in his creative aspect as being superior to his preservative (the Christos) and his destructive (the Jehovistic) aspects.

When the true relationship existing between the various members of the Creative Family (the Trinity) has been established, the real significance of the doctrine of salvation through grace is at once apparent. Ancient philosophy concerned itself with this problem of the Demiurgus, and the method of evading the doom awaiting those caught in his net of illusion. Hence, philosophy was, primarily, a discipline evolved to elevate man above the Demiurgic level and enable him to dwell in the realm of spirit over which the Lord of Form was powerless. In other words, salvation was achieved by escaping from the material self; by liberating the eternal Knower from its noneternal sheath. Christendom believes that this escape was made possible through the incarnation, death, and resurrection of Jesus Christ, who by rolling away the stone from his sepulcher liberated all mankind from bondage to the concept that death was the finale to life. Only such as believe in death can actually die and they alone are actually in slavery to the world and its Regent. Thousands of years, however, before the birth of Jesus Christ, pagandom "liberated" man from servitude to his inferior self, creating by means of the Mysteries that "royal road" leading upward to permanence from impermanence. By an infinite grace the door between the dark world below and the bright spiritual sphere above was thus left ajar, and through this mystic portal passed the illumined of the ages.

When Jesus Christ as the personification of the qualities of the rational soul is made to say: "I am the way, the truth and the life: no man cometh unto the Father, but by me" (St. John xiv:6), it is abundantly evident that he spoke in a figurative sense and that the saving principle thus referred to is not to be understood as a personality. The "way" here signifies the spiral path of attainment established in the world coincident with creation itself. This way—which is in truth the plan of salvation itself—can scarcely be regarded as a man, even though a highly illumined one. Nor can "truth" be conceived of as an individual, for truth is the unchanging nature of things as they actually are—a concept transcending the comprehension of mortal creatures. Finally, the mystical "life" by which the regeneration of the individual is wrought is unrelatable to any personality, since it obviously exists as an all-pervading principle. In this enigmatic fashion is set forth the fact that Christ (the Christos) signifies the procedures and qualities of that cosmic rationality which, according to the Greeks, had its seat in the rational soul of all men but which manifested itself only in those who through the disciplines of philosophy had lifted their irrational selves to a state of participation in the effulgence of the rational soul. In the Greek *Cabala*, the numerical value of Christ (Christos) is 888 which means the higher mind, and which the Greeks conceived to be the spiritual Knower complemented by rationalized, or regenerated, intellect.

As rationality is at first latent in all irrational things, new light is thus thrown upon the statement, "Christ in you, the hope of glory." In other words, the rationality in you is the saving "grace." The word *grace* has two distinct shades of meaning. It may be considered as the mercy of God by which he chooses to pardon those parts of himself which momentarily displease him. In its æsthetic sense, however, grace becomes an actual attribute of the internal nature itself. Sometimes we use words better than we know. The ninth definition of *grace* in Webster's *New International Dictionary* reads:

> "Attractiveness; charm; esp., the æsthetic value shown in suppleness and ease, spontaneity, and tactful harmony; the charm of congruity, harmony, and pliancy in beauty as distinguished from sublimity or force; beauty as displayed in free flowing curves, easy and natural contours, fluent color, or felicitous and musical diction; as applied to persons, manners, etc., easy and natural elegance; in a weakened sense, propriety; seemliness; comeliness."

It is thus evident that the grace by which man is saved may be considered not only as an attribute of Deity but also as an attribute of man himself. From the latter point of view man works out his own salvation through aesthetics, in which his own innate grace actually becomes his redeeming virtue. If we correlate the triune nature of God to the One, the Beautiful, and the Good, the quality of grace in the light of the definition quoted at once becomes synonymous with the Beautiful. Thus, microcosmically, grace is the rhythm in the human soul, and macrocosmically, the universal harmony by which the divine beauty of the Plan is revealed as coessential with the divine order of the Plan. It will yet be philosophically established that the grace which man himself develops in his relationship to the manifold problems of life will be the grace by which his salvation is assured.

The popular concept that belief in the divinity of Christ is a prerequisite to virtuous living may be interpreted in a way which casts considerable light upon an otherwise obscure subject. In this case all depends upon the interpretation of the word *belief*. If belief is regarded as merely an intellectual acceptance of the truth of a statement, then the entire subject simply resolves itself into another theological absurdity. If, however, belief takes the form of an inner realization of the spiritual truths involved, then indeed it is a spiritual power. Belief in immortality must precede knowledge of immortality. That faith upon which man establishes his philosophy of life and which gives him the courage to sacrifice all in the quest of that which is the greatest good, is indeed a sustaining faith. For example, the neophyte entering the House of Wisdom assumes the disciplines of philosophy because he has faith in the efficacy of philosophy; he believes that the path he has chosen will ultimately lead him to where faith will be exchanged for understanding, and belief for knowledge. Belief, then, in the reality and faith in the attainability of achievement—these are indispensable to accomplishment. Faith in self and belief in the divinity of self—these must precede perfection. But faith without works is dead, and belief is valueless unless it inspires to the attainment of the thing believed in.

According to the vicarious atonement, one just man expiated the sins of an unjust world. In the Orphic philosophy a mysterious agency—which men indiscriminately call love, beauty, or harmony, but which the Greeks termed the *rational soul*—descended out of the perfection of Deity where it had existed in an undivided state and was scattered like seed throughout the substances of the inferior world. As the Demiurgus could control only matter, these seeds from a higher sphere were of too exalted a nature to be dominated by his

THE DOCTRINE OF REDEMPTION THROUGH GRACE 163

edict. These seeds remained apparently lifeless, however, through the dawn period of the world, the Demiurgus molding the substances of matter at his pleasure and ignoring the germs lying dormant therein. Worlds and men were thus gradually fabricated until the whole genera of life appeared, but still the seeds remained inactive. Man wandered hopelessly in the gloom of mortality, living and dying without light or understanding in his servitude to the Demiurgus and his host of spirits. At last the spirit of rebellion entered creation in the form of Lucifer, who in the guise of a serpent tempted man to revolt against the mandates of Jehovah (the Demiurgus). In Greece this character was known as Prometheus, who brought from the gods the impregnating flame that would release the life latent in this multitude of germlike potentialities. In Christianity, Christ (the Christos) is the divine fire which, striking the latent germs of immortality, liberates them from their ages of impotency.

As man emerged from barbarism and began to cultivate what may be called the intuitional, or soul qualities, an environment of beauty was thereby created wherein the germ of the rational soul could be stimulated and made to grow to the point where it would completely remold the life of man in terms of the beautiful and the true. In a purely technical sense there are three definite methods by which man may impregnate this germ of spirituality within himself. The first method is known as *works* and in antiquity was symbolized by the soldier who went forth to "fight the good fight." The age of chivalry was the natural product of the ideal that the greatest good could be accomplished by destroying the forces of evil and thus attempt to re-establish the golden age upon earth. The second method is *love,* under which heading is included the factors of faith, belief, and service. Through prayer and devotion to noble ideals a certain glorification is awakened in the life. Love is elevated and impersonalized until it becomes a great spiritual urge stimulating all that is true and noble within the soul. The third method is *philosophy.* The venerable sage, contemplating the wisdom of the ages, thus sought to elevate his rational nature until it could gaze unafraid upon the vastness of Being. The understanding thus created excites a noble intellectual passion which brings with it the stimulation of the soul qualities. In all three methods there is a crowning state—a condition of apotheosis or ecstasy in which for a moment man actually dwells upon the plane of his ideals. The knight in deadly combat rose to heights of heroism wherein he gladly gave his life for principle. Those in whom faith is the dominant factor are elevated to a condition of overwhelming proximity to Deity, as testified to by the enraptured visions of the mystic. To the philosopher there comes the gradual realization of cosmic immensities; and at length the sublime spectacle of it all picks him up and sweeps him into the philosopher's heaven —a state where all thought is clarfied and the rational faculties become momentarily able to cope with the riddle of existence.

Regardless of the means by which this clearer and larger vision is attained, its purpose is ever the same. The ecstatic state becomes like a bolt of fire which, striking the germ of rationality within the physical nature of man, causes them to burst open and release that universal redeeming and rationalizing power which was mixed with primordial matter before it was molded into worlds. Thus what Jacob Boehme calls "the tree of the soul" has its beginning. Its roots are in the dark earth of mortality, but gradually the tiny shoot—whose very nature is Divinity—grows upward to blossom forth into a beautiful and noble plant. When once this seed of Divinity has been quickened the power of the Demiurgus is broken. The Lord of the world may thunder his displeasure. Though he slay man a thousand times, yet shall that man live, for life has been awakened within him. Though all the furies of creation may attempt to destroy that tiny soul-plant, yet shall it prevail against them, for it is composed of the substances over which death and destruction are powerless. Through the disciplines of the Mysteries this redeeming plant—which the Christians have called *Christ*—is caused to increase in power and magnitude until in its perfected state it absorbs into itself all of the irrational nature upon whose substances it was formerly maintained.

When it is realized that antiquity postulated a period called the *golden age* during which the rational soul so controlled universal manifestation that all things lived together in a state of harmony, beauty, and goodness, all the elements necessary to complete the world drama of salvation are at hand. The rational soul is therefore the beloved of the Father, dwelling with God (the One) in a state of absolute felicity. Again, the spirit of beauty and truth is symbolized as the beloved son of the Universal Spirit through whose rhythmic principles the immeasurable dignity of the First Cause is most adequately manifested. Then came the symbolic "fall" of man foreshadowed in the incarnation, death, and resurrection of the spirit of universal harmonics. As Bacchus was torn to pieces by the Titans and his dismembered parts scattered throughout the universe, so the principle of redeeming beauty (or love) was disseminated as the aforementioned seeds throughout the irrational sphere. When man reawakens (resurrects) this spirit of universal love, it ascends into the presence of the Creator, there to intercede for that regenerated one.

The newly unfolded realization that beauty is the most powerful of all agencies is itself the redeeming grace, and the vicarious atonement merely signifies that there is a spirit of beauty resident in mortal man which can accomplish for mortal man what he cannot accomplish for himself. Two natures reside in every individual: one, as Goethe says, to the heavens aspires, the other in the earth suspires. The heaven-man (the Christos in us) is not born of woman but is conceived of the Holy Ghost. This spiritual agent becomes our redeemer when of our own free will we elect it to be the master and director of our activities. Thus the just man in us redeems his own sinful shadows. He descends into hell and forever abolishes the power of evil; he ascends into heaven and pleads our cause in the firmament. Through him we partake of Divinity even as through our outer natures we partake of humanity.

As man increases in rationality the spirit of the beautiful begins its ministry of transmuting the baser elements of the not-self. The uncouthness of the nature gradually disappears, and tinctured with the grace of the indwelling Divinity the outer nature is transformed. The rationality within permeates the entire structure causing it to sing with a new harmony and establishing a more perfect symmetry between its component parts. Thus mortal man who is nothing of himself, is brought into proximity with the sky-man, who is the spirit of life and truth. When the union of the two is effected and the animal nature—the relapsed heretic of the ages—is at last converted to the true faith, then the miracles so eloquently described in Scripture take place. Those who are mentally and spiritually crippled are healed; those who are blind to the greater realities of life are made to see; those driven frantic by the seven devils of worldly desires are freed from their bondage to the senses; and those tainted with the leprosy of ignorance are cleansed. Furthermore, those who hunger for the food that satisfies the inner self shall be fed by that inner knowledge which is the true bread of life.

When rationality—not in the sense of intellectuality but of true and beautiful *knowing* in the sense of identity with spirit—assumes the reins of human life, then that life becomes beautiful and happy in the fullest and truest sense. From this and other evidence it can be established with philosophic certainty that Christ is indeed the spirit of truth, which few recognize but which when recognized becomes the redeemer of the life. He who desires to recognize this truth must realize that it is the supreme goal of all endeavor. He who would succeed in his quest for it must first of all develop one peculiar faculty which we will term *appreciation*.

It has often been said that appreciation touches off endeavor, but here again is a word with two meanings. We ordinarily conceive appreciation to mean the esteem felt by others for ourselves, but what it actually means is the esteem we feel for others. The heart that is receptive to the beautiful in life will achieve unity with the object of its desire. Man possesses the power to appreciate and recognize the goodness and beauty of existence. This power which makes realization possible is itself the blood of the divine Bacchus—the god-soul—who through its blood in man shall redeem the world. There is in us a certain spiritual capacity: the power to be more than we are, the power to be more than simply a crawling worm bowing humbly before the despotic Regent of the world. This power to transcend our mortal selves is symbolized by the blood of the godman that, freed by the spear of necessity, pours down into the cup of matter, there to remain as the cleansing blood.

Age after age finds mankind soaring to nobler heights, and each passing generation shows some marked progress in the realization of new ideals. Let us then realize that this power to increase; this power to elevate us so high that even the stars cannot restrain us; this power to be magnified until the very universe becomes a confining wall; this power which enables us to face our Creator unafraid; this rational Knower who is limitless—this is the Universal Savior, the Christ, which in the magnificence of itself ultimately atones for all that has gone before and by right of its very existence makes man partaker of all good things to come. Man cannot be destroyed by his gods because his gods are within himself. By his incarnation, Christ (the rational soul) infuses into all creation a quality as immortal as the gods themselves. By right of this capacity for divinity within himself man may not be cast aside, but is entitled to infinite opportunity and divine protection. Thus is the symbolism preserved whereby a man through the Christ in him shall arrive at the condition of that glorified perfection which is now the object of his faith. Each of us is struggling to be free from the bondage of his mortal sepulcher. The skyman yearns for the stars, and if he be lifted up to his true estate of first place in the constitution of man will draw all the rest unto him that all good works may be brought to speedy consummation. The science of redemption may be said to embrace any and all means by which the dormant germ-like potentialities of Divinity resident within all human nature are first awakened and then stimulated to divine perfection through aspiration. In summing up it follows, therefore, that such diversified elements as beauty, belief, grace, faith, love, appreciation, labor, and thought—all being expressions of rationality—are indispensable to the perfection of the whole.

THE ORPHIC EGG

The Universal Germ, stirring within the Egg of Creation, established the worlds and generations by three "gestures." It fashioned the souls of things according to Virtue, the bodies of things according to Beauty, and the laws by which souls and bodies are maintained according to the Necessary. Together these comprise the Work which is called *The Good*.

CHAPTER EIGHT

The Mission of Aesthetics

AESTHETICS is that branch of philosophy concerned primarily with the intrinsic nature of beauty, its place in the Divine Plan, and the processes whereby beauty can be created or caused to manifest where previously it did not exist in a tangible state. That beauty produces a profound effect upon the entire nature of man is too well established to be questioned. Just what constitutes beauty, however, and why it wields so profound an influence is still a subject of controversy. Is environment the basis of an aesthetic standard; that is, does the familiar become the standard of aesthetic propriety? In a limited sense this must be true. On the other hand, man has been surrounded for ages with such familiar themes as war, disease, and decay; yet he has never come to regard these as beautiful, at least not in his lucid moments. Beauty, declared the ancients, results from the harmonious correlation of parts; the spectacle of the mutual agreement of all the elements involved in a common pattern creates a pleasant reaction in the sensory organism of man. That the urge toward what man terms the beautiful is universally present in Nature was also asserted. Certain natural processes were cited in support of this belief. For example, vines and creepers rapidly grow up to hide the gaunt outlines of a rotted tree, and flowers in profusion blanket the shell-torn fields of Flanders once made horrible by the unleashed fury of man.

Standards of beauty vary with the evolutionary status of races and individuals. The preference displayed by the nobility of Hawaii for stoutness of figure proved rather embarrassing to the court of Queen Victoria. The hennaed whiskers of the Rajput gentry, while very chic in Rajputana, are a striking incongruity to Western standards of aesthetics. The quaint African custom of distending the lips and ears by the insertion of loops of bone or pliable wood is productive of a type of beauty totally beyond our Occidental comprehension. Furthermore, though our poets wax eloquent over the graceful lines of a swan's neck, the Burmese belles (who achieve the literal effect by stretching their necks with iron rings) find our modern verse-mongers strangely unresponsive to their charms.

It is difficult—perhaps impossible—for the individual to view life with any aesthetic standard other than his own. If it were possible to analyze the sensory organism that can see symmetry in the bound and distorted foot of a Chinese lady, one great mystery of aesthetics would be well-nigh solved. The gradual evolution of man's concept of beauty seemingly depends upon both the power of observation and the sense of proportion. For example, the child recapitulates, in some measure at least, the racial evolution of which it is a product. Children, while fond of drawing, are generally incapable of recognizing perspective, and among primitive types nearly all art is two-dimensional. When a child designs a crude little house the size of a postage stamp and draws a man beside it several inches high, it senses no inconsistency in the possibility of the man to enter the house. In a similar way the little girl regards her doll as alive and intelligent, although well-aware that its head is made of porcelain and its body of sawdust. Great battles are fought with little tin soldiers on a nursery floor, and both the little chinchilla bear and wooden horse are endowed by their juvenile owner with all the qualities of their living prototypes. The sculptor of the Stone Age, probably likewise unaware of the crudity in his technique, evidently viewed his art as a striking reproduction of the person or principle he sought to portray. When the mediaeval artist drew upon canvas faces which were as expressionless as eggs he endowed them, so he believed, with all the beauty and vividness of his model. The evolving standards of symmetry, however, have outgrown his ideal, making the products of his brush now valuable for their oddity rather than their merit. Thus, while we are able to estimate the inconsistencies of the past when contrasted with the apparent consistencies of the present, we are wholly unable to realize how inconsistent the present will appear in the light of future standards. Some may still recall the time when Dame Fashion decreed bustles and leg-of-mutton sleeves for milady, and when gentlemen had the creases pressed out of their trousers lest they be suspected of buying ready-made clothes. While all admit the revolutionary changes of fashion, the mental process that justifies these changes and ridicules that which it previously justified is more difficult of analysis.

The average individual believes that beauty in style is established by the caprice of the modiste and fashionable tailor, who find it lucrative to cater to the love of novelty innate in human nature. While this may be the superficial explanation for these cycles of change, the definite trend of the centuries is produced by certain psychological tendencies. In discussing such problems of aesthetics as simplicity and complexity, a modern writer has arrived at some remarkable deductions. Simplicity has long been accepted as the chief prerequisite of beauty. This is definitely opposed to the barbaric tendency toward adornment. It is reasonably certain, for instance, that clothing (except in the most frigid zones) is the outgrowth of the desire for ornamentation rather than the dictate of utility. The theory is also now advanced that complexity is used to conceal weakness, and simplicity to reveal strength.

The evolutionary trend of aesthetics is obviously toward simplicity, for complexity invariably creates the sense of discord by scattering the faculties of comprehension. Man originally conceived ornamentation as complementing his personal dignity; he considered adornment a setting wherein he might be shown to better advantage. Illustrative of the degree to which this element has eclipsed the personality is the story of two ladies watching a third go by wearing a very expensive ermine cloak. Turning to the second lady, the first remarked: "Did you see that magnificent cape that just passed by?" Thus, in the effort to be beautiful, humanity has become a race of *mannequins*, hopelessly enslaved to fads and styles which, if not actually detrimental, are at least unnecessary. Greek supremacy in aesthetics is based upon the fact that they achieved the objectification of the beautiful while at the same time preserving utter simplicity. Never did they permit principles and ideals to become involved in complicated forms of manifestation so that they were even partly obscured. In Greek art the idea was ever apparent, and with the objectification of that ideal labor forthwith ceased, for beauty was recognized to be a principle so elusive that it invariably escaped if the means to capture it were unduly stressed. Apropos of this truth is the saying that it requires two men to paint a great picture: the first is the artist; the second, a near friend whose duty it is to shoot the artist at the psychological moment.

The plea of Greenwich Village, "Art for art's sake," while it expresses a theoretical ideal, is often misapplied. There is a tendency to produce technicians who become so skilled in the manipulation of various mediums that they overlook the fact that all mediums are useful simply for the expression of an idea. The great artist is not necessarily a great technician; he is rather a man with a great idea. It is a curious, but nevertheless noteworthy fact that those with the best knowledge of grammar and composition seldom write the best books. Those who become slaves to means or methods are prone to lose sight of ends. Words are sound mosaics which by their combinations create pictures in the mind of the one who hears them. It is the ability of the speaker to create this picture in the mind of his audience that is of prime importance. His greatness is measured by the sublimity of that picture.

What words are to the orator, pigments are to the artist. Through their infinite combinations eternal and intangible verities are expressed in a language comprehensible to the understanding soul. All the arts and sciences are such mediums of expression, fulfilling their purpose when they are developed not for their own sake but for the sake of those inner convictions which through them alone can be shadowed forth to become an impulse or urge in the external life. It is his own shortsightedness which invariably thwarts the ends of the technician. A certain thrill which accompanies the possession of an intricate and adequate mechanism of expression has a tendency to fascinate the mind and hold it as in a hypnotic spell. The fact that words, like colors, are susceptible of such a variety of combinations often intrigues the mind from pursuit of an ideal to lose itself in the maze of approaches to that ideal. The desirable knowledge of method is thus acquired, but the chief purpose has been frustrated: namely, arrival at the true goal. The result is a wasted life in the sense that self-expression has failed to be objectified. To the ancients, the arts and sciences were all sacred to the gods, and upon being admitted to apprenticeship the future craftsman dedicated whatever proficiency he might later acquire therein to the service or expression of eternal truths. Man studied that he might not only learn but that he might use intelligently. And what may be termed intelligent use? The answer is: a use that is beautiful, virtuous, and necessary, since these are the true characteristics of Divinity; for God was regarded as the most beautiful, the most virtuous, and the most necessary of all things.

In its truest sense, therefore, aesthetics may be considered a philosophic discipline by which the consciousness of man is equipped to estimate the degree of beauty, the degree of virtue, and the degree of utility inherent in the nature of an object; also the power to discern how these qualities may be increased to ultimate perfection. The first work is to establish the nature of beauty, virtue, and utility in their most comprehensible sense. Before beauty is cognizable in other than its transitory and inconsequential sense, the consciousness must be elevated to that level of rationality on which the principle of beauty exists, dissociated from the clumsy efforts of man to express its qualities. Upon the basis that only the beautiful is capable of recognizing the beautiful, the assumption of the philosophic life is regarded as indispensable to the recognition of the aesthetics of Divinity.

Socrates would have conceived beauty as expressing itself in the social fabric as utility and in the moral fabric as virtue. To be beautiful is the natural state of all that is good, in that good must manifest good; and beauty most adequately expresses, and is the inevitable attribute of the good. One of the primary axioms of geometry—that things which are equal to the same thing are equal to each other—may be profitably applied to this Socratic triad. So, in answer to the question, What is the most beautiful of all things? philosophy says that which is the most virtuous and the most necessary. What is the most virtuous of all things? That which is the most beautiful and the most necessary. What is the most necessary of all things? That which is the most beautiful and the most virtuous.

The truth of these assumptions is self-evident. Never has the world realized more clearly the utilitarian value of beauty or how necessary virtue is to the survival of the whole. Much of the crassness with which modern civilization is cursed has resulted from the divorce of beauty and utility, in which the spirit of aesthetics has been sacrificed to what we foolishly term the "practical." Some years ago I visited a state prison, and upon being taken into that section reserved for those commonly called "lifers" I was struck with the pathetic effort of the convicts to preserve the spirit of beauty behind the drab stone walls of their penal institution. The men had built little wooden flower boxes, fastening them to the foot of the grating of their cell doors. In these boxes were planted creeping vines which, growing upward, entwined themselves about the gratings and made of the iron bars a trellis. Also in the tenement districts of large cities where thousands are huddled together in an atmosphere of squalor and vice, the little potted geranium on the fire escape is a familiar spectacle, bearing witness to that spark of aesthetics which the Lord of the Whole hid deep within each human heart.

Although to a certain degree an intangible asset, beauty is the molding factor in racial and national life. As long as the spirit of the beautiful shines forth through the bodily structure of peoples and institutions, these increase in power and glory; but when aesthetics dies, the very structure of society deteriorates and begins its march toward inevitable oblivion. Beauty is a soul quality, and like the soul is visible only in its tincturing effect upon its immediate environment. When life is actuated by the spirit of the beautiful, the entire organism—social as well as individual—is the beneficiary of a definite grace and charm which render a relatively imperfect body not only endurable but even attractive. It is not given that all human beings should have beauty or symmetry of form and features. As we pass through the Hall of Fame where the likenesses of the world's illustrious are preserved for the admiration of posterity, if mere physical symmetry be regarded as the sole criterion of excellence many of these geniuses were but rude caricatures of men and women. Carved deeply in the marble of immortality we find the crude and distorted face of Socrates, a little farther down the gaunt figure and aquiline features of Dante, while from his niche stares great Milton whose sightless eyes could yet envision paradise. More recent additions to the immortals are the lank and raw-boned Lincoln and the crippled Steinmetz. Why have the beautiful so often mounted to power through tyranny and oppression, while the deformed have nobly and unselfishly served mankind? The answer seems evident. Beauty has regarded its own existence as a substitute for merit, and fascinated by its reflection in the mirror of vanity has therefore passed into oblivion. On the other hand, those of unsightly mien have struggled for that transcendent internal beauty which has elevated them to chief place in the hearts of men.

That man has a compound nature is difficult for most people to understand. In other words, man is not merely an individual; he is many individuals considered as one. With similar propriety we might refer to an army as a single entity, disregarding the fact that an army is really an aggregation of entities. The brain of man is actually composed of over forty lesser brains, each a specialized organ of thought. Each of these complete thinking organisms vies with every other to dominate the entire organism of thought, and through this competition of parts the compound mental attitude is established. Unaware of what may be termed the ethical code in the relationship of these brain parts to each other, man believes himself to be the master of his thinking processes, when in reality he is frequently the victim of their machinations.

Throughout the entire constitution of man there is a continual plotting for precedence. To a certain degree each part victimizes its associates, with the result that the organism is a seething maelstrom of biological intrigue. In similar fashion the social order—which is really a vast body—may be likened to the fabulous dragon whose seven heads are continually biting at each other.

While the interdependence of parts prevents an open outbreak, there are few bodies in which even a comparative degree of harmony can be said to exist. The compound human organism may be fair to gaze upon but this does not necessarily prove that the various strata of its microcosmic social system are on amicable terms with each other. The human body is one of many examples of the failure of the democratic theory, for nothing could be more tragic than the picture of man's hands or feet liberated to work out their own destiny irrespective of the welfare of the rest. Only because there is within each of us an autocrat who binds the various members to the accomplishment of its own ends can even a semblance of order be maintained. When it is further realized that this autocrat is itself capable of error (in fact, almost incapable of anything else!) we may better grasp the problem presented by the government of man's functions. The wonder is not that man manages his affairs so poorly, but that he manages them at all! An individual whose own internal parts are so bady disorganized as to make rational functioning impossible cannot but reflect his own indecisions into the social order of his civilizaton. The codes by which he lives, being the product of his own internal disquietude, thus engender national and international friction with their resultant crime, war, and disease.

Like individual power, racial power must result from the autocratic usurpation of authority by some figure—no matter how despotic and arbitrary—who grasps the reins with a strong hand and drives the whole toward the consummation of its own desires. Men like Alexander the Great, Cæsar, Genghis Khan, and Napoleon, represent the personification of a racial urge which Nietzsche might call "the will to power." These men gathered up the belligerent elements which had previously expended themselves in a guerrilla-like warfare of factions and directed them toward the goal of world conquest. While this procedure proved most distressing to the strangers without the gates who were its luckless victims, it alone preserved the political integrity of the exploiting powers.

The moment either an individual or a nation ceases to struggle against external obstacles, internal dissensions arise. As soon as the Christian Church stopped fighting the pagans, it began fighting itself. As rapidly as nations reach the point where they are strong enough to maintain an isolated individualism, they are destroyed by civil war. It is sad, but nevertheless true, that up to the present time conquest has been the only force strong enough to surmount national prejudices and cement them into national alliances. There is undoubtedly a certain relationship between this fact and the well-known adage that the devil finds mischief for idle hands to do.

As the individual is likewise a nation in miniature, he is only capable of maintaining the efficiency of his separate organisms while these organisms as a whole are directed toward the achievement of a definite end. Though the lodestar of both nations and individuals, ambition has also proved to be their undoing; for, having outdistanced their resources, they were unable to maintain the positions they had gained. An ancient philosopher once said, "If you want to humble your adversary, give him power." Power may be defined as the privilege of self-expression. Only the wise, however, can express themselves and still be great; the remainder reveal their own ignorance and thereupon tumble from their gilded thrones. To the question, what is the most powerful thing in all the world? the financier would answer, money; the general, guns and men; the religionist, the church; the scientist, knowledge; the philosopher, reason; the mystic, love; the aesthetician, beauty.

Money, while not inherently evil, has been the motivating principle behind nearly every form of crime known to man.

Guns and men, as we know all too well, have become the elements of a gigantic destructive science which may hurl millions of living things to a horrible death in order to establish a diplomatic technicality.

The church, founded originally for the worship of God and the service of man, has now become an arrogant institution, looking with contempt upon those who supply it with the wherewithall of its very existence.

Knowledge has deteriorated until it is simply a dust-covered stack of dry and worthless notions.

Reason has degenerated into debate, wherein minds which should be directionalizing their efforts toward the good of the whole, huddle together under the cloak of learning and mumble their absurdities.

Love, the most sacred of all emotions, has been dragged from its lofty pedestal, and crimson-robed lust seated in its stead.

As for beauty, it has sunk to depths so low as to be considered the vicarious atonement for irrationality.

That beauty is a power is undeniable, but the magnitude of that power is as yet unsuspected. As the proper directionalization of beauty is a potent factor in the civilizing of races, so the misuse of this agency results in a corresponding degree of depravity. External beauty combined with the insolence of internal pride produced a Lucrezia Borgia who, with a face as beautiful as that of a saint, poisoned without a qualm of conscience all who stood in her way. Yet it is written of Lucrezia Borgia that despite her surpassing beauty there was an intangible something about her which filled everyone in her presence with indescribable fear and loathing. Thus the internal nature is impossible of total concealment, and where the outer beauty does not complement the grace within the soul, an incongruity surrounds the personality like an intangible miasma.

The warring segments of a personality, as has been suggested, can only be unified by a common purpose which will enlist the sympathetic co-operation of all. *Right motive*—one of the eight noble paths of Buddhism—can be made to unite all the diversified faculties and members of the nature and directionalize them toward achievement of the greatest good.

The consciousness that steadfastly contemplates only good through all its diversified perceptions may be said to have united its various parts into a pattern worthy to be designated beautiful. Co-operation only can be conceived of as beautiful, for competition must ever manifest as a grotesque absurdity. Only a propaganda-ridden world could possibly imagine war to be beautiful, and competition is merely a bloodless war in which the soul and not the body is slain.

While contemplating the nature of the Supreme Good, the Neoplatonists of Alexandria also philosophized with rare lucidity upon the nature of the beautiful. Plotinus writes concerning the order of the beautiful as it emerges from the first Beauty: "And in the first rank we must place the beautiful and consider it as the same with the good; from which immediately emanate intellects as beautiful. Next to this we must consider the soul receiving its beauty from intellect; and every inferior beauty deriving its origin from the forming power of the soul, whether conversant in fair actions and offices, or sciences and arts. Lastly, bodies themselves participate of beauty from the soul, which, as something divine, and a portion of the beautiful itself, renders whatever it supervenes and subdues, beautiful, as far as its natural capacity will admit."

Beauty, existing independent of form and as a divine principle, is likened to the fountainhead of existence, from which streams of beauty flow forth to permeate and beautify the whole inferior creation. Furthermore, the beauty of the inner nature greatly transcends the beauty of the outer, for the spiritual essences constituting the supersubstantial man, being more proximate to Cause, partake more fully of the nature of Cause, which is true Beauty. Hence, as Plotinus also observes, there are those who "on perceiving the forms of gods or dæmons, no longer esteem the fairest of corporeal forms."

The quest of the truly beautiful is therefore identical with the quest of Self, for Self in its perfect and universalized sense —the all-pervading Consciousness postulated by the sage—is the perfect source of all beauty and therefore partakes in perfect measure of all that which is manifested from itself. That this supreme truth was taught by the sacred institutions of antiquity is further evidenced by Plotinus, who continues: "Just as those who penetrate into the holy retreats of sacred mysteries are first purified, and then divest themselves of their garments, until some one, by such a process, having dismissed everything foreign from the God, by himself alone, beholds the solitary principle of the universe, sincere, simple, and pure, from which all things depend, and to whose transcendent perfections the eyes of all intelligent natures are directed, as the proper causes of being, life, and intelligence."

The Neoplatonists did not confine themselves solely to a theoretical consideration of mystical truths; they deemed it also essential that the disciple learn to actually partake of the verities disclosed by intellectual contemplation. If perfect beauty was synonymous with perfect good, then the achievement of perfect participation in its effulgence was of first importance. As the ephemeral beauties of the outer (or material) world were sensed chiefly through the eyes, so the eternal beauties of the inner (or spiritual) world could only be sensed through a mystical perception which they termed the "eye of the soul." "We must enter deep into ourselves," again says Plotinus, "and leaving behind the objects of corporeal sight, no longer look back after any of the accustomed spectacles of sense. For it is necessary that whoever beholds this beauty should withdraw his view from the fairest corporeal forms, and convinced that these are nothing more than images, vestiges, and shadows of beauty, should eagerly soar to the fair original from which they are derived. For he who rushes to these lower beauties, as if grasping realities where they are only like beautiful images appearing in water, will doubtless, like him in the fable, by stretching after the shadow, sink into the lake and disappear. For by thus embracing and adhering to corporeal forms he is precipitated, not so much in his body as in his soul, into profound and horrid darkness; and thus blind, like those in the infernal regions, converses only with phantoms, deprived of the perception of what is real and true."

While the Alexandrian mystics shared the Oriental attitude concerning the attainment of Reality through rejection of the illusions of sense, they had more definite conclusions as to the method whereby the Causal Beauty was to be realized. Their instructions read thus: "Recall your thoughts inward, and if, while contemplating yourself, you do not perceive yourself beautiful, imitate the sculptor; who, when he desires a beautiful statue cuts away what is superfluous, smooths and polishes what is rough, and never desists until he has given it all the beauty his art is able to effect. In this manner must you proceed, by lopping what is luxuriant, directing what is oblique, and by purgation illustrating what is obscure; and so continue to polish and beautify your statue until the divine splendor of Virtue shines upon you, and Temperance, seated in pure and holy majesty, rises to your view."

To the ancients aesthetics was not only the science of beauty, but that discipline whereby each individual in his quest for truth might elevate his own level of functioning so as to become luminous with the reflected light of Universal Beauty, and ultimately identical therewith. Two forms of beauty were postulated: that which is intrinsic to the nature of a body, and that which is extrinsic or communicated from some external source. In man, for example, beauty was the natural attribute of the spiritual nature, but the material nature partook thereof only by reflection. Being a rational creature manifesting through an irrational animal organism, man has the capacity to recognize and estimate the excellence of order, symmetry, and grace. Even as that which is base finds response in the baseness of the material nature, so that which is beautiful awakens a pleasant reaction in the rational part. As Bacchus was dismembered by the Titans and his parts strewn throughout the irrational sphere, so the rational soul of man is scattered throughout the substances of his irrational animal nature. To the presence of this element of confusion is referable the inability to recognize or appreciate such soul qualities as harmony and beauty.

The pleasurable sensation which beauty awakens in the beholder was said by the Greeks to arise from an internal symmetrical nature beholding an external body with qualities similar to its own. As the internal nature dwells in perfect order, it thus rejoices in order and recoils from disorder. To a certain degree beauty is order, and as such is compatible with that internal orderliness which inevitably follows the liberation of rationality from the disorganizing effect of matter. Beauty rejoices in its own nature and even the faintest shadow of it awakens a glad response. The infinite diversity of standards by which beauty is measured result from the various combinations of rationality and irrationality present in the soul. That which is beautiful to one is not necessarily beautiful to another, and yet beauty as a principle is common to all. We consider that to be beautiful which approaches most closely the symmetry of our own internal natures; and as the inner nature evolves more perfect harmonies we become more discriminating in our responsiveness to external stimuli. Gradually symmetry of form gives place to symmetry of thought, and the beauties of the inner nature are then revealed as surpassing the beauties of the outer form.

The Neoplatonic theory of beauty may be summed up as the rationality of the beholder rejoicing in the evidence of rationality in the thing beheld. Grace, symmetry, harmony, and order are unquestionable evidence of a rational consciousness, and we rejoice in this evidence to the same degree that we possess the ability to recognize them. That is most beautiful, therefore, which elicits most perfect response from our inner perceptions. Through philosophy we ascend from that beauty communicated from an external source to the recognition of that beauty identical with Source itself. Having ultimately attained through right thinking, right feeling, and right living to the condition of the beautiful within ourselves, with enraptured vision we can respond in perfect measure to the eternal beauty which flows from the inexhaustible fountain of the one Good.

In the present century two great opposing systems of thought are struggling for supremacy. On the one hand is idealism, which declares that to be practical which is beautiful; on the other hand is realism, which asserts that to be beautiful which is practical. It is difficult to estimate the profound effect caused by this simple interchange of the words *practical* and *beautiful*. Practicality must be interpreted to imply the greatest good to the greatest number, and there is no question that, if so interpreted, that which is of the greatest good to the greatest number is the beautiful necessity. However, we may well ask if what we now term practical is actually fulfilling this ideal. Much of the structure of modern civilization is revolting to the finer sentiments of humanity. Elbert Hubbard can hardly be censured for defining civilization as "a device for increasing human ills; a machine for the perpetuation of the weak; an ingenious contraption for spreading disease and hunger." Men and women of vision all realize that modern civilization is doomed to collapse under the weight of its own infirmities. Like the mighty Juggernaut, it is rumbling down the hillside of Time to vanish ultimately in the vale of oblivion below.

The reason civilization must crumble is because it is not beautiful; and lacking the order, harmony, symmetry, and grace which collectively constitute beauty, it will be disintegrated by the friction of its own individual parts. Like the scaled, fire-belching dragon of mythology, it is the jealous guardian of the tree upon whose branches hangs the Golden Fleece. Even today the Argonaut sets forth. Man in his quest for happiness—which alone makes life endurable—is determined, like Jason, to wrest the highest prize from the clutches of the monster he himself has created. The future dragon-slayer is first born in the human soul as the spirit of revolt against the crushing weight of the artificial world which man in his folly has raised, Babel-like, to rival the glory of the heavens. Man has built a house whose bricks are made of mud and held together by slime. Indifferent to the laws of social architecture, he has raised this mighty edifice upon shifting sand, and now its walls of their own weight threaten to collapse about the heads of the foolish builders.

Seated on their golden thrones the Titans of finance gaze down, like the huge stone Memnons of Egypt, upon a devastated land. Like the Pharaohs of the ancient Nile their sandals are pounded from the golden crowns of vanquished kings.

Wall Street may be likened to that gloomy ravine which led down to the depths of Dante's Inferno. Here souls lost in the maze of their own greeds and passions wander in the dim light that finds its way down between the towering skyscrapers that rise cliff-like on either hand. Wall Street is a most appropriate symbol of the path of glory which General Wolfe declared leads but to the grave; for at one end of that short but awful thoroughfare lay the murky and polluted waters of the river; at the other stand the crumbling and moss-covered headstones of Trinity's churchyard. There is a common saying upon the "Street" that those who succeed are laid away in pomp to the chime of old Trinity's bells, while those who fail are found floating upon the turbid breast of the river.

As one gazes downward upon the teeming world maelstrom of human endeavor where millions of creatures in ant-like confusion struggle to survive, with no time, no strength, no opportunity to dream, to hope or to aspire, he can better sense the incubus of civilization. To what end all this cyclopean struggle in which destruction is ever the victor? As one regards this seething cauldron where, like the witches of Macbeth, the three sisters—ignorance, superstition, and fear—brew their poisonous broths, he cannot but recall the prophetic words of Prospero in *The Tempest*:

> The cloud-capped Towers, the gorgeous Palaces,
> The solemn Temples, the great Globe itself,
> Yea, all which it inherit, shall dissolve,
> And like this insubstantial Pageant faded
> Leave not a rack behind: we are such stuff
> As dream are made on; and our little life
> Is rounded with a sleep.

When the Bishop of Ripon suggested to the British Association for the Advancement of Science that it take a ten-year vacation for the good of the human soul, this venerable churchman precipitated a storm of protest. "The very greatness of his [man's] recent achievements," declared the Bishop, "would seem to make his ruin more certain and more complete." While any cessation of man's effort to improve his own status would undoubtedly prove disastrous, there is no doubt that the Bishop has sensed an impending catastrophe—that ever-widening gap between the spiritual and the material life of man.

Man's internal progress has failed to keep abreast with the growth of his conveniences. With the advent of the washing machine it cannot be said that we have registered corresponding improvement in our standards of beauty, ethics, and aesthetics. The popular superstition that if the body is comfortable the spirit will take care of itself has not been justified by experience. Although too many churchmen wander in a maze of theological complexities, still for the most part they recognize the need of spiritual education. If his inner nature fails, man perishes; and while in the last analysis failure can only be temporary, still to disregard the sciences of the higher life is but to prolong the agonies of the unillumined state.

The enlightened theologian does not desire to tear down the achievements of science or belittle the blessings that it has conferred upon mankind. The true spiritual thinker merely affirms the necessity of elevating the sciences of the soul to a parity with those of the body. He regrets that man should learn to live so well only to ultimately die as badly as before. Whereas, according to the theologian, man may live in this world but a few score years, he is predestined to endure in a transcendental state throughout all eternity. If he is willing to spend so great a part of his life equipping himself for the little span of earth life, should he not, argues the Bishop, also give some consideration to that greater life of which the present is but the vestibule?

A just criticism against modern science is that as it magnifies by its repeated emphasis the importance of terrestrial concerns, it belittles in like measure the still nobler concerns of the spirit. Savants are too prone to solve the problem of the after-death state by disdainfully rejecting the concept of immortality as but another survival of primitive superstition. Thus the day of greatest physical light bids fair to become the day of greatest spiritual darkness. It is questionable if science will ever be able to make the earth such a desirable locale that world-worn souls will not ultimately be glad to escape from its stifling environment.

The goal of science apparently is perpetuation of the physical life, which seemingly is the only life of which it is sure. Since woman is devoting more of her time to consideration of world problems she may be gratified to learn that one scientist assures us that within the next century babies will be manufactured in the laboratory to meet any and all specifications. Physical immortality, therefore, may be regarded as the ultimate goal of science, which can conceive of no other form of immortality. Thus, the modern scientist actually seeks that same elixir of life which he ridicules the mediaeval alchemist for declaring to be a reality.

The church very properly opposes this so-called practical attitude, since if physical immortality be the real goal of existence the universe is without integrity, for how can the dead past share in the immortality of the unborn future? The mystic also realizes the insufficiency of this new physical urge which worships a word and pays homage to its own achievements as summed up in the term *practical*. To him the word is a synonym for the prosaic in whose presence the finer qualities of life must inevitably languish and die. No sane man would block the progress of human thought or condemn any real contribution to the life, happiness or efficiency of the race. Men and women with vision would, however, rejoice if they could see growing up in the world an institution both vast and beautiful which would serve the aesthetic needs of the individual, and would insure that life would be not only efficient but also beautiful; that man would enjoy not only health of body but be possessed of healthy emotions and ideals. The population of earth is sufficient to assure science that it will never be without a body of informed men and women to carry forward its ideals. There are enough also to form another group as strong, as noble, and as true to preserve those aesthetic principles which existed long before the dawn of modern thought and without which science as an institution could never have existed.

When by some joyous exception of Nature we find the scientist in whom the beautiful is an awakened and radiant force, there results a type of mind as constructive as any modern society can produce. It will yet be demonstrated that no scientist can achieve to the highest in his chosen field until he acknowledges the existence of a superphysical nature which survives the dissolution of its temporal parts. Even as men in primitive times fashioned crude images and then bowed humbly before their own creations, so the scientist of today has but elevated his superstitions to a more dignified level; for having fashioned with his own reason the entire body of science, he now contemplates with an awe approaching blind adoration the craftsmanship he has wrought. Without doubt the prosaic attitudes of scientific men have done much to turn thinking minds from the contemplation of aesthetics to the more utilitarian themes of biology and physics. Science has the unquestioned advantage of tangible evidence of its utilitarian value. We are ever surrounded by the examples of scientific accomplishment, while the accomplishments of aesthetics, being largely limited to the internal nature, make no showing impressive to the uncultured.

With its emphasis solely upon the practical, the realistic interpretation of life over-justifies existing conditions; for it assumes that because deformity exists it must be necessary and, being necessary, it must be beautiful. Dr. Will Durant has defined the true offices of realism and idealism. Existing conditions, he declared, should be analyzed in the terms of realism and reconstructed in the terms of idealism. There is an element of precocity among civilized peoples today which is most unseemly; sophistication is everywhere. The surfeit of advantages which we have enjoyed has brought in its train the state of boredom. Nothing pleases, nothing suffices, nothing intrigues. The race has an inclination to sit around and await dissolution as the one remaining experience that may contain the element of novelty. College youths finds it necessary to murder in order to create a passing thrill. Externally we are simply over-civilized; internally we are morons. The very people who suffer most keenly for this chronic ennui, who are satiated with the entire subject of life, have never really experienced in their thoughts, feelings or actions any of the more profound verities of existence.

Turning from the sordidness of realism, let us look at the world through the eyes of those dreamers who have dared to believe that the good in human nature would ultimately blossom forth and regenerate the entire social system. Beauty, declared the ancient philosophers, was the only offering acceptable to the gods. Furthermore, beauty being the environment of Divinity, God himself was present in every manifestation of the beautiful. In the Scriptures it is written that if the temple is built according to the Law, the living God will dwell therein. The Greek Dionysiacs symbolized the establishment of world harmony by the erection of a temple to the Unversal Creator. Upon the theory that like attracts like they philosophized that when the world was made beautiful, souls of the nature of beauty would incarnate to people it. Because of their belief in reincarnation, the Greeks taught that rational souls incarnated in harmonious environments, whereas discordant areas were populated with irrational creatures whose own internal discord attracted them to a discordant sphere.

The remarkable physical symmetry for which the Greeks are justly famed is ascribed to a peculiar practice. Prospective mothers were isolated from the confusion of the community life and spent their days in secluded gardens filled with statuary representative of the ideals of grace and beauty. They were not permitted to look upon any asymmetrical object lest it mark the coming child. In some communities they went so far as to destroy at birth the crippled or unsightly. This was done not only to prevent the suffering resultant from such affliction but also that society might not through the sight of such malformations perpetuate that which was not beautiful.

Much of our crime and degeneracy can be traced to home environment. Mystical philosophy declares heredity in its conventional sense to be a fallacious doctrine. We do not actually inherit the traits of our ancestors; rather, these traits are environments which call into incarnation souls of a like degree of rational development. A home in which dissension reigns attracts to itself a soul equally discordant. When upon reaching maturity such a soul exhibits the traits of its parents, such traits are erroneously ascribed to the previous generation by such as do not realize that each evolving consciousness has its own definite temperament and does not receive its temperamental bias from another.

The collective attitudes of nations, generations, and races result in their drawing into objective manifestation all subjective qualities consistent with their own. When a nation gives itself over chiefly to problems of finance, souls who conceive money to be of primary importance incarnate therein until ultimately the entire fabric of that people is permeated with this common attitude. Souls in whom corresponding interests do not exist depart from such people and either appear in other races or else in anticipation of a better day resign themselves to patience.

If we truly wish to beautify our present civilization we must realize the necessity of creating an environment which will draw into objective manifestation the nobler souls whose rational faculties have been unfolded to a comprehension of the harmonious and the good. This same environment will further stimulate to rationality those who have not yet fully achieved to this exalted state. Philosophy was the dominating passion of ancient Greece and so intense was its attractive power that it drew into incarnation the greatest number of noble thinkers the human race has ever produced. If we would endure as a great people, we too must realize that as qualities increase in excellence they also increase in permanence, and that a civilization established upon virtue, beauty, and utility will endure long after the structures erected upon the foundations of finance and war have vanished from the earth.

Today the philosopher in search of reality must retire deep into the recesses of his inner self and thus escape from the discordances of the outer life. If he would think, he must depart from the mob which in its non-productive scrambling scatters the faculties of the mind and robs man of his most precious gift—the power of thought. It should not be necessary for man to leave the world in order to find himself, for his world should be a place where his true nature may mingle in concord with the true natures of all other beings.

The sham of civilization is apparent when we realize that it forces the majority of people to assume false lives, to live in conflict with their inner convictions. The idealist must keep silent or be reviled; the thinker must hold his peace or be persecuted; the mystic dares not share his vision with the world which, though aware that he is right, will crucify him if not in body at least in soul. Hence, those with little knowledge babble continuously and their words become the laws of men, while those of nobler vision must remain unknown, unhonored, and unsung. Never can we rise to the true heights seen by the eyes of the idealist while we are in servitude to the inferior part of ourselves.

Man does not realize the weight of that curse by which he was cast forth from the light of truth to wander in the darkness of his own making. He feels helpless in the presence of the vast industrial mechanism which has required centuries for its perfection and which has now assumed an appearance so formidable that even those who consider themselves its masters tremble and are afraid. Philosophy knows that before man can really live, the machine must go; and if humanity is incapable of self-emancipation it must wait until the mechanism grinds itself to pieces.

It is predestined that the *golden age* shall come again; that men shall live together in love and understanding, and the earth shall become once more a garden of surpassing beauty as it was in the beginning. In that time men shall learn all that they learn now. There shall be great institutions for research and record; the arts and crafts shall flourish. But unlike preceding generations this era shall not pass away; for the God of it shall be Beauty and where Beauty in its various aspects rules a people, that people shall remain as permanent as eternity. It is not necessary that we tear down the entire structure of our present system or revert to some savage type and start anew. It is merely necessary that we tincture utility with beauty; that we add the soul qualities of symmetry and grace to the products of our schemings.

Beauty is the deadly enemy of every excess, for into its constitution enter the elements of grace, proportion, symmetry, and harmony. A thousand means have been suggested by which the injustice of men may be offset, but all these must ultimately fail unless aesthetics becomes an integral part of our social fabric. Until the soul reaches that degree of rationality wherein it is able to recognize the supreme importance of the beautiful, it cannot withstand the urge of selfishness and greed which ever lure nations as well as individuals to their destruction. When we love the beautiful as we now love the dollar we shall have a great and enduring civilization. When we adore the God of harmony as we once worshipped the God of vengeance, we shall know the inner mystery of life. When we create with symmetry, preserve with integrity, and release with joy, then only are we good. Never until we have become one with the good can we be happy, for happiness is the realization of internal beauty which joyously goes forth to mingle itself with the beauty that dwells in space.

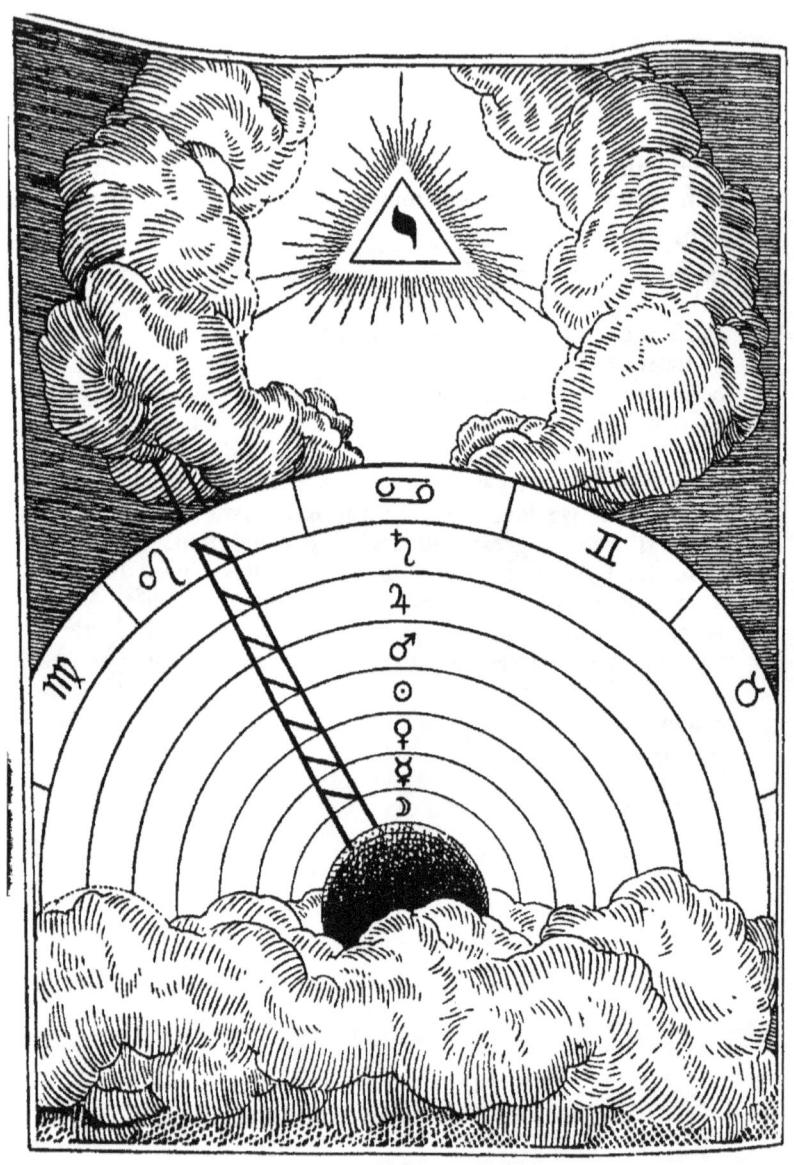

THE LADDER OF LIFE

Man is ever ascending from an inferior to a superior state according to a law which was established coeval with the foundation of generation. This law is the philosophic ladder which is treated more in detail in Chapter Seventeen. It is likewise the mysterious Masonic ladder—that ancient symbol of the Secret Work.

CHAPTER NINE

The Cycle of Necessity

WHAT relationship does the little life we know bear to that vaster existence which is our hope and which Rabelais would call "the Great Perhaps"? Three questions have ever vexed the rational faculties of mankind: *Life* is the beginning of what? *Love* is the fulfillment of what? *Death* is the end of what? The essential attribute of an enduring religion or philosophy is the rational solution which it offers to this threefold riddle. If physical existence be regarded as the whole of life, then the hopelessness and inconsistency of the scheme is apparent, for as Manilius writes: "We begin to die as soon as we are born, and the end is linked to the beginning." Hence universal order can only be restored when we regard physical existence as a fragment of a nobler and more complete cycle of duration. Somewhere in the chain of his speculation the philosopher will ask: Is the corporeal state natural or accidental to man? In other words, is man destined by virtue of inherent qualities to abide forever as a terrene creature, or is he—like the hero of that Gnostic classic, *The Hymn of the Robe of Glory*—an exiled prince seeking the way which leads back to his Father's kingdom, the spiritual Dawn Land?

Knowledge of the purpose of life is essential to right living. Unless we comprehend, in part at least, the order of which we are a minute but consequential part, we cannot achieve the greatest good here and now. The past and future like mighty trees meet overhead and shadow the present. The field of today's endeavor is bounded on the one hand by unborn tomorrow and on the other by dead yesterday. Our attitudes toward these opposites—the fateful past and the destined future —must be the measure of our present achievements. When he says, "The present only is great, the past is dead," the opportunist little realizes that he himself is the past; for all that goes before lives again in that which follows after. The today man worships is but a fleeting second, yesterday was without beginning, and tomorrow without end; yet all are embraced within the span of the eternal philosophic NOW. From the obscure fountains of futurity the waters of time flow down through the turbulent cataracts of present endeavor to mingle finally with the boundless ocean of the past.

All men worship either life or death. Philosophers worship life by affirming it to be imperishable; the non-philosophic worship death by accepting it as a reality. Being essentially incorporeal, life is not limited to place, but in the terms of Neoplatonism is "everywhere, not with interval, but impartibly." In his *Auxiliaries to the Perception of Intelligible Natures*, Porphyry tells us that "things essentially incorporeal are not locally present with bodies, but are present with them when they please; by verging toward them so far as they are naturally adapted so to verge. They are not, however, present with them locally, but through habitude, proximity, and alliance." Being free from the limitations of place (used in its Platonic sense) life animates forms by approaching them, and by its subsequent withdrawal into its own nature causes the forms to exhibit the phenomenon called death. In its physical sense life results from the temporary association of an incorporeal agent with a corporeal patient. Bodies, being corporeal, occupy place, and an interval exists between them regardless of their apparent proximity. When life which exists without such interval, animates form, an illusion is created which causes the uninformed to assume that life itself is subject to the confining bounds of place.

Being incorporeal, the gods were not limited to place but exercised their azonic privilege of being distributed according to will throughout the entire substance of creation. This explains the popular belief that God is everywhere and hence with equal efficiency may be addressed by multitudes in various places simultaneously. While life is essentially ethereal and in constant activity, form is essentially dense and static. In combination wtih form, life animates form to a certain degree; conversely, form is an impediment to the flow of life. The result is that physical manifestation is a paradoxical state wherein life appears less than itself and matter more than itself. At death, form reverts to its natural state of inertia, while life returns to its normal condition of uninterrupted flow.

In his treatise, *On the Wanderings of Ulysses,* Thomas Taylor, drawing upon *De Ulyxis Erroribus,* the work of an anonymous Greek writer declares that Homer used the Trojan war as a symbol of the battle between the rational faculties (the Greeks) and the irrational faculties (the Trojans). Thomas Taylor notes that Homer is reputed to have been blind "because, as Proclus observes, he separated himself from sensible beauty, and extended the intellect of his soul to invisible and true harmony. He was said, therefore, to be blind because *that* intellectual beauty to which he raised himself cannot be perceived by corporeal eyes." In the *Thirteenth Book of the Odyssey,* Homer describes in veiled language a mysterious cave by which the Orphic philosophy concerning the mystery of life and death is obscurely set forth:

> High at the head a branching olive grows,
> And crowns the pointed cliffs with shady boughs.
> A cavern pleasant, though involv'd in night,
> Beneath it lies, the Naiades' delight:
> Where bowls and urns of workmanship divine
> And massy beams in native marble shine;
> On which the Nymphs amazing webs display,
> Or purple hue, and exquisite array.
> The busy bees within the urns secure
> Honey delicious, and like nectar pure.
> Perpetual waters through the grotto glide,
> A lofty gate unfolds on either side;
> That to the north is pervious to mankind;
> The sacred south t' immortals is consign'd.

In his essay on *The Cave of the Nymphs,* Porphyry discusses at some length the occult significance of Homer's cavern. The gist of Porphyry's conclusions, (which he derives from various ancient authors—Egyptian, Greek, and Persian) is as follows: The ancients consecrated caves as symbols of the world in that, like the world, they were produced from an internal and not an external cause. The Persian mystics signified the descent of the soul into the sublunary regions, and its regression therefrom by initiating their mystics in caverns. As temples, groves, and altars were established in honor of the gods, so grottoes were also dedicated to the Nymphs, or Naiades, because of the water which trickled down the walls. In the seventh book of his *Republic,* Plato writes: "Behold men as if dwelling in a subterranean cavern, and in a den-like habitation, whose entrance is widely expanded to the admission of the light through the whole cave."

The ancient theologists considered caverns as appropriate symbols of mundane powers and of the sensible world, because these rocky openings are dark, stony, and humid. Furthermore, the dampness existing in the cave was analogous to the humidity of the world, which the Greeks conceived to be indispensable to the generation of souls. The soul may be Platonically defined as "the first of bodies" and the individualized source of bodily life. Heraclitus says: "That moisture appears delightful and not deadly to souls." The etheric humidity which incarnating souls find indispensable to their body-building processes caused the philosophers to declare that these souls must be profoundly steeped or drenched in moisture as they enter into the sphere of generation. But pure souls do not desire to generate and hence absent themselves from the sphere of humidity, which causes Heraclitus to remark: "A dry soul is the wisest."

Porphyry then declares that souls proceeding into generation and enveloped in this ethereal moisture are properly called *Naiades.* The Naiades are Nymphs, presumably water spirits, and their esoteric meaning as given above was revealed only to the initiated. The cavern is therefore a temple sacred to the processes of generation and signifies not only the world in which generated souls reside, but (although Porphyry does not bring out the fact) also the womb from which the philosophic-elect are liberated by the second birth. The bowls and urns which, according to Homer, are contained in the cave, are not only appropriate emblems of the aquatic Nymphs but are also symbols of Bacchus, and being composed of baked earth signify the bodies into which the corporeal souls descend. Here we have the vessels of various shapes which Omar Khayyam refers to in his *Rubaiyat*.

Homer then describes the purple webs which the Nymphs weave on marble looms. The spinning of the web represents the building of the fleshly body with its arteries, veins, nerves, and muscles upon the shining framework of the bones. This is the garment with which the incarnating soul is to be invested but which, alas, is to prove a net to ensnare and hold captive the rational virtues. The heavens are called a veil by the ancients, by whom they are regarded as the vestments of the celestial gods.

The honey which the busy bees store away in the bowls and amphorae has two significances. Honey was regarded by the ancients as both a preservative and also a purifier. The Persians used honey in their sacrifices as a symbol of the preserving and defending powers. Honey further signifies mortal and transitory pleasure as distinguished from divine and enduring pleasure. In the ancient mythology Saturn, being intoxicated with honey sleeps, and while in this condition is robbed of his empire by Jupiter. This fable obscurely intimates that the soul is robbed of its divinity when it becomes intoxicated by the illusionary happiness of the corporeal sphere.

Porphyry also gives a third interpretation to honey, which he declares was used to signify death—an interpretation dependent upon the previous assumption that it befuddled the divine perceptions. Gall he declares to be a symbol of life, adding, in comparing the two, that the life of the soul dies through pleasure (honey) but through bitterness (gall) the soul resumes its life. Bees (here termed the *ox-begotten*) are symbols of just souls entering into generation both because of their industry and because they instinctively return to that place from which they first came, for the just soul instinctively returns to its divine and unlimited condition.

In his *Scholia on the Phaedrus of Plato*, Hermias declares that the nectar and ambrosia of the gods are to be understood as possessing a profound philosophic meaning. He writes: "Ambrosia is analogous to dry nutriment and on this account it signifies an establishment in causes; but nectar is analogous to moist food and signifies the providential attention of the gods to secondary natures."

Referring to the gates leading into and out of the cavern, Porphyry declares them to represent the winter and summer solstices—Capricorn and Cancer respectively—adding that as Cancer is nearest to us it is very properly attributed to the moon which is the nearest of the heavenly bodies to the earth; but as the southern pole by its distance is invisible to us, Capricorn is attributed to Saturn, the most remote of the planets. The Orphic theologists add that Cancer is the gate through which souls descend into generation, and Capricorn the gate through which they ascend again, in that the north is appropriate to descend but the south to ascend. The north gate of the cavern is therefore said to be pervious to the descent of men, but the south gate is called the avenue not of the gods but of souls— the immortals—ascending to the gods. The ancients likewise connected the winds with souls proceeding into generation or escaping therefrom, declaring that the north winds aid generation and refresh the dying, but the south winds dissolve life.

But one symbol remains to be explained: namely, the branching olive that grows above the cave. The olive is the plant of Minerva, and Minerva having been produced from the head of Jupiter is the proper symbol of wisdom. It was customary to place this plant over the gates and arches to signify that the universe (the world symbolized by the cavern) is not the product of casual effort or the work of irrational fortune, but the offspring of an intellectual nature and a divine wisdom. The olive is also the plant with which the victor in the race of life is crowned, thus revealing the mystic fact that he who vanquishes or outruns his lesser nature will be rewarded with wisdom's crown.

The *Cycle of Necessity* is the term applied to that period or condition through which man must pass in the attainment of conscious immortality—conscious in the sense of illumined realization as distinguished from that immortality of which we all partake in common but which remains unrecognized until philosophic perception grasps its true import. In his pilgrimage to the Holy City man must pass through the valley called Jehoshaphat or, the "place of dry bones." Here grisly specters rise from their moss-grown sarcophagi to perform the weird gyrations of the Dance of Death. Every gesture of the irrational life is part of a ghastly pageantry, for the cradle stands within the open grave. Philosophy alone can bestow upon man the precious gift of immortality; for though every human soul is innately divine and beyond dissolution, it cannot partake of its own permanence without those perceptions which philosophy must confer.

As long as man believes in death, there is no life; and what man affirms to be existence is actually the gloomy vestibule of oblivion. Buddhism became the faith of half the world because it assured man that death was but a dream and mortality an empty lie. The power exercised by Christianity over the Western Hemisphere results in great measure from its claim that for those of sufficient faith death has been forever vanquished by the resurrection of the holy Nazarene.

It is not sufficient, however, that man be simply immortal, for immortality is merely the means to an end—the infinite opportunity for achievement of ultimate perfection. It is not sufficient that man go on living after he is dead, for this would only perpetuate on a more attenuated sphere the miseries of his present state. Nor is it reasonable to presume that the phenomenon of death can produce any definite cultural results. Theology fails to interest the modern mind because it postulates an after-death state which is but small improvement over corporeal conditions. What shall it profit a man if he leave a static earth to wander around in a static heaven? Yet philosophically, theology is nearly correct in its depiction of the so-called celestial state, for heaven is an attenuated earth where life continues on practically the same ethical and aesthetic levels as during physical existence.

The mortal sphere consists of two parts: one visible, the other invisible, but both alike illusionary and material. It follows that he who gives up the illusions of mortal life must also give up the illusions of mortal death. So the philosopher who transcends the imperfections of mortal existence transcends also the corresponding imperfections of immortal existence. Heaven and hell are woven on the same loom and he who renounces the latter must renounce the former with it. Ignorant man may go to heaven, but his heaven—like his earth—is inconsequential. The heaven whose praises are so often sung is designed primarily to augment the comfort of the animal man, to cause only pleasing reactions in the emotional nature and afford expression for desires and impulses which have their origin in the irrational soul. It therefore follows that it is an animal paradise and becomes insufficient the moment the rational soul in man is liberated from its bondage to bestial instincts.

Among the ancient Vikings, for example, heaven was regarded as a hall of gluttony where heroes gorged themselves from a magic larder which ever replenished itself. Heaven, moreover, even co-operated with the feasters by making appetites more and more insatiable, the warriors only leaving their feasting long enough to stage gladiatorial combats wherein they dealt each other mortal wounds which healed immediately. It is evident that this heaven was as much a part of the irrational sphere as the physical earth itself, for it offered but enlarged opportunity for intemperance and sensuality. Would not Plato who transcended the sordidness of earthly excesses also transcend a heaven which existed merely to satisfy the unquenched fires of animal desire?

At the entrance to the Elysian Fields, where the souls of the blessed dead picked daisies and eternally chanted hymns to the deities, the Egyptians placed a great judgment hall built of rocks as solid as that of Karnak. Here Osiris, painted white and having upon his person more eyes than Argus, sat in judgment upon the shades of earth's illustrious, weighing their souls in a pair of ordinary scales. A jury and a motley group of immortals watched the proceedings with keen interest for probably the hundred millionth time. Does not such a picture afford ample evidence that man's ignorance, unaffected by such episodes as birth and death, continues until the advent of rational consciousness?

At this stage a logical subject for speculation is what happens to an individual who, believing in the reality of the theological heaven, starts out after death in search of the pearly gates and golden streets. Does their nonexistence disappoint him? Philosophy answers no, for as the illusions of physical life here are perfectly tangible and real to those who *believe* in them, so the heavenly city with its foundation of precious stones opens its imaginary portals to all who have convinced themselves that such portals exist. As surely as humanity can delude itself with the belief that there is such a thing as a rich man, it can believe that the gods are richer still and hence can bestow wealth untold upon certain favored dead. We all live in a world of make-believe, and as we pass from the make-believers of life to the make-believers of death we simply step up our imagination to a higher level and keep right on dreaming, declaring that to be true which never had and never will have aught of fact within its fabric.

Conversely, hell is simply that state which is created for us by our own realization of the fact that if the universe has any integrity whatsoever we deserve to burn for a few milleniums at least! Stupid fears generate our hells and inane wishes our heavens. In what manner would the plan of existence be glorified by having the souls of men roasted on hot spits throughout eternity because they broke some imaginary statute of the celestial code; or, in what way would the glory of God be magnified if more fortunate souls were given grandstand seats and permitted to witness the inspiring spectacle of the devil, sitting as high inquisitor, meting out perdition?

When Parsifal, standing in the enchanted garden of Klingsor, the evil magician, elevated the holy spear and traced with it in the air the sign of the cross, the chimerical world of the sorcerer disappeared. The enchanted garden vanished, the flower maidens faded into thin air, the great gloomy castle was shaken and the liberated stones came tumbling down to vanish like mist before the rising sun. So it is with these spectral worlds—heaven, earth, and hell—which the senses have taught us to believe are real.

With the opened eye of his rational perceptions the sage gazes out upon a very different world. First, with mortal eyes gazing upon the illusion are seen all those treasures which in our ignorance we have held dear. But gradually as the eyes of the flesh are closed, the eye of the soul is opened, and like a dream the spectacle of wordliness fades and in its place the permanent universe is revealed. The souls of men are seen passing back and forth through the swinging veils which divide the chamber of mortal existence into two compartments. Carrying the burdens of life, bent with the responsibilities of years, obsessed with the reality of matter, the tired and toilworn wanderer exchanges life for death. But as he passes through the veil he still carries with him the old perplexities of his mortal incarceration. We may see him still bent, still broken, still afraid, creeping through the tiny rent in the veil of his existence to continue on the other side the life he cannot cast aside until he rises above his lesser self. To him death is the promise of fulfillment. So he brings with him his empty money bags that they may be filled; he seeks the waters of Lethe where resting in that state of forgetfulness of all that engenders sorrow he seeks to assuage the aching of his heart, still the spinning wheels of his mind, and realize thwarted desire.

The invisible world gradually assumes the appearance of the office where he labored during the years of earth life. Still the ticker sounds in his ear, telephones ring, and vast projects torment his tired mind with their complexities. A little while and this soul drifts into a great vortex of endeavors, vain struggles, and loosened passions. Like a mighty whirlwind his soul in company with the souls of millions is swept about in hopeless confusion in the after-death chamber. The sighing of the wind is the mourning of deluded souls. Suddenly the curtains begin to sway and through them sweeps the torrent of air back into the world of the living. A little child creeps through a tiny rent and burdened still with the affairs of life crawls into mortal existence. The years pass and the child again becomes a man. Still the tickers sound, still the struggle for gain goes on, again the back is bent by responsibilities, the life soured by unfulfilled desire until at last, carrying with him the same possessions that bowed his back before, the soul creeps away again to rest. Yet what is rest? Just more longing, more desire, more unrequited love. Thus age after age the Wheel of the Law goes round; age after age man comes and goes, bound to its spokes of agony, and this fools in their folly have termed *life*.

All this the opened eye of philosophy lays bare; all this the sage perceives with enlightened vision. He knows the unreality of heaven as well as hell. He realizes that both are but projections in the substances of a more subtle element of the same impulses which have taken a beautiful earth and made of it a breeding ground of greed and a house of discord. Death is not a liberation from ignorance, nor is it a solution to man's problem; neither is it the end of anything. Death is but an exchange of vestments; it is no cure for that sickness of the soul which the wise term *ignorance*. Back and forth between the chambers of life and death man passes until he wears ruts in the stony floor he treads. Yet he is never free for he escapes one prison but to enter another. With perennial hope he faces each new scene, only to find that he exchanges bad for worse.

Birth and death are illusionary in that they seem to be a change of state when in reality they are but a change of place. Though man were lifted to the heights of Olympus he would not be greater than himself; and though he were hurled downward to the depths of the inferno, no virtue that is innately his could be taken from him.

The philosopher realizes that these extremes are but illusions of his own mind and remains unmoved by either the sense of height or depth. Having mastered those attitudes and perceptions by which man is enslaved, he is free from life and death alike. He has found another door, so that he no longer travels between the two halves of the mortal sphere; but leaving the whole chamber of the world behind he ascends into that vast domain where walls are as distant as eternity and where limitations are measured by space alone. Therefore of him it is said that he has stepped down from the wheel and has broken the fetters that once bound him to necessity, for he has accomplished the necessary end: namely, realization of the unreality of mortality. He knows the import of the sage's words, that though a man die a thousand times yet shall he live; for he himself has died many times while still fastened to the wheel of sense. Reborn through the disciplines of philosophy he is no longer subject to death because he is no longer capable of desire. Desire breeds death, and he who has liberated himself from desire has liberated himself from death. Ignorance and death—which are synonymous in their inner nature—are indeed the last great adversary. He who vanquishes this twofold monster by that power which is the inevitable product of right-thinking, has achieved conscious and enduring immortality.

Life and death as we know them are but passing phases of existence. This does not mean that the philosopher achieves to the state of physical immortality, for no one who is wise desires to live forever in any one state. It means that the rational soul, neither slumbering nor sleeping but forever awake and contemplating the face of Truth, has been so liberated from the limitations of erroneous perceptions that, though bodies come and go, it remains unmoved, preserving forever that unobscured vision and unbroken continuity of reflections which alone constitutes immortality.

A quality characteristic of the gods is endurance, and man approaches to divinity when he increases the span of enduring consciousness. Physical matter must abide by the law of its own substance; hence to all things composed of physical substance dissolution is inevitable. As the animal nature is, philosophically, an exudation of the mortal substances, is ultimately dissipated with the decay of forms. Consequently, he who has placed all his faith in this decaying part shall experience mentally the blight of death for he shall behold the disintegration of that which he has pleased to term himself. If, however, he has established his rational and divine part as real, he shall remain unmoved when its inferior vehicle is dissipated, and because his faith is vested in Reality shall dwell forever in rapturous contemplation of permanence.

Life and death are measured by our belief, permanence is determined by our consciousness, and perfect immortality is achieved by perfect realization. Strangest of all, perfect immortality is synonymous with ultimate dissolution, and of all the illusions that must go, not the least is the illusion of individuality. Having completely mastered this, the last phase of death is conquered; for as long as man believes in individuality he fears that unknown but certain ultimate when individuality is dissolved back again into the universal state. It is strange but true that all the things man fears become the instruments of his liberation. Man fears the loss of individuality, yet perfection is not attainable without it. Man fears death, yet death is simply the necessary polarizing of life that he may endure until he has learned to exchange the living death of form for the deathless life of spirit. If it were not for the opportunity that death gives us to go behind the scenes occasionally, we might become so obsessed with the dream play of mortal life that we would never wake up to its unreality.

The process of alternating manifestation between the visible and invisible spheres of the inferior universe is erroneously termed metempsychosis. A swinging pendulum has been employed to symbolize that monotonous motion of the unawakened soul which results in the phenomena of successive lives and deaths. In the East Indian classics it is written that certain is death for the living and certain is life for the dead; but though the wheel spins incessantly, by the very nature of its motion it ends where it began. When the philosophers describe the descent of the soul into generation they do not mean what is now termed incarnation, but rather that the rational part has become immersed in the substances of a generated and generating world where it must remain until through the liberation of its innate rationality it escapes from the tangled web of sense and circumstance.

Pythagoras tells us that the sphere of Hades or Pluto extends downward from the Milky Way through the rings of the zodiac, the orbits of the planets, and the spheres of the elements. Pluto's domain is therefore synonymous with matter, not only matter that is physical but also its invisible counterpart from which the so-called invisible world is fashioned. The sphere of generation merely signifies that inferior part of Nature wherein manifestation depends upon the generation of vehicles. Generation is limited to the world of forms in that all forms are generations, being the temporary vehicles of ungenerated and immovable "souls". Physical bodies as we know them are generations in that they are the fashionings of an invisible agent who creates them for the peculiar workings of its will. The fact that the soul can fabricate a physical body is proof itself that the soul is manifesting upon the level of generation, and incarnation is that process whereby the spiritual nature establishes itself upon the level of generation in order to become the formator of innumerable corporeal vehicles. Having assumed the *idea* of generation, the soul is capable of generating, and bodies are its generations. In order to generate, the soul becomes individualized and ultimately abstractly personalized. Therefore it is said arcanely that there is a continuity of personality throughout the cycle of incarnation, but this personality is the soul personality posited at the apex, or causal point, of the triangle of the generating sphere.

The ancient philosophers affirmed that 777 physical earth lives constitute the incarnation of the human soul. Each of these earth lives is divided into a physical and superphysical part—life and death. Occupying the middle ground between the spiritual part and its generated vehicles, the soul hangs suspended from its own cause, and from it are suspended the physical personalities which manifest for a day, only to be dissolved by death into their primordial state. From this it is evident that the physical phenomena of life and death have little effect upon the spiritual status of the individual, for this status is actually measured by the degree to which he has disentangled his soul from the illusion of generation, and has no reference to the corporeal or incorporeal condition of his body. The true "fall" of man was the descent of his soul into the Cycle of Necessity or sphere of generation, and his true resurrection is the ascent of the soul to its former state of noninvolvement. Thus, life—both before and after death—is simply an allegorical ceremony during which, as in the pageantry of the Mysteries, a curious ritualism is performed which recapitulates upon the physical level the entire story of man's superphysical dilemma. The bodies shadow forth the rationality of the soul. While the idea of generation is upon the soul the bodies manifest the qualities of materiality. When the soul shakes off the drowsiness of the state of generation, the physical personalities which it objectifies manifest in an idealistic and spiritualized manner.

The consciousness of man is said to exist in three general states: in an unawakened state, an awakening state, and an awakened state. Those whose souls are wholly immersed in the illusion of form are declared to be asleep. Although they may manifest activity in the phenomenal sphere, this activity being of their outer and not their inner parts, is not regarded as an evidence of wakefulness. Such souls are symbolized as lying asleep throughout the span of life. Occasionally they are depicted as covered with cobwebs as symbolic of the weaving of their own fancies. Their bodies also are partly buried in that dust which collects upon all inert objects. This dust represents that inactivity which soon dulls the perception of the unwary, but which the just man shakes off by endeavor. Those to whom beauty means nothing, in whom there is no desire to better an imperfect state, who live but to gratify the appetites of the flesh, are the sleeping ones who, after passing unawakened through the span of physical existence enter into the invisible world, there to lie in rows still sleeping as they slept while in the physical world. After a time these sleeping souls

drift back again, take upon themselves bodies, sleep through another life cycle, and continue this procedure until finally innate Divinity, by the agency of some dire necessity, is aroused and animated to cast off its robes of lethargy.

The second group—the wakening souls—are those in whom realization, while not perfected, has become an element in the cultural life. Physical existence has come to be recognized as a period of endeavor through which the divine potentialities must be liberated from the winding-sheet of matter. Through the periods of both life and death such a soul is consecrated to the attainment of wisdom. All change is regarded as fresh opportunity, and with faith in ultimate perfection the seeker eagerly pursues the quest of Self.

The third group—the awakened souls—are those who have cast off the graveclothes of limitation and made their escape from generation, exchanging the alternation of mortal life for the continued awareness of the inner existence. They are masters not only of the so-called terrestrial state, but having liberated their souls from the idea of generation they ascend to that truly incorporeal world where the soul is united with the true substances of its own being and where, dwelling in its own state, it is said to abide in a state of perfect felicity.

Let us next consider the role played by love in the periodic comings and goings of the soul while in the state of generation. The law of the intellect is reason, the law of the soul is love, and the law of the body is generation. It follows that while each of these spheres is amicable toward its own qualities, when these qualities are combined to form a compound, friction results. Paracelsus tells us that the elementals, or Nature spirits, live for hundreds of years because, composed of a single principle, there is the minimum of friction between their parts. To reason, established in its own essence and functioning according to its own laws, love is thus inexplicable; likewise, the physical nature, which is established in and exists through generation, views both reason and love as antagonistic. The plans of reason are frequently thwarted by the claims of love; and both reason and love are often overwhelmed by the dictates of the animal nature, though reason unfailingly reminds the latter of its own insufficiency. Hence, the inconstancy of human attitudes is primarily due to the lack of a common denominator.

Plato defined love as the longing of diversity for unity; the desire of parts to be brought together to form wholes; the instinctive urge of all creatures toward a perfect state. Realizing that reality increases in proportion as diversity is overcome, the rational soul rejoices in the union of incomplete natures; for even the least perfect of such unions contributes to the unity of the whole. The same urge that first causes souls to come into generation and unite themselves with corporeal substances later causes them, after they dissociate themselves from corporeal substances, to rise toward and mingle themselves with spiritual Reality.

As the essential unity of reality is apparently broken up by its descent into the sphere of generation, a condition ensues common only, however,, to such as have assumed the reality of diversity. Laboring under the illusion of separateness, the fractional parts function in the consciousness of isolation. Probably no feeling can sweep over the nature of man more terrifying than that which causes him to feel absolutely alone. This *aloneness* means the stifling of all expression. Joy and sorrow alike must be relieved by expression; otherwise they infect the temperament with a curious disease which Robert Burton rather inadequately terms *melancholy*. This feeling of isolation is invariably accompanied by one of utter hopelessness, for man is essentially a social animal. While his unenlightened animal sociability causes him to seek the companionship of the phantoms of matter, still it is a necessary though imperfect expression of that spiritual quality which will ultimately unite him with the whole order of being.

Physical life may be likened to a gloomy dungeon where those convicted of "materiality" sit in solitary confinement, each in his own little cell. Like the prisoner of Chillon, who vainly longed for the blue sky and the comrades of yore, the soul of man locked in the life of form yearns for companionship and understanding. In the Tarot cards is one called Temperance, showing a winged figure pouring water from one urn into another. In the Cabala also it is declared that Chochmah flows into Binah; that is, Wisdom flows into Understanding. As man at Nirvana inverts that bowl which he calls himself, and pours his soul into the Infinite, so throughout all the ages of his unfoldment there is within his life an inherent urge to flow forth and mingle with other lives in a mystical communion.

The irrational soul is ever building walls which the rational soul is ever tearing down. The irrational soul is ever emphasizing the intervals which separate living creatures, which intervals the rational soul annihilates by the realization that the divine nature can be limited by no place or condition. The mythological "marriages" of the gods signify the union of a principle with its form, for the god is a creative principle and his consort is the vehicle of that principle. Thus when the soul enters into generation a mystic marriage takes place in which a rational agent is wedded to the sphere of generation which is to be its vehicle of manifestation. At death when the rational soul casts off generation another marriage takes place in which the rational agent, having divorced its inferior part, is united by a symbolic ceremony to the sphere of liberation.

Several philosophies differ as to the place occupied by sex in the Cycle of Necessity. Those who assert that sex is differentiated in the spiritual nature itself maintain an untenable hypothesis, since it is philosophically evident that spirit, which partakes of the divine wholeness though containing the potentiality of diversity, does not manifest that diversity while in a spiritual state. While *androgynous* may not be the true defining term, it may be employed to express the undivided state of sex in spirit, where it exists in no form other than that of a latent attribute. This theory brings up the inevitable question: If spirit is inherently androgynous and perfect, why should it manifest through a vehicle less perfect in gender? The common theory of a divided spirit, with the resultant quest of the severed parts for each other, has proved to be more poetical than practical; for unity, which is the primary attribute of the causal nature is destroyed if two complete organisms are postulated as manifesting independently from a single cause. The modern woman, moreover, has registered in unmistakable fashion her dislike to be considered a subordinate or vagrant fraction of the masculine temperament.

The secret schools of ancient philosophy postulated man as a twofold entity, which when masculine in its outer nature was feminine in its inner nature, and vice versa. In each sex, therefore, one pole is objectified and the other subjectified—one nature facing outward and the other facing inward. Each sex possesses the qualities of the other, but manifests them in an inhibited degree. Human love may be defined as a reciprocal emotion in which the subjectified nature of one person is stimulated by contact with the objectified nature of another. Affection is therefore an activity, both synchronous and reciprocal, in which the subjectified nature in one person flows toward its own objectified fullness in the other, while its own objectified fullness flows into the privation of its own quality; namely, the subjectified nature of the other.

Among the secret instructions of the Mysteries was one concerning the law which is known to various schools as the Law of Consequence, Compensation, Karma, or Cause and Effect. That a principle flowing from itself must always act in conformity with the laws responsible for its own existence, is undeniable. For example, good must always manifest according to the nature of good. But as the flow recedes from its own source it partakes ever less of the virtue of proximity to that source, and consequently may exist in every conceivable degree of its own quality. Each active agent is surrounded by its own effulgence. This effulgence is the natural radiance of life, and "tinctures" according to the nature of the radiating agent all that is brought into proximity thereto. The agent may therefore be conceived as the *cause;* the inevitable flow of the agent in conformity to its own nature, the *effect.* Hence karma may be defined as ignorance moving in accordance with its own nature, and producing conditions in harmony with its own inherent state.

The doctrine that "Whatsoever a man soweth, that shall he also reap" is based upon the Law of Consequence—the inevitability of action following reaction and reaction following action *ad infinitum*. A vicious circle is thus created in which every cause becomes an effect and every effect becomes a cause. Here again is the Cycle of Necessity—a wheel of incident without beginning and without end. It is as necessary to step down from the wheel of cause and effect as it is to leave the wheel of life and death; for in the last analysis cause and life and effect and death are correlative terms. As life generates death and death generates life, so action generates reaction and reaction generates action; and to this sequence there is neither beginning nor end. Melchizedek, the Initiate-King of Salem, was declared to have been "above the law"; for karma has no control over such as are reborn out of the irrational into the rational state. Karma is the law by which irrationality multiplies itself, perpetuates its kind, and ultimately dissolves all creation in a holocaust of retribution.

Karma is the law of generation applied to action by which deeds are caused to reproduce their kind. It has been well said that laws are made for those who break them. This is particularly true of karma, which applies only to those irrational creatures who, due to the clouding of their rational perceptions, are capable of functioning in a manner productive of destructive reaction. It is also stated that there is not only "evil" karma but also "good" karma. In the same way "good" karma is simply constructive action generating its own kind. But as action, both destructive and constructive, partakes of the illusion of matter—for action is the motion of material agents—so the laws of action ond reaction, like those of life and death, are dissipated by philosophy which, by annihilating diversity, destroys the field in which these illusionary elements arrange themselves in complicated pattern.

Action is a dependency of place, for it signifies the flow of a life or condition out from self into not-self. Diodorus declared motion to be impossible in that it depended for its reality upon the passing of a body from the place where it is into the place where it is not, and all bodies must ever occupy the place where they are. While this statement may appear ridiculous to the uninitiated, it is based upon the philosophic verity that life is without interval, and consequently incapable of action. For example, the processes taking place within life itself by which it generates form, cannot actually be termed action in that they are fourth-dimensional, coming under none of the recognizable classifications of physical activity. Bodies, however, existing in place are capable of rearrangement and of being moved about through the medium or interval in which they exist. Among the ancients activity was considered an attribute of form and karma its correlative. The philosophic discipline consequently liberates man from all the confining bonds of matter, elevating him to that estate wherein he may truthfully say, "I am the master of my fate, I am the captain of my soul." It should not be inferred, however that philosophy liberates man from the natural reactions of his actions, but rather that it liberates him from that sphere of activity which is productive of reaction.

To escape from this vast turmoil of ephemeral agencies which we call mortal existence, it is necessary to discipline the rational faculties to the realization of permanence. In other words, the disciple must come to *know* that he is an enduring and imperishable creature entirely beyond the reach of demons dwelling in the darkness of the corporeal sphere. Like Dante, he wanders through an inferno which has no power over him other than the power he bestows upon it by acceptance of its reality. Though man be in the world, he is not of the world. That part of him which is fabricated from the illusional substances is, like Caliban, but a grotesque and unruly monster which must serve the will of the enlightened *magus*. To know the actual relationships existing between the parts of ourselves gives the power to directionalize these agencies toward the accomplishment of our own purposes. He who knows his body to be a body has a useful, if somewhat temperamental, servitor; but he who conceives his body to be himself has elevated a moron to power, and is destined to feel the iron heel of an irrational despot upon his neck.

It is essential that the student of ancient metaphysics regard himself as a permanent and immovable point which from the exaltedness of its own dignity gazes forth upon the phantasmagoria of outer existence. Such a one regards his own bodies as shadows that encircle him, as planets encircle their sovereign sun. All his forms he views as something apart from himself for he is formless, and though functioning in a sphere of generation he is not deluded by his workmanship. Gazing upon the personalities he has objectified, he must say:

"I am not they. They come forth from me to do my bidding and furnish the garment of my experience. They are like hands and feet which move at my command, and withdraw themselves from outer objects at my will. These shadows live and die, yet I am not born with their birth nor do I cease with their dying. Their coming and going alike are incidental, and have no effect upon my solidarity. Immersed in the confusion of mortality these shadows experience the twin illusions of joy and sorrow, health and sickness, gain and loss. Yet if they gain all the shadows of possession and encompass the whole illusion, they are no greater than before; for the thing they gain is nothing and the thing they lose is of equal value. If one of these shadows rises to great dignity and becomes a ruler of all the rest, what is he but nothing ruling nothing? If in despair these shadows wander about, is not their despair—like their joy—but a dream which fades into the nothingness that is its essential nature when the dreamer awakes? I close my eyes and, lo, a world of phantoms is imaged in the nothingness that I behold. These phantoms engage in intensive labors, concerning themselves with the weighty problems of their dream existence. At last I tire of sleeping, and exhausted with my own rest I open my eyes. The empire of my sleep dissolves as though it had never been; the vast but ghostly enterprises have no more substance than those who served them. In the daylight of conscious wakefulness all the shadows of the darkness melt away, to leave in their stead only a vast expanse of luminosity. The many have vanished and the one remains. Instead of worlds there is only the I—the eternal and unchanging Self which dreams creation, and upon its awakening dissipates the whole."

But woe unto him who in his dream unites himself with his shadows and loses sight of his mastery over them; for he then assumes the concerns of his phantom forms. He struggles for the achievements of ephemerality; he seeks to build empire out of a dream, only to finally discover the senselessness of the fabric with which he wrought, since permanence cannot be fashioned out of impermanent stuff. Then the self is tormented with every problem of the not-self; the joys and sorrows man images become so real that the goodness of life is blotted out, and crushing despair broods over all. The wise live not in dreams nor in the world of dreams, but in Reality. They have opened their eyes and scattered forever the shades of night; they have left behind the trooping pageantry of incident, and upon the solid foundation of eternal and enduring Self have builded a destiny that shall not pass away.

THE VARAHA INCARNATION OF VISHNU

There was once a Daitya who desired to rule the earth. He grew so powerful that he stole the planet and carried it with him into the depths of the ocean. Vishnu, in the form of a boar, dived into the abyss and slaying the evil one restored the earth by raising it upon his tusks.

CHAPTER TEN

Pagan Theogony and Cosmogony

FROM the Greek mythology that had its genesis in the revelations of Orpheus and its efflorescence in the erudition of Plato, the Neoplatonists extracted a sublime philosophy. In his introduction to *The Six Books of Proclus on the Theology of Plato*, Thomas Taylor writes: "According to this theology, therefore, from the immense principle of principles, in which all things casually subsist, absorbed in superessential light, and involved in unfathomable depths, a beauteous progeny of principles proceed, all largely partaking of the ineffable, all stamped with the occult characters of deity, all possessing an overflowing fullness of good. From these dazzling summits, these ineffable blossoms, these divine propagations, being, life, intellect, soul, nature, and body depend; *monads* suspended from *unities*, deified natures proceeding from deities. Each of these monads, too, is the leader of a series which extends from itself to the last of things, and which while it proceeds from, at the same time abides in, and returns to its leader. And all these principles and all their progeny are finally centered and rooted by their summits in the first great all-comprehending one. Thus all beings proceed from, and are comprehended in the first being; all intellects emanate from one first intellect; all souls from one first soul; all natures blossom from one first nature; and all bodies proceed from the vital and luminous body of the world. And lastly, all these great monads are comprehended in the first one, from which both they and all their depending series are unfolded into light. Hence, this first one is truly the unity of unities, the monad of monads, the principle of principles, the God of Gods, one and all things, and yet one prior to all."

The concluding sentence of the quotation establishes beyond all cavil the monotheistic foundation of Greek philosophy. In fact, to the discerning it is basically a philosophic atheism, for this Supreme Deity actually is neither a personality nor a principle, but the principle of principles, the most abstract of the most abstract, so universalized and unlimited in its inherent nature as to be incomprehensible. When such a deity is compared with the popular theological concept of a personal God, the supremacy of philosophy's God is at once apparent. The God of ancient philosophy is the Deity whose sufficiency will yet be vindicated by modern science. Men will never outgrow the God of Plato, but one by one the Gods of creeds and sects will be driven from their thrones by the unfolding intellect of man. The modern world already demands the abdication of that despotic regent who has ruled the universe for the past few thousand years.

The foregoing quotation also reveals how from this first and perfect unity infinite diversity proceeds in sequential order. Simple monotheism thus manifests through a complex polytheism, and the gods are demonstrated as philosophically necessary to the orderly workings of the Divine Plan. On the subject of the gods proceeding from the nature of simple unity, Thomas Taylor further writes:

"For if whatever possesses a power of generating, generates similars prior to dissimilars, every cause must deliver its own form and characteristic peculiarity to its progeny; and before it generates that which gives subsistence to progressions far distant and separate from its nature, it must constitute things proximate to itself according to essence, and conjoined with it through similitude. It is therefore necessary from these premises, since there is one unity the principle of the universe, that this unity should produce from itself, prior to everything else, a multitude of natures characterized by unity, and a number the most of all things allied to its cause; and these natures are no other than the Gods."

The principle of emanationism as unfolded in the Orphic theogony became the vital doctrine of the Gnostics, who conceived a spiritual hierarchy as occupying each degree of the interval between the extremes of First Cause and Nature. The seven grand divisions into which existence is divided are termed in Neoplatonism: (1) The Principle of Principles, which is inscrutable and analogous to the threefold darkness of the Egyptians; (2) Being, the first point of the Triad of Cause; (3) Life; (4) Intellect, which completes the Triad of Causes; (5) Soul, which is the apex of the Triad of Generation; (6) Nature; and (7) Body, which completes the Triad of Generation. Thus is revealed the order by which Cause flows into Generation and eventually produces bodies, the latter being objectifications in matter of superphysical paradigms or archetypes.

As certain monadic forces are thus suspended from the Supreme Unity, so this design of diversity suspended from unity is an invariable pattern throughout creation. Each item of diversity then becomes in its own nature a unity, from which is further suspended another chain of diversity, and so on *ad infinitum*. For example, from the immense Principle of Principles as the Supreme Monad are suspended the divine principles of Being, Life, Intellect, Soul, Nature, and Body. Each of these becomes, in turn, a monadic unit. From Being are suspended beings; from Life, lives; from Intellect, intellects; from Soul, souls; from Nature, natures; and from Body, bodies.

It naturally follows that all bodies partake of the qualities of the principle of Body and are manifestations of it; all souls partake of the principle of Soul; and all beings partake of the principle of Being. The principle of Body exists throughout all the chain of emanations intervening between its primal manifestation from the Absolute and such bodies as stones and trees which exist temporarily in this ephemeral sphere. There are divine bodies, luminous and splendid; there are immortal bodies, transcendent in power; and there are mortal bodies, subject to continual evil and decay. The greater the interval between the principle of Body and the subordinate body suspended from that principle, the lower the quality and organization of that body. The world as a body and the worm as a body are both suspended from the principle of Body. The worm, however, is suspended from a monad far more remote from the principle of Body than is the world, for the worm, being part of the life of the world, is a minute part of the diversity from one of the countless monads suspended from the body of the world itself. Herein is revealed the mystery of Adam, for as Philo Judaeus affirms, Adam is actually the monad of mankind. Human beings therefore derive their human qualities from their participation in the nature of this prototypic monad. Thus from the Adamic monad are suspended the hundred of millions of individualized men and women who, when considered as a unit, constitute a single male and female creature—the first and supreme man, the *idea* of mankind, the Adamic unity.

The theogony of Orpheus as set forth by Hesiod and interpreted by Proclus is divisible into three major parts, of which the first (in the words of Rev. James Davies) is concerned with cosmogony, or the creation of the world, its powers, and its fabric. The second part, or theogony proper, is concerned with the generations of the gods, and records the histories of the dynasties of Cronus and Zeus. The third part is concerned in a fragmentary way with the generation of heroes, who sprang from the intercourse of mortals with immortals. Both space and the purposes of this chapter limit us to a consideration of the first (or cosmological) division, together with a brief outline of the generation of Cronus and the rebellion of the Titans.

In the beginning, declare the Orphic fragments, was the Absolute—unborn, unaging, and undying Time. Here Time is conceived to be in a state of suspension; for as Time depends for its reality upon the succession of incidents, it cannot exist actively until the establishment of the worlds. Time is the perfect *Wholeness* which encompasses all manifestations as a mysterious intangible envelope. Within the divine sphere of Time existences live and move and have their being. From this inscrutable *Wholeness* there issue forth two agents designated Ether and Chaos, or the *Bound* and the *Infinity*. Thus in the terms of the ancient symbolism, "the One becomes the Two." The first of these agents—Ether—is called the *Bound* because as a symbol of primordial activity it is limited as to place, condition, and duration. Chaos, which in some systems of cosmogony is elevated to the position of first deity, takes second place, when compared to the enduring *Wholeness*. Being unlimited, unorganized, and without sense of Time, it is properly termed *Infinity*.

These two opposites—*Bound* and *Infinity*—acting each upon the other, destroy the placidity of the eternal state. Ether, the active agent, is symbolized as a vast whirlwind which moves the surface of Chaos, and out of its unorganized substances forms a great ovoid, termed by the ancients the Orphic or Cosmic Egg. This Egg is usually represented as encircled by the coils of a great serpent (the Ether). The substances of the Egg, having been impregnated by the divine Ether, "increase from within outward." The fertilized Egg expands and finally bursts asunder to reveal the Triple-Dragon God *Phanes*, who is called the "Divine or Absolute Animal." Phanes is described as "an incorporeal God, bearing golden wings on his shoulders; but in his inward parts naturally possessing the heads of bulls, upon which heads a mighty dragon appears, invested with the various forms of wild beasts." The point is also repeatedly emphasized that Phanes, while possessing wings and a human head, is without a body, his entire being consisting of a vast ring of radiant effulgence. The ancient commentaries (especially those of the Neoplatonists) identify Phanes with the Cherubim of Ezekiel and the composite monster of the Chaldaic-Egyptian Mysteries. The bull's head signify the constellation of Taurus; the lion's head, which Phanes is sometimes said to have, is the constellation of Leo; the dragon is the constellation of Scorpio; and the human head with wings upon its neck is the constellation of the god-man, Aquarius. Thus the four hierarchies called the Lords of Generation are set forth.

In the Christian system these animals and winged creatures are ascribed to the four Evangelists to indicate that the Gospels are the source of spiritual life. The specially emphasized fact that the head of Phanes is without a body reminds the disciple that the lower or bodily universe has not yet become objectified, but remains as an unapplied idea of the first deity. Several early mythologists divided the Egg of Cosmos into an upper and a lower hemisphere, the upper composed of gold and the lower of silver. Similarly, in the images of Zeus the eyes are sometimes inlaid with silver to indicate his sovereignty over the inferior (or lower) hemisphere of creation. It is also stated that after breaking open to release the radiant Phanes, the upper part of the Universal Egg became the Intellectual Universe and the lower part the Sensible Universe. This is paralleled in the story of creation according to Genesis, where it is related that the waters which were above the heavens were divided from the waters which were below the firmament. The interval between the two sundered hemispheres of the egg was called Heaven, and here the light of Phanes was diffused throughout the elements of the Intelligible Sphere. It is most significant that Heaven should be located between the extremes of Intellect and Sense, since its correlate in the body—the heart—is situated between the intellectual nature above and the animal nature below.

Phanes is referred to as the "triple God" because he is a triad of powers, with himself as the principle, or monad, and Ericapaeus and Metis as his lesser aspects. As Phanes represents spiritual light and life, it is natural that his consort, or *Sakti*, should represent spiritual darkness, or the medium through which this light manifests. The Mother of the Gods was therefore called Threefold Night, and she alone mingled in perfect union with Phanes, who is described as giving to her his scepter that she might in queenly manner rule his world. By right of her threefold powers Night brought forth two children, the first of her progeny, called Heaven and Earth. The latter is to be understood as a divine cosmic earth, and not the terrestrial globe with which we are familiar. One of the chief sources of confusion in the study of ancient systems of cosmogony arises from the effort to relate such terms as *earth* and *world* to our own physical system, when in reality they refer to invisible superphysical spheres—the archetypes of the inferior generations which are to follow. The Heaven and Earth born of the union of Night and Phanes are the spheres of the *noumenon* and *phenomenon* which form such essential elements in the philosophy of Immanuel Kant.

Heaven and Earth are then united in marriage, and in the words of G. R. S. Mead, "From their union arises a strange and curious progeny, the Fates (Parcæ), Hundred-handed (Centimani), and They-who-see-all-round (Cyclopes). * * * The Fates are the Karmic Powers, which adjust all things according to the causes of prior Universe; while the Centimani and Cyclopes are the Builders, or rather the Overseers or Noetic Architects, who supervise the Builders of the Sensible Universe. * * * These were the first progeny of Heaven and Earth, and were cast down to Tartarus, for they worked within all things, and so, as evolution proceeded, permeated every kingdom of nature. But then, without the knowledge of Heaven, Earth brought forth, says Orpheus (Proc. *Tim., iii.* 137), 'seven fair daughters, bright-eyed, pure, and seven princely sons, covered with hair;' and these are called the 'avengers of their brethren.' And the names of the daughters are Themis and Tethys, Mnemosyne and Thea, Dione and Phœbe, and Rhea; and of the sons, Cœus and Crius, Phorcys and Cronus, Oceanus and Hyperion, and Iapetus (Proc. *op. cit.*, v.295). And these are the Titans." (See *Orpheus*.)

Under the leadership of Cronus all the Titans save Oceanus rebelled against Heaven and established the Material Sphere. Cronus became the ruler of the Titans, which position he held until Zeus, leading his giants, overthrew the empire of Cronus and established the Physical Universe. We are told in the commentaries that the last of the heavenly line is Bacchus, in whom the generations of Uranus, or Heaven, are complete. In the Orphic theogony then follows the order of the supermundane and mundane gods, with accounts of the heroes and those who were elevated to a parity with divinity because of the immortal spirit that led them to the pinnacle of achievement.

This sublime philosophy, which clothes cosmic processes in personalities and reveals by their combinations the wonders of the Intelligible Sphere, has been debased to the point where it is now regarded as merely a collection of myths suitable only for the amusement of the adolescent and the dotard, or to furnish poets with the inspiration for a bare existence. Perpetuated thus in all its outer form in Bullfinch's *Age of Fable,* the theology by which Plato lived and died is now looked upon as something outlived or as having overshot the mark. The Orphics, however, thought truly and wrote well. Their theology cannot die, but shall survive every device created to destroy it, and in a more philosophic era in the future shall shine forth again with splendor undiminished.

It is now established beyond reasonable doubt that the Vedic writings of the Hindus were the chief contributions to the exalted structure of Orphic theogony. It is even asserted that the first Orpheus was a Hindu. A number of early Greek philosophers, moreover—prominent among them Thales and Pythagoras—were initiated into the Mysteries of the Brahmans. There is also a legend to the effect that Osiris, the black god of Egypt, journeyed to that land from Asia, establishing in the Double Empire of the Nile his Mysteries patterned after those of the Brahmans. Whether these founders of philosophic systems were actual personalities or personifications of their doctrines cannot be determined definitely at this late period. It is not at all improbable that the journeys presumably taken by such demigods as Orpheus and Osiris arcanely signify the migrations westward of the cults of the primitive Asiatic Aryans. When compared with the Oriental creation myths it is evident that the Greek fables appear fragmentary and obscure; for the early Brahman sages were unquestionably the greatest abstract thinkers whose doctrines have survived to this day.

That eminent student of Vedic philosophy, the Hon. H. H. Wilson, in a footnote on Indian mythology and tradition was moved to write: "As, however, the Grecian accounts, and those of the Egyptians, are much more perplexed and unsatisfactory than those of the Hindus, it is most probable that we find amongst them the doctrine in its most original as well as most methodical and significant form." Having given a brief outline of the Orphic cosmogony, we next turn to the more ancient Brahman theory in order to make possible a comparison between these two philosophic systems. The Vedic creation myth as set forth in the opening chapters of *The Vishnu Purana* may be summarized as follows:

The sage, Parasara, discourses with his disciple, Maitreya (not the Bodhisattva), concerning Vasudeva (the indwelling radiance) and how it came forth to manifest creation. Parasara begins his account with this prayer:

"Glory to the unchangeable, holy, eternal, supreme Vishnu, of one universal nature, the mighty over all: to him who is Hiranygarbha, Hari, and Sankara, the creator, the preserver, and destroyer of the world: to Vasudeva, the liberator of his worshippers: to him whose essence is both single and manifold; who is both subtle and corporeal, indiscrete and discrete: to Vishnu, the cause of final emancipation. Glory to the supreme Vishnu, the cause of the creation, existence, and end of this world; who is the root of the world, and who consists of the world."

Upon completion of his prayer Parasara enters upon the main theme of his discourse with the declaration that Brahma —the supreme, eternal, unborn, imperishable, and undecaying lord—first exists in the forms of Purusha (spirit) and Kala (time). From Purusha next proceeded two other forms called the discrete and the indiscrete. Thus primary matter, spirit, visible substance, and time, are declared by the wise to be the pure and supreme condition of Vishnu, which is Brahma in the state of quiescence. In his opening prayer Parasara refers to Vishnu (who, in the terms of the Greek Platonists would be the Power, or second person of the Brahmanic Triad and consequently its active part) as Hiranygarbha (meaning the Brahma who is born from the golden egg), Hari (which is Vishnu as the lord of goodness), and Sankara (or Shiva, the destroyer). Taking upon himself the capacity of Brahma, Vishnu becomes the creator; assuming the nature of Shiva, or Rudra, he is the destroyer; and in his true nature as Vishnu he is in equilibrium between them.

In a footnote to the description of the four elements composing the nature of Vishnu, Prof. Wilson states that the Purusha, or spirit of the Hindus, is analogous to the Phanes of the Orphics; Pradhana or primary matter, to the Orphic Chaos; and Kala, or time, to the Orphic Cronus. As Phanes consisted of a triad of powers, so Pradhana is declared to be endowed with three qualities in equilibrium, and to be the mother of the world. Therefore it is written: "There was neither day nor night, nor sky nor earth, nor darkness nor light, nor any other thing, save only One, unapprehensible by intellect, or That which is Brahma and Puman (spirit) and Phadhana (matter)."

It is then written that the supreme Brahma of his own will enters into spirit and matter, and the season of creation having arrived, agitates the mutable and immutable principles. This is accomplished in an occult manner. "As fragrance affects the mind from its proximity merely, and not from any immediate operation upon mind itself: so the Supreme influenced the elements of creation." From these equilibrated qualities proceeds the unequal development of these qualities, which is termed the principle Mahat or Intellect. The creator then invents the great principle Intellect, which is termed Iswara, the manifested creator. Mahat then becomes threefold, and its phases are termed the threefold Egotism.

The Vishnu Purana continues: "Elementary Egotism then becoming productive, as the rudiment of sound, produced from it Ether, of which sound is the characteristic, investing it with its rudiment of sound. Ether becoming productive, engendered the rudiments of touch; when originated strong wind, the property of which is touch; and Ether, with the rudiment of sound, enveloped the rudiment of touch. Then wind becoming productive, produced the rudiment of form (colour); when light (or fire) proceeded, of which, form (colour) is the attribute; and the rudiment of touch enveloped the wind with the rudiment of colour. Light becoming productive, produced the rudiment of taste; whence proceed all juices in which flavor resides; and the rudiment of colour invested the juices with the rudiment of taste. The waters becoming productive, engendered the rudiments of smell; whence an aggregate (earth) originates, of which smell is the property."

When the rudiments had united themselves with the properties here described they assumed the character of one mass which, directed by spirit and with the acquiescence of the indiscrete Principle, Intellect, and the rest, formed an egg which gradually expanded like a bubble of water. "This vast egg, O sage, compounded of the elements, and resting on the waters, was the excellent natural abode of Vishnu in the form of Brahma; and there Vishnu, the lord of the universe, whose essence is inscrutable, assumed a perceptible form, and even he himself abided in it in the character of Brahma. Its womb, vast as the mountain Meru, was composed of the mountains; and the mighty oceans were the waters that filled its cavity. In that egg, O Brahman, were the continents and seas and mountains, the planets and divisions of the universe, the gods, the demons, and mankind. And this egg was externally invested by seven natural envelopes, or by water, air, fire, ether, and Ahankara, the origin of the elements, each tenfold the extent of that which it invested; next came the principle of Intelligence; and finally, the whole was surrounded by the indiscrete Principle: resembling thus the cocoanut, filled interiorly with pulp, and exteriorly covered by husk and rind."

Vishnu as the principle of immeasurable power and the quality of goodness preserves these creations through successive ages until the end of a Kalpa, or period. Then he assumes the form of Rudra and swallows up the universe. "Having thus devoured all things, and converted the world into one vast ocean, the Supreme reposes upon his mighty serpent couch amidst the deep: he awakes after a season and again, as Brahma, becomes the author of creation. Thus the one only god, Janarddana (the object of mortal adoration), takes the designation of Brahma, Vishnu, and Siva, accordingly as he creates, preserves, or destroys. Vishnu as creator, creates himself; as preserver, preserves himself; as destroyer, destroys himself at the end of all things."

The Kalpa (or day of Brahma) is the period of manifestation of a creation, and at the end thereof the Mighty One retires into himself for an equal period, after which he comes forth again in a new creation. From the method employed to calculate time in *The Vishnua Purana,* figures are obtained which are overwhelming in their magnitude. For example, each year of human reckoning is divided into two parts to signify the six-month periods during which the sun is north and south of the equator. These periods are called respectively a day and a night of the gods. Twelve thousand divine years, each year consisting of 360 such days of the gods, constitute a great age (or aggregate of four lesser ages called Yugas) by which the activity of the world is measured. A thousand of these great ages are termed a day of Brahma, and fourteen lords, or Manus, rule over this vast period. Prof Wilson estimates a Kalpa to be 4,320,000,000 years, or the great day of Brahma. The life of Brahma consists of one hundred years made up of such great days, or 155,520,000,000,000 mortal years. The last great Kalpa (which is called Padma, or the lotus) closed the first half of Brahma's existence. The present Kalpa (which is called the Varaha, or boar, Kalpa) ushers in the second half of Brahma's life.

Parasara then describes how at the beginning of the present Kalpa, Narayana (he who moves upon the waters) brought forth the earth and re-established the generations. It should be borne in mind that the beginning of a Kalpa is the reawakening of Brahma from his night of rest, and is not a complete creation; for things already exist in a suspended state, in which condition they have remained through the sleep of the gods. At the beginning of a Kalpa, therefore, the creation is in reality a reorganization of already existing elements. It is written: "At the close of the past (or Padma) Kalpa, the divine Brahma, endowed with the quality of goodness, awoke from his night of sleep, and beheld the universe void."

Realizing the earth (in the sense of cosmos) to be concealed in the depths of the great waters, Brahma assumed the figure of a huge boar, as in previous Kalpas he had taken upon himself other forms. Thus embodied he plunged into the great ocean.

The earth, beholding his approach to restore her to her ancient dignity, recited a hymn in his honor in which she glorified his powers. The mighty boar, pleased with the chanting, emitted a low murmuring sound and then lifted upon his ample tusks the globe of the world. Filled with delight at beholding the trembling boar as he rose up dripping with moisture, the sages residing continually in the sphere of the saints sang praises to the stern-eyed upholder of the universe after this fashion:

"Triumph, lord of lords supreme; Kesava, sovereign of the earth, the wielder of the mace, the shell, the discus, and the sword: cause of production, destruction, and existence. THOU ART, oh god: there is no other supreme condition, but thou. Thou, lord, art the person of sacrifice: for thy feet are the Vedas; thy tusks are the stake to which the victim is bound; in thy teeth are the offerings; thy mouth is the altar; thy tongue is the fire; and the hairs of thy body are the sacrificial grass. Thine eyes, oh omnipotent, are day and night; thy head is the seat of all, the place of Brahma; thy name is all the hymns of the Vedas; thy nostrils are all oblations: oh thou, whose snout is the ladle of oblation; whose deep voice is the chanting of the Sama veda; whose body is the hall of sacrifice; whose joints are the different ceremonies; and whose ears have the properties of both voluntary and obligatory rites: do thou, who art eternal, who art in size a mountain, be propitious."

Quickly raising up the world the great boar placed it on the "summit" of the ocean, where it floats like a mighty vessel sustained by its expansive surface. Then "he who never wills in vain" divided the world into portions, seven in number (the planes). He likewise created the spheres of the elements and the worlds of the immortals, and prepared for the coming of organized life which was to blossom forth again spontaneously after the Pralaya (or sleep of the great night). From this point Brahma concerns himself with the orders of mundane life and the re-establishment of his faith and order among men. (Those who desire complete details of the story are referred to *The Vishnu Purana* as translated from the original Sanscrit by H. H. Wilson, or the *Vishnupuranam* in prose English translation by Manmatha Nath Dutt.)

Whereas the Greek and Brahman creation myths are comparatively well-known to scholars, the subjects of Chinese cosmogony and theogony have received little or no consideration in the Western world. Hence in the study of comparative cosmologies we may consider with profit the Chinese doctrine concerning the origin and procession of the worlds. For such purpose no more ancient or venerable authority can be found in Chinese literature than the *Yih King,* or *The Classic of Change,* which is devoted to an interpretation of the trigrams of Fuh-He and which also contains a lengthy commentary by Confucius. Upon approaching this subject the student is surprised at the definite and direct treatment, reminiscent of the Greek style, that pervades the entire scheme. The purity, the simplicity, and the dignity of Chinese philosophy are a real joy to the Occidental thinker, as well as a pronounced relief from the involved and rambling procedures of Western cults.

By way of introduction, the whole pagan universe is regarded as being alive. Nowhere in it is death to be found—only continual change accompanied always by a certain sense of continual improvement and a hazy, yet intriguing, promise of ultimate accomplishment. It is unfortunate that Christian theology could not have perpetuated the magnificent pagan concept of a pulsating, vibrant universe instead of a world in which everything is dead except God in his threefold nature, man, the angelic orders, and a motley assortment of devils. In China there is a famous saying: "The *living* Heaven and the *living* Earth." The Rev. Canon McClatchie, for 25 years a Christian missionary, and a student of Chinese philosophy, writes: "Our Christian ideas teach us that the Heaven above us, and the Earth beneath our feet, are composed of dead matter; whereas the pagans one and all, have ever regarded these as Beings endowed with life, and informed by a living soul (or 'Mind' as they generally designate it) which rules and governs the world just as the soul does the human body."

Western theology ostensibly postulates the earth as simply a mass of inert substance slipped in under a falling humanity to prevent it from dropping through space indefinitely. Not so long ago theologians viewed heaven as a great dome with the constellations suspended like elaborate chandeliers from its inner surface, these lights owing their existence presumably to the fact that Divinity trusted creation so little that he feared to leave his children alone in the dark. Somewhere also in this most substantial vault was a ventilator or skylight which could be opened to permit the descent of the New Jerusalem suspended on four cables and a windlass. Invidious comparisons made by Christian writers as between pagan and Christian theoolgies demonstrate the perennial difficulty of creeds to see the beam in their own eyes; for in no respect is the heaven of theology a worthy substitute for the heaven of pagan philosophy, and nowhere among the cultured pagans do we find a concept of the universe so hopelessly inadequate as that assumed by Christendom. To exchange the oppressive atmosphere of an inanimate universe for the sweep of that animate world of the Chinese, is to escape from the prison-house of sense into the larger world of mind and spirit.

The unsolvable problem for theology is how the Creator could fashion the universe of things out of the vacuum of nothing. Such an achievement must indeed be ascribed to Divine legerdemain. Again, if nothing pervaded all eternity, then even the substance of Deity itself becomes a legitimate question. According to this theological concept, the Creator is a vast personality with abstract parts and members more or less, who in some unaccountable manner must have issued forth from the very emptiness with which he is enveloped. The element of rationality is nowhere apparent in the theory of a Creator who dwells alone forever in the void of nothingness, but who occasionally amuses himself by manifesting mud pies out of this nothingness, and then with childish fretfulness resolves them back again into the nothingness from which they came. The asseverations of the Church to the contrary notwithstanding, this primordial nothingness can scarcely be conceived of as a pliable or workable substance, nor can the procession of universes said to issue from this literal vacuum be regarded as other than a miracle which would overtax the capacity of even the Deity. And yet the Rev. McClatchie blandly assures us that "The Biblical student, for example, is aware that one of the most essential and important doctrines taught in the first verse of Genesis is the non-eternity of Matter; but, in translating a pagan Classic, he should be acquainted with the fact that all heathen systems without exception assert the eternity of Matter, and that this is one of the most prominent differences between the Cosmogony of Moses, and that of all pagan writers. If Matter is eternal it must necessarily be divine and a God; and hence it is altogether vain and fruitless to expect to find, in heathen materialism, any Being whom it is not idolatrous to worship."

The eternal duration of Matter (here regarded as synonymous with the Absolute, and in reality man's negative approach to the Absolute) is philosophy's answer to this dilemma of a spontaneous creation from nothing as maintained by theology. Modern science agrees with pagan philosophy that there is an ever-existing substance, the nature of which is as yet undefinable but which provides the common seed-ground from which grow the myriads of manifesting spheres. When the pagan thus affirmed the existence of an undying substance—Universal Root Matter—which after passing through an infinite diversity of modes ultimately returns to its primordial state, they established the Wheel of Eternity and founded the doctrine of world transmigration. Far from being "nothing" this Universal Root Matter was all things, and because it was only capable of negative definition was termed "No Thing." From this eternal Matter—not matter as defined by the physicist but rather as the ever-enduring, undifferentiated life—creation comes forth, and after manifesting the latent urges inherent in its parts ultimately returns to its primordial state. This philosophic Matter—the undefined Monad composed of an infinitude of germinal units in abstraction—offers both a rational and effective solution to the problem of First Cause, thus leaving the mind free to contemplate the processes by which this First Cause fashioned the tangible universe. This hypothesis supplies Deity with the substance of his own nature, the origin of his own divinity, and the materials with which he is to fabricate cosmos.

The Supreme God of China, like the first deities of Greece and Egypt, must be this ever-enduring Matter to which is applied the term *Tien*. It is the inner heavens in the sense of quality, and the outer heavens in the sense of quantity—the Universal Parent, the infinite capacity, the undifferentiated Cause, the ever-flowing fountain. From the nature of this universalized divinity emanated the organized creation by an orderly progression. To begin with, there came forth two principles called *Airs*, by which this universal essence opposes itself to itself, and in the field of this opposition establishes the generations. These two, called *Heaven* and *Earth*, are to be understood as actuating Spirit and receptive Matter. Their proper names are the Great Father and the Great Mother, which together form a vast anthropomorphic deity whom the Chinese call *Shang-te*, or the Sky Emperor. Shang-te, the heavenly ruler of the celestial empire, is revered through his positive aspect (Heaven) and is therefore termed the Emperor of Heaven. His descendant upon the earth, the human emperor, is called the Son of Heaven and rules by right of the authority vested in him by his Sky Father. In his aspect of Heaven, Shang-te consists of a triad which is termed Heaven, Earth, and Man. The third member of this trinity is the world emperor who, as a sort of Platonic monad, contains within himself all mankind. The elements of the Brahmanic system—primary matter, spirit, visible substance, and time—have their parallel in the Chinese Tien, Heaven, Earth, and Pwan-koo, which together are termed Shang-te, the Creator.

As the Great Father (Heaven) consists of a triad of qualities, so the Great Mother (Earth) also manifests three natures which complement the three principles of the Great Father, resulting in what are called the eight trigrams or figures, of which Kheen (the Father) and Khwan (the Mother) are the origin. In the Chinese *Cabala*, Kheen, the active principle, is symbolized by three unbroken lines, and Khwan, the receptive principle, by three broken lines. These lines are arranged in six other patterns, called respectively the three sons and three daughters. In the more profound interpretation of this philosophy Chaos is the eternal Deity or divine Matter which causes to exist within itself two Airs, one termed subtle and the other coarse. The subtle Air is spirit and its name is *Yang;* the coarse Air is matter and its name is *Yin*. From the intimate mingling of these two Airs all the phenomena of generation have their origin.

In terms of Platonism, these two Airs would be the rational and the irrational souls respectively which, as Confucius declares, are never discoverable separate from each other. It is possible, therefore, to divide diagrammatically the Chinese universe into three spheres corresponding to the three worlds of Pythagoras; i. e., the Supreme World, the Superior World, and the Inferior World, all of which exist within the nature of absolute and unchanging Matter, which is both the first and the last, the unborn and the undying. Thus within the great Egg of Chaos exist three moving agents which are the spirits of the world. The first, which is synonymous with the will of Deity, is called *Le,* or Fate, and is the driving power that moves all things to their predestined end. The second, Wisdom, is Shang-te, which is referred to as a horse upon which Fate rides to the accomplishment of its ends. The third, Activity, is called the body of Shang-te and is ruled over by Pwan-koo, the Demiurgus or Lord of the World, the Protogonas or First Man.

Wherever Matter is considered to be an eternal element, and manifestation a periodic blossoming forth of the creative energies of this ever-existing state, we have the law of Kalpas, or successive creations. In the Chinese system the *Yuen* (Kalpa) is considered analogous to the natural year, which therefore becomes its symbol. As the year is divided into twelve periods, corresponding to the months and the signs of the zodiac, so the Yuen is divided into twelve divisions called *Hwuy,* each consisting of 10,800 years. The four seasons become symbolic of the four grand periods which correspond to the Hindu *Yugas,* or divisions of life—birth, growth, maturity, and decay —the Four Horsemen of the Apocalypse. Thus in the period termed spring cosmos comes forth into manifestation. During the summer the phenomena of growth and expansion take place; during the autumn the fruitage of effort is reaped; and during the winter the retirement of cosmos into its primordial nature is consummated. The spring of the world is symbolized by the color blue, the summer by red, the autumn by white, and the winter by black. Four great kings or regents, corresponding to the four Maharajahs of the Brahmans, each painted the respective color of his season, rule over the cardinal angles of the heavens. In their midst sits the great "Yellow Emperor"—the Brahman *Mahat* or Intellect, the Mind of the Universe.

The twelve signs of the zodiac are divided into groups of three to represent these seasons. The twelfth, first, and second signs (which are to the north) form the winter season, with the first sign due north. The third, fourth, and fifth signs (which are to the east) form the spring season, with the fourth sign due east. The sixth, seventh and eighth signs (which are to the south) form the summer season, with the seventh sign due south. The ninth, tenth, and eleventh signs (which are to the west) form the autumn season, with the tenth sign due west. It is evident that this diagrammatic arrangement, which resembles a horoscope, is a figure by which may be estimated not only the duration of world periods, but of every order of creation, greater and lesser. Thus the life of every atom is a Kalpa; likewise the life of man, the life of the race, the life of the planet, the life of the solar system, the life of the universe, and the life of cosmos itself. As will be noted, throughout all manifestation each of these Kalpas is a fractional part, in turn, of a still greater one, until at last time—which is their basis and indispensable to their existence—is so merged into eternity as to be incapable of further differentiation.

Every twenty-four hours the whole cycle is re-enacted in mortal time. The smallest Kalpa may be but the fraction of a second's duration, while the greatest may endure for countless milleniums. While in time and magnitude these periods differ widely, still the diagram is a proper symbol of them all; for regardless of their magnitude all obey the same principle of periodicity and manifest the same general mathematical characteristics of form and progression. For example, the rotation of the earth upon its axis causes one of the twelve signs of the zodiac to rise sequentially every two hours upon the eastern horizon, so that the twelve complete their revolution in twenty-four hours and thus make a minor Kalpa, or period. In its revolution around the sun the earth also passes through the twelve signs of the zodiac in twelve months, thus constituting a greater Kalpa. Again, through the precession of the equinoxes the sun retrogrades through the twelve signs of the zodiac in approximately 25,000 years, which is therefore called a great sidereal year, and by which a still greater Kalpa is established. From such well-known illustrations we may gain some slight idea of the complexity of celestial dynamics as disclosed by the principle of Kalpas.

In the first sign (which is due north) the Chinese universe had its genesis. The Universal Power (Heaven) came into manifestation and a new day of wandering began. In the second sign the earth issued forth, and in the third sign (which is the first of the spring months) Pwan-koo appeared. This Kalpa then continued and the generations came forth, and through the spring, summer, and autumn months lived, reached maturity, and entered upon the inevitable decay. At last in the twelfth sign (which is the first of the winter months) came the great Deluge, which marked the close of that Kalpa. All living creatures were destroyed except Pwan-koo, who is the undying or unchanging creature. After a period of rest the new Kalpa was ushered in and Pwan-koo in the third period came forth again to be the progenitor of human life. In this lesser reappearance (in which the Kalpa of the earth rather than the universe is signified) the principle of Pwan-koo became Fuh-he, the first Emperor. It is said that the previous Kalpa was destroyed because of its wickedness, but the Archetypal Man with his family—the eight diagrams of the *Yih King* —was preserved through the Deluge to perpetuate creation. We are informed by the secret doctrine that Pwan-koo is the Sky Man, or the Monad of human generation. From Pwan-koo descend upon threads (as in the Platonic system) a number of subordinate powers called by the Brahmans the Manus, or the First Men. There are fourteen such Manus to a great Kalpa, and one comes forth at the beginning of each round (or day of manifestation) and also at the establishment of each root race. Thus the Noah of the Jews is the Vaisvata Manu of the Brahmans. He is the undying man whose progeny gradually increases to the dignity of a race.

In the present cycle Pwan-koo, the Eternal Man, came forth in the form of Fuh-he, the Manu, to establish the new humanity. Hence Pwan-koo is Adam and Fuh-he is Noah or the second Adam, who preserved the generations through the Deluge which marked the close of a lesser Kalpa. Fuh-he, while generally regarded as the first Emperor of the imperial line, is really an avatar or incarnation of the Grand Man. His color is blue like that of Krishna, and as Vishnu came forth at the beginning of his worlds in the form of a fish, so we are told that Fuh-he, the indigo Emperor, had the body and tail of a fish. A similar philosophic basis exists for the legends of Dagon, Oannes, and the fish-gods of antiquity; yes, even Jonah, who in the third sign (or period) was cast out of the whale's belly.

An analysis of these various cosmological and theogonic systems shows the ancient pagan philosophers to have been unified in their concept of the principles by which the universe was called forth out of the Abyss of Absolute Matter. Though the natural differences of terminology are obvious, and though the allegories have taken on local color, still their common underlying truths are evident even to the uninitiated. These ancient sages have thus met the exact requirements prescribed by Socrates in the *First Alcibiades* for all instructors: namely, that "they must agree together and not differ." That which men know is the basis of their agreement; that which they do not know is the cause of their disagreement. That sages, widely separated geographically and with diverse environments and temperaments, should arrive at the same general conclusions attests the accuracy of their findings. Being for the greater part superficial-minded, modern thinkers do not arrive at any such unanimity of agreement, but grope their way in a maze of contradictions which they impart to the young under the guise of education. Thus in their frantic quest of the new or the spectacular, modern philosophers fabricate theories expressive more of the bizarre than of rationality.

While all speculation regarding the infinite may be regarded as inconsequential when compared with the necessity of solving the problems of daily life, such rumination is essential to right perspective; for by it the mortal creature is raised from the state of some eyeless earthworm to the estate of a participator in the whole pageantry of universal procedure. In the past man has been oppressed by his own sense of inferiority. During the Dark Ages it was presumptuous to the point of heresy to speculate either upon the eternal laws by which he was governed, or the nature of that vast power which brooded over him and measured both his comings in and his going out.

Today this bogy of fear persists only in a few isolated districts where the earthworm still wriggles in his native habitat, declaring that there is no sun because he cannot see it! The world is now coming to realize that thought is not heresy, but that not to think is to live in a concept of existence equivalent to the grossest blasphemy. There is nothing terrible or vengeful about the universe, nor does it turn disdainfully from the honest searcher into its mysteries. Creation stands forth unafraid and welcomes analysis of all its parts. It is said in Holy Writ that none shall look upon the God of Israel and live. But Israel's God was the Lord of another day, and woe unto him who shall turn back from this new day to worship the irate gods of yesterday; for he shall perish from the narrowness of his own vision!

The God of tomorrow stands forth in all its majesty of suns and moons and stars. Its extent is from space to space, and eternity alone confines it. Man, gazing into the eyes of man, beholds therein his Maker. His Creator sings to him with the voice of the wilderness, and descends upon him from the stars that spangle the heavens by night. This God is not hidden behind flowing draperies, nor are his ministers avenging angels. Unmoved by the passing of ages he contemplates the worlds that are his substance, and through his own mind in man seeks to probe the depth of his own reality. This Vast One has written his law in the heavens where they shall endure long after earthly codes have been erased from the memory of man. This God manifests his will in the endless progression and change by which things are moved from Then to Now and from Now to Then. This Universal Creator fears not man's effort to understand him; telescopes and microscopes may scan his features without offence. For what is the quest of knowledge but the God in man seeking the God in All? God is; man is. Therefore, man is God and God is man. But before man may consciously enter into his divinity he must gaze upon himself in the All without fear and recognize himself in the All gazing back without hate. Steadfastly and unafraid, the rational soul thus gazes upon those glorious beings whose radiant natures are that mystical light which is the life of the beholding soul.

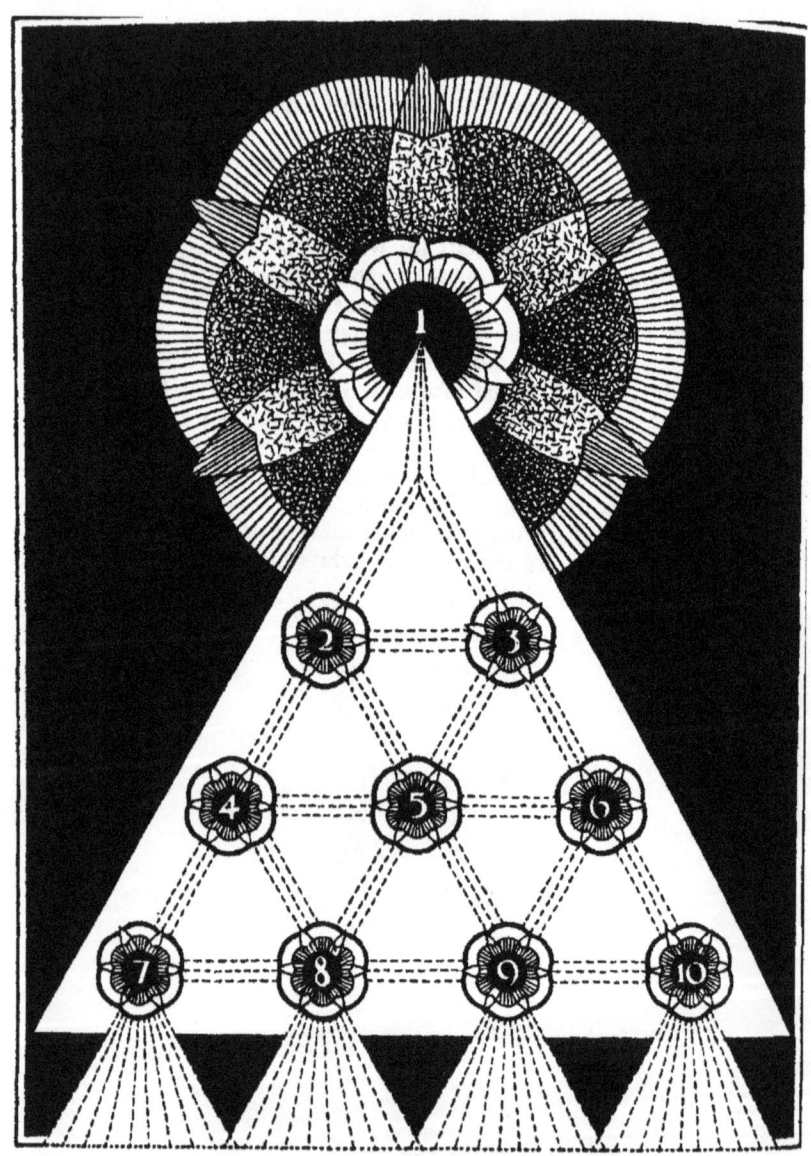

THE PYTHAGOREAN TETRACTYS

From the contemplation of the order and progression of the Numbers out of the Monad may be discovered the true relationship between natures and their Cause. He who understands this mystery is of all men the wisest. Numbers are the keys to the flow of Universal Energy.

CHAPTER ELEVEN

Mathematics, the Master Science

THE Pythagoreans defined mathematics as the science of magnitudes and multitudes; for by its principles might be determined not only the number of constituent parts, but also the degree to which one part differs from another in length, breadth, thickness, or weight. Mathematics also makes it possible to compute the interval in time between incidents, and in distance between bodies and places. It was regarded as the divine science because order was established by its means throughout the nature of being. All the arts and sciences depend upon this order for their survival. History, for example, is simply a chain of incidents whose order is preceded through arbitrary sequences of time. If this element of time is removed and the incidents are not preserved in chronological order, history becomes valueless, for the proper relationship between episodes is thus detroyed. Only by mathematics, then, is it possible to construct the chain of sequences that will show the definite relationship between a cause and its effect, an action and its reaction, a beginning and its end.

Antedating the age of history is the age of fable, from which the time sequence is largely absent, with the resultant confusion concerning theological origins; for the creative processes that required hundreds of millions of years to consummate their work were so thrown out of perspective that up to the last century Christendom actually believed the earth to have been fashioned a little over six thousand years ago. Fortunately the laws of Nature were their own historiographers, and we find the records of countless ages written in the enduring substances of fossil and geologic strata to refute the erroneous conclusions of men.

To the trained thinker mathematics is obviously limited to the realm of form, or to those departments of manifestation where numbers as diversified elements exist suspended from common Unity, which is their monad and which was termed by the Pythagoreans *Number*. As all individual minds are suspended from the principle of Mind, so all numbers are suspended from the principle of Number. Number is consequently divine and founded in the archetypal sphere, from whence its radiations (or principles) descend into the sensible world, there to manifest as the exactitudes of mathematical procedure. By some, Number was considered synonymous with God in that the first motion of Deity establishes Number, which becomes the mode whereby the magnitude and duration of that motion are rendered conceivable. Hence motion does not exist unless the cause is aware of its own extension or induces awareness in the substances through which the extension is taking place. Motion and Number, therefore, are of kindred nature and form the monad from which is suspended all diversified activity—which is Number in motion, or the numbers.

From the fathomless and unknown beginning the principles of mathematics existed as a divine, unnamed reality. The man accredited with its discovery simply extracted from the infinite the principles of universal order and christened them the science of mathematics. This new science thereupon became a hypothetical monad, and diversity took place within it, arithmetic, algebra, geometry, trigonometry, and calculus becoming the vehicles of its expression in the sphere of mental activity. These are the lesser monads suspended from the body of the parent monad. As gold exists in the dark earth long before the miner's pick bares it to the light of day, so all the truths revealed to man in the past and to be discovered by him in the future are eternal, and as divine principles were the media in the beginning by which the Creator flowed into Being from the eternal state of Not-Being. In its exact sense, Truth is therefore the way of God in *all* things and truths the ways of God in *particular* things. The forms of learning which mortals term science, philosophy, and theology are simply aspects of divine procedure on the physical, mental, and emotional planes respectively. As Number becomes numbers, so Truth becomes truths and the subordinate monads suspended from Truth become that which is real upon each of the countless levels of existence. Wherever one of these facts is established, it becomes the monad or radiant center from which flows forth a number of secondary agencies. The moment this lesser establishment and flow take place, mathematics is again manifested. From the monad of theology, for example, are suspended the religions, of which there are not less than seven major bodies. The flow of theology into any one of its religions establishes a new vortex, thereby giving expression to another suspended element of mathematics. Each of these major divisions of religion becomes, in turn, the monad of a still greater order of diversity, a notable example being the Christian faith whose branches number several hundred. Each motion of Truth out from itself toward that infinite diversity which is the inevitable circumference of Unity is thus measured, determined, and directionalized by Number moving through its own vehicles—numbers and their infinite combinations.

The Pythagoreans termed the number 1 as the apex of the pyramid of numbers, since it is the first manifestation of Number. It is Unity established in place, for in its perfect and abstract sense Unity is unlimited by place or condition. Thus, Number that is all-pervading becomes the 1—the first numeral to stand alone. Being the least of diversity, the numeral 1 is therefore the spirit of the numbers; for like spirit it is universal life limited to the sphere of generation, or the apex of the pyramid of phenomena. About the central axis of the 1, or Tree of Being, moves the whole order of the numbers, which are suspended from the 1 even as the 1 itself is suspended from the principle of Unity, of which it is the primary mathematical manifestation.

Since the 1—which signifies the wholeness of the numbers—is equivalent to Divine Unity, it is apparent that all the other numerals are fractional parts of this primordial wholeness, and not multiples of the 1 as might first be supposed. Thus, 2 is in reality Unity considered in terms of halves, 3 is Unity considered in terms of thirds, a billion is Unity considered in terms of billionths; for the imperishable whole, which can never increase or decrease, is always the sum of conceived or conceivable parts. In philosophy the 2 cannot be greater than the 1; for in that event, spirit would exceed the sum of itself and an amount would be greater than its own stated quantity. If the 1 is the symbol of the All in its least conditioned state, the 2 cannot be the All doubled, but is rather to be understood as the halving of the Absolute within its own nature whereby the All becomes manifested in the least number of parts of itself. Diversity, as symbolized by the numbers, can exist temporarily within the nature of Unity, yet the number of the parts can never exceed their own sum, for the integrity of the whole must be preserved.

By philosophic addition, therefore, the sum of all the parts (or numerals) must always be the 1, or wholeness. Likewise when parts (or numerals) are subtracted from parts the remainder must be 1, or wholeness, save when the whole is subtracted from the whole; in which event the cipher, or Absolute, is left, for when the conditioned is subtracted from the conditioned the Unconditioned remains. When parts (or numerals) are multiplied by parts, the product cannot exceed the 1, or wholeness; and when parts (or numerals) are divided by parts, the quotient must be the 1, or wholeness.

The order of the numerical pyramid is thus revealed, for from the apex, which is wholeness, it diverges to the base, which consists of an infinity of fragmentary parts. This is the arcane significance of Herodotus' strange statement to the effect that the Egyptians in building their pyramids commenced at the top and worked downward—a method which, because it is an architectonic absurdity, cleary demonstrates that Herodotus wrote history with an ulterior motive. Thus while the prestige of history may have suffered at the hands of this first historian, the body of philosophy has been enriched by his labors.

As the numbers are all contained within the numeral 1, so the pyramid is contained within its own apex, from which it flows down to mingle itself with the rock upon which it stands. In this manner is established the philosophic fact that Unity is synonymous with Cause and diversity with effect.

As the alchemist employed chemical terms to symbolize the various elements of life, so the Pythagoreans gave to the creative sphere the appellation of *Number*, and to the creation which issued therefrom, *numbers*. The Divine Mathematics dealt not with sums calculated upon paper nor carried in the mind, but rather with the order and arrangement of corporeal bodies, their mutual relationships, and the proximity of each to its own cause. Though any one of the arts or sciences is capable of thus becoming the outer garment of the secret doctrine, the various Greek schools employed particularly mathematics, music, and astronomy in this manner. Like Herodotus, they frequently confused the elements of the science itself in order that the esoteric principles—which were often diametrically opposed to the exoteric application—might be presented to such as were able to interpret the symbolism.

Through mathematics, then, is set forth the system of philosophic monadology, the principles of which were arcanely hinted at by Leucippus and Democritus. From the doctrine of monads sprang the theory of atoms, which are simply these archetypal unities of wholeness vested in matter and established as the principles of substance. These atoms exist in concatenated order from the infinitesimally small to the unmeasurably great, each of the greater being compounded according to atomic law from a prescribed number to the lesser. An important point is established when the question is asked, "What do all of these atoms have in common, leaving out of consideration the factors of size and order?" Two things: their participation in the all-inclusive atom composed of their sum; the condition of individual wholeness which each atom occupies in relationship to itself, though to greater unities it occupies the relationship of a part.

This *quality of wholeness*, which is the common property of these diversified and otherwise irreconcilable bodies, becomes as it were, their common denominator. Though wholeness is present in all natures it is not an attribute of natures. This wholeness is an archetypal quality—an attribute of Deity. Regardless of the nature of its expression, every activity, quality, or condition is essentially a wholeness. This wholeness is made manifest by a division within itself whereby its nature becomes a mass of innumerable fragments, each of the fractions partaking of the quality resident in the original wholeness, and manifesting it through the wholeness of its own fractional part. For example, Man is a wholeness possessing and manifesting certain rational qualities and characteristics. This archetypal wholeness, flowing into diversity, breaks up to form men. Each individual, by virtue of his own inherent wholeness, shares in the virtues resident in the wholeness of the archetype; and by virtue of his participation in the one causal nature moves in the rhythm of the archetype, which archetype manifests through such laws as polarity, generation, rationality, morality, and such other ideals and practices as are the common property of all men.

Let us take the principle of unities, or wholes, and apply it to the subject of duration. Man forever struggles against the illusion of time. He views the marching years as relentless enemies conspiring to prevent achievement; his eyes forever watch the clock's swinging pendulum which ticks his life away. In the third part of *King Henry VI*, the monarch indulges in this soliloquy:

> See the minutes, how they run,
> How many make the hour full complete;
> How many hours bring about the day;
> How many days finish up the year;
> How many years a mortal man may live.

The great expanse of duration, in which like a great sea all existense is immersed, is divided by the unenlightened into three hypothetical intervals: the past, the present, and the future. These intervals were personified by the Greeks, who called them the *Fates* and invested them with power over the destinies of all mortal creatures—or more correctly, the mortal parts of all creatures. To most men the past is a period of vain regrets, the present a sterile struggle against apparently insurmountable obstacles, and the future that fourth-dimensional vista where alone dreams come true.

Thus hope, faith, and charity come into their own; for with his hope posited in tomorrow, his faith supporting him in today, and with charity toward yesterday, man faces the illusion of years, at the end of which Cronus (Time) awaits to devour his own progeny. Every moment both marks the beginning of a new period of Time and also the close of some expiring interval. Upon this intricate background of minutes, hours, and days, humanity fashions strange workmanships—the products of its imagings and its imaginings.

Time is both a creator and a destroyer, for it is a perpetual beginning as well as an end to something. In Time all that is false shall pass away, and in Time all that is true shall be realized and established. Time is the acid test, and only that which can survive its ravages is worthy to be termed permanent. Time has dominion over all that is untrue, unreal or perverse. One by one the fallacies of life fall beneath the reaping scythe of Time, and are garnered into the capacious bin of oblivion. In Time all forms must die; in Time all worlds must cease; in Time the very universe will be resolved back into its primal state; in Time are contained all beginnings and all ending, for Time is the lord of the illusion of beginnings and endings. Time is the master of the mortal sphere and all that exists within it. Time preserves for a little while the perishable only that ultimately it shall perish more completely.

Within form, however, there is that which is without beginning and without end; something that laughs at the years and mocks destroying Time. This enduring quality is that wholeness which rejoices in the annihilation of those forms which are the diversity temporarily established within the sphere of this all-containing Unity. From the viewpoint of wholeness, the more that is destroyed the more remains, until when everything has been destroyed, all remains; for as the unity of Number is broken up by numbers, so the unity of life is broken up by forms. Hence, by destroying form, Time restores life to its perfect wholeness.

Mortal creatures come and go in kaleidoscopic diversity; yet in the midst of this ever-changing scene is an intangible but all-pervading and inclusive permanence—the divine Reality, the Self, the perfect Wholeness. Unborn and undying, the Self is neither old nor young. Its condition never changes; for though all things pass away, it endures. It is wholeness, and being wholeness is sufficient unto itself; for that which is complete is sufficient and that which is all is enough for itself. As Time is the measure of parts, it cannot affect that which is superior to the existence of parts and which consequently knows no Time.

Time is recognized and measured by the markings it leaves upon the face of ephemeral being. Though it deeply scores the surface of all material life, it can have no effect upon the enduring nature of Reality; for wholeness, being wholeness, includes Time. The parts can have but a fractional share of the attributes of the whole, but the whole partakes of the attributes of the parts in fullness and perfect harmony. Hence the whole is the master of its parts, which must bow before its dictum and are powerless to force their fragmentary agencies upon the structure of wholeness itself.

Those who live material lives—who think and feel in terms of matter and estimate permanence upon the basis of corporeal substance—must forever fear Time which sooner or later will wrest their possessions from them and scar their personality with its blows. But those who have risen above the illusion of years realize, as they gaze upon the immeasurable vistas of eternity, that the law of the spirit is permanence and the law of matter is change. Time may well be the measure of corporeal being, but what is Time to that which remains unmoved and against which impotently pound the waves of interval!

MATHEMATICS, THE MASTER SCIENCE 249

Numbers partake of the *maya* of diversity, for they are infinite in their combinations, and their progression is limited only by the rational capacity of the mathematician. So we find the Pythagorean declaring the monad, or the 1, to signify Reality; but the duad, or the 2, illusion. Coincident with division, the ephemeral state is manifested; for the laws of polarity for which the 2 stands limit the generating soul to the narrow confines of definite procedure, which procedure at best can but inadequately represent the essentially unimpeded flowing of the causal nature.

An attempt has been made to demonstrate that Time is the mysterious fourth dimension so long sought by philosophers. The proponents of this theory declare that it is impossible to completely isolate any existing object from the element of Time, and that the failure to include this element destroys the congruity of the object under consideration. Time is a phase or manifestation of place; for that which because of its abstract nature cannot be said to exist in place may, however, be localized in Time. For example, the moment an incident is closed or a personality is dissipated, it may be considered to have disappeared from place but to be still definitely situated in Time. Time is an elastic quality which is ever great enough to include both place and occurrence. Therefore an object may be declared to require four descriptive properties in order to render it intelligible to the senses: length, breadth, thickness, and place. Neither Time nor place, however, can be conceived of as actually fulfilling the conventional requirements of dimensions; and in approaching the problem of the fourth dimension, it is evident that we are attempting its solution with a three-dimensional consciousness. Hence our methods of approach must necessarily be through hypothesis and negative procedure.

Let us assume two cubes of the same size to be composed of spirit and matter respectively. Cube A (spirit) is the causal nature of cube B (its material vehicle). The all-permeating quality of cube A permits it to occupy the same place that is occupied by cube B, so that by virtue of their composition both bodies may occupy the same place at the same time. But cube

A and cube B are not the same; consequently, an interval exists between them—the same type of interval that might exist between two mentalities, one of which is highly evolved and the other of comparatively negligible development. The interval between spirit and matter is, therefore, an interval of quality, and when so considered may be as incalculably great as is the interval between God and man. How shall we measure this interval; how shall we accurately ascertain the distance between two bodies occupying precisely the same place at the same time, yet separated by a chasm so vast that the one may be totally unaware of the existence of the other?

Throughout creation there are distances which are purely qualitative. In estimating the nature of an object, length, breadth, thickness, and quality reveal more of its nature than do length, breadth, thickness, and time or place; for both time and place are environmental attributes, while quality is purely intrinsic. It is not a justifiable inference, however, that quality is the fourth dimension, but rather that the interval of quality is the field whose true dimensions, proportions, and conditions can only be estimated or measured by a fourth tool of the reason—an instrument akin to reason itself. In addition to the properties of length, breadth, and thickness, every object has also a quality extension toward the nature of perfect Good. This quality extension comes under the influence of Time only to the degree that quality determines permanence and Time measures the degree of impermanence.

The *theory of relativity,* by establishing the fallibility of present methods of estimating the relationships between objects, proves that all conclusions concerning celestial dynamics must be relative, or true only in part. Relating two bodies to each other is a comparatively simple problem, however, to that of relating an object which is in place to a spiritual principle which is universal. If a spiritual principle is omnipresent at all times, then no object can ever be moved so that it either approaches closer to or retires farther from spirit; for spirit has its center everywhere and its circumference nowhere. The interval between spirit (cube A) and matter (cube B) is, therefore, hardly a proper subject for relativity, but must be regarded rather as a lapse of quality. In other words, it is an interval which exists without distance, since distance cannot exist unless both objects under consideration occupy place. To attempt to establish distance between these two opposites of quality represented by spirit and matter would be like standing in a certain spot and asking the question, "How far is it from here to everywhere?" The correct answer, "As far as here is less than everywhere," is almost as baffling to the faculties of comprehension as the question. Such an interval can only be properly surveyed and subdivided by one fortunate enough to possess the fourth-dimensional consciousness, which would enable him to travel through the quality interval with the same facility that we pass through the place interval. The popular fallacy that God dwells in the furthermost angle of the heavens and must be hymned in triple fortissimo arises from the dimension limitations of human consciousness, for the mind untrained in abstractions, confuses the interval of quality with the interval of distance. The mind concludes that if evil be near, good—its opposite—consequently must be far removed, and the distance between them can be estimated by a highly spiritualized yardstick.

Thus distance may be defined as the interval between two given bodies, places, incidents, or conditions. The methods employed to measure these intervals differ, according to the nature of the intervals themselves. For example, the interval between bodies or places may be estimated by the arbitrary standards of distance; the interval between incidents by the arbitrary standards of time, and the interval between conditions by the arbitrary standards of quality. When limited to the interval between physical objects or places, distance can be calculated with reasonable accuracy, for men have established definite laws of measurement by common agreement. Such methods of computation, however, are wholly inadequate in the almost unexplored spheres of consciousness and mind, concerning the natures of which most men differ widely one from the other.

It has been said that the philosopher may travel around the world while seated on his own hearthstone, for thought annihilates the interval of distance. A man thinks of China and, behold, he is in China; for he must always dwell in the midst of his own thoughts. But with what subtle instruments shall we measure the wide interval through which thought sped in its instantaneous passage to Cathay? Certainly the tape is not made that meets the need. Again, realization eliminates the intervals in consciousness, for through realization the one realizing becomes identical with the thing realized, and thus spans the superphysical interval between the Self and the not-self. Into this interval Self is ceaselessly flowing, and by the gradual elimination of this qualitative interval the fractional part ever mingles itself more completely with the whole. Nirvana may be defined as the ultimate annihilation of every interval of quality, for it marks the point to which the lesser self has been caused to approach, and finally to be merged with its ultimate goal—the Greater Self.

Mathematics enables the investigator of the abstract verities of the philosophic sphere to organize his findings and present them intelligently to a world so limited in consciousness that it is incapable of imagining conditions apart from place, or intervals unmeasurable in terms of distance. In presenting any abstract reality for consideration by the concrete faculties, something must necessarily be lost; for truth cannot be brought down to the level of ignorance without the element of ignorance entering into the equation and thereby detracting from the integrity of truth. Mathematics, however, offers a medium whereby such pollution is reduced to a minimum. For example, it would be highly ridiculous to attempt to estimate in terms of physical distance how far life is from death, heaven from hell or opinion from fact.

Recognizing that the law of generation works through the principle of opposites, it is nevertheless a justifiable assumption that the total interval between two opposites is equivalent to unity, or the One. This totality is then capable of being reduced to halves, quarters, and other forms of division. The numbers will then represent concatenated degrees of quality, and a definite scale is thereby established which will permit the various forms manifesting these qualities to be accurately determined in relation to the scheme through which they are moving. Thus, while it is difficult to compute the distance between growth and decay, maturity may be fixed as the halfway point.

The evolution of human consciousness may be measured in a similar way, for the entire interval between unconsciousness and consciousness can be conceived of as divisible into thirds. The first division confers no realization beyond the limitations of place, the second no realization beyond the limitations of interval, and the third no realization beyond the limitations of quality. By such mathematical procedure it is possible to determine the age of a soul; for the interval between beginning and end, being understood as a wholeness, the position of the manifesting life at any given time may be determined by the degree of its own quality in relation to the total privation of that quality—which was its source—and the fullness of that quality—which is its ultimate.

Philosophy employs such terms as "young" souls and "old" souls. A young soul is one who in quality is more proximate to source than to ultimate, or in whom the degree of privation of a given quality exceeds the amount of the quality itself. If there is more of the absence of a quality present than there is of the quality itself, then the quality is declared to be negative. If the reverse is true, the quality is declared to be positive. Using 100% to represent the sum total of the interval between any two conditions or states, the relative perfection of a life in the plan of progress is determined by the proportion its position bears to the total interval. Thus, an individual manifesting 90% of a certain quality is nine-tenths of the way across the interval that lies between the total privation and the fullness of that quality. To summarize, the intervals of quality (in common with the calculations of all superphysical elements) must be established upon the basis of totality or wholeness, and growth or change is always computed as a percentage of that basis. Hence, in calculating spiritual progress, each of us must calculate it in terms of fractions, parts, or percentages as related to the wholeness of Being.

At this point it may not be out of place to reproduce Proclus' encomium to the science of mathematics: "Hence, the business of this science is apparent from its name: for it moves knowledge, excites intelligence, purifies the dianoetic part, unfolds the forms which we essentially contain, removes the oblivion and ignorance which we possess from generation, and dissolves the bonds with which we are held in captivity by an irrational nature. And all this it effects according to a real similitude of that divinity (Mercury) who leads into light intellectual gifts, fills all things with divine reason, moves souls to intellect, excites them as from a profound sleep, converts them by inquiry to themselves, perfects them through obstetrication, and through the invention of pure intellect conducts them to a blessed life."

In the Platonic theory of converging nullities is revealed a strange doctrine concerning negative affirmations and affirmative negations. The number 1 is a positive affirmative number in that it sets forth in unequivocal terms certain divine attributes of Reality: namely, unity, inclusiveness, priority, and stability. On the other hand we may have a negative statement, as "God is no thing." This is an affirmative negation in that *no thing* exceeds *thing* in the quality of excellence, for the removal of a definite state leaves an indefinite state partaking more perfectly of divine qualities. Whereas the 1 is similar to the nature of Divinity, the 2 is dissimilar in that it is the symbol of contraries and separation. Hence, while Divinity can be defined affirmatively by the 1, it must be defined negatively by the 2; for God is like the 1 and unlike the 2. In other words, numbers define Deity negatively; Number, affirmatively. The numbers, consequently, are negative affirmations, and Deity is defined negatively by every form in the universe; for forms resemble Deity in their unity and differ from Deity in their diversity.

An affirmation is a definite declaration of opinion, belief or attitude, and, if true, inclines toward and becomes identical with truth. If the affirmation be false, however, it retires from truth as though abashed, thus negatively affirming truth by declaring itself to be dissimilar. A negation is an affirmation through denial, and is the only method by which the Absolute may be approached. When the negation verges toward the thing negated, it nullifies its negative correspondences in that thing so only that which *is* remains. Thus affirmatives give definition by investing power with place, condition, and quality; while negatives, by divesting the Absolute of these defining limitations, restore it to the estate of supreme dignity. In this manner is created the paradox that affirmations pertaining to First Cause are negations, and negations are affirmations.

Theological systems founded upon the premise of an anthropomorphic deity assume duality to be ultimate and therefore invest the 2 with a dignity superior to the 1, which is a concept Platonically unsound. The 2 is the symbol of good and evil and the entire illusion of sequences has its foundation in the duad—the monad of diversity. According to the Pythagoreans, the 2 is an evil or unholy number because it is the archetype of separateness and produces from itself a dual standard which is now accepted as the manifestation of a dual creative principle. Thus we are given a key to the intrinsic natures of good and evil; for good continually inclines toward unity or wholeness, and being ever the same amalgamates with everything good, so that diversity can never exist therein. Evil, on the other hand, is widely diversified and may exist in many conditions or states, all of which are irreconcilable not only to good but also to each other. While the body of good is always a unity, the body of evil is always a diversity; for evil does not co-ordinate with itself. For example, a virtue is good, and the manifestation of virtue produces an action to which the nature of good is intrinsic. Blending with the ever-existing good, the good act becomes a part thereof, thereby enriching, strengthening, and increasing the entire body of good. Conversely, a vice is evil and must remain as an isolated activity, since it is incapable either of being accepted into the nature of good or of attaching itself to the body of evil, as the element of concord is not common to the intrinsic nature of evil.

Hence, good ever fortifies its own nature, while evil undermines itself by the ceaseless warfare between its own parts. In the unification of one good with another, the power of good is accordingly magnified. When one evil comes in contact with another evil, in the ensuing struggle each evil destroys the effectiveness of the other. In this way it becomes apparent that good, possessing the virtue of unity, must ever increase until it includes everything within its own nature; while evil, in which the principle of diversity is inherent, will ultimately destroy itself by the continual controversy between its parts. It has been well said that two evils do not make one good, but attacking each other achieve their mutual destruction, and by self-elimination thus prepare the way for the irresistible progress of good.

For this reason the Pythagoreans declared that the perfect numbers (the sum of whose fractional parts is equal to themselves) are the most rare; whereas the superabundant numbers (the sum of whose fractional parts is greater than themselves) and the deficient numbers (the sum of whose fractional part is less than themselves) are most common. This is based upon the fact that there are many ways by which any definite end may be accomplished, but only one of those ways is the best. Consequently he alone is wise who can recognize the best, and he alone is strong who has the courage to use this method, regardless of the personal peril or responsibility involved. Therefore, while all natures partake to some degree of the good, only that is true which partakes in fullest measure of the good, and only one who is qualified to recognize good can make a rational choice between a number of bodies with qualitative differences.

Concerning the doctrine of perfections as revealed by numbers, Thomas Taylor, in his *Theoretic Arithmetic,* sums up in the following words the opinions of Nicomachus, Macrobius, and Theon of Smyrna: "Perfect numbers, therefore, are beautiful images of the virtues which are certain media between excess and defect, and are not summits, as by some of the ancients they were supposed to be. And evil indeed is opposed to evil, but both are opposed to one good. Good, however, is never opposed to good, but to two evils at one and the same time. Thus timidity is opposed to audacity, to both (of) which the want of true courage is common; but both timidity and audacity are opposed to fortitude. Craft also is opposed to fatuity, to both (of) which the want of intellect is common; and both these are opposed to prudence. Thus, too, profusion is opposed to avarice, to both (of) which illiberality is common; and both these are opposed to liberality. And in a similar manner in the other virtues; by all (of) which it is evident that perfect numbers have a great similitude to the virtues. But they also resemble the virtues on another account; for they are rarely found, as being few, and they are generated in a very constant order. On the contrary, an infinite multitude of superabundant and diminished numbers may be found, nor are they disposed in any orderly series, nor generated from any certain end; and hence they have a great similitude to the vices, which are numerous, inordinate, and indefinite." (For further details on this subject consult the chapter on *Pythagorean Mathematics* in my recent work, *An Encyclopedic Outline of Masonic, Hermetic, Qabbalistic and Rosicrucian Symbolical Philosophy.*)

As the 1 represents the monad of unity, so the 2 as the monad of diversity is the moving spirit of irrationality. The conflict between rationality and irrationality may be likened to the proverbial concept of the two ends fighting the middle. Extremes are basically irrational, and only the point of equilibrium may be said to be established upon an enduring foundation. Furthermore, as the extremes pertain to the secondary creation, they are illusional when compared to the center, which is the primary and enduring creation. Thus height and depth are both opposed to the center, for depth departs from the center in a downward course, and height in an upward course. That which departs from center departs from balance, which is a principle exploited to its ultimate by Akiyama Shirobei in the theory of *Judo* or *Jujitsu*. The theory underlying Judo "start from the mathematical principle that the stability of a body i destroyed as soon as the vertical line passing through its cente of gravity falls outside its base." Once the individual is lure into jeopardizing his equilibrium, he becomes his own wors enemy and requires little outside assistance to bring about hi downfall.

The philosophic truth here revealed applies not only to th body but to the consciousness as well. When the self in equi librium, signified by the 1, is intrigued to incline from its pei fect state toward the extremes, signified by the 2, it jeopardize its stability and is at the mercy of its adversary, diversity. Le the 1 signify permanence and the 2 life and death. Both lif and death share the common vice of impermanence, as the both lack the common virtue of permanence. Therefore, it i as fatal for the 1 to incline toward life as toward death; for ii assuming life it assumes that which must die, and in assumin death it assumes that which is corruptible and changeable Only when dissociated from both is the perfection of endui ance assured. Thus is revealed the stability of Number and the instability of numbers, for all numbers (save the 1) partak of the common evil of manyness and are involved in the proces of generation, whereby imperfection perpetuates itself since it i incapable of enduring in its own nature. The self exists in dependent of generation in that, being indivisible, it is incoi ruptible; but the not-self, being divisible and corruptible, de pends for its endurance upon generation and the renewal of it transitory bodies.

Between the rational soul and mathematics is the sympa thetic bond of similars. Preciseness—which is an attribute c the good—delights in precision; and order—which is a qualit of Number—rejoices in the continuity of similars and retire from the malarrangements of dissimilars. In facing inward tc ward its own intrinsic perfection, the self becomes Numbe regarding No Number, or that Cipher which precedes numera tion. But facing outward toward bodies, it encounters th numerical classifications of orders and projections, and therefor stands in equilibrium between Not-being (which is the perfect and eternal Being) and transitory being (which, in the terms of the ultimate, is not-being). Thus self (the individual) is the monad of secondary natures and the paternal foundation of progeny, which are tertiary natures. Hence the 1 (which is the monad or archetype of good) and the 2 (which is the monad or archetype of evil) are both declared by the Pythagoreans to be no numbers but sacred qualities—namely, the primary and secondary natures. The 3, or monad of tertiary natures, was regarded as the actual parent of numbers, or progeny, for 3 is a blending of similars (the 1) and dissimilars (the 2) and is consequently the proper foundation of compound bodies, which compounds must always consist of similars and dissimilars, similars being the spiritual and abiding parts and dissimilars the material and transitory parts. From the various orders of similars and dissimilars issue the multiplicities which are alluded to as the cogitations of Divine Mind. Thus, the first Trinity consists of the Monad (the Father) the Duad (the Power) and the Triad (the Mind or Monad of Generations); for all generations consist of a rational nature (the Monad) immersed in an irrational nature (the Duad) toward some phase of which the Monad inclines, or seems to incline, during the irrational epoch. Liberation, therefore, is the retirement of the Monad from proximity to opposites, and the re-establishment of its own self-sufficiency by which it is capable of assimilating the qualities of the dissimilars and returning to its true abiding condition as the paternal foundation of generations.

Syrianus, the Pythagorean, declared that the wise, turning from the vulgar paths, delivered their philosophy in secret to those alone who were worthy to receive it and exhibited it to the rest of mankind through mathematical terminology. Forms therefore, they called numbers as being the first things separated from impartible union; for such natures as are above form are also above separation and consequently pertain to the sphere of Number itself. The sacred decad, or 10, is generated from the sum of the first four numbers (considering the 1 and 2 as numbers)—1, 2, 3, and 4. The 1 was termed the first point, the 2 the first interval, the 3 the first superficies, and the 4 the first solid. Thus Aristotle declared that the first permanence is the dot, the first length the duad, the first breadth the triad, and the first depth the tetrad. The nature of the tetrad, being that of the first solid or body, reveals why it is declared to be the symbol of God. The 4 is the Demiurgus, whose substantial nature is the proper field of mundane fabrications. As four surfaces are the least number that can enclose an area, so the Demiurgus is the first of areas or fields; and consequently the one in whom we live and move and have our being.

Pythagoras further declared that knowledge existed in four states. The first, similar to the monad, was called *intellect;* the second, similar to the duad, *science;* the third, similar to the triad, *opinion;* and the fourth, similar to the tetrad, *sense*. It is evident that intellect partakes of the solidarity of the monad, for it is the immovable contemplation of relative mutations. The duad even fulfills the Baconian requirements for the constitution of science, for the 2 establishes the comparisons essential to the accumulation of knowledge through observation and experimentation. The 3 consists of three monads separated by two intervals. These intervals become the proper symbols of opinion; for opinions are founded not upon facts (monads) but upon the intervals between them, and two intervals are necessary for opinions in that opinions exhibit the qualities of dissimilars. The 4 consists of four monads and three intervals, which intervals may be likened to the dimensions—length, breadth, thickness; for the monads are qualities manifesting in intervals or dimensions by which they are rendered appreciable to the sense perceptions. Thus the hidden symbolism of the tetractys, or pyramid of ten dots, is unveiled. The four rows of dots further signify four qualities—form, order, beauty, unity —imperishably related to Number. These qualities partake of excellence, and through their participation in the order of creation render the whole felicitous to the internal constitution. Their presence insures the comparative excellence of forms and bodies.

As already intimated, every compound body is composed of the qualities of the monad and the duad. Aristotle reminds the disciple that a number, such as the 6 for example, partakes of the nature of the duad in that it is composed of parts; i. e., 6 monads. But it also partakes of the monad itself in that these parts form a whole—the 6—and the question naturally arises: By what virtue do a number of monads group together to form a definite wholeness to which an arbitrary term is given? In other words, why do 6 monads make 6 rather than simply 6 monads, for the 6 is not denominated six 1's but a unity composed of 6. As the Pythagoreans explain it, the 6 monads may be considered as six pieces of wood from which is fashioned a chair which we will call the number 6 itself. By what virtue do these six separate objects form a new and definite pattern, and why should they not always remain simply a bundle of wood? If the numbers were merely aggregations of monads, they would all be bundles, differing simply in the number of their parts. By virtue of a divine order, however, these parts are made to pattern themselves into new terms. The Platonists declared that as a carpenter fashioned a new object out of the separate elements, so a mysterious agent called the *Numerative Soul*—being itself a monad and consequently a wholeness composed of infinite diversity—gives form and subsistence to all numbers according to definite divine laws. "But," Thomas Taylor concludes, "in this only consists the difference, that the carpenter's art is not naturally inherent in us, and requires manual operation, because it is conversant with sensible matter; but the numerative art is naturally present with us, and is therefore possessed by all men, and has an intellectual matter which it instantaneously invests with form."

In the light of Pythagoreanism, it is no cause for amazement that 6 monads are never without the innate sense of *six-ness;* for the moment a certain number of units are combined they are ensouled by the quality equal to their sum, and invested with an organized formative nature through which they manifest a wholeness where previously they manifested a separateness. It follows that with the establishment of sums these sums are automatically invested by the rational soul of man himself with the sense of wholeness equal to their number. If 3, for example, be taken from 6, that which remains is immediately invested with the wholeness of 3. We must give form to numeration, for "our soul cannot endure to see that which is formless, unadorned, especially as she possessess the power of investing it with ornament." The soul naturally desires the adornment of wholeness, and recognizing this intrinsic urge is pleased to confer it upon other natures. Forms are consequently the sense of wholeness superimposed upon parts by the rational soul, to the end that these forms are no longer regarded as bundles of monads but as definite structures.

To summarize, the world is an infinite number of monads grouped into an infinite diversity of patterns, each pattern invested in a quality called form, which quality is measured by the quantity of the monadic parts. The world is adorned with numbers which hang upon it as ornaments upon the person. Each group of numbers is capable of infinite division, but whether in its divided or undivided state, it in turn is adorned with an infinite diversity of unities or wholes which issue forth in response to the urge of the rational soul to clothe abstractions in denominating natures. Thus the law which governs the increase and decrease of wholes, and the superimposition of wholeness upon number, is a manifestation of a divine urge within the numerative monad, which is termed Number and is a definite attribute of Cause itself.

In this manner we see mathematically demonstrated how Man, the unconditioned principle, is obscured by men, the infinite diversity; how mind, the Yellow Emperor, is hidden in the midst of minds which think in many terms and with many results, but which reason all toward the same end. We behold the Creator so veiled by his creations that his own dignity is no longer apparent but is absorbed into the effulgence of his spheres. As we gaze forth upon the universal vista we see the veils behind which stand the divine principles—the immovable causes of motion, the ungenerated causes of generation, the undying causes of life and death. Our external parts reach forth to grasp the external substance of the All, our tiny fingers reach out to pluck the stars from their thrones, and our outer being bows with veneration before the outer substances that are its very self and from which it was mined in the Primordial Day. Meanwhile our inner selves—the invisible cause of our visible activity—yearn to be mingled with the Spirit of Cosmos.

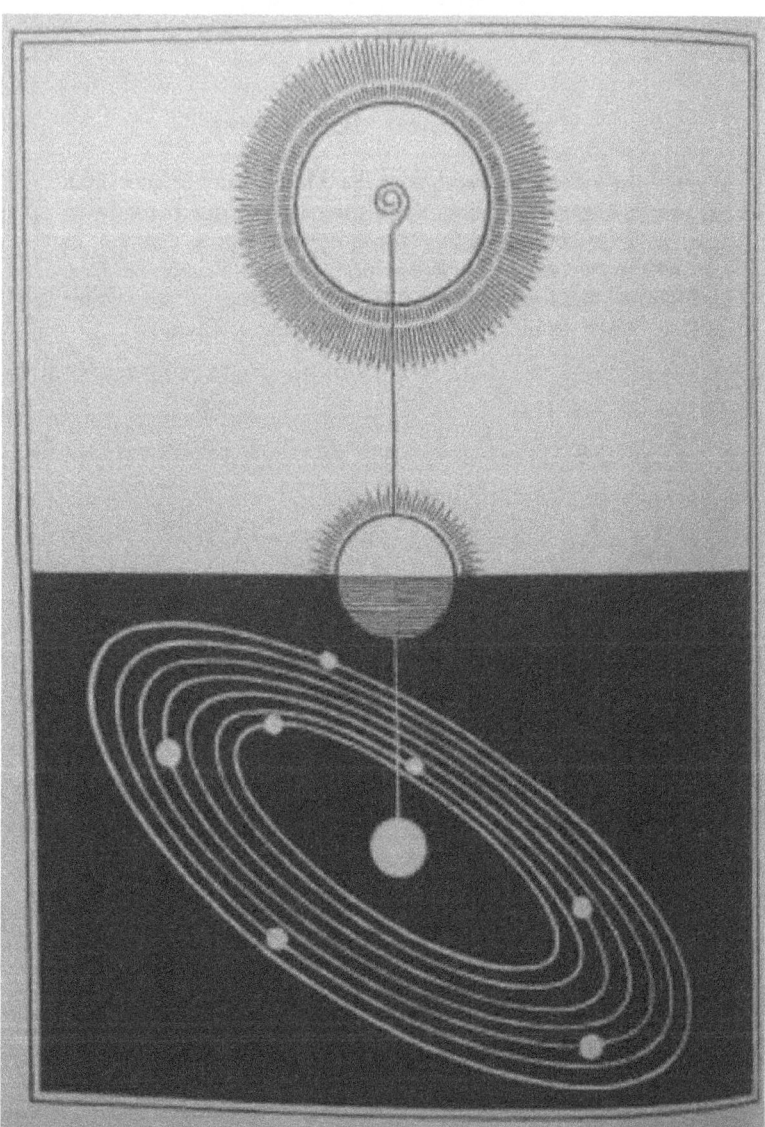

THE GOLDEN THREAD

The upper and light half of the diagram represents the causal universe. The thread of manifestation is seen unwinding from the archetypal germ to descend into the globe of the soul. From thence it falls into the irrational sphere to end in the radiant solar center.

CHAPTER TWELVE

Demigods and Supermen

WHEN Socrates declared irony and inductive reasoning to be the peculiar instruments of philosophy, he implied far more than the words convey to the average layman. As previously stated (pp. 189) the soul of man when immersed in generation manifests according to the laws of the generating sphere. Hence man can only liberate himself from corporeal conditions by first freeing his rational part from mundane entanglements. The personality with its numerous attributes is suspended from the generating soul, and consequently the clarification of consciousness is attainable only by the liberation of the self from the generating principle. While invested with the substances of the generating sphere, the rational soul is capable of objectifying an infinite diversity of forms or bodies. These the generating soul spontaneously evolves from its own nature by virtue of its inherent formative qualities. As forms and corporeal natures continuously flow from the soul thus invested with generating attributes, it is evident that any attempt to escape diversity by dispersion of the forms is futile. The generating soul is like the fabled dragon—for every head that is cut off two more grow to take its place. Inhibitions and austerities are efforts to combat the processes of the generating soul by destruction of the generations as they come forth. But the task is never finished, and no permanent victory is ever won. The remodeling of character through the despotism of will is therefore, at best, an imperfect and inadequate procedure. To arbitrarily remove the ends, while the means which produce those ends are permitted to remain, is to imperil the entire nature in which such inconsistency exists.

In a certain sense man is an appendage of impulse; hence the regeneration of character must be through the reformation of impulses and not their inhibition. A certain consistency must exist upon all planes of activity. The animal soul must ever express itself through animal instincts, the generating soul through the instincts of generation, and the rational soul through the urge to rationality. For the internal nature thus to function upon one level of consciousness while the external nature attempts to exist upon another, is to create a confusion which must inevitably result in disaster. Socrates maintained that the rationalizing of the individual must take place in the causal nature which, flowing downward into the corporeal constitution, will speedily mold the inferior into the image of the superior. Hence his emphasis upon the efficacy of irony and inductive reasoning. Irony is here to be understood in the sense of fate, which philosophers have ever declared to be ironical. Fate effects the liberation of the rational part by revealing that all things are destined to return to their own natures (or origins) in spite of every effort to nullify this design. Ultimate achievement is hence unavoidable, and is the certain end of all beginnings; but incalculable is the interval that must elapse before the operations of divine procedure restore all things to their primal state.

Irony, therefore, is the long way around—the path of the drone. It is beset with every obstacle that materiality can contrive; it leads through death and sorrow, and he who chooses to take the buffetings of destiny must be prepared to withstand the blasts of outrageous circumstance. Ironically, he who chooses to do the least must accomplish the most; for none shall labor as hard as the sluggard or struggle as intensely for liberation as the one content to drift upon the sea of Providence. Whoever chooses to escape the responsibilities of life exhausts himself in his efforts to dodge inevitables.

For the foolish, then, the ironic road; for the wise, the true Socratic path—the theory of inductive reasoning. Establishing his entire philosophy upon man—consequently upon a particular—Socrates reasoned therefrom to generals, thus establishing a procedure to which Francis Bacon added the essential element of analogy. Induction infers a process of thought whereby the rationality which is posited in particulars is urged or impelled to retire along the line of its own flow, and verge toward the monad (or general) of which it is the particular. In other words, Socrates sought to arrive at divine realities by causing particulars to retire into their own general state. While the monad might erroneously be considered a particular, it is in reality a general, and the manifestations which emerge from it are the particulars.

The ancient Socratic philosophy involved, therefore, the correction of particulars by the renovation of generals. Affirming all particulars to have their origin in generals, it is evident that man as a particular is founded upon Man as a general, and hence that which influences the general must necessarily influence the particular. The reverse, however, is not essentially true; for the lesser cannot dominate the greater but must be dominated thereby. Philosophy, accordingly, is peculiarly adapted to the fields of generals, while science has an affinity for the field of particulars. Hence science is founded in philosophy and must receive its particular truths by adaptation from general verities. Philosophy, consequently, is not individualistic in the commonly accepted sense, but regards individuals as dependencies of universals, and seeks to achieve the liberation of individuals by the reconstruction of universals.

Descending to the level of man himself, we must then regard man as a general; his parts, members, and attributes as particulars suspended from his general, or rational, nature. Man is not simply a personality; he is a personality, an individuality, and a universality in one. His universality verges toward universals, his individuality verges toward individuals, and his personality verges toward personals. Each of these natures in turn has its own dependencies which verge toward it and toward which it also apparently verges. From the subject matter of the previous chapter it is evident that generals partake of unity or wholeness; and particulars of diversity; for as diversity is contained within unity, so the particulars are contained within the general. Impulses which impel the consciousness toward particulars consequently incline it toward diversity and illusion, while impulses which impel the consciousness toward generals, incline it toward wholeness or reality.

How, then, shall man stimulate his inferior nature to verge toward its own superior part and thus accomplish philosophic growth? The answer is evident: By permeating the consciousness with the realization of wholeness, or by the instinctive inductive process of reasoning toward generals. Personalities are particulars; principles are generals. Hence to reason toward particulars is to reason toward personalities. Personalities are infinite diversity, and the contemplation of them is a philosophic error whose reward is an involvement therein which jeopardizes rationality. By inclining toward generals, however, we approach principles, and in the sphere of principles we approach wholeness; for a principle is a wholeness which may manifest as a diversity in application, but which in its own nature is an essential unity. Involution is consequently the inclination of the rational soul toward diversity (particulars). Its nadir is corporeality, where dissimilars manifest as an infinite diversity of forms. Evolution, conversely, is an ascent to principle, in which the rational soul verges toward the principle of wholeness, thereby uniting itself with natures of ever-increasing permanence and lucidity.

It follows that growth inspires the contemplation of wholes, or unities, and that contemplation of wholes inspires, in turn, growth. Thus a benevolent circle is created which gradually accomplishes the unification of parts and elevates the abiding genius (the rational spirit) to the contemplation of abiding monads, or wholes. From the standpoint of pure philosophy it is useless to affirm wholeness or deny diversity or platitudinize concerning either. The realization must flow downward from the apex of the individual self, where it has become established as the object of the rapturous contemplation of the rational soul. By verging toward the realization of wholeness the rational soul is drawn out of the quagmire of generation, regaining thereby the control of certain functions and members rendered impotent by the embrace of generation.

As particulars depend from generals, so all natures exist suspended from principles, and before the mind is capable of rational functioning it must be established upon the foundation of familiarity with principles. It follows that intellect founded upon principle cannot deviate from that which its own rationality has approved. Consequently minds founded in principles are certain to function in harmony with the flow of principles, and the inevitable result of intellect functioning in harmony with such a flow is reasonableness of conclusion. In the last analysis that which is reasonable is true if the reason itself be established in principle; for no part can deviate from the wholeness from which it is suspended, and principle is always sufficiently inclusive to circumscribe exception. In simple words, then, *the establishment of the mind in wholes (unities) is essential to right thinking, and is the master key to the rational cognizance of the order and sequence of parts—the monads of particulars.*

The haphazardness of modern philosophic speculation is due to ignoring the necessity of founding intellection in wholes or unities. A mind which does not reason from generals to particulars is always in danger of elevating a particular to the dignity of a general, thus creating an exclusive rather than an inclusive general. In other words, when the emphasis upon a part causes this part to appear as a wholeness to the perceptions of a specialized intellect, the result is a wholeness which is not inclusive in that parts do not contain each other. If a part, therefore, be raised to the dignity of a wholeness, then another part may also be similarly elevated, the result being an infinite diversity of wholes, which is a philosophic absurdity in that the element of diversity cannot exist in wholeness. When a part is so raised above the level of its own dignity we find a system of thought which seeks to reduce universals to the estate of parts; to interpret the whole in terms of the fraction; to explain the whole by the laws of the part; or to invest the whole with the limited attributes of the part.

All this results in the concept of an *all* which is not all-inclusive and which consequently finds it necessary either to manipulate universal laws so that they conform to the imperfect attributes of the part itself, or to ignore those phases of universal activity whose manifestations are beyond the province of the part. For example, to the ancient philosopher science was a part of the body of knowledge. It was therefore a dependency of reason and an instrument of erudition. By the modern scientist, however, science is elevated to the dignity of wholeness, and regarded as the actual monad of rationality rather than a dependency thereof. The resultant confusion is foreshadowed. The field of phenomena includes a multitude of activities outside the province of science as a particular. These are naturally excluded from science when it is regarded as a general. Hence scientific men are prone to ridicule the concept of the immortality of the soul, because such concepts do not come under the jurisdiction of science as a particular; and when science is thus elevated to the false dignity of an absolute state the doctrine of the soul is necessarily outlawed from universals.

The inadequacy of science is thus demonstrated, for it is indisputably established as a particular and not a general. There is a natural tendency of the mind to elevate its own particular to the estate of a general. This is the inevitable outcome of founding knowledge upon particulars. The philosophic perspective is lost and short-sightedness ensues. From short-sightedness itself as a monadic entity, are suspended such particulars as bigotry, intolerance, and rational injustice.

In America today we have a deluge of cults—literally hundreds of minor creeds, orthodox as well as heterodox, which have sprung up from an over-emphasis of the Baconian doctrine of particulars. Analytical reasoning is largely responsible for this unfortnate condition, for analysis is a separative impulse whose natural trend is to break up similars into dissimilars and thereby unduly emphasize them. On the other hand synthesis is an unceasing impulse toward the establishment of wholes or unities. This does not necessarily imply that the philosophy behind the procedure is at fault; for the microscope, while ever revealing particulars, at the same time reveals also the unity of those particulars. If parts be invariably regarded as wholes, and each new division be likewise invested with the sense of wholeness, then the present analytical process, through the reformation of its theory, would automatically become a synthetic process.

In religion this practice of elevating parts to the dignity of wholes is most common. Every little motion is thus raised to the dignity of a divine edict; every little whim rooted in a spiritual certainty; and every infinitesimal belief so highly magnified that it eclipses the entire body of universal order. If every individual nail in the rim of a wheel should conceive itself to be the hub, imagine the dilemma of the wheel at finding itself expected to revolve upon a score of different hubs simultaneously and make definite progress!

The mind naturally thinks in terms of particulars; it is consequently incapable of ascending to that sphere of rationality where dwells the spirit of intellectual justice. Justice does not necessarily result from a full comprehension of wholes, but rather from the realization of the equality of parts. Thus in philosophy there is a democracy of parts and an autocracy of wholes; for parts are equal to parts but inferior to wholes. St. Paul epitomizes the philosophy of the "Master Builder" concerning this subject: "For we know in part, and we prophesy in part. But when that which is perfect is come, then that which is in part shall be done away." (I Cor. XIII : 9-10) In this case that which is "perfect" signifies the state of wholeness. These words have been interpreted by the Christian Church to signify the ultimate unification of all men under its own banner, unmindful of the obvious fact that it is but a "part" itself and can endure only until "that which is perfect is come."

The elevation of isolated fragments to a position of supremacy over wholes is the sequel to the overemphasis of individualism; for individualism, while it properly emphasizes the wholeness innate within parts, fails to emphasize the greater wholeness that is the sum of parts. The natural supremacy of the Platonic system of reasoning over the more popular Aristotelian method thus becomes self-apparent. Reasoning *a posteriori* is characteristic of modern thought, whereas the ancient Mysteries owed their excellence largely to the *a priori* method. The *a posteriori* method inclines toward separateness, egotism, and selfishness; the *a prori* toward dignity, humility, and unselfishness.

All systems of thought which ascribe to the parts a power equal to the whole are productive of despotism and the false usurpation of power. Tyranny is an oppression, and the limiting boundary of parts oppresses the limitlessness of wholes. From this insufficiency is born rebellion, for that which is unduly bounded bursts its bonds and escapes into an area sufficient for its expression. When inferiors are ruled by superiors, order reigns; but when superiors are ruled by inferiors, chaos prevails. If man is ruled by the laws of the universe he is justly dealt with; but if the universe were subjected to the laws of men, sufficiency would be oppressed by insufficiency. When particulars are ruled by generals, rational order is the product; but when generals are ruled by particulars, the despotism of irrationality destoys all rational congruity.

When the individual essays the philosophic life it is first necessary that the mind be trained to think in round terms; for roundness partakes of the nature of wholeness because the circle or sphere (like wholeness) is without beginning or end. To think in round terms may be interpreted to mean keeping the mentality upon the level of greatest inclusiveness, ever striving to attain fuller inclusiveness since perfect inclusiveness alone qualifies the intellect to descend to the contemplation of parts. For example, when thinking of religion, do not think of Mohammedans, Brahmans, or Christians, but think of religion as the universal adoration of creative principles common to all mankind, and found in a rudimentary form even among the higher animals, such as the anthropoid ape.

Having first established the universality of veneration, we have founded our comprehension upon the wholeness of the subject. From this point we may then rationally descend to the consideration of religions, thereby escaping the pitfall o. intolerance resulting from basing the study of religion upon a religion. When viewed from the exalted level of wholeness, such issues as the possible priority of the Presbyterians over the Methodists not only become inconsequential, but retire beyond the vanishing point of philosophic concern. Yet men who have termed themselves rational, who have been entrusted by their communities with positions of importance and the administration of justice, have waged bloody warfare and unreasonable persecution over such trivialities. Competitiveness is thus demonstrated to be natural to parts. Hence the mind that thinks in terms of parts makes continual comparison between them; whereas the highly evolved intellect, recognizing that co-operation through which the parts are caused to form the whole, thinks and lives in terms of tolerance and magnanimity.

Philosophic discipline therefore requires that the intellect be rationalized through familiarity with unities, and permitted to express its natural amity toward them. Being itself a wholeness, the rationality has an affinity for wholeness, and rejoices in its contemplation. This rational desire for completeness is opposed, however, by the irrationality of the animal soul. Limited to the plane of sense and beholding only diversity, the principle of unity is inconceivable to the animal soul because its nature and perception function in terms of isolated individualism. Stimulated by philosophic discipline, the rational faculties are caused to assert their intrinsic preference, thereby inclining the entire mental organism toward recognition of the supremacy of wholes. Having thus established its preference, the mind gradually comes instinctively to function in harmony therewith. The result is mental benevolence, which manifests in the outer life as that nobility of temperament which irresistibly attracts, and is concordant with, the subconscious unity existent in all human nature. The nobility of the inclusive intellect is undeniable, and opposition to its conclusions is usually based upon cupidity or egotism, for it can never be rationally opposed.

Another point of major importance is that a mind established upon wholes is never forced to reconstruct its attitudes toward particulars, for these attitudes are continually held in suspension. As the mind increases in its knowledge of particulars it simply pours them into the capacious wholeness, which is always sufficient to include the nature of the parts. As a result, it is impossible to outgrow a doctrine or be forced to reconstruct it; for the mind, moving in certainties, builds in from universals and does not arrive at particulars until it is capable of recognizing and organizing their diversity.

In the preceding outline the processes of inductive and deductive reasoning may appear to be hopelessly confused. Here again it must be realized that reason itself is also a wholeness, of which induction and deduction are parts. Hence, as Confucius noted, the positive and negative are never found to be totally isolated, so induction always partakes to some degree of deduction; while deduction, inclining toward induction, finds its opposite essential to the philosophic unity. Induction—which is the pure Socratic method—while it reasons from particulars to generals, does so with the definite purpose of establishing generals. It is possible for the mind to ponder upon particulars without emphasizing the quest of wholeness—in fact, particulars may be traced toward their own cause without the realization of wholeness being established; for in this case particulars merge into particulars instead of generals, and the entire universe continues to be regarded as a mass of particulars rather than a wholeness.

True induction, however, is the quest of wholeness through particulars—the decision to establish the rational code in the sense of generals. Upon reaching this state the mind has realized the true end of the Socratic process or the Aristotelian mode. On the other hand, having established rationality in generals, the mind assumes the Platonic mode and begins to reason toward particulars. This procedure ultimately results in the establishment of consciousness at a point of equilibrium midway between induction and deduction, where both are shown to be contributing factors in the unfoldment of the process of rational thinking.

The natural flow of existence is from the prior to the subsequent or from the cause to its effect. Pythagoras, however, recommended the retrospective mode whereby the subsequent is caused to flow back into priority. The mental reactions caused by these two processes are far-reaching. To establish a cause through its effect awakens a reaction wholly different from that created by the picture of a cause flowing into its effect. The former is an impulse far more definite than the latter, due possibly to the unnatural order which emphasizes the intensity of the elements involved. The flow of cause into effect is so common as to become monotonous; the mental faculties, therefore, become oblivious to the drone of the natural or normal sequence. When, however, the process is reversed, the mental faculties are startled into activity by the unfamiliar —and consequently discordant—note.

Retrospection is an inductive procedure which, by revealing the effect before its cause, emphasizes the enormity of consequence that can be suspended from the mote of cause. The effect of such revelation is to overawe the intellect with the sense of responsibility. It demonstrates that though man has a certain province for the exercise of despotic agency, he is powerless to control the destiny of his fabrications or determine with certitude the ends at which his beginnings shall arrive. Man's sphere of influence is as far-reaching as creation, and what we first agitate diverges to the shores of eternity like the ripples from a stone thrown upon the surface of some placid lake. That which we have thus enlivened with our own potentialities we can never overtake until at last we mingle with it in the Absolute.

The living are ruled by the dead; the present is ruled by the past; and, as Omar Khayyam says, that which the first man wrote, the last man shall read. Under the moldering headstone in some obscure churchyard may rot the mortal remains of some petty despot whose royal edicts still survive to afflict unborn generations with their absurdities. Huge enterprises may go awry, yes, empires perish through the insidious consequences of a few hastily spoken words or a single irrational act. Retrospection warns men so to regulate their thoughts and actions that the afterglow of their achievements shall not be tinted with a lurid or unnatural hue. Though man loses control over the seeds of action which he has sown in the fields of space, he is forever the victim of his self-generated consequences. Those careless in thought or deed will sometime curse the Providence that heaps upon them the unwelcome fruitage of their own folly and forces them to live in tolerance with their own progeny.

Elsewhere are described (pps. 52, 53) the orders of the gods, demigods, supermen, and mortals. Descending from his spiritual state, man was established in irrationality, a condition from which he seeks to escape by inclining himself toward superior natures and ascending to the seat of rationality. The gods differ from man in that their realization of wholeness or unity is intrinsic, and their consciousness is incapable of descending to terms of diversity. They are consequently unable to exist, think, or feel in terms of particulars, since by virtue of their establishment in wholeness they are without the appreciation of parts. A simple illustration of this attitude is man himself, who finds it difficult to realize the existence of individuality within his own nature. He cannot conceive of independent cellular or organic function within his own body. He may affirm his intellectual belief in the individuality of parts, but his consciousness does not supply him with any definite reactions along this line. As man—the corporeal unit—is incapable of descending into and coming *en rapport* with the consciousness of a single cell of his own body, so the gods—or units of spiritual consciousness—have no rational perception of the diversity suspended from their own natures.

When we realize the gods to be wholes or unities we can better comprehend why they abide in immortality and are not subject to dissolution. The dignity of gods over men is equal to the superior dignity of wholes over parts. As wholes can never be less than wholes, it is evident that the gods cannot descend to men; but as parts are capable of being merged into wholes, so man is capable of ascending into the presence of the gods. When he has accomplished this he is immortal—not absolutely in his own right but in the immortality of the god from whom he is suspended. Immortality is consequently the merging of a mortal nature with an immortal nature, whereby the nature of the immortal is caused to extend and include the nature of the mortal. What was formerly impermanent thus becomes permanent by its mergence with the nature of permanence. Natures become immortal by retiring into their own causes; for causes partake of immortality and are proximate to the One Cause toward which they themselves incline to partake of the fullness of Being. Though men (the fractional parts) come and go and their span is but a little while, Man (the principle) endures for an interminable period of time. By elevating themselves to wholeness men are able to partake of the immortality of their archetype. Thus men and women as isolated personalities are not immortal, but their immortality is assured through their foundation in the causal nature.

According to the ancients the universe contains, in addition to the myriads of natural creatures (who inhabit its inferior part and are visible to the perceptions of the normal human being) other orders, hierarchies, or species of life beyond the perception of the limited faculties now at man's disposal. Socrates declares that there are orders of life which dwell along the shores of the air as men dwell along the shores of the sea. Dwelling in a subtler stratum, these beings are seldom given to contention, but live together in amity, worshiping the gods and serving the beautiful.

To assume the visible to be the all is to deny even the most rudimentary instincts of human nature. Mankind dwells in a vale, as it were, and on every side rise high mountains which obscure from view that which lies beyond. Yet by what right shall we deny the existence of broader vistas beyond the circumscribing walls of our sense perception? Is it not reasonable that the interval between wholeness and diversity is filled with a concatenated order of generations—some verging toward wholeness and proximate to it; others verging toward diversity and filled with its quality? Degrees of wholeness are the spiritual impulses which manifest as the various genera composing physical life. There are degrees of wholeness requiring vehicles of expression far more refined than man's bodies, even as there are degrees of diversity, which like the grain of sand call for a structure less complicated.

Are the gods then to be considered as arbitrary creations, or simply the hypothetical divisions erected by philosophy for the purpose of classifying the proximity of various natures either to their substance or their shadow? Through the centuries men have pleased to worship gods as proxies of the One Indivisible and Omnipotent Nature. Being posterior to the One, are not the gods themselves natures? Though elevated to divine dignity from their proximity to wholeness, are they not, like men, orders of dependencies suspended in the abyss of interval, there to generate within their abundant natures a numerous progeny which they tolerate and ultimately cause to flow back again into themselves?

Let the contemplation of divine natures, therefore, be approached in the spirit of reasonableness, bereft of that awe and diffidence which has marked such contemplation in the past. Like the Cyclopes, the wholes (or unities) stand regarding through their unified perceptions the transcendent nature of the First Wholeness. An analysis of the natures of the gods is essential to an understanding of human nature; for through them we partake of the fullness of all good, and in them is the field of both our present labors and our future endeavors. Wholeness is not a personality. The gods, therefore, do not partake of the attributes of personalities. They are not vengeful principles, nor are they inclined to be moved by the piteous supplication of the inadequate. Like the carved Rameses of Egypt, they sit immovable, sufficient, and all-sufficing. Of their immeasurable dignity we may not know all; but through philosophic discipline we may equip ourselves to understand, in part at least, the magnitude and tranquillity of their abidance. Regardless of the degree or dignity of the parts, the wholeness from which they themselves are directly suspended is their

God, their Father and their Mother, their beginning and their end. Thus the gods are legion. Merging into each other, these wholes verge toward their common First Cause; and as the gods retire into God, so God, in turn, retires into that which was, is, and ever shall be, yet is not.

The already well emphasized point that the gods are principles rather than personalities is confirmed by the evidence of Iamblichus, who attacked the concept popular among the uneducated masses that *places* could be assigned as divine habitats, or that certain communities enjoyed the patronage of the celestials. One of the erroneous beliefs was that Athena Parthenos (Minerva) was the guardian spirit of Athens. Iamblichus reasoned thus: As the gods permeate the entire structure of being, and as universals are unlimited as to time and place, how can any locality be sufficiently privated of their influence to require the appointment of a superessential protector? Being everywhere at all time and in all place, the gods are inherently omnipresent, nor can their influence be either increased or diminished. This theory is the rational foundation upon which must yet be erected the structure of universal religion. It unmasks the fallacious conceptions of racial or national gods; for it demonstrates that although men may differ concerning the attributes and number of their divinities—even attempting to distribute the universe among various deities—the divine principles themselves remain undivided and unchanged, with their presence equally common to all men and to all places.

Iamblichus further likens the celestials and their abiding natures to the zodiac and the other heavenly bodies, whose influences (according to the astrologers) modeled sidereal nature into the tangible likenesses of various abstract qualities and conditions. As the stars abide in their enduring causes and are ever the same, so the gods abide upon their immovable thrones; for their unchangeableness is an essential attribute of their own divine natures. But as the mutual intermingling of the attributes of the abiding stars results in a countless order of diversified manifestations, so while the divine natures (the gods) remain unchanged, those participating in their manifold virtues assume a variety of aspects to them and, dependent upon their proximity (which is measured by rationality) either enjoy the benevolent dispositions of these abiding divinities, or suffer from the deprivation of these influences.

These relationships between abiding principles and non-abiding personalities are capable of measurement according to certain abstract principles, which the ancient philosophers concealed under the symbolism of Time. These abstract mensurations (which must never be confused with literal calculations) are arcanely designated by the philosophers as the "birthdays of the gods." Deities are said to be "born" at the moment when the unfolding rationality of the aspirant first participates in their effulgence or comes into harmonious correlation to their power. Thus the celebration of the divine birthdays does not signify that the deities were actually created upon these days; for if actually born they would thereby partake of the nature of generation and also be subject to the unstable laws of generation and decay. In Christianity, for example, although the 25th of December is celebrated as the birthday of Christ, even the least informed layman knows that *natus solis invicti* signifies merely the descent of an eternal principle into the sphere of temporal agencies where the rationality of man may partake of its attributes and qualities. Christ is declared to have existed in the presence of the Father before the beginning of Time, and after his death and resurrection to have reascended into the sphere of endurance, there to remain throughout all duration unaffected by Time and not subject to the laws of incident and change. This concept is in harmony with the Platonic theory that the virtue of the immortals lies in the fact that they are *unborn*, having the apex of their period of activity posited in undivided unity or (as the Egyptians pleased to call it) *unaging Time*—duration that does not pass.

In describing how inferior natures, or corporeal constitutions, become filled with the superabundance of celestial natures (thereby partaking of and manifesting the celestial sufficiencies) Proclus in his *Theurgy*, translated by Ficinus in his *Excerpta*, writes in substance as follows: As those who love gradually advance from the admiration of sensible forms to the admiration of divine principles, so the initiated priests, discovering the sacred truth that *all things subsist in all things,* advanced from this conclusion to the fabrication of the sacred science founded upon the principles of mutual sympathy and participation. Because of their understanding of the fourth-dimensional universe, they realized that as far as the element of place is concerned heaven was in the earth and the earth in heaven; that principles continually permeate both places and things; and that places and things endure their natural span immersed in the very substance of principle. Hence, the superior forever rules the inferior. Inferiors are ever paying homage to their superiors either consciously (as in the case of illumined men) or unconsciously (as in the case of the elements), the latter voicing their admiration by assuming the appearance and reflecting the attributes of divine qualities.

Thus, observes Proclus, the sunflower pays homage to the solar orb by inclining itself toward the source of its own being. A piece of paper, if preheated and then brought close to fire, will suddenly burst into flames even though it does not actually touch the fire. This is an arcane hint that divine natures (the fire) communicate themselves to such corporeal bodies (the heated paper) as have rendered themselves capable of their reception. The flaming paper further represents the deification of mortals whose divinity, by mingling itself with the causal flame, vanishes away into its own beginning, leaving naught behind but the ashes. The lotus also unfolds its petals with the ascent of the sun toward the zenith, closing its petals when the sun retires to the western corner of the heavens. This gesture of the plant is as much a "hymn to the sun" as the prayers and praise of men. Again, the sunstone imitates with its golden rays the luminosity of its namesake. Another curious gem, the eye-of-heaven has a form within it which resembles the pupil of the human eye and emits a brilliant ray. The lunar stone, by certain changes inherent to itself, also modifies its rays by the phases of the moon, and the stone called *helioselenus* changes its color with the celestial moods of the sun and the moon. By such occult means do irrational natures manifest the abundance of superessential virtue imparted to them out of the fullness of divine natures. (For further details consult the notes at the end of the 1821 Edition of Thomas Taylor's translation of *Iamblichus on The Mysteries of the Egyptians, Chaldeans and Assyrians*.)

As previously suggested, the virtue of the gods springs from their abundant unity. It is a Platonic axiom that "the principal (chief) subsistence of everything is according to the summit of its essence." In other words, all bodies and constitutions are to be measured by the dignity of their first principles or natures; for this principle is the true measure of the capacity and limitation of the thing suspended from it, because no thing can become greater than its source. To mingle with superiors it must cease, therefore, in its own nature. Emerging from the indivisible unity or wholeness, the gods thus partake of the virtue of this their summit. They, accordingly, differ from man in that while man has for his apex the rational mind, the gods flow downward toward rationality from a far more exalted sphere. Philosophy is a discipline which impels all activities to flow toward their own causal principle. Its chief province, therefore, is to restore all natures to their origins and thus accomplish the perfection of natures; for that is perfect which has been accepted back into the fullness of its own unity.

Among the most mysterious symbols employed by the Egyptians were two pyramids united at their apexes, one inverted and the other upright, to signify the interchange of divine and natural powers. While this particular symbol has already been briefly discussed, it will not be out of order to amplify the previous description. The inverted pyramid, with its foundation in the superior sphere, they termed *inspiration;* the upright, with its foundation upon the inferior sphere, they termed *aspiration*. Hence both of these forces commingle in natures. From the inferior the urge of the rational disciplines is toward the elevation of natures; from the superior (which is an attracting agency) the urge of inspiration is ascent toward divine perfections. If the symbol be closely examined we become aware of a more archaic meaning; for recognizing the pyramids as flowing from their own apexes, we discover that the central point from which both diverge is the abiding place of the superiors. From this superior point one pyramid—usually shown as dark—flows upward, its color signifying the occult nature of its properties which must forever remain dark and mysterious to the intellections of unillumined mortals. The second pyramid flows downward, becoming the tangible universe which is luminous to the many and susceptible of a certain degree of analysis by even those who are unenlightened.

These two pyramids represent, therefore, the duad existing within and flowing from the monad—polarity manifesting out of simple unity, through which manifestation the universe came into being. Between the unseen sphere of principles above and the visible sphere of personalities below is a ceaseless interchange of activities. Separateness being the law of personalities and unity the law of principles, it is evident that while each body occupies *some* place, each principle occupies *every* place. All principles are therefore capable of manifesting in each body. Upon this fact was based the philosophic deduction that place is of relatively small importance in matters pertaining to the higher sciences. Socrates was once accosted by a seeker after truth, who asked him where could be found the best place in which to learn. The great Skeptic instantly replied: "Where thou art;" for, whereas the learner was in place, learning was everywhere. The two consequently awaited the unifying effect of rationality, which when present links place with everywhere.

Theology particularly has become a servant to the concept of place. Among nearly all religious peoples it is a common practice to sanctify places of worship and be in attendance at the performance of certain holy offices in such places. The tombs of the saints are also hallowed, and there is a widespread veneration for sacred objects of every description. A visit to Jerusalem will demonstrate the influence wielded by such veneration for place. Here every pebble is more venerable than a boulder elsewhere, and even the filth spreads piety instead of plague! Theology also limits the mind to the concept of time as a factor in religious place. Witness the "holy days" when prayer is presumed to have especial efficacy and the celestial hierarchies are said to be peculiarly receptive to the whining importunities of men. Assembly for the common purpose of worship may confer certain ethical and sociological virtues—for instance, by inspiring the courage born of numbers—but little importance can be attached to the practice if viewed from the standpoint of spirit. In the terms of pure metaphysical philosophy, the gods as causal agencies are both omnipresent and omniscient. Free from time and place, above condition, and incapable of such purely mundane concepts as pleasure or displeasure, they flow unimpeded through the many dimensional vistas of eternity. If would-be reformers can correct the theological absurdity that the gods are localized like the weather, systematized like industry or dispositioned like ward politicians, there is still hope for the religious instincts of the race.

Plutarch of Chaeroneia, one of the early Gnostic Fathers, in his *Vision of Aridaeus*, describes an excursion made by a benighted soul into the realm of Hades, where with the aid of the "single (or psychic) eye" he perceived many things with greater clarity than is the fortune of most mortals. Aridaeus (the man who had the vision) is supposed to have died and found himself in a great sea of light, "of objects with which he had been previously familiar, he saw none save the stars; they were, however, of stupendous size and at enormous distances from one another, and poured forth a marvellous radiance of colour and sound, so that the soul riding smoothly in the light, as a ship in calm weather, sailed easily and swiftly in every direction. Omitting most of the things he saw, he said that the souls of the dead, in passing from below upwards, formed a flame-like bubble from which the air was excluded; then the bubble quietly broke, and they came forth with men-like forms and well-knit frames." (See *The Vision of Aridæus*, translated by G. R. S. Mead.)

Compiled during the first century of the Christian Era, this curious allegory is of particular interest to the modern student of Platonic philosophy; for the bubble-like souls with flaming luminosity that flowed past Aridaeus represent the spheres of isolation within which the rational nature must remain during the period of irrationality—that is, before the *one* hears the call of the *All* and chooses to mingle its destiny with the common cause. This "flame-like bubble" constitutes the interval between man as the partly-illumined creature and the gods as divine potentialities. Although man exists in these god essences, he cannot be united with these infinite certainties until he causes this bubble to "quietly break." This is a direct allusion to the rites of the Mysteries, and we suspect that Plutarch wrote not of the after-death state but of that secret ritualism whereby the dead soul in a living body is liberated to the contemplation of divinities. As institutions of illumination, the Mysteries are agencies appointed to prick the bubble of self-conceit that envelopes the average soul, and thereby renders it impervious to divine ministrations.

The well-formed bodies seen by Aridaeus coming forth out of the broken bubbles represent the organized rationalities which are manifested after the consciousness has been liberated from the inferior sphere—that iridescent world which, mirror-like, shows man only the reflection of himself, leaving him unaware of the Great Within in the nature of which he floats. The sea of luminosity in which the soul floats like a ship represents the causal universe whose divine agencies, manifesting first as colors and sounds, mingle in an exotic symphonic profusion. Aridaeus also declares that in this luminous world he felt as though he was breathing all over, for his whole body was filled with a life-giving air that gave the sense of buoyancy and freedom from every oppression of matter. Air is the ancient and secret symbol of rationality, and represents the intangible illumined mind that is declared to be absent from the contents of the bubbles (the symbols of irrationality). The free air of the spirit comes to relieve man when he is willing to renounce the oppressed atmosphere of the body. This is the secret of the "enthusiasm" of the ancient Mysteries—the ecstasy that came upon those who "breathed in" the gods—for by divine enthusiasm was signified unity with God, as the word itself implies (*en theos,* in God.) Those who were in the nature and consciousness of Cause thus ceased to move of their own accord, but their frantic gyrations were regarded as evidence that a divine spirit was agitating and mingling them with universals.

When Socrates declared that where thou art is the place to learn he thereby revealed the universality of Cause. The fact that all men do not actively partake of the all-permeating learning implies a barrier between learning and the learner; between life and the living; between the good and those who strive for virtue. This barrier is the quality interval referred to in the preceding chapter, to be overcome only by the disciplines of the Mysteries; for alone and unaided, men cannot sufficiently organize their internal natures to achieve this most necessary end. The gods are presumed to be superior to these intervals of quality, and hence mingle not only with each other but each with All in a perfect unity. With few exceptions pagan philosophic systems discovered that man exists within the opalescent globe now termed the *auric egg,* or soul envelope. This auric egg (its lower sheaths at least) totally isolates man from the rest of the universe, admitting through its poles only sufficient of the Universal Agent to maintain him in his isolated embryonic individualism; for this auric egg is the womb in which the prenatal life of mortality is passed.

As long as he remains an individual, man is an embryo; as long as he is in this embryonic state he is a mortal; and as long as he is a mortal he must exemplify the mortal principle of separateness. While he may fit together with the other parts so as to form a comb-like fabric, he can never actually mingle his own nature with that of any other creature. Men mix with each other as oil mixes with water; but the gods mingle as oils for all have the same essential base. Divinity, exemplifying similars, forever mingles with itself; humanity, exemplifying dissimilars, may be brought together, yet a certain separateness inevitably remains as long as humanness remains. It is because man is separate from man that he is not a god. To the degree that he overcomes the sense of separateness he overcomes his humanness and rises to the state of immortality—a state in which he comes proximate to the gods, converses with the immortals, and beholds those great Causal Principles which, like mighty pillars, sustain the universe in its appointed place.

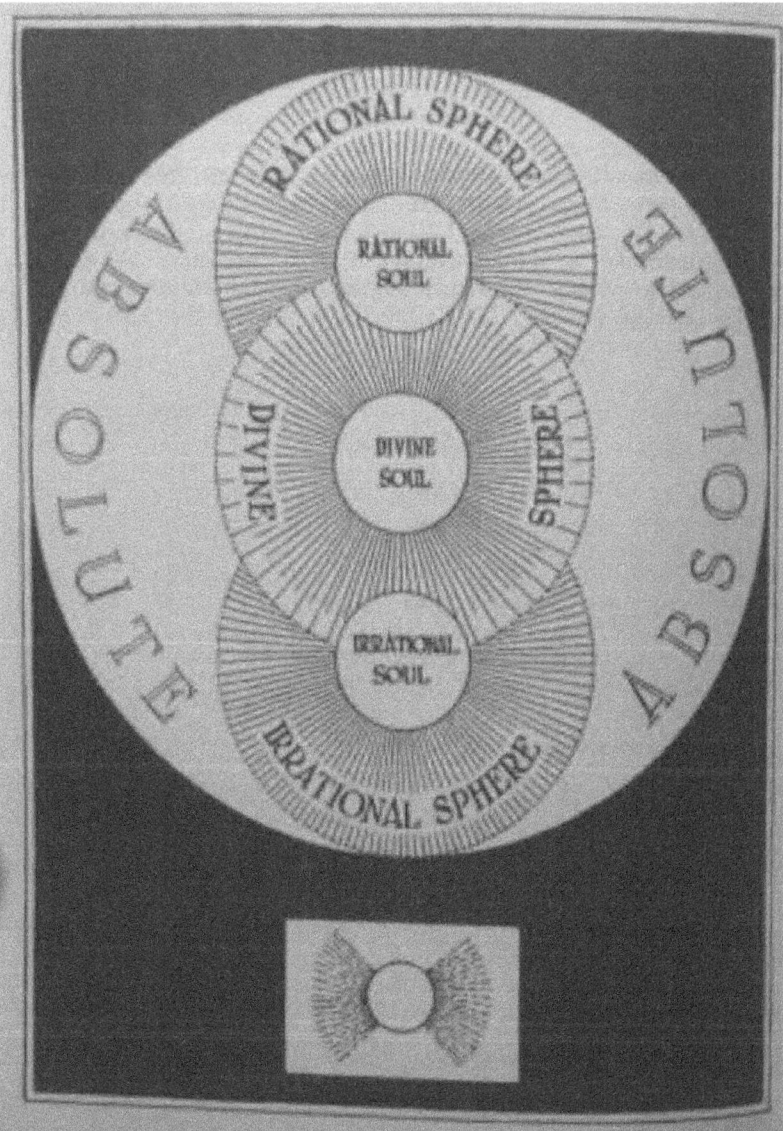

THE SPHERE OF THE SOUL

The sphere of the Absolute is here shown centered as a radiant power denominated the Divine Soul. While this Soul maintains its equilibrium, spiritual consciousness remains unbroken; but by the soul inclining toward the extremes is created the illusion of the rational and irrational souls as positive and negative poles.

CHAPTER THIRTEEN

EMERSON'S CONCEPT OF THE OVERSOUL

IN every human nature abides a Cyclopean self with whom, at long intervals, the mortal part of man communes. With this thought is introduced a new phase of Greek metaphysical speculation. The instructors in the Mysteries declared that at birth each individual was assigned an invisible patron spirit called the *natal daemon*. This entity was analogous to the *totem* of the North American Indians, except that the totem was invoked by prayer and fasting, while the daemon—being coexistent with the generating soul itself—became, as it were, the identity of the senses. By some this natal daemon was considered the personified aggregate of past experiences or the summation of previous lives; it was synonymous with the instinctive impulse-nature—that inevitable product of existences which stands behind and urges the issues of the outer life. This natal daemon is the composite self; the sum of countless previous selves; the personality compounded of multiple personalities; the thinking, feeling, and actuating sensory organism of material urge; the superphysical by-product of temporal achievement. The natal daemon is the god who protects the fool, making it impossible for man to actually undo himself beyond redemption. It is the patron saint of the outer life; the intuitively sensed superiority; the intangible authority by which mortal man is given courage to assert his participation in a divine energy. According to the Egyptians the natal daemon is created by the converging celestial rays at the time of nativity. It becomes the intangible cause of dispositions, and through its agencies two individuals, though similarly organized, neither think nor feel the same, but work out their diverging destinies motivated by this daemoniacal part.

"Plato," writes Apuleius on the *God of Socrates*, "asserts that a peculiar dæmon is allotted to every man, who is a witness and a guardian of his conduct in life, who, without being visible to any one, is always present, and who is an arbitrator not only of his deeds, but also of his thoughts. But when, life being finished, the soul returns [to the judges of its conduct], then the daemon who presided over it immediately seizes, and leads it as his charge to judgment, and is there present with it while it pleads its cause. Hence, this dæmon reprehends it, if it has acted on any false pretence; solemnly confirms what it says, if it asserts any thing that is true; and conformably to its testimony passes sentence. All you, therefore, who hear this divine opinion of Plato, as interpreted by me, so form your minds to whatever you may do, or to whatever may be the subject of your meditation, that you may know there is nothing concealed from those guardians either within the mind, or external to it; but that the daemon who presides over you inquisitively participates of all that concerns you, sees all things, understands all things, and *in the place of conscience dwells in the most profound recesses of the mind.* For he of whom I speak is a perfect guardian, a singular prefect, a domestic speculator, a proper curator, an intimate inspector, an assiduous observer, an inseparable arbiter, a reprobater of what is evil, an approver of what is good; and if he is legitimately attended to, sedulously known, and religiously worshipped, in the way in which he was reverenced by Socrates with justice and innocence, will be a predictor in things uncertain, a premonitor in things dubious, a defender in things dangerous, and an assistant in want. He will also be able, by dreams, by tokens, and perhaps also manifestly, when the occasion demands it, to avert from you evil, increase your good, raise your depressed, support your falling, illuminate your obscure, govern your prosperous, and correct your adverse circumstances."

The natal daemon is declared by Olympiodorus to be the supreme flower of the soul, for it is the blossoming of soul qualities. To a certain extent the soul is generated from the interplay of action and reaction in the sphere of sense. The soul is the garment woven from the threads of incident; the natal daemon is consciousness born of experience—the realization begotten of necessity. The natal daemon is the diamond soul, the transmutation of corporeality into incorporeality, the regeneration of bodily quantities into bodiless qualities; for the natal daemon is the wholeness of consciousness which must ever result from the co-ordination of heterogeneous parts. In the terms of mathematics the natal daemon is the spirit of the number 6, which is invoked by the coming together of six monads and is inseparable from them as long as they continue to constitute a unit or wholeness. The natal daemon must therefore be regarded as the consciousness of the senses conceived as a monad and established at the summit of the pyramid of sense, from whence it flows downward to tincture with that understanding based upon experience the entire structure of the corporeal perceptions. The philosophers declared that a natal daemon, or *familiar*, is assigned to every man, with whom it remains until the rational soul, having been elevated above the sphere of the senses and having achieved comparative illumination, turns to the contemplation of superessential verities. Upon one who had achieved this distinction the Greeks conferred the appellation of *hero*.

A hero was one who had heroically turned from the contemplation of the temporal to the contemplation of the eternal, and consequently was dedicated to the service of the gods. Gazing rapturously upon the faces of the Ungenerated Ones, the heroes verged toward certain divinities with more ardor than to others, thus expressing the innate preferences of their dispositions. The heroes, therefore, were divided among the orders of the gods, each serving his own preference and by degrees coming to be identified with the qualities of his chosen deity. As the gods themselves are incapable of descending into the corporeal sphere, they incline toward it through their vassals, the heroes. As a result certain men have come to be revered as divine incarnations and the creative principles venerated under their similitudes. Unable to discern that the hero is not a god, the nonphilosophic have befogged the issues of theology, with the result that men have become the worshippers of men and have propitiated mortal heroes before the superessential gods.

While ordinary mortals, being as yet rationally unawakened, depend largely upon their natal daemon, the heroes—or those already approaching liberation—are the beneficiaries of a more exalted genius, denominated the *essential daemon*. The Father-Star of the Neoplatonists is this essential dæmon, into whose nature the natal daemon has been merged by a process in which the lesser is mingled with the greater, and their issues become one. The essential daemon is unapproachable by him who is still a servant to his sense perceptions. Nor can the essential daemon descend into man, but as a Silent Watcher must brood over the irrational soul until, emerging from its chrysalis of materiality, it spreads its spiritual wings and soars swiftly to the source of its own light.

In Homer's *Odyssey*, Ulysses is revealed to be a mortal aspiring to the estate of a hero, which end he attains by his perilous voyagings through the seas of temporal uncertainty. As the senses must be mastered before that which is above the senses can be liberated, one of the labors of Ulysses was the blinding of the Cyclops. This giant signified Ulysses' own natal daemon—his self-will—whose power must be destroyed before divine will could be seated in its place. The Cyclops is, therefore, a monster of the astral light, the shadowy giant who abides amid the shadows of man's own being and whose "single eye" is the pineal gland—the only organ with which he discerns the outer universe. But it is possible for the eye of the natal daemon to see two ways. By turning inward it ceases to serve the Cyclops, and fixes its gaze upon the splendid features of the essential daemon who, abiding in the sphere of pure intellection, is the Father-Star—the Pole-Star by which the mariner of life steers the bark of his own soul into the safe harbor of divine perfection.

The philosophy of daemons is the outgrowth of man's natural veneration for the rationality manifest in every order of life and form. The very clouds scudding across the sky exist by virtue of the intercession of rational intelligence, and upon fulfillment of their destiny are dissipated by the activity of this selfsame intelligence. A peculiar Providence equips every organism with the instruments of its own survival. The plant's vital seed is protected by a stalwart husk, and the life of the Crustacea by its defensive shell. The urge that causes irrational nature to act in a rational manner we call *instinct*. To the ancient philosopher, however, the flowering of plants, the propagation of species, the tinting of rocks and crystals, the motions of the elements, and the emotions of the soul—all these were regarded alike as evidence of the presence of invisible but powerful spirits (daemons) who, seated in the causal nature of the manifesting sphere, guided primitive lives to the fulfillment of the predestined ends of uinversal procedure.

Some of these daemons are analogous to the elemental spirits of Paracelsus, with whose characteristics the great Swiss physician was made familiar by Arabian sorcerers. Recognizing all diversified activities to be suspended from causal unities, the philosopher of antiquity realized that while green, for example, dominates the color scheme of numberless organisms, green is itself a monad or unity, its intrinsic nature being coetaneous with a rational daemon. The orderly or rational distribution of green is thus effected through the ministrations of this guardian spirit, which is synonymous with the very nature of green itself. To attribute rationality to a tube of pigment at first may appear to be a baseless concept. Those who have experimented most with colors realize, however, that they have an inherent orderliness and are very much alive, possessing the power to excite pleasure or displeasure, and through their intermingling to demonstrate various complexions of universal order. As the salamander is born by the very friction that ignites the sulphur match, so a daemon is spontaneously produced through every combination of forces, substances, or circumstances, becoming the patron of such combinations and remaining with them until divine procedure returns these combinations to their original simplicity.

The belief in guardian spirits is a very lofty one when the unfolding rationality of man permits him to regard these entities as ever beautiful and virtuous. On the other hand, untutored peoples consider these transcendental entities to be innately malevolent, conspiring against human beings and seeking to spread sorrow and mischief throughout the world. The idealism of the Greek aestheticians enabled them to recognize divine agency in all that was beautiful, in that divinities rejoiced in the harmonious combinations of substances and circumstances. Accordingly, a place of beauty must needs be the dwelling of a thing of beauty. In somber groves dwelt grave dryades formed of the soft shadow that lingered there; in the high-flung spray of waterfalls nymphs disported themselves, while diminutive but pompous gnomes industriously hoarded beechnuts against the possibility of seven lean years. Though these creatures were invisible to the normal sight, man was conscious of their presence. They were indeed creations of place—the products of environment and necessary to the setting of the picture. All these creatures are daemons of different orders; for there are not only vast spirits whose bodies are stars, but daemons so small that they seek the shelter of toadstools or play hide-and-seek among the blades of grass. The daemon is the spirit of feeling that is born of, and is inseparable from, the circumstance that gives it birth. It is the preserver of universal order in the lesser, the untiring minister to parts, the protector and patron of unfolding life.

Just what relation, then, does the *Oversoul* of Emerson bear to the God of Socrates, that strange yet exalted spirit which impelled the Athenian commoner to a martyr's end? Emerson, the Occidental Orientalist, thus defines what he conceives to be that common oversoul of whose nature we all partake, and which is the common measure of us all: "The Supreme critic on all the errors of the past and the present, and the only prophet of that which must be, is that great nature in which we rest, as the earth lies in the soft arms of the atmosphere; that Unity, that Over-Soul, within which every man's particular being is contained and made one with all other; that common heart, of which all sincere conversation is the worship, to which all right action is submission; that overpowering reality which confutes our tricks and talents, and constrains every one to pass for what he is, and to speak from his character and not from his tongue; and which evermore tends and aims to pass into our thought and hand, and become wisdom, and virtue, and power, and beauty."

It is a philosophic axiom that as we verge toward Cause we verge toward simplicity, and as we depart from Cause we incline toward complexity; for all things are simple in their beginnings, complex in their midmost parts, and simple again in their ends. As man passes from childishness through maturity to childishness, so life (according to the doctrines of Herbert Spencer) is from simple homogeneity to complex heterogeneity and from heterogeneity back again to homogeneity. Approach to simplicity, then, presumes an ever-decreasing number of parts, until ultimate simplicity is utter privation of partition. Emerson clearly senses the common unity of Cause —that vast Monad which is our common parent and whose sufficiency is the one noble Reality. This is indeed the Great Daemon, the Supreme Soul invoked by existence, whose ministrations we manifest in common and whose edicts are the code of our lives. As we increase in rationality we become diffused among or enter into the inner nature of an ever-increasing number of organisms, thereby becoming capable of knowing and feeling the impulses which actuate these organizations. Thus Man became the Oversoul of men—the Adam, or archetypal one from whom issue the many; the Protogonas from whose nature as from the pores of the skin come forth the "sweat-born" and the establishment of generations.

Thus Man—the Oversoul—is the *anthropos*, or daemoniacal spirit which is the common father of infinite progeny; the vast sphere of influence which men can never escape, but which is their allness and against the sovereignty of which they vainly struggle, ignorant of the fact that it is their common life. The Oversoul alone is Man, for men are but fractional parts of themselves and are never complete until all together form one grand nature. Therefore, while all men differ in their outer lives, in their inner life there is this common ground whereon all stand together and upon which they must erect the citadel of their strength. Only to the dreamer, who sees not with his eyes, but with his soul, is the dignity of the *anthropos* apparent; only the mystic can comprehend that vast being which towers above the puny sensibilities of mortals and from the lofty place broods over the body of its sovereignty. This *anthropos* exceeds men to the degree that the whole exceeds its parts, for each part contributes to the sufficiency of the sum.

The Neoplatonists differed from the Egyptians in their definition of the *anthropos*—or the nature of the all-containing self—when related to the status of men. According to one group, all of man descends into the sphere of generation, there to wander for a given time in the confusion of sense, and later by rational procedure to escape therefrom and reascend to the sphere of spiritual sufficiency. The more profound philosophies, however, declared that the ungenerate can never actually generate, nor can that which abides in the contemplation of perfection ever become immersed in the delusions of mortality. While the inferior nature of man, suspended from its monadic cause, may thus struggle for a brief period in the darkness of the moral sphere, the true self remains throughout this period in the presence of perfect order and adequate comprehension. According to this viewpoint all of man does not descend into the realm of his corporeal limitations, but rather broods over the incarnating part, and from its own state of detachment contemplates the attachments which involve the inferior self. Thus man is more than man; he is like the oft-employed simile of the iceberg, of which only a fractional part of its great bulk is visible. This invisible greatness of man—unmoved and uninvolved, and residing in the pure rationality of the supreme sphere—is termed the "Silent Watcher," the *Atman* who is the true man, and of whom the lesser part becomes increasingly aware as it ceases to be conscious in its animal part. In this manner is man, the comparative physical nonentity, suspended from Man, the actual spiritual immensity. Is it not this overbrooding divinity which man senses when he explores the depths of his own feeling and seeks to measure the magnitude of his intellect? Is it not this transcendent superpersonal one who is the true substance of man's hope and the body of his aspirations?

Picture, then, the mortal nature of man who, obscured by the insufficiency of his physical perceptions and crawling wormlike upon the surface of earth, dares to believe in his own thoughts and assume the reasonableness of his own contentions. Then conceive the blind mortality which men call life to be directed by a great and observing spirit which, grasping the lesser life by the hand, gently leads it toward comprehension and realization. Imagine that behind the little you at all times stands the greater You—majestic, illumined, magnificent—who communicates to the earthiness which is your mortal body a splendor more than sufficient, and through whose greatness the little you is made partaker of the greatness and goodness of all things. This is the *anthropos*, the Heavenly Man, the Supreme Manu, from whose presence man departs for his terrestrial wandering in the prodigal's sphere.

While Emerson conceives this soul to be within man, in philosophy we prefer to conceive of man as within this soul. As through philosophy we increase the dimensions of our internal selves, we gradually annihilate the interval between our human souls and this Oversoul. Our internal selves take on the stature of this nobler part until, though our body be still of mortal size, the scope of expanding consciousness becomes tions of inspiration. We then understand the qualities which inspired Emerson to pen these words: "The soul looketh steadily forward, creating a world always before her, and leaving worlds always behind her. She has no dates, no rites, nor persons, nor specialities, nor men. The soul knows only the soul. All else is idle weeds for her wearing."

We now turn to a more detailed consideration of the intrinsic nature of the soul and the position it occupies in the composite structures of both man and the universe. As already defined, the soul is the first and chief of the generations. It abides in its own essence at the apex of the pyramid of form. If the soul, then, be a generation and not an eternal principle, of what is it generated and why is it superior to other generations? That which is generated receives its life from another. Having had this active agent once imparted to it, it is thenceforth capable of separation therefrom. On the other hand, an ungenerated being—because its life is inherent—must ever abide in that life and that life in it, and hence is incapable of dissolution. Being a generation, the soul must consequently be included under the classification of bodies. Yet it is different from bodies; for being the chief of them, it possesses a fullness of virtues which exceeds the fullness of any other body. Of inferiors, then, the soul is the superior, and by virtue of its disposition occupies a midmost place between abiding life and unabiding form. As the physical man is clothed in a vehicle composed of the objectification and substantial counterpart of his superphysical corporeal impulses, so an invisible body generated of attributes too subtle to assume physical aspect envelopes the spiritual part as with an appropriate robe. Virtue, for example, is irreducible to physical perceptions. Seated, however, in the invisible nature, it manifests as an intangible and definite attribute of the self. Man is as surely clothed in the garments of virtue as he is in the garments of the physical; they are vehicles of his expression no less real than are the members formed of bone, flesh, or sinew.

Besides the physical, man is the owner of many bodies, invisible however to those whose perceptions are limited solely to the earthly senses. Each of these bodies is the vehicle of

definite potentialities which are slowly being manifested
through appropriate organisms. Man lives in many worlds
simultaneously, but of this fact he is unaware until he comes
to realize that every phase of his temperament attunes him to
a different level of universal activity. A concatenated chain
of vehicles extends upward from the dense physical organism
to the attenuated superphysical organism of the soul. These
bodies originally issued forth from the soul and to the soul
they must return—or rather, we should say their essences verge
—for soul existed before bodies and shall endure after bodies
have ceased to be. Yet the soul is profoundly influenced by its
bodies, and its nature is subjected to change by the reactions
of bodily conditions. As the proper monad of bodies, the soul
causes to issue out from its own being all that is inferior to
itself. And by the same course that dominated their issuance,
the soul reabsorbs these selfsame bodies back again into its
own essence; for by this reabsorption is the perfection of bodies
consummated. Man cannot enter into the presence of Reality
while still invested with body, for body can never contemplate
the bodiless, form the formless, or the generated the ungenerated. As bodies, forms, and generations are thus transmuted
into soul (more correctly, reabsorbed into the soul substance)
man creates for himself a new and more subtle garment—a
luminous sheath, a bodiless body, a form verging toward the
formless, by which it is enabled to contemplate formlessness
with comprehension. The soul, then, is the all-sufficient body;
it is form elevated to the vanishing point; it is nature retired
into its own apex and thus rendered capable of contemplating
its own cause. Through progressive sublimation bodies are
caused to retire from their own materiality and incline themselves toward that spirituality from which they derived their
actuating principle.

If the fruitage of physical experience were apprehensible
by the physical nature alone, then life would be but a span
of useless suffering, for the deed would perish with the doer
and the self be left as impecunious as before. Though every
tangible evidence of physical achievement must be discarded

by the decarnating spirit, yet there is carried forward into the invisible a subtle substance or pabulum extracted from incident and assimilable by the soul nature. Every incident, every experience, every conclusion of the physical life has its own soul nature, to be extracted therefrom by a strange distillation. The vapors thus distilled are inhaled by the soul even as the physical body subsists upon the material atmosphere. The distilled essence of incident thus becomes the essential nutriment of the soul, and the experiences of life are ultimately metamorphosed into soul qualities, becoming psychical urges and influences by which the outer nature is inclined hither and thither.

As polarity exists throughout the sphere of generation, it follows that the soul itself though intrinsically a monad, must manifest through the duad—the positive and negative channels of expression. The soul is accordingly symbolized as two creatures: one a beautiful and radiant spirit subsisting upon the manifesting virtues of the life; the other an evil and rebellious spirit fostered by every unworthy thought or deed. These two guard the mystic gate between the outer and the inner self; for, as the soul, they are the portal through which the polar forces of cause and effect pass in mutual exchange. The radiant soul fashioned from the very substance of achievement becomes the animating principle of intuition; for what is intuition but a kind of memory in which particulars are forgotten but principles remembered? The mind may lack the power to reason through, and the outer nature be uninformed regarding the solution of perplexing problems. But based upon ages of endeavor, intuition unerringly points out the law of probability; for by virtue of ripe experience it inclines with more certitude than the reason, and with more discretion than the thinking but inexperienced personality.

The evil part of the soul speaks also, and its voice is conscience. Conscience is the still, small voice of unremembered suffering which, long vanished from the conscious mind, yet lives in the deeper recesses of the nature, where it warns of impending catastrophe and whispers to such as will listen the standards of right and wrong as established by experience. Men and women of normal intelligence never commit wrong deeds which they do not know are wrong before their commission. We may dissemble or feign ignorance, but all too often we realize that we lie even while we speak. The mentor of ages dwells within, and irrespective of our pretensions its words are audible to our inner selves. What is that accusing self from which the malefactor can never escape and which hounds the evil-doer to the bitter end? It is the soul. Living its own life consistent with the principle of Truth, the soul will never let us rest until our outer lives are rendered harmonious with the code within. Why are some happy, though surrounded by all manner of misfortune and sorely oppressed by offending circumstances? Because the soul, satisfied with the behavior of the life, bestows the sense of satisfaction upon these outer sensibilities so keenly vexed by an unkind Providence. The all-sufficing realization of accomplishment flows from the soul, and like the balm of Gilead assuages the torments of the material Tartarus. The persecuted parts are imbued with fresh courage and conviction, and given new strength to meet every emergency. On the other hand, why are so many who are fully blessed with this world's goods, and possessors of all that should bestow happiness and tranquility so miserable, so abject, so afraid? Because the soul, dissatisfied, refuses to allow an outer complacency to silence its accusations. When man's soul thus convicts him of misdirected living, there is no tribunal to which he can appeal for mitigation of his offence.

Shall we then wonder that the Greeks declared conscience to be a daemon that eternally whispers in the ear of the mind, and intuition a guardian deity that can conduct the life through the perils of the physical universe? Intuition and conscience are the tangible expressions of the intangible soul by which man is made to realize that from every act a residue remains which shall influence his doing unto the end of time. Nothing that we accomplish is lost; nothing that we achieve is forgotten; for while the particulars may vanish away, the principles involved are interwoven into the fabric of an invisible vestment that clothes the self in the ample folds of experience, and insures that spirit shall never be without a counselor, or life without a patron.

We have already set forth the triform constitution of the Divine Agent who through the One, the Beautiful, and the Good creates, preserves, and destroys the innumerable orders of beings. Apuleius, in *The Metamorphosis*, sets forth in allegorical terms the inner mystery of the soul. The legend of Cupid and Psyche existed, however, prior to the time of Apuleius, being preserved inviolate by the philosophers lest a profane world desecrate the sacred truths.

A king and queen had three daughters (so the story goes), of whom the youngest, Psyche, was of such surpassing beauty that mortals paid her a homage that elevated her above the dignity of even Venus herself. The indignant goddess of beauty thereupon dispatched her winged son, Cupid, to humble the pride of Psyche by infusing her with a passion for some gross and unnatural being. Invisible to mortals, Cupid entered the apartment of Psyche to carry out his mother's mission, but became so enamoured of the beautiful maiden that he repented of his role and schemed to win Psyche for himself.

Suffering from the enmity of Venus, Psyche found no love among mankind, and in obedience to an oracle which declared that she would never be the bride of a mortal lover but that her husband would be a monster whom neither gods nor man could resist, she ascended the mountain upon which it was decreed she should await the coming of her unnatural bridegroom. As she stood upon the mountain top the god Zephyr picked her up and bore her into a flowery dale, in the midst of which stood a grove of tall and stately trees and a magnificent palace which was not the work of mortal hands. The palace roof was supported by gilded columns, and the walls were ornamented with tracing of beasts and strange creatures. Vast treasures of gold and jewels were also gathered there, and Psyche was served by invisible attendants who gratified her slightest wish.

Psyche never saw her husband, who came only at night and departed before dawn. She begged him to permit her to look upon his face, but he declared that she must be content with his love and never try to see him. Desirous of putting at rest the worries of her family Psyche sent for her two sisters, and these, jealous of her fortune, incited her to make an effort to see her husband. So one night when he was asleep she lit a lamp, and carrying a knife with which to slay the evil monster described by the oracle, stole into her husband's bedchamber and discovered him to be Cupid, the son of Venus, and the most beautiful of all the gods. As she stood watching him a drop of hot oil fell upon his body, and awakened by the pain Cupid spread his downy wings and fled through the window, sorrowfully reminding Psyche that love cannot dwell with suspicion.

The palace thereupon vanished and Psyche found herself in a field near her father's city. Broken-hearted, she began a quest for her lost lover, first seeking the help of Ceres who suggested that if she go humbly to Venus and surrender to her dictates she might regain Cupid's love. Desiring the discomfiture of Psyche, however, Venus made a servant of her, setting her almost impossible tasks which Psyche in every instance accomplished with the assistance of sympathetic gods. Her first task was to separate a vast quantity of mixed grains; her second, to gather golden fleece from a large flock of vicious rams; and her third, to descend into Hades and bring back from Persephone, the goddess of the underworld, a casket filled with beauty.

Still inquisitive, however, Psyche opened the casket in spite of the warning given her by the tower god who had aided her in the adventure. Instead of being filled with beauty the casket contained a Stygian sleep which loosed from the box, overcame Psyche so that she fell unconscious on the path. Cupid, coming to her rescue, returned the sleep to the box, and interceding with Jupiter for her hand, both finally reconciled Venus to the match. Psyche was then given a cup of heavenly drink which conferred upon her immortality, and in common with all fairy stories the two lovers lived happily ever afterward.

In the interpretation of this fable of the soul's descent into generation—more correctly, its descent into the concept of generation—we must reiterate certain of our earlier assumptions. In the words of Thomas Taylor: "In the first place, the Gods, as I have elsewhere shown, are super-essential natures, from their profound union with the first cause, who is super-essential without any addition. But though the Gods, through their summits or unities, transcend essence, yet their unities are participated either by intellect alone, or by intellect and soul, or by intellect, soul, and body; from which participations the various orders of the Gods are deduced. When, therefore, intellect, soul, and body are in conjunction, suspended from this super-essential unity, which is the center, flower, or blossom, of a divine nature, then the God from whom they are suspended is called a mundane God."

The Platonists further affirmed that the human soul was born from the intellect and soul of the world, but that its direct parents were the intellect and soul of a certain star, which is its Father-Star and from which it first descended into the sphere of non-tranquility. As the soul is suspended between intellect and body, its "fall," so-called, represents its inclination toward body. Therefore the mundane soul and the intellectual (or supermundane) soul are identical in essence, but verge in opposite directions. The fall, or descent, of the soul into materiality is the result, consequently, of its contemplation of body; and conversely, its liberation from the mundane sphere is accomplished by turning about to the contemplation of intellect. The soul is an immortal mortal, for when mingling with the immortals it shares their permanence and transcendency. When mingling with mortal concerns, however, it is bereft of these endowments, becoming susceptible to a certain degree of mortality by which its luminosity is destroyed and its wings are clipped. From this we understand how it is possible for a soul to fall from its estate and yet still remain in that estate; for though it may verge toward the intellect or the body, it is still essentially in its own estate and remains soul regardless of the nature with which it mingles.

Apropos to the subject matter, we have the remarks of Aristides concerning the descent of the soul. "The soul," he says, "as long as she is seated in a purer place of the universe, in consequence of not being mingled with the nature of bodies, is pure and inviolate, and revolves, together with the ruler of the world; but when, through an inclination to these inferior concerns, she receives certain phantasms from places about the earth, then she gradually imbibes oblivion of the goods she possessed in her former superior station, and at the same time descends. But by how much the more she is removed from superior natures, by so much the more approaching to inferiors, is she filled with insanity, and hurled into corporeal darkness; because through a diminution of her former dignity, she can no longer be intelligibly extended with the universe; but on account of her oblivion of supernal goods, and consequent astonishment, she is borne downward into more solid natures, and such as are involved in the obscurity of matter. Hence, when her desire of body commences, she assumes and draws from each of the superior places some portions of corporeal mixture."

The same author continues his description of the descent of the soul through the orbits of the divine planets, from each of which—as in the story of Ishtar at the seven gates and also the descent of the soul in *The Divine Pymander of Hermes Mercurius Trismegistus*—the soul receives a luciform and enveloping nature. At last, approaching the sphere of the moon, the soul becomes of such corporeality that a certain gravitation draws it into the rhythm of the physical world. The soul then loses its spherical form and assumes the human shape, the luciform and ethereal substances gathered from the stars first becoming fetal membranes and later definite parts of the physical structure of the outer nature and psychical qualities in the inner nature. For, as Aristides again remarks, the shell-like vestment of man is nourished from its own root, which is the descending soul.

Psyche (or the soul) is described by Apuleius to be of royal parentage, thus arcanely intimating that she is of a divine line, for royalty here signifies the spiritual lineage. That which has its foundation in the gods is declared to be of kingly order, for the gods were the patrons of rulers who thus administered their kingly office by divine right. In contradiction, mortals were regarded as creatures of common birth to signify that their mother was the earth and they themselves earthborn and not—like the gods—the sons of heaven. Psyche is further described as the most beautiful of all mortals, so far surpassing all other earthly beings in loveliness that men venerated her as a goddess and made her offerings similar to those with which Venus, the Mother of Generations, was propitiated.

The soul is thus represented as exceeding in perfection all other material bodies, its beauty being due to its proximity to the fountain of beauty, of whose harmonies it partakes and whose excellence it reflects into the inferior sphere. The perfections of the soul surpass the perfections of the body even as the qualities of the superior nature surpass the qualities of form. In Book X of the *Laws,* Plato puts into the mouth of the Athenian stranger the following words: "And if this is true, and if the soul is older than the body, must not the things which are of the soul's kindred be of necessity before those which appertain to the body?" Cleinias answers "Certainly." "Then," rejoins the Athenian, "thought and care, and mind and art, and law will be prior to that which is hard and soft, and heavy and light."

Here Plato emphasizes the doctrine of the excellence of the soul over the body; for the concerns of the soul are more noble, more lasting, and more satisfying than are the concerns of the mortal nature. As mental activity is more beautiful than physical activity, and virtue more excellent than pulchritude of person, so the ancients ascribed to the soul a transcendent and luminous beatitude. Sensing the felicity of this inner part, the outer nature regarded the soul as a divinity—in some cases, as *the* Divinity. This misdirected homage is said to have "vexed" the higher gods who, since they greatly exceeded the virtue of the soul, should properly be the recipients of a fuller and more perfect devotion.

If the gods, however, be impersonal principles, how shall we interpret that vexation which prompts them to divert their benevolence and leave the offending mortal deprived of their qualities? When man in his quest of realities exalts secondary natures—such as the soul—and loses sight of the divine origin and wholeness from which souls are suspended, he reaps for his imprudence irrationality, or the suspension of rational activity. Thus is his mind continually vexed by its own unsoundness, and such disquietude in the rational faculties is declared to represent an offended intellect or an indignant divinity.

The goddess Venus manifests a twofold disposition. The superior phase liberates souls from material generation and elevates them to those superessential generations which subsist from the apex of the generating sphere. The other, and lower, phase of Venus inclines souls toward corporeality and binds them in servitude to the generating nature, for which reason the goddess was regarded by the ancients as a personification of carnality. The great dragon or monster whom the oracle prophesied was to become the husband of Psyche signified materiality—the mortal nature with whom she must be wedded at the time of her entrance into physical life. The fabulous monsters of the ancient Mystery rituals—such as *behemoth, leviathan,* and the *hippocampus*—all signified the mortal sphere that devours the souls descending into generation, and like the Minotaur claims for its own the fairest and bravest of every age.

Psyche is led forth to the top of a high mountain, there to wed this strange creature decreed by the gods, that her spirit might be duly humbled, and that she might realize that only the immortals can escape the limitations of matter and the ravages of time. From this mountain top Psyche is borne downward by Zephyr, the west wind, into a beautiful valley where stands a mighty grove of oak trees. This valley signifies the mundane sphere or lower world into which the generating soul is conducted. The east is the portal of generation, for it denotes the place of the nativity in a horoscope. So the west wind blows the soul gently into birth. The grove of trees signifies creation, which is, as it were, a clump of mighty agencies. In the midst of this grove is the palace of the world, where there are vast treasures and the jewels of the stars. The tracings upon the walls of the palace are the constellations—those vast signs upon the walls of heaven which hem in our solar system and are the limits of the mundane house.

Here Psyche is served by invisible beings whose voices she hears; for having descended from her true estate, the spiritual agencies which are her excellence are no longer visible. But their voices still speak to her inner nature, even as the gods still speak through the oracle of the human heart. Psyche, however, is not yet physical and mortal; hence the physical agencies of creation are also invisible. Suspended thus between two spheres, she wanders in the Great House of Life which she is eventually to discover is the dwelling place of Cupid.

Cupid is chiefly familiar to the 20th century as the matchmaker supreme, but in antiquity he played a most significant role. He is the symbol of love which, according to philosophy, has a duality of natures. The first is that supernal passion by which the soul is moved while still pure and undefiled in the luminance of the soul sphere. The second is mortal love in which the soul—deluded by the findings of sense—exchanges for the adoration of internal qualities the infatuation for external appearance.

Married to an invisible being, Psyche thus becomes the bride of spiritual love, into which union the element of form or materiality has not yet entered. She dwells in a beautiful astral palace, served by creatures whose natures have not yet been invested with mortal fabric. Here she remains until her sisters—who signify mortal instincts—begin to pull her downward into the sphere of sense.

When Psyche beholds the physical form of her husband, spiritual love is changed into material passion. She is forthwith precipitated from her heavenly palace into the broad meadow of the earth where broken-hearted she wanders in search of the happiness she foolishly sacrificed by listening to the voices of worldliness. She then becomes a servant of Venus, who sets for the unfortunate girl a number of difficult as well as dangerous tasks. These tasks represent the labors of life; the misfortunes of existence which generation heaps upon those who come beneath its sway. In each instance, however, she is assisted by a heavenly voice which, representative of the ever-present daemon or divinity, with its greater vision leads the soul befogged by matter through the tortuous byways of existence.

When Venus enslaves Psyche, the lower love becomes master of the soul qualities, and the shackles of desire hold the will in bondage to the animal propensities. The last task set by Venus for Psyche to perform is the journey to Hades to bring back with her from the sphere of the dead a casket filled with beauty. This casket signified physical life, which the ignorant soul believes to be the receptacle of happiness and beauty but which proves, upon opening, to contain only an evil and stupefying spirit. Seizing the soul, this spirit causes it to descend into the very depths of corporeality, there to remain until Cupid (or love) comes to awaken and elevate it to its lost estate.

Cupid, the invisible god, is rational love—that affection which is seated in the true qualities of the soul. This higher and more divine emotion, rousing the rational soul as from a stupor, communicates its vitality thereto and thus enables the soul by rational procedure to cast off the lethargy of the illusions of the flesh. Upon completion of this task Psyche placates the angry Venus and even wins favor in the sight of awful Zeus, the Demiurgus himself. Thereupon she is given the heavenly drink and ceasing to be a mortal verges toward the immortals. She thus becomes the mother of joy, which is born of the union of the rationality in each soul with that greater rationality which is the invisible but all-potent god of intellectual love.

Thus is set forth the story of a prodigal daughter whose experiences parallel those contained in the biblical allegory of the prodigal son. Here also is the key to the allegory of Lohengrin; for the young prince of the Holy Grail is divine and unnamed love, which is destroyed or forced to retire when its nature is brought within the sphere of denomination.

From the foregoing it is evident that the integrity of man is posited in his superior part, and regardless of the physical inhibitions by which the flow of his divinity is impeded, that which is essentially good and true must perforce ultimately dominate the entire character. Not without just cause does man instinctively turn to his own soul for consolation and guidance. While he may not consciously realize the immensity of Reality, he senses an expansive principle which, residing within the innermost recesses of his being, is ever ready to incline him toward perfection.

Life posits its own awareness in the soul quality; through the soul, spirit learns of its own apparent aloofness from, yet its actual identity with, matter. Clothing its own transcendency in soul, spirit gives its impersonal self into the keeping of a personal nature; clothed with the rationality of a personal nature, spirit descends into the inferior universe to fulfill the natural law of being, that in the nature of perfect existence there shall constantly manifest generations. The Divine Plan includes an order of forms through which life principles continually flow from awareness through the vale of unawareness back to awareness again.

In philosophy, therefore, we labor without ceasing to stimulate our higher natures and thereby rouse the soul from the lethargy of materiality; permit it to ascend from personals to impersonals, from forms to the estates of the formless, to be finally reunited with that sovereign voice of rational, or intellectual, love—that passion of the soul for Reality, that impulse to verge toward those natures partaking most fully of the permanently beautiful. Thus, within human nature, which is incapable of appreciation in its fullest sense, dwells an all-comprehending power—the human soul—which ever seeks reunion with that omniscience to which each action of universal agency is, in turn, the object of a profound appreciation. This greater soul, this mysterious Cupid; this formless being which man may not behold without destroying; this least of forms and most of spirit—this is the true Oversoul in whose intellection we are perpetually immersed and of whose transcendency we continually partake.

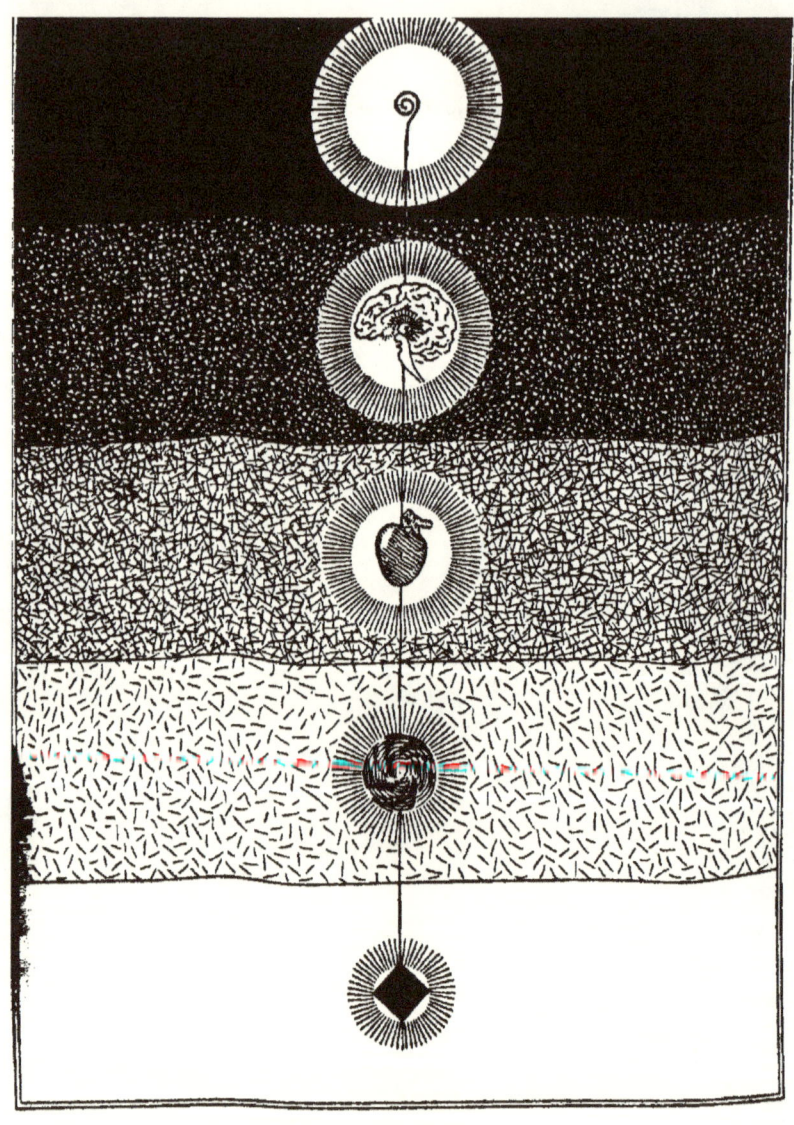

THE PLANES OF THE GENERATING SPHERE

Assuming the illusion of form, the spiritual life descends out of its own radiant nature and takes upon itself in sequential order a mental constitution, an emotional (or astral) constitution, a vital constitution, and, lastly, a physical constitution. These four constitutions are united to the non-incarnating spiritual self by a thread of life.

CHAPTER FOURTEEN

Exoteric and Esoteric Knowledge

IN Plato's *Charmides,* wisdom is declared to be the science of itself and also the science of other sciences; furthermore, the science of the absence of science and the science of mental temperances. While all other divisions of learning are concerned with objects, substances, places or conditions, wisdom is concerned with its own nature. From it flow however all other sciences, and by it is determined not only the knowable but the unknowable; not only the extent of that which is but also the extent of that which is not.

Defined as the proper temperance of the mind, this wisdom, verging toward neither extreme but abiding in perpetual equilibrium, may be likened to the monad of knowing, the unity of rationality, the summit of all sciences and speculations. Today we have preserved those sciences which are properly termed the classifiers of extraneous facts, but that form of wisdom which is primarily concerned with the substance of erudition itself has vanished from the institutes of man. As Plato further observes, a wise and temperate man is one capable of correctly estimating the extent not only of his own knowledge or ignorance but also of performing the same service for others. No one is wise who is not as fully acquainted with the extent of ignorance as with the extent of wisdom; for in mortal concerns wisdom is an inconsequential area of rationality existing in an infinite expanse of ignorance.

Temperamentally a skeptic, Socrates infers that wisdom is not the knowledge of things but the knowledge of the condition of knowledge with respect to its absence or presence; an observation plainly intimating that wisdom deals with generals and not with particulars. Wisdom may therefore be considered as composed of the universals of knowing and the sciences of the particulars of knowing, which as the practical are suspended from theory. Exoteric knowledge then, can be defined as the knowledge of particulars—a familiarity with those arts and sciences arrived at through application and concentration upon external natures. Conversely, esoteric knowledge is concerned with the inherent nature of knowldge itself and is limited to those acquainted with the more profound issues of philosophy and rational theology. Lest the reader grasp too much of this sublime teaching, Plato causes Socrates to refute the statements concerning this abstract science of knowing, thus making it perceptible only to such as are in turn able to refute Socrates.

When he claimed for science that it would wrest from theology the entire domain of cosmological theory, Professor Tyndall would so magnify the part as to swallow up the whole. The puerility of such an assumption is self-apparent, for science by virtue of its very nature has not and cannot invade the realm of true theology. Science may overthrow the false gods and dogmas of creed, but the mysteries of the divine spheres elude the grasp of corporeal learning since they belong to a more subtle and esoteric realm. Never until knowledge is capable of analyzing itself can it retire into its own causal nature and behold the luminous and stupendous wholeness from which beings are suspended by most intangible threads. Thus while the knowledge of external natures and the classification of objective phenomena are the definite province of science, none but the Mysteries held the true keys to wisdom. They were the custodians of secrets most arcane. Through peculiar disciplines they equipped certain selected mortals with rational instruments by which to measure, estimate, and classify those internal facts which forever elude the intellect delimited by its training to the phenomena of the exterior universe.

Founded, according to Sanchoniathon, in the night of Time, the Mysteries were established upon the premise of this twofold wisdom, of which the greater phase was committed to their reverent custody and the lesser revealed to all men without discrimination. The world, however, was not left wholly devoid of truth, for the secrets of the inner life were set forth under the guise of theological fables that those whose rational faculties were awakening might sense and incline toward the more sublime verities. Sallust declares the fables of the wise to be of five orders, of which the first is the theological; the second, physical; the third, animastic or psychical; the fourth, material; and the fifth, of a mixed order. Many generations often elapsed between the appearance among men of exalted intellects able to comprehend and reconstruct from the figures and metaphors of mythology the hidden body of this spiritual learning, belief in which is now regarded as one of man's most tenacious superstitions. Yet shall we consider as pure figments of the imagination those theological systems which wholly occupied the intellectual faculties of such men as Pythagoras, Plato, Aristotle, Socrates, Proclus, Porphyry, Cicero, Epictetus, Crantor, Atticus, Galen, Plutarch, and Boetius? Is not the rational proof advanced to support the existence of this esoteric knowledge as valid in its own field as the proof adduced by science and now regarded as infallible evidence of scientific erudition?

That knowledge is not the common property of all is evident from the natural superiority of one mind over another, for no two individuals possess equal faculties of comprehension. These intervals of intellect, manifest to even the most obtuse senses, can never be annihilated save by a definite process of improvement by which the lesser self equips itself to comprehend the findings of the greater. The line of demarcation then, between the hidden and the revealed, is not to be considered definite but rather relative, for the unfolding rationality is ever rejecting the old in favor of the new which, half-defined, is scarcely tangible enough to support the intellect. Thus the individual is ever engaged in tearing away the veils that drape the Saitic figure of knowledge. Yet in the words of Sir Edwin Arnold, "As veil upon veil he lifts, he finds veil upon veil behind." The elements of realization are forever elusive, and greatness or littleness of thought is dependent upon comparison for its estimation. Man is increasing in his ability to comprehend things, to orient himself in relation to place, and to estimate quantity and condition. Though the conceivable universe is actually but an anthill in cosmos, inquisitive humanity in the interests of science will eventually explore that universe to its outermost fringe and fling itself therefrom into eternity.

As long as the human intellect thus involved in its own insufficiency communicates its opacity to all external natures, the term *esoteric* should not be applied to that which is simply unknown, but rather to that which in terms of mortal intellect is unknowable. We have but begun our struggle to master the phenomena of the physical universe; milleniums must pass before we can hope to classify its infinite diversity and cope with the problem of eternity. Although the universe envelopes us as with a vast mantle of obscurity and isolates us in the midst of our insufficiency, yet no phenomena discoverable either by scientific apparatus or philosophic deduction can be classified as truly esoteric. The building of an improved telescope with lenses powerful enough to reveal a galaxy of stars at present invisible would in no way encroach upon the province of esoteric knowledge, for the fact that these stars may be seen if the physical apparatus is sufficiently acute assigns them to the category of exoteric knowledge.

The term *exoteric* covers the area of communicable facts and includes every form of knowledge discoverable to the intellect through the sense perceptions or the physical mind. That which has been, is now, or can ultimately be recorded upon paper, discoursed upon in the lecture room, debated by polemics, or dissected by the anatomist, must perforce belong to the inferior sphere of speculation where these activities are common, and hence be exoteric. That which can be couched in the language of the mortal sphere pertains to the mortal sphere; but that which pertains to the higher spheres can never be caught upon the surface of grosser substances or sensed by duller perceptions. In one sweep the self-recommended vendors of things esoteric who herald their coming with 24-sheet posters, are thus eliminated. The communication of esoteric knowledge requires a method far more than any at the command of metaphysical mountebanks. The proper custodians of this knowledge—the ancient Mysteries—realized too well that its transmission and perpetuation were the most difficult of all tasks, in many instances bordering on the impossible. How shall we reveal to another that which entirely transcends the province of the senses, that which is nonconvertible into mundane terms, and with which nothing physical is comparable?

Hence the secret schools of antiquity instituted systems of definite discipline by which the whole nature was dissociated from the elements of exoteric knowledge, and through protracted effort elevated to the level of supersensuous comprehension. Having reached this state, the principles of higher knowing were then communicated to the neophyte by a method almost as arcane as the secrets themselves. A strange telepathic system was developed whereby the findings of the subtler inner perceptions were communicated without passing through that place interval which exists between ordinary intellects—an interval which must be filled with words or other symbolic forms in which the esoteric matter is necessarily lost. How then shall we define esoteric knowledge? It is the classification of those superessential elements of the pure intellect sphere where form, as man recognizes it, does not exist. It must be communicated by a method which, while it awakens no response in the sensory organisms, renders knowledge comprehensive to the inner perceptions. The subject of this inner knowledge and its method of communication has long confounded men of letters. Science cannot conceive of the human mind functioning independently of matter; nor, if consistent to their premises, can men of science admit the possibility of the mind thinking in terms independently of form. In other words, they cannot dissociate the rational processes from the similitudes of phenomena and the laws of comparison that dominate the field of material thought.

According to science the human mind instinctively clothes its conclusions and reactions in the vestments of form, so that even before the thought is registered by the outer nature of the thinker it is habited in familiar, yes, even trite and conventional forms. What science really means, however, is not that thoughts are necessarily always related to form, but rather that until they are clothed in the elements of form they are incommunicable. In other words, thoughts for which there are no form associations must die at birth. Dominated by the laws of generation and under the patronage of the goddess Demeter, the physical sphere will permit no energy to exist within its domain unless that energy abide by the dictates of matter by being clothed in the substances of matter. When thoughts abide in the mind they are thus launched into generation through words, these words—which are their bodies—dimming, like the mortal vehicles of man, the lucidity of the inner nature. Like the human soul, word-souls function imperfectly while enveloped in the grosser substances of the generating sphere.

Thus, while the mind under certain conditions is capable of receiving into itself definite superphysical stimuli, it cannot communicate these attenuated impulses and still preserve their integrity. A notable example is that of the eminent psychologist Henry Havelock Ellis who, as the result of intense functioning in the realm of psychologic idealism, became so sensitized that to him occurred what is classified under the general heading "mystical experience." In his book, *The Dance of Life*, he writes: "My self was one with the Not-Self, my will one with the universal will. I seemed to walk in light; my feet scarcely touched the ground; I had entered a new world. The effect of that swift revolution was permanent. At first there was a moment or two of wavering, and then the primary exaltation subsided into an attitude of calm serenity toward all those questions that had once seemed so torturing. * * * Neither was I troubled about the existence of any superior being or beings, and I was ready to see that all the words and forms by which men try to picture spiritual realities are mere metaphors and images of an inward experience. * * * I had become indifferent to shadows, for I held the substance. I had sacrificed what I held dearest at the call of what seemed to be Truth, and now I was repaid a thousandfold. Henceforth I could face life with confidence and joy, for my heart was at one with the world and whatever might prove to be in harmony with the world could not be out of harmony with me."

Similar experiences are recorded in the lives of Meister Eckhart, Emanuel Swedenborg, Dante Alighieri, and Martin Luther. Scientists regard the "mystical experience" in a troubled sort of way; those savants more generously-minded cherish the vague hope that some such experience may be their lot and thus afford them opportunity to analyze first hand its attendant reactions. Unfortunately, the "mystical experience" does not occur to such pedants as are minded to dissection, or whose paper learning causes them to view lives as simply complicated mechanisms. When, therefore, the apparently miraculous does transpire, the men of letters congregate to marvel and debate, desirous of scoffing but withal perturbed. To them spirit is so intangible and the bugaboo of superstition so tenacious that they fear even to register an interest in things superphysical lest they be accused of mental senility.

In the light of the persistent drift of modern thought toward materialism, it is not difficult to understand why the ancient systems of learning mean so little to the modern mind. Firmly posited upon what it terms the *practical*, science can discover no purpose in ceremonial or symbol, nor can it conceive any tangible good to result from chanting grave rituals to the accompaniment of the lyre. The professional standing of Pythagoras the philosopher was almost irremediably impaired by the discovery that he advocated dancing as essential to education, and that even in his advanced years he was accustomed to invoke Terpsichore with true scholastic measure. Modernity cannot picture such profound and serious-minded men as Plato and Aristotle, or even the skeptical Socrates, capering with aesthetic abandon in some moonlit grove. Yet we have not the slightest evidence that the accuracy of their philosophic deductions was adversely affected thereby. Pythagoras declared, upon the authority of Empedocles, that every individual who is to achieve greatness must be capable of expressing rhythm in some proper manner; that the soul which cannot so acutely sense the exalted tempo of the celestial spheres that he is possessed therby, can never hope to so approach the soul of things as to reach the summit of achievement in any form of learning.

Pythagoras realized what the modern gownsman has ignored: namely, that none is capable of knowing in great measure who is incapable of intense feeling. Learning acquired in an aesthetic atmosphere is far more valuable than that gained in the severe or lifeless schoolroom. In the effort to preserve its integrity, science posits its dogma upon the infallibility of material evidence, which is presumed to increase in accuracy as it departs from sentiment, and is most valuable when most cold. Add to this a second premise—that of the impossibility of knowing beyond the sphere of phenomenon—and you have the schoolman's dilemma epitomized.

A transcendent form of knowledge demands for its expression a transcendent form of communication. Vocabularies are created to supply certain needs, and are useless beyond the confines of these ends. Language is intended to transmit the more common attitudes of mankind, but for those rare souls who have elevated themselves beyond the level of common attitudes the language of the herd is wholly insufficient. Thus in ages past philosophy evolved its own language—an unspoken tongue—a method of communication which was mostly a communion by which the unutterable was transmitted. In the initiations of the ancient Cabirian Mysteries of Samothrace, knowledge was disseminated by a curious method not unlike a highly perfected radio. The instruments of this unique procedure were the rational faculties of the disciples themselves, and the activating agent was a mysterious electric fluid which the priests had learned to capture from the atmosphere and direct by impulses of the will. It has been clearly demonstrated that the Greeks were familiar with electricity, a knowledge secured by them from the Egyptians. This accounts for the peculiar veneration accorded amber by early priestcrafts, for this substance had been found to possess the quality of capturing and storing electricity. Among carvings and figures of the Samothracian Mysteries are several depicting what is called the "electric head." The face is surrounded by a circlet of hair which is standing on end as though galvanized by an electric current. In one symbolic group the hierophant is seated in the center like the sun in the midst of the zodiac. This venerable one is giving the instruction and his appearance is that of singular repose; yet the forcefulness pervading the figure is arcanely significant of the concentration of the will upon the dissemination of the Great Work. Gathered about him are the disciples who have the appearance of being electrified. Each individual's hair is standing on end as though caused by a current of electrical energy, in each instance flowing away from the central figure from whom the current emanates.

To the initiated beholder the picture is evidence that the central figure is creating and disseminating rings of electrical energy which, passing outward in ever-increasing circles, moves through the bodies of the disciples and produces the appearance of electrification. Ancient sculpture also abounds with these electrified heads, whose significance thus far has been almost entirely overlooked by modern students of the Mysteries. It is evident, nevertheless, that these heads and the pageantries in which the electrified hair is shown represent efforts to portray the method employed in the communication of esoteric philosophy. The doctrines, projected like an electric current, thus stimulated certain rational faculties in the inner natures of the disciples. As a result of such internal stimuli the disciples were enabled to sense, feel, or intuitively grasp that which was incommunicable by any objective means. Only when the disciplines of the secret schools had stimulated the internal centers of consciousness to a point where it was possible for the neophytes to be brought *en rapport* with the inner perceptions of the hierophant could this body of secret tradition concerning formless and eternal truths be communicated from one to another.

Mystical philosophers have demonstrated that proficiency in certain arts and sciences stimulates the sensitivity of the superphysical rational faculties. Because of the definite impulse toward orderliness and exactitude conferred by the study of mathematics, this science was elevated to chief place among the stimuli to rationality. Sculpture, similarly, was highly venerated, for it was a medium by which beauty could be liberated from the shapeless block of marble. The sculptor was not regarded as a creator of beauty but rather as one who chipped away the rough exterior and thus brought to light the concealed symmetry of an inner nature. In short, the statue existed in the stone before the artist released it and made its symmetry apprehensible to the casual observer. Dialectics also stimulate the subtler phases of rationality by causing them to rise in defense of principle or premise. Through dialectics the mind is rendered flexible and sufficient for any and every contingency. Schooled in the thrust and parry of dialectics, the mind produces "a Roland for every Oliver" in the intellectual *affaire d'honneur*.

The ideal educational system by which the cultural standards of our youth are to be molded is the stimulation of these inner perceptions and the preparation of the mind for the contemplation of life's broader and profounder realities. For the most part, however, modern institutions of learning fail to accomplish this *summum bonum* because they are regarded as ends rather than means; they are considered capable of educating the mind, when actually their sole province is to prepare the intellect to receive into its own substance those impregnations of the rational self upon which all true mental excellence depends. Mathematics *per se*, for example, leads to ends comparatively mean and insignificant, yet nearly all great mathematicians have developed some phase of clairvoyance or clairsentience as the result of their application to its principles. Gradually the inner perceptions assert their sovereignty, and through a concrete mental organism rendered supersensitive by mathematical speculation, become aware of the polydimensional vistas of the higher and more spiritualized sciences. The musician is similarly subjected to a sublimation of feeling. Through protracted application to the principles of harmony and rhythm the musician so refines his own emotional nature that it comes to be ensouled by universal concords, and the musician himself is moved as though possessed by universal agencies. Thus the mind that has given itself over to the rather prosaic science of harmonics is instinctively caused thereby to verge toward universal rhythm and actually hear the music of the spheres.

Standing in the place of the wise and discoursing to his students upon the profundities of divine order, the philosopher suddenly discovers that he speaks better than he knows, becoming, as it were, a disciple of himself. He finds new meanings in his own words; he becomes aware that his mortal mind is being moved by an immortal agent, and that by some indefinable circumstance he has become the very mouthpiece of the ages. Thus, while the exoteric learning disseminated by our public schools and universities inclines the whole nature toward mental illumination, only through the Mysteries is that inclination brought to the high tide of expression—namely, that point where the principles by which eternal verities are maintained and proceed according to their own essences are rendered apprehensible to limited human comprehension. With rare exceptions, eminent educators admit that our schools are primarily intended to be stimulators of internal faculties, which faculties alone are capable of inducing the state of knowing. In the majority of cases, however, even our comparatively sufficient educational facilities are productive of results either abortive or hopelessly mediocre. Too often the student is simply introduced to those phases of learning which are definitely applicable to the utilitarian problems of the age. His education is consequently considered complete when he is schooled in any subject sufficiently for it to serve as a livelihood. Only occasionally do we find the man or woman whose knowledge of any particular subject is profound enough to support the mind in a state commensurate with its dignity.

The lack of rational philosophy common to this age is most evident in our educational systems whose object ostensibly is to superimpose extraneous thoughts upon those half-awakened adolescent minds groping for substance amid the shadow of their own immaturity. Educators presumably have adopted Locke's theory that the juvenile mind is a blank sheet of paper upon whose receptive surface must be scribbled conventional platitudes, premises or admonitions. Regarding the intellectual equipment of youth as a sort of highly attenuated putty, instructors subconsciously relegate to themselves the molding of this mental stuff into the likeness of the conventional, the substantial, and the prosaic—what they esteem as the outstanding characteristics of sound and useful thought. Under the molding influence of the old, it is thus assured that the new life will be a replica of those inadequate generations which rise from their stupor only to blight futurity.

When philologic pedagogues have finished poking their intellectual fingers into the plastic substances of his brain, its youthful owner is prepared to go forth into the world and repeat every imprudence which marred the tranquillity of his ancestors. The dire circumstances that torment each succeeding generation are thus reinvoked and perpetuated. This mental overshadowing renders its beneficiary incapable of originality even in vice; he cannot even make his own mistakes but must continue to repeat the errors of the ages and bow beneath such time-honored institutions as war and competition. With the possible exception of theology, nowhere outside the realm of education does man's egotism find more grandiloquent expression. Here fools in purple doublets sanctimoniously bestow their foolishness upon posterity. Having lost sight of the true purpose of education, these pedants regard him well-cultured who thinks least and remembers most while in the schoolroom but who, having matriculated into the greater concerns of life, there conveniently acquires the knack of forgetting even the little he once remembered. With the ends of education thus most effectively obscured, the means by which these ends should be attained are at best but highroads to nowhere. Education has become a vicious circle wherein the ignorance of one generation is transmitted like a hereditary taint to its progeny. Every form of social evil is made to thrive exceedingly, and the racial virtues are periodically threatened with extinction.

Interpretation is the preponderant factor in modern teaching. The instructor perforce acts as an intermediary between the complexity of a science and the insufficiency of a partly-developed mind. To interpret adequately is a divine gift bestowed by the gods only upon those whose attainments rival the heroic deeds of myth and legend. A great interpreter is no less a master than a great originator; for only a mind as great as the conceiving mind can intelligently interpret the concepts of that conceiving mind. A proper instructor of the young is born, not made. His genius is supreme, for not only must he be able to grasp the infinite complexity of a subject, but he must also reduce that complexity to an orderly simplicity. He must think downward to those intellects that still verge upon the state of thoughtlessness, inclining them gently, reverently, yet unmistakably, toward rational procedure.

Plato was dead five hundred years before an interpreter was found worthy of the task of revealing the intellectual achievements of this illustrious mortal. Of all the Platonic successors, only Proclus sensed the significance and magnitude of Plato's contribution to human knowledge. Each century gives birth to but one or two truly creative or interpretive minds. All other claimants to proficiency and conversance are merely meddlers in matters of the mind—dabblers, dilettanti, veritable parasites upon the bodies of art and science. They suffer from that most loathsome and fatal of all diseases: ignorance of their own ignorance. *The prime requisite of every great exponent of an art or science is that he shall recognize and emphasize its aesthetic and ethical aspects.* Even such prosaic arts as carpentry and cookery may become media by which the mind can be introduced to the beautiful, the noble, and the good.

Failure to perceive the substratum of divine agency below the surface of every physical procedure is to demonstrate one's disqualification to instruct in the elements of that procedure. Therefore none but the idealist who can see the beautiful in all things should be entrusted with the education of a child in whose nature it is hoped that the spirit of beauty will take up its abode.

Of Greek philosophy it has been said that its interpretation was "reserved for men who were born indeed in a baser age, but who being allotted a nature similar to their master were the true interpreters of his sublime and mystic speculations." (See the introduction to the *Select Works of Plotinus*.) Of education in general, as of jurisprudence in particular, it is all too evident that the spirit is dead and only the letter remains. Those dependent upon it for intellectual sustenance sicken and ultimately become intellectual corpses from whom the rational life has fled. As without the fructifying principle the germ of potentiality cannot burst its confining walls, so without the higher ethics of philosophy the seed of divinity resident in man can never be quickened. Only a comprehending soul rendered aware of the luminous realities behind the veil of form through the disciplines of right-thinking, can dispel those illusions which, like the monsters of a fabled age, guard the adytum of the sacred sciences.

The corruption that crept into its ethical institutes was the direct cause of the decadence of pagandom. Those custodians of the secret doctrine—the venerable hierophants of the Mysteries—left their schools and hied themselves to the remote corners of the earth. Deprived of their inspired leadership, the Mysteries became mere mongers of empty words. After courageously passing all the hazardous trials of the ancient rituals the enthusiastic neophyte did not receive at the completion of the rites the promised esoteric knowledge. Sanctimonious priests could only drone garbled fancies, or whisper with bated breath elegant nothings in his ear. In the quest for truth men will risk much, but even the most intrepid soul will hesitate to jeopardize life or limb for such dubious returns.

A similar betrayal of trust also awaits the modern seeker after Truth. The ends to be gained by modern education are so doubtful that there is much justification for the revolt of youth against a system which, in exchange for some eighteen years of application, leaves him as unfitted for life as before. While the social standing of the well-educated man may be a trifle more impressive and his earning capacity exceed that of his less schooled brother, he does not necessarily excel him in an understanding of those deeper issues of life with which higher education should be, but unfortunately is not, concerned. College men are quite as unhappy as illiterates; in fact their capacity for sorrow is enlarged, for their curriculum has acquainted them with a legion of miseries to which the uneducated are immune. All too often schooling complicates uncertainties, multiplies doubts, generates disquietudes, and verifies the growing suspicion that all creation is awry. Instead of solving problems modern education complicates them. Reacting to this divergence of dictum and tenet, the mind schooled beyond its capacity either rejects them *in toto* to become a philosophic atheist, or making a show of digesting them becomes unbearably sophisticated. The defection of modern youth from education is more than a surface symptom. The student is content to slip through college with mediocre grades because he is firmly convinced that all the knowledge he can ever hope to secure is nugatory in solving the imminent problems of his life. Hence the chief incentive for distinction in scholarship is removed.

When the modern college rose as a substitute for the ancient *collegia*, it fell heir to its task but not to its toga. While the *collegia* of Greece and Rome were the domiciles of a transcendent learning under the patronage of the gods and heroes, the colleges of today are but hollow imitations of these older and nobler institutions. In comparison to that sublimer knowledge disseminated by these ancient schools, modern houses of learning have become dispensaries of but the husks of knowledge. The illustrious record of the past must not be erased from man's memory; modern methods on the other hand must be recast into a more sufficient mold, for the morbid materialism of this age can only be dispelled by educating the juvenile mind in the principles of higher rationality.

In antiquity the roads of lower education led, like the converging spokes of a wheel, toward the Mysteries. Knowledge was then an actuality, and the byways of speculative thought, though tortuous, eventually led to the open gates of operative knowing. Those who excelled in temporal education, by right of their superior mentality and integrity were permitted to enter that inner sanctuary where the principles of divine knowledge were unfolded. Here the mind was diverted from the course of materiality, and initiated into those secrets of spiritual comprehension which bestows tranquility, compassion, and comprehension. Higher education began where lower education ceased, and all who sincerely desired to know were privileged to receive knowledge up to the limits of their own capacity. The arts and sciences of men were revealed to be but outer garments of a divine spirit—the concealments of a superior science, the science of living. Today all this has been swept aside, and the advanced bodies of learning are unable to confer that more adequate interpretation, for lack of which education necessarily fails. How little true incentive there is for scholastic greatness when he who has learned all that men can teach finds naught but disenchantment in the inadequacy of the whole system. When the masters of a science confess their ignorance of the very principles which are the daily subjects of their speculations, what shall it profit a man to sit at their feet and spend his years in the determination of the exact degree of ignorance possessed by his mentors?

Is it not possible that man comes into this physical world better fitted to function in harmony with rationality than after passing through what we like to term our course of culture, wherein the divine impulses toward the virtuous and the beautiful are stunted and the integrity of the nature incurably upset? Man is fortunate indeed if his education does not render him incapable of knowing. As Paracelsus might have said: "He is best served by education who is least injured by it."

A great thinker is one who by some strange Providence has escaped the pitfalls of mediocrity unwittingly dug by men to entrap genius. "All the world," wrote Emerson, "is at hazard when God lets loose a thinker." Humanity seems to fear an intellect which is great enough to destroy our prevalent sense of smugness and complacency. We are naturally inclined toward inertia; whether comfortably or uncomfortably we prefer to vegetate, and woe unto him who dares disturb our proletarian serenity. Humanity chooses to languish in the darkness of things as they are for fear that the godlike splendor of things as they might be will also uncover humanity's foibles and impose the burden of their correction. Knowledge is a responsibility, and responsibility is a term formidable and disquieting.

No better epitome of the enslavement of the intellect by education can be found than Alexander Pope's excoriation of pedantism in the fourth book of *The Dunciad*—The Epic of the Dunces. The pedagogues of every land are here personified by a specter whose index finger the virtue of the dreadful wand holds forth, and whose beavered brow a birchen garland wears. Preceptor of an awful knowledge, the bloodless lips of this spectral doctrinaire speak out the mandates of the superficial.

> Since man from beast by words is known,
> Words are man's province, words we teach alone.
> When reason doubtful, like the Samian letter,
> Points him two ways, the narrower is the better.
> Placed at the door of learning, youth to guide,
> We never suffer it to stand too wide.
> To ask, to guess, to know, as they commence,
> As Fancy opens the quick springs of Sense,
> We ply the Memory, we load the Brain,
> Bind rebel wit, and double chain on chain,
> Confine the thought, to exercise the breath,
> And keep them in the pale of worlds till death.
> Whate'er the talents, or howe'er design'd,
> We hang one jingling padlock on the mind.

How utterly we have become the servants of words, elevating mere terms to the degree of infallibility! While it is fitting that we should regard them as media of intercourse, is there not an understanding which is superior to words—a silent language by which comprehension blends with comprehension, a transcendent mode by which the within which is *you* communes with the within which is *I* and we together commune with that within which is *All?* Do not the stars upon their lofty thrones commune by a strange silence with each other, by wordless tongue and soundless voice uniting in a common knowing far beyond the ken of mortal apprehension? With upright larynx, does man so greatly excel all other creatures that he shall achieve glory by virtue of his lips alone? If he earns a crown, must he wear it on his tongue?

Words are but the infinite diversity of sound, and by many a curious gasp and rattle do we make our whimsies known. We live in a universe of words; terms and letters continually intervene to become the agencies of endless misunderstanding. As the memorizer of words is not a thinker, so the cloth of philosophic terminology cannot make the philosopher. Words are but names for unknown quantities and conditions—no more; for words are powerless to acquaint us with the inner natures whose qualities they bound. In Genesis it is declared that Adam went forth and named all creatures, and following his example men have never ceased to coin appelations with which to designate or describe the objects and conditions of environment. By appropriate terms the heaven and earth came to be defined, but how different from wordy definition is the comprehending nature of those polynomial powers which, founded in eternity, verge toward time just enough to be vaguely apprehensible.

Picture the enlightenment of the proverbial inquisitive schoolboy who, pointing to a growing mystery of leaves and stems, presents his instructor with this poser: "Master, what is this living, unfolding thing?" And he in whom the acumen of the past is presumed to be concentrated can only reply: "My boy, that is a tree!" The teacher might also very consistently have added: "We know it is a tree, for we named it ourselves." Groping after realities the juvenile mind is confronted with nothing but the limiting, strangling bonds of terms. As he passes through the various stages of education the pupil is familiarized with all the relatively inconsequential opinions we share concerning the subject of trees. Through a cross section of their trunks he studies their inner constitution, and with the microscope may see the roots that terminate in hungry mouths, or the infinitely minute life-particles that conspire to produce leaf and stem. Yet of tree itself—the mystery of that intangible something which expands from a tiny seed and surrounds itself with bark—man can discover nothing.

Thus education turns us from the consideration of living realities to cherish the baseless notions of our sires. While the heavenly orbs march on in majestic file to a glorious and unlimited destiny; while the whole universe, celestial and terrestrial, thrills with vibrant actualities and thunders on in concord with cosmic principle, humanity concerns itself with the trivialities of its cultural codes. Men turn their backs upon the midnight sky, whose immensity frightens them and dissipates their bombast, to the infantile task imposed by their culture of choosing the proper fork or frock for a formal banquet. Having familiarized themselves with the decrees of fashion in these respects, such little minds rest upon the oars of petty accomplishment until natural decay returns their ashes to the common Mother. Fascinated by the insignificant and bewildered by the real, oblivious to the distant and terrified by the imminent, mortals live by the meanest of their codes and choose mediocrity as the path of ease.

The value of present-day education is not to be discounted, but its superficiality is to be condemned. It may have value as a means, but it is wholly inadequate as an end; for it cannot supply that knowledge indispensable to right-living. If permeated by a sort of philosophic optimism concerning the ultimates of knowledge, and leavened by the ancient procedures and disciplines, material education could prepare its votaries for those loftier forms of learning for lack of which the nations perish. So long as education assumes that knowledge beyond its own prescribed domain is unavailable, it is false to the great need of humanity. Unfortunately, this is the assumption prevalent in the bodies of so-called higher learning. Ridicule is heaped upon the ancients for their "superstitions"; the esoteric doctrines are declared to have been idle rumors generated in the perfervid imaginations of unbalanced fanatics, who were consequently branded charlatans, adventurers, and impostors. Mindful of the claims of consistency, should we not condemn as impostors those schools which supply mere notions in lieu of actual knowledge and declare the individual to be "educated" though totally ignorant of every vital issue of existence? Graduates of modern educational institutions are presented with impressive diplomas, which too often are the most tangible evidence of scholastic attainment.

In his *Discourse on Initiation,* Hermes elucidates to his son Tatian the subject of spiritual education. The oration moves rhythmically and majestically upon the theme of appreciation, and may be summed up in the single thought that appreciation for Universal Good is the beginning of wisdom. Education is here revealed as the discipline whereby man is rendered capable of appreciating divine order and made susceptible to its redeeming impulses. Tatian is instructed by his immortal father in the discovery of God in these words:

"If thou wouldst contemplate the Creator even in perishable things, in things which are on the earth, or in the deep, reflect, O my son, on the formation of man in his mother's womb; contemplate carefully the skill of the Workman; learn to know him according to the divine beauty of the work. Who formed the orb of the eye? Who pierced the openings of the nostrils and of the ears? Who made the mouth to open? Who traced out the channels of the veins? Who made the bones hard? Who covered the flesh with skin? Who separated the fingers and the toes? Who made the feet broad? Who hollowed out the pores? Who spread out the spleen? Who formed the heart like a pyramid? Who made the sides wide? Who formed the caverns of the lungs? Who made the honourable parts of the body conspicuous, and concealed the others? See how much skill is bestowed in one species of matter, how much labour on one single work; everywhere there is beauty, everywhere perfection, everywhere variety. Who made all these things? Who is the mother, who is the father, if it be not the only and invisible God, who has created all things by his will?"

Alcibiades, the Greek patrician who nursed within his breast senatorial aspirations, submitted to an inventory of his mental and ethical qualifications at the hands of Socrates, who thereupon demonstrated that the sole asset of the youth consisted of a vague proficiency in strumming the lyre, the ability to recite poetry not too badly, and an indifferent prowess in the gymnasium. Holding up the mirror of rationality before Alcibiades, Socrates convinced the would-be guardian of the sovereignty of Athens that he lacked sufficient intelligence to administer his own affairs, let alone those of the Athenian commonwealth. Times have changed since those golden days when Skeptic and Peripatetic roamed the Athenian byways, but the spirit of Alcibiades still lives. What matters it if his lyre has now become the saxophone, his quoit and javelin the ball and bat, and his poetic fancies chiefly concerned with carolling the virtues of his Alma Mater? The 20th-century Alcibiades still goes forth full of purpose but woefully empty of knowledge and for lack of a Socrates may actually become a senator and tax the resources of Providence to preserve the integrity of the commonwealth.

The universalization of educational opportunity is the exalted purpose of today. The body politic enthusiastically supports every issue which encourages and facilitates the promulgation of learning. Impressive institutions for the instruction of the young are the civic pride of every community, and like the cathedrals of medieval Europe shadow the teeming city spread out around them. We have deified education and built temples to the spirit of wisdom even as antiquity gilded shrines for the gods of yore. Nevertheless, to us education is still but a word—a wonderful word, truly implying all that is noble, all that is beautiful, all that is true. Yet how far does the practice fall short of the premise; how vast the interval between the implication and the fact! The education for which men have even given their lives and which they have preserved at fearful cost through the world's Dark Ages; the education which the seekers of every age have sought with whole-souled longing; the education that was the very bounty of the gods and the evidence of their perfect covenant with men—this education has failed from the earth. Knowledge has retired again into that Stygian darkness from which the first philosophers called it forth by strange rite and sacrificial deed. We live in a day of material enlightenment, but profound indeed is our ethical and philosophic benightedness.

There is a supreme Educator, an all-knowing Preceptor, an all-wise Counsellor, an all-sufficient Guide, whose integrity dwarfs that of any mortal man. Deep in the inner recesses of our own souls, but obscured by the hallucinations of the senses, is Mercury's inexhaustible pitcher—an infinite capacity which, though ever flowing, is ever full. Man's only educator is this inner self which alone is capable of sifting fact from fancy. The drawing forth of this inner knowledge and its establishment as the ever-sufficient and comprehending director of the outer life is the true office of education. *Educo*, then, signifies to draw forth; and education is that mental process of the outer mind by which is evoked as though by magic the mighty genius that, like a sleeping giant, is man's unsuspected strength. Truth, then, comes from within, fancies from without; and never will education fully solve the problems that are its peculiar province until it equips unfolding manhood and womanhood with the keys by which this treasure house of inner potentialities may be unlocked. As through a glass darkly can even now be glimpsed that tomorrow of education when, grasping with fuller realization the purpose of its own existence, the school assumes the fullness of its role by becoming the dispenser of those disciplines by which man may release the greater Thinker within.

How removed from the frenzied searcher after temporal knowledge is the calm and certain Master of the Hidden Path! The philosopher does not gaze at the stars through man-made telescopes alone, but by the transcendency of his internal faculties he is lifted up and taken into the very soul of the star itself. He feels its life throbbing through him, and from his place within its very heart he learns its innermost secrets. Mingling through his inner self with the inner selves of all things, the truly educated one thus exchanges vain fancy and speculation for the perfect understanding. The soul in him communes with the soul in his world, and both share in a common felicity. He sees, he senses, and he feels, thus coming into possession of countless esoteric secrets which, though his very own, he cannot impart to others nor even explain to that inferior self which is in bondage to the sphere of ignorance.

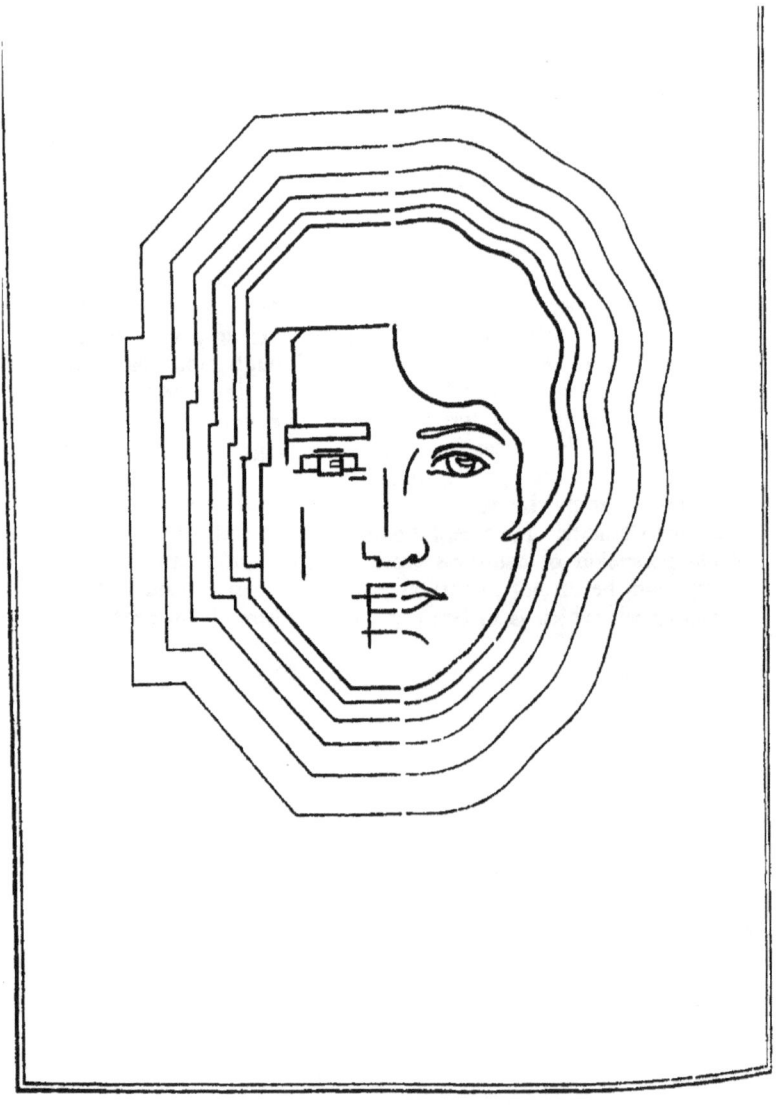

A STUDY IN ANGLES AND CURVES

In symbolism the straight line is considered masculine and significant of strength, the curved line feminine and significant of beauty. In the Cabala the two pillars, Strength and Beauty, support the arch of the Universal House. In the above face the male and female elements are combined, and thus Cosmos, the Divine Androgyne, comes into being.

CHAPTER FIFTEEN

Symbolism, the Universal Language

A SYMBOL is a form designed to portray some abstract quality. A symbol must convey an impression; it must cause the mind to see something which, though not actually in the symbol itself, is suggested by the symbol. Through the familiar is thus shadowed forth the unfamiliar; through the commonplace that which is not commonplace is made evident. Symbols are forms, but the principles for which they stand so transcend the boundaries of form that they can only be sensed by reading into the symbol certain abstract elements, or by grasping with internal comprehension that greater profundity which the symbol does not contain but whose existence it intimates. Symbols are also employed to epitomize. A whole universe may be summarized in a single star, and vast issues by being reduced to their simple elements may be rendered intelligible. By clothing the unfamiliar in terms of the familiar the mind is enabled to grasp with a certain measure of accuracy the significance of the unknown.

We must re-emphasize the point stressed in our opening chapter; namely, that as symbols increase in complexity they decrease in power. Thus the simple figures set forth immensities; the compound figures parvitudes. Increasing definition causes qualities to verge toward form; hence the more intricate the figure the more it is concerned with particulars and the narrower becomes the scope of its symbolism. One of the true purposes of symbols is to preserve ideas in an indefinite state so that their lucidity shall not be obscured by unnecessary form involvement. Between symbolism and caricature there is a slight fundamental difference. As a personality may often be most truthfully depicted by the exaggeration of certain characteristics, so symbols may convey an adequate likeness of a quality and still in no appreciable way resemble the quality. In the last analysis, man is not simply a body but rather a bundle of characteristics which confer upon his objective nature a certain temperament or individuality. By deftly accentuating the idiosyncrasies of character with a few heartless lines, the caricaturist exposes the deformities of rationality and thus portrays the man as he really is. The art of caricature follows certain cardinal principles in recognition of the impressions innate in forms and orders. Breadth, for example, is always associated with optimism, length with pessimism. Hence to broaden the head gives the impression of mental sufficiency, or broadmindedness; to broaden the body suggests a certain substantiality. To narrow the head causes the impression of intolerance, or narrowness of outlook; to lengthen the body oppresses the mind with a feeling of melancholy. Angles convey the impression of strength; curves of beauty. Harmonious combination of angles and curves invoke concord; inharmonious combinations produce discord. Definite reactions are thus produced by simple lines or combinations of lines. Colors and sounds also possess similar powers of mental and emotional stimulation.

Consciously or unconsciously, the shape and arrangement of bodies with which we come in close contact thus profoundly influence our dispositions. Definite mental reactions are caused by contemplation of the symmetrical Pythagorean solids, for all natural bodies contain a force generated by their own organization which leaves its subtle record on the inner sensibilities of man. By accentuating this force according to a definite procedure certain mental attitudes can be stimulated, and in recognition of this principle the Mysteries recommend that their initiates meditate upon certain emblems or figures prepared with this end in view. In common with the laws of caricature, symbolism secures emphasis by distortion, harmony by conventionalization, and force by simplicity. In great measure, art is the process of elimination. Symbolism reveals the necessary by eliminating the unnecessary, and emphasizes the real by disregarding the superficial which obscures the real. In this respect symbolism verges toward the diagrammatic, for through diagrams processes are made evident. Phenomenon when stripped of its outer part reveals the laws by which it exists and manifests. Being chiefly concerned with those few primary principles which are the basis of infinite diversity, philosophy finds in symbolism not only a language singularly qualified to disseminate fundamental premises, but a method whereby universal ideas are communicated without passing them through the sphere of particulars.

Symbolism thus embodies most fully the requisites of the perfect medium of education. Every symbol is a definite stimulus to the mind, and has the delightful faculty of reflecting the moods of the mind attempting to analyze its parts. In other words, a symbol always means what we think it means. Dealing with incorporeal substance, it takes on, chameleonlike, the interpretive attitudes of its interpreter. Through the symbols the individual thus discovers not what symbols mean but rather what he knows himself. In the effort to understand what the first symbolist concealed under his figures, the resources of the mind are stimulated to reveal their own fecundity. Thus emblematic figures and fables draw out from the individual analyzing them the sum and substance of his own understanding. By studying symbols men learn about themselves; for they read into the figures their own hopes and aspirations, their own concepts of universal order, and their own understanding of divine agency. To some degree is thus explained the diversity of codes by which the affairs of men are regulated. Life itself is a symbol, and each must interpret it according to the convictions of his own soul. As we look about we see a universe which, whether we know it or not, is simply our inner convictions reflected back to us from the polished surface of nature.

In *Lazarus Laughed,* Eugene O'Neill causes his hero to thus taunt Gaius Caligula, the heir of Tiberius Caesar: "But what do you matter, O Deathly-Important One? Put yourself that question—as a jester! Are you a speck of dust danced in the wind? Then laugh, dancing! Laugh yes to your insignificance! Thereby will be born your new greatness! * * * Tragic is the plight of the tragedian whose only audience is himself! Life is for each man a solitary cell whose walls are mirrors. Terrified is Caligula by the faces he makes! But I tell you to laugh in the mirror, that seeing your life gay, you may begin to live as a guest, and not as a condemned one!"

The nonphilosophic suffer from a disease which may best be termed *superficiality*. Man's thinking ever fails because of its shallowness. He often mistakes breadth for depth, believing that with but a hasty scrutiny he can become familiar with any object. Superficiality generally springs from indifference, and necessarily produces mediocrity. Our interests ever lie with the familiar, and for the unfamiliar we have no emotion save indifference. By stimulating interest, philosophy causes man to regard an ever-widening circle of incident as a proper field for his speculation. Thus the man, formerly oblivious to the wonders of the universe about him, suddenly comes to realize their existence, and with growing enthusiasm applies himself to the garnering of knowledge. The study of symbolism causes the mind to develop what may be defined as *philosophic suspicion*. Instead of accepting things at their face value, the symbolist searches for their hidden motives—those invisible agencies which are the animate causes of apparently inanimate objects. When the mind comes instinctively to regard forms as the outer garments of realities, great strides have been taken in the rationalization of the entire nature. Man begins to know as soon as he divests himself of the illusion that the universe is material and matter the divine reality.

From this realization it is but a step to the comprehension that truth does not exist in matter but must be sought for behind the veil of matter. The physical (or irrational) mind is incapable of comprehending a single absolute fact; for abiding in the sphere of relative conclusions it necessarily lacks the accuracy of exact procedure. Symbolism discloses the relationship of an intangible agent to its tangible subject; it renders conceivable that interval between the invisible—which is the fact—and the visible—which is the fancy. Even a photograph is fanciful and misleading when compared to a cleverly drawn caricature; for while the caricature may but slightly resemble the physical appearance it is still more discerning than the camera's eye. Our physical personalities thus reveal us as we seem to be, but our intangible individualities continually reveal us as we are. Unfortunately for others, but comfortable for ourselves, the number able to read the intangible characteristics are few; otherwise our mortification would overwhelm us. Yet, in reality, our truest friend is the one who points out to us that which it is so difficult for us to estimate for ourselves—namely, the quality and compatibility of our intangible parts.

Symbolism should be employed throughout the process of education, for by it two definite ends are attainable. First, the student will instinctively reveal to the teacher the constitution of his reasoning part by the interpretation he places upon the symbols; second, the student will be stimulated to originality and thereby preserve the peculiar technique of his own rational processes. The death of originality is the death of genius. Symbolism encourages originality, and hence is productive of genius. Symbols can be devised to induce almost any desired phase of thought or emotion. By the use of emblematic figures alone, abnormality can be corrected and subnormality raised to a normal state. Paracelsus discovered that words written upon parchment when held up before animals produce as definite results as though the words were spoken, although it is evident that the animal cannot read. Combinations of letters, magical symbols, and curious figures, radiate definite impressions, and from the realization of this fact must ultimately emerge a new form of corrective therapy in which the medicine will be administered through the channel of sight. The eyes are peculiarly responsive and the process of visualization already borders upon the psychic, for the impressions transmitted by the eyes to the brain are exceedingly subtle and powerful beyond imagination. The reactions set up through the sight of definite forms or patterns have not yet been thoroughly catalogued. When this work is finished we will understand far more intelligently the motives producing joy and sorrow, sickness and health, vice and virtue. The environment contacted by the individual through the medium of the eyes molds him profoundly, and even his status in the world itself is a key to the temperaments that surge within his breast.

In his *General Introduction to Psychoanalysis*, Freud attempts to relate certain primitive motives of the soul with dreams, in this way disclosing a subconscious faculty of association in the human mind by which external objects, through either appearance or use, become media for the expression of psychic impulses. Freud is dealing with what Plato would call the *animal soul*—that part of the psychic nature which has assumed the idea of generation and which constitutes the ceaseless urge toward the establishment of forms. Obsessed with the idea of polarity, the generating soul causes to flow from itself those impulses which Freud analyzes under the general subject of sex psychology. He maintains that the peculiar soul power which manifests while the functioning organism is asleep is concerned primarily with the principles of generation, and the sleep symbols are largely of a phallic nature. This is incontestible evidence that the earliest religions of mankind were priapic cults and based upon the generating urge of the soul. Clothing itself in appropriate forms, this impulse resulted in strange fables and figures which are now almost dissociated from the primary impulses that inspired them. Though having but few interests, the animal soul often employs a diversity of symbols to signify its attitudes. Thousands of emblems and figures are used to represent a single idea. The animal soul is interested in neither religion nor philosophy, and our mental concepts are its playthings. The animal soul is primarily concerned with the laws of attraction and reproduction; its duty is to perpetuate the species and it knows no ethics beyond this limited field.

Freud infers that dream symbols can be reduced to a very simple alphabet of symbolism. Clothing its urges in the familiar, the soul creates its alphabet during physical infancy and childhood and retains it throughout life. As humanity thus preserves in its religion and philosophy the simple elements which dominated its attitudes during the most primitive periods, so the adult man or woman clothes these soul impulses in those figures and similes which were impressed upon the outer nature during adolescence. It is comparatively easy to understand how most symbols come to have a phallic import. All forms are generations, and all generations are emblematic of the processes by which they themselves came into being. To the individual who functions in the animal nature—that is, where the rational soul has not disengaged itself from the involvements of the corporeal senses—there is no sphere of interpretation above that of generation. To those who by the disciplines and procedures of the higher life have transmuted or regenerated their inferior natures, a loftier sphere of interpretation is rendered apprehensible. Transcending the idea of generation, the philosopher discovers in the symbol a meaning more exalted than that concerned with reproductive processes. Not only is there the animal soul which clings tenaciously to form, but there is also the divine (rational) soul which verges ever toward Reality. Above that part which conceives generation to be the supreme function there is that which contemplates the deathlessness and permanence of the Supreme Good, realizing that Divinity is ungenerate and transcends in every respect the limitations of mortal procedure.

Symbols consequently change their meanings according to the level of intelligence upon which their interpreter functions. The purpose of symbols is to uncover the limitations of mortal consciousness by continually emphasizing the insufficiency of the interpretations placed upon them. Confronted by a symbol, every man recognizes the uncertainties of his own nature. Being never sure that he is correct in his interpretation he is made to realize his heritage in that common uncertainty shared by all ages and all men. The insufficiency of modern so-called knowledge is evident the moment the mind is invited to reflect upon problems involving certitudes. Thus faced, the intellect hesitates and becomes confused. Our thinking is sufficient until it becomes necessary to trust ourselves to its mercy, when it retires abashed, informing us unmistakably of its incapacity. The paradox of knowledge is that knowledge does not exist, for we claim already that for which in reality we are searching. Modern knowledge is not a discovery of facts but the effort to discover facts, and there are great moments when the truth of this apparent contradiction is brought home to us.

There is a popular fallacy that we grow by change. Like the ironic method described and employed by Socrates, change is inseparable from the elements of pain and sorrow. We advance but slowly when every new discovery must contradict those gone before; when every new philosopher must give the lie to his predecessors and every new order depends for its success upon the destruction of previous orders. A little apple tree does not change into a lemon tree while in the process of becoming a big apple tree, nor does truth change its identity in the process of being understood. Every great mind evolves by a sequential process; it does not tear down previous conclusions to make room for new. A growing tree increases from a single shoot to a miracle of branches and foliage, yet nowhere is there any inconsistency or contradiction in the process. The trunk is not destroyed that a new branch may come forth, nor is the tree uprooted to make room for its own fruit. Each manifestation depends upon that which preceded it, and in turn finds its consummation in that which issues from it. From the first quickening of its seed the tree moves inevitably toward a single end; at every step of the way its procedures complement each other and unite in the realization of that end. This perfect co-operation of parts results not only in the tree maintaining its homogeneity and attaining its end with the least expenditure of energy and time, but demonstrates the exactness of the power that willed it into being. Never will the world think well until men reason as trees grow—causing to issue from the single trunk of rational certainty the foliage of thoughts which, clustered symmetrically about their center, impart grace and dignity to the whole.

In their ignorance men make laws, only later to find them faulty. Then, lest their infractions of these laws seem too flagrant, they amend their former errors with fresh errors in the effort to render their own conceits endurable. The various schisms in the body of religion seek to mollify their differences by resorting to condescension or modification. Their compromises, however, are a glaring confession that neither possesses enough of fact to insure survival. So age after age man —who according to the pagan astrologers was fashioned under the influences of Cancer—still demonstrates his kinship to the crab by making most of his progress in a backward fashion. It is more than a seven days' wonder that institutions of importance have to be saved from extinction by periodic renovation, or have their authority curbed lest their intolerance overshadow and endanger personal or national liberties.

Philosophy declares that the first step in the development of rational powers is to establish them upon an immovable foundation, so that the mind in its unfoldment will not be forced periodically to overthrow previous attitudes, but continually to supplement and justify them. *To realize this ideal it is necessary that the first postulations of the intellect shall be vast enough or sufficient in scope so that all subsequent thinking will not be forced to exceed the boundaries of these first assumptions.* Men waste a lifetime devising new methods of thought, only to realize at the end that they have outgrown their own premises; that their building is top-heavy; and that in the architectonics of intellect their edifice of theories is grotesque and inharmonious. As all the agencies of the tree conspire to consummate its purpose—namely, fruitage—so all the agencies of thought conspire to produce the fruitage of the mind. Lacking the wisdom of the tree man all too often finds his roots and trunk structurally too insecure to bear the weight of the ripening fruit.

The eclectic spirit prevalent in this century is largely responsible for this condition. *Men do not think their thoughts through*. Viewing a fractional part of an idea, they are content with its apparent consistency, failing to realize that it may have no place at all in that greater picture composed of infinite ideas combined in most complex patterns. We do not apply Immanuel Kant's *Critique* by which he measured the justifiableness of assumptions. We might ask ourselves, "If the whole universe were run by the same principles as my own little notions, would the world still be sufficient to meet the needs of the vast order which it maintains; if my little whim were elevated to the dignity of a divine reality, would it serve all men; if my thoughts were laws, would there be justice in creation?" These are the questions which intrude their presence upon the mind seeking to *think things through*, often to their bitter end. It is not sufficient that an idea should tickle our sensibilities or give us a pleasant emotional thrill. It is necessary that the idea should stand the acid test of analysis. It must survive the heartless process of *thinking through*. We say "heartless," for few notions—except that they proceed from rationalities so noble that notions have become permissible to them—can survive even the first stages of analysis.

Symbolism re-emphasizes the necessity of approaching every issue with an adequate philosophic background. Confront the untrained mind with some symbol or fable, and it will construct a confused and meaningless explanation, usually far more complex than the figure warrants, and as senseless as a macaw's chatter. Few of us have had the success of Samuel Johnson in protecting the intellect against the assaults of words. In the preface to his dictionary he writes: "I am not yet so lost in lexicography, as to forget that words are the daughters of the earth, and that things are the sons of heaven." The superficial thinker reasons in terms of words alone; the profound thinker so venerates the meaning of words that he conserves his language. We must all realize that it is beyond man's province to comprehend one third of what he says and sacrilegious to talk much with little understanding. Whereas the mediocre intellect is capable of ministering to physical

needs, it is decreed that in the more exalted realms of rationality the mediocre shall pass into the oblivion of the disqualified.

Man can never hope to escape the limitations of his own irrationality; whenever he attempts to transcend himself, his insufficiency blocks his way. The struggle must ever be to overcome insufficiency; to establish within the self an intellectual adequacy in which the mind acquires a competency for its problems. Symbolism stimulates the healthy mind that has been introduced to the disciplines of philosophy, but bewilders the unorganized thinker. No mind is really sufficient for its own needs until it has learned to act as a connective tissue between ideas. Isolated thoughts are comparatively valueless, for the probability of error is too imminent. An impractical thought, then, is one that can survive only in an isolated state; a practical thought one that survives repeated contact with competitive ideas. To study symbols is dangerous for the immature mind, for the practice will only compound absurdities and establish more firmly irrational habits of thought. Hence the ancient Mysteries circulated among the masses definite interpretations of their symbols and allegories, encouraging the untrained thinker to accept these expositions and wonder no more on the subject. Had this not been done a wild orgy of misinterpretation would have followed, and erroneous speculations without number would have found lodgement in minds incapable of recognizing and protecting themselves against these incongruities. Thus in symbolism the profound investigator will discover that the real is ever concealed beneath the superficial. He who is contented with the superficial will consequently never discover the real, and so from age to age the arcana of ancient philosophy have been preserved inviolate at the hands of the unprepared. These secrets are their own custodians, revealing themselves only to such as refuse to accept any substitute for truth, or any part of knowledge less than all.

Two oft-repeated questions are, "Why is it so easy to deceive people in matters pertaining to religion or philosophy," and "Why are the best educated the most gullible?" The answer to the first is self-evident. Theology and philosophy are sciences dealing with intangibles. There is no criterion by which their integrity can be questioned or established save that of a rational mind qualified by its own integrity to weigh and pass judgment upon the elements involved. These divine sciences so completely transcend the limitations of the sense perceptions by which mortal concerns are estimated that every code of physical integrity is inapplicable to them. There is nothing tangible and evident with which to associate these abstruse verities, and the investigator must appoint himself their inquisitor. As all life's great realities exist in this intangible sphere—which we like to term the invisible or causal universe —the problems of existence can never be actually solved except by the exploring faculties of a rationalized intellect. The second question is based upon the unfortunate fact that education, while in some instances increasing the tolerant attitude, all too often fails to increase the integrity so that it can properly direct tolerance. The educated man is usually one who has been instructed in the enormity of his own ignorance, and is therefore inclined to believe that anything may be true. On the other hand, the uneducated man is generally very set in his opinions and hence difficult to convince even of demonstrable facts. A scientist is frequently a disillusioned man. He has been undeceived as to the sufficiency of knowledge and is correspondingly gullible. Camille Flammarion declared that there was but one attitude of the mind more dangerous than that which accepted everything: namely, the attitude that accepted nothing. The materialist who understands practically nothing believes practically nothing.

The ignorant must ultimately become his own executioner. Thus the struggle for knowledge becomes identical with the struggle for survival; for only knowledge insures survival. We are as permanent as the realities that have come to be established in our own natures; we are as impermanent as the fancies that incline us one way or another, only to eventually leave us as ignorant as before. The rational faculties are man's sole hope of ultimate accomplishment, and this accomplishment is identical with happiness; for the changes necessary to establish harmonious physical relationships must first descend from the rational sphere and come into physical manifestation through minds specially trained in philosophic procedure. Every child that is born is a potential instrument for the salvation of the world, and remains an unknown but all-powerful quantity until our physical cultural processes destroy those sensitive instruments of erudition by which the imperceptible verities of the rational sphere can be sensed. Humanity's most precious assets are those developing physical brains, which as focal centers of mental energy radiate thought throughout the substances of the inferior sphere. The answer to every problem, therefore, must be considered as existing in the rational sphere, awaiting that day when unfolding human brains shall be so disciplined in the procedures of rational thought as to become adequate vehicles for the manifestation of this superior knowledge in the physical world.

Rendered prophetic by the luminosity of their inner natures, the sages of antiquity discoursed with rare acumen upon the fate of the sacred sciences at the hands of generations then unborn. In the *Asclepian Dialogue* is preserved a prophetic picture of the decadence of knowledge in baser ages to come. In those days "no one shall look up to heaven. The religious man shall be accounted insane, the irreligious shall be thought wise, the furious brave, and the worst of men shall be considered a good man. For the soul, and all things about it, by which it is either naturally immortal, or conceives that it shall attain to immortality, conformably to what I have explained to you, shall not only be the subject of laughter, but shall be considered as vanity. Believe me, likewise, that a capital punishment shall be appointed for him who applies himself to the religion of intellect. New statutes and new laws shall be established, and nothing religious, or which is worthy of heaven or celestial concerns, shall be heard, or believed by the mind. There will be a lamentable departure of the Gods from men; noxious angels will alone remain, who, being mingled with human nature, will violently impel the miserable men [of that time] to war, to rapine, to fraud, and to everything contrary to the nature of the soul."

Much of this prophecy has already been verified, for during the Dark Ages capital punishment was meted out to those who dared apply themselves to the "religion of intellect." Philosophy was swept from the face of Christendom and the voices of the gods were drowned out by the hymns of the martyrs. Fleeing before theological fanaticism, the custodians of the *arcana imperii* took refuge in the Arabian desert, finding Islam more receptive to philosophic instruction. Accepting Greek philosophy as a sacred trust, the Sons of the Prophet, when carried into southern Europe on the high tides of their fortunes, established in Spain universities far excelling contemporary Christian institutions of learning. To the colleges of the Moors came scholars from every part of Europe, and the lips of men again taught the inspired doctrines of Plato and Aristotle. Islam realized that the teachings of Plato and his illustrious disciple assisted man to liberate his soul from the entanglements of idolatry, for the four Caliphs had set for themselves the task of exterminating idolatry from the earth. Proclus declares that the philosophy of Plato was given to men for the benefit of their terrestrial souls; that philosophy might be authority instead of statutes, rationality instead of temples, understanding instead of sacred institutions, truth instead of mortal leaders of salvation, that the men who are now, as well as those who shall exist hereafter, might not wander about the earth destitute of intelligence.

The literalist is an inveterate profaner of the beautiful. His attitude is a supreme blasphemy, for his art is to limit all natures to the narrow confines of form. He sees nothing beyond an appearance, mistaking the outward show for the inner quality and the dimensional as the only certainty. Whereas the idealist ever strives to elevate man to the estate of gods, the literalist would drag the immortals from their Olympian heights and debase them with the similitude of man. The literalist emphasizes inconsequentials; to him every jot and tittle is a fetish. To the literalist, symbolism is inscrutable, for he is incapable of distinguishing between principle as an abstract reality and form as the transitory vehicle of that principle. Religious stagnation is the wayward child of literalism. As long as theology clings to the blasphemous idea that to think is to usurp a divine prerogative, theologians are restrained from reasoning on the logic of the law, and only the saints are accredited with sufficient sanctity to contemplate the sandal thongs of the Lord. Quaking under their cowls, the pious clergy read and reread the ominous lines from Revelation wherein it is written. "If any man shall add unto these things, God shall add unto him the plagues that are written in this book." Little wonder that the divine science of interpretation failed amid such hostile environment; that symbols became fearful images of literal terrors and the gods came to have as many hairs in their beards as some inspired artisan might carve into their Carrara features.

Maimonides, the most learned of the Rabbins, who devoted a lifetime to contemplation of the Scriptures, writes thus of its hidden meanings and secret imports: "We should not take literally that which is written in the Book of the Creation [Genesis] nor entertain the same concepts of it as are common with the vulgar. If it were otherwise, our learned ancient sages would not have taken so much pains to conceal the sense, and to keep before the eyes of the uninstructed the veil of allegory which conceals the truths which it contains. Taken literally, the work contains the most extravagant and absurd ideas of the Deity. *Whoever can guess at the true meaning should take care not to divulge it.* This is a maxim inculcated by our wise men, especially in connection with the work of the six days. It is possible that by our own intelligence, or by the aid of others, some may guess the true meaning, in which case they should be silent respecting it; or, if they do speak of it, they should do so obscurely, as I myself do, leaving the rest to be guessed at by those who have sufficient ability to understand me."

While the literalist may believe he is defending the integrity of the gods, he is actually detracting from their magnificence by presuming them to be speakers of words when in reality they are disseminators of ideas. Origen asks: "What man of good sense will ever persuade himself that there has been a first, a second, and a third day and that these days have each of them had their morning and their evening, when there was as yet neither sun, nor moon, nor stars?" Even the great St. Augustine admitted the Scriptures to possess profound and unsuspected meanings, at the same time maintaining with characteristic inconsistency that both their literal and historical accuracy also should be affirmed. We shall yet realize that man cannot live by history alone, even though that history be declared sacrosanct. To studious Christian and pagan alike, symbolism becomes a philosophic stone whereby literal absurdities are transmuted into allegorical realities. While little minds may thus thread their way through religion, those of greater vision—recognizing in symbolism a golden key to the treasure house of the world's thought—studiously apply themselves to the principles according to which all fables, allegories, and emblematic figures are erected.

Another phase of symbolism presents itself for consideration. The literalities of one generation become the allegories of the next. The changing customs, the periodic redirectionalizing of interest, and the reinterpretation of the meanings of words and figures, make it most difficult for any generation to understand its forebears. Hence to interpret the ideals of one century in the terms of another is to lose a certain intangible atmosphere which cannot survive the vicissitudes of time. Consequently, to secure an accurate translation of Greek philosophic writing does not necessarily imply that we possess the information embodied in those writings.

It has been said that no philosophy can survive translation, for no sacred teaching can ever be actually understood except by one able to transport himself into the locale and time in which the material was originally indited. Hence arose the practice of perpetuating the inner doctrines through oral tradition, for it was presumed that each generation would reclothe these basic ideas with proper vestments and thus preserve them free from distortion at the hands of time. To understand the

Mysteries we must cease to live in America of the 20th century and assume the temperaments, attitudes, interests, and environments in which the Mysteries were first established. To understand Greek philosophy we must understand ancient Greece and its people. The secret teachings are always clothed in the terms of the familiar when revealed to the multitudes, and the familiar terms of yesterday are not the familiar terms of today. The same is true of the Bible. The archaic Hebrew of the pre-Christian period interpreted the ideals of an older people of whom not one true vestige now remains. The Pentateuch is the living remnant of a world long dead; of interests which have outlived their time; of attitudes archaic and ethics extinct.

If we would release the spirit of beauty locked within the ancient characters and make it serve this generation, we must divest it of its ancient robes and reclothe it in the familiar habiliments of today. With rare discrimination we must separate the principle from its form, the living from the dead, the eternal from the temporal. Only the symbolist has developed that fine faculty of dividing the relevant from the irrelevant and prudently preserving that which is usable. As the archeologist sifting the ashes of dead civilization recovers therefrom priceless evidence of things no longer evident, so the symbolist studiously examining the intellectual remains of vanished orders rescues from oblivion those fragments of rationality which will contribute to the right-thinking of the world. As the earth is built up of geologic strata—the rot of milleniums—so the body of world thought is composed of an infinite number of layers, in each of which may be seen the half-disintegrated remains of vast institutions and noble intellectual procedures. In things of the mind the past has not lived in vain. Those who live best today live by the world's first thoughts, and the foolish of today still commit the same grave errors that the first philosophers decried. There is no such thing as modernism in human thought, for minds have labored since the beginning and the world's first thinker reasoned out the same problems which the world's last sage must ponder. The future will perpetuate the quest of the past, and tomorrow is but the knowledge of today plus an added period for contemplation.

A few simple rules will be of value to those desirous of assuming the mantle of philosophy. There are many queer pockets in its ancient folds, and only when they are investigated in order will their contents prove of highest value. It has well been said that there are tricks in every trade. These tricks are a certain "knowing how" by which accomplishment is facilitated. In accordance with the ancient Pythagorean law it is first necessary to establish the triangle before the solution of any problem is possible. The science of symbolism is accordingly based upon a threefold premise. Once the mind is familiarized with this triangular foundation, integrity and industry will discover the correct solution.

> First, *every substance, object, element, and agent in the universe is capable of instructing man in those phases of divine order which are involved in its own constitution.* In other words, everything can teach us of itself, and as all natures differ from each other to greater or lesser degree, each performs a definite ministry of instruction. From an earnest consideration of their constitutions and procedures man is enabled to familiarize himself with those laws of being to which he himself is also subject.
>
> Second, *the more fully an individual is acquainted with the operations of the inferior universe, the better qualified he is to contemplate the constitution of the causal spheres.* This is a development of the Hermetic axiom of analogy; namely, that the above is like the below and the below like the above. The knowledge of inferiors is necessary to the knowledge of superiors. The danger arising, however, from the analysis of inferiors is that the mind may form an attachment for them and thus be rendered incapable of turning from them to the consideration of superiors.

Third, *all natures should be regarded as worthy of profound analysis, for the deadly enemy of all proficiency is a superficial attitude toward any phase of existence.* The true source of man's education is not to be found in books, but lies in his observation of natural phenomena and his attempt to estimate its significance. Failure to regard any object as worthy of particular attention is to lose the opportunity to understand the superphysical function or characteristic which is the intangible but all-powerful cause of the object itself.

Symbolism, when thus regarded, is elevated to the dignity of a religion, or more correctly, it becomes the means to the end of religion. To the philosophic atheist symbolism occupies the middle ground between knowledge and ignorance, becoming the divine instructor through whom the mysteries of the inner spheres are made apparent to the outer sense perceptions. Thus, instead of waiting for the heavens to open and permit an angelic visitant to deliver homilies from an ambo supported by some cumulus cloud, the symbolist liberates through rational procedure the ideas resident in form. These ideas thus freed preach their own silent but all-informative sermons. To the one capable of discerning God, Deity is omnipresent in His own handiworks. The philosopher is the continual recipient of divine revelation, and the gods are proximate indeed to that illumined sage who sees God in the fire and hears Him in the wind.

The Phrygian Dactyls (physicians by magic) employed symbols because of the remarkable therapeutic powers they possessed. The figures drawn upon parchment and papyrus, or carved into the forms of medallions and talismans, were applied to the diseased members or attached to the persons of the sick, and thus by necromantic means dislodged the evil agencies conspiring to drive the spirit from its infected nature. Paracelsus, who secured from the Arabians many secrets of pagan theurgy, describes in detail the remedial agencies reposing in the ancient metals, and their alloys, particularly electrum. Of the virtues of electrum (which he declared to be composed of the seven planetary metals) the great Swiss physician writes: "Vessels fashioned from electrum render their contents safe from poison and from sorcery, for this alloy has great sympathy for the human race. The ancients fashioned from this mystical substance rings, bracelets, medals, seals, figures, bowls, and mirrors, all possessing most wonderful virtues. A ring formed of electrum and worn upon the finger will cure lameness, paralysis, and the epilepsy. I have seen a ring of electrum put on the ring or heart finger of a person afflicted with a secret disease. The ring immediately began to sweat and became spotted and even went out of shape with sympathy for the sufferer."

Forms, declared the Mysteries, possess strange virtues, and the tracing of these forms intensifies these virtues and renders them potent ministrants to human ills. The Idaean fingers of the Samothracians and other curious effigies of human members were magnetized with medicinal virtues and possessed by a spirit whose strength was sufficient to avert plagues or pestilences and liberate the flesh from all manner of infirmity. Not only was it essential that these devices be made out of the proper substances, but they must be fashioned into definite shapes commodious to the astral light which, flowing through the symbol, was conjured thereby to manifest as a preservative or curative agent. Manipulated by the hierophants—the *Patars* who received their wisdom "through a keyhole"—these models and figures became as though alive. They were charged as with an electric current, at times glowing or radiating showers of sparks and miniature lightning flashes. As forms are the projections of invisible forces, so their artificial construction invokes invisible natures adapted to their geometric patterns. These supermundanes ensoul the objects and lend their power to the *magus* whose knowledge is sufficient to control them.

This explains the strange phenomenon of the talking images, the vocal mechanisms of the ancients, the urns of prophecy, and the nature of oracles; for even openings in the earth, apertures in walls, and the concavities of vessels, became the abode

SYMBOLISM, THE UNIVERSAL LANGUAGE   357

of genii conformable to those capacities. Moving within their appointed vents and orifices, these spirits caused the phenomenon of winds and strange sounds in sealed *amphorae* and subterranean crypts. Such forces are too intangible, however, for mortal perception, unless by secret rituals the genii have been invested with a certain amount of terrestrial substance. We shall yet rediscover the secrets of the talking urns that spoke with the voice of ages and through whose lips issued the words of men long dead. By this the ancients did not infer that the dead spoke through these urns, but rather that the words spoken during the lifetime of these men had been preserved in the subtle ethers of cosmos and through specially patterned instruments could be rendered audible again after the lapse of centuries. Science, the necromancy of the 20th century, will yet accomplish by physical means that which the ancient hierophants performed by their rational knowledge of the inner construction of the universe.

Symbols are oracular forms—mysterious patterns creating vortices in the substances of the invisible world. They are centers of a mighty force, figures pregnant with an awful power which, when properly fashioned, loose fiery whirlwinds upon the earth. Pythagoras foretold impending disasters by hydromancy, for he possessed a brazen bowl which, when filled with water, became strangely agitated, the surface of the water being continually moved as though a spirit were breathing upon it. Gazing upon the agitated water the Samian sage foretold by the ripples in the water things which were to come.

Pythagoras was also one of the "veiled" philosophers who revealed his instruction from behind a curtain, permitting only certain favored disciples to behold his face. Those desirous of receiving his words were instructed by an intermediary who stood without the door and heard the illumined discourses "through the crevices in the locks." Hence the thought of the "keyhole" philosophers or hierophants who, never beholding the immortals, were the doorkeepers of the *arcanum arcanorum*. Of this order was the Apostle Peter whose name, PTR, was the common appellation bestowed upon the instructors in the sacred rites, who were indeed the "living rock" upon which the House of Wisdom was raised.

Christianity, as we have it today is a philosophy revealed through a keyhole—a few mysterious words caught by an eavesdropper. This allusion, however, has a symbolic rather than a frivolous import. The eavesdropper was a privileged listener permitted to hear that which he could hear, for while he listened without "the banquet of the gods" was going on within. But only when the divinities shout most lustily do mortals catch even the faintest echo. Symbols are keyholes to doors in the walls of space, and through them man peers into Eternity. Only to a few, however, is the privilege given to take the gold or silver key of the Cabalistic light and with it draw back the bolts that hold securely the portals of the *domus sancti spiritus.*

Symbolism, then, is the divine language, and its figures are a celestial alphabet by which those upon the seats of the mighty trace their will in the fabric of the worlds. Though the patterns be infinite and man finite, still in the marvelous pageantry of emblems and figures human creatures may behold the workings of their heavenly masters. The meditating seer beholds strange figures in the sky. There are also signs upon the earth as well as in the heavens, and he who can read them is lifted up and transported into this sphere of reality.

The Buddhist mendicant pays homage to the footprints of his Lord; the Egyptians caught upon stone with mallet and chisel the shadows of the gods; and the rational soul gazing out into a universe of images beholds, as it were, a mirage hovering above the expanse of the earth. In this dream-world dwell the luminous rishis of the Brahman's contemplation; here in majestic file pass the mild-faced bodhisattvas in their pilgrimage through Eternity. Gazing downward from this mystery above, the symbolist sees faintly shadowed on the plains of earth this passing pageantry of supermundane things. To the discerning few the outlines of the gods may ever be traced in the flora and fauna of Nature. Hovering above terrestrial concerns, the divine orders are sensed by the inner perceptions and rendered knowable by the forms which perpetuate their impulses.

It is said that in ancient days God walked in the Garden, and the light that was with him illumined the parts thereof. Nor is Deity today any more distant than yesterday, for the Maker of things still blesses his creations with his proximity. The growing grain, the ripening fruit, the tender shoots rising from the dark brown mold, the soft-eyed kine grazing on the hillside, the laughter of men—all these bear evidence of the invisible but ever-present Maker. God is in his world, and although men cannot gaze into his face and live they may gaze upon his works, and if they look rightly shall receive life more abundantly.

The world is a symbol of the permanence of God, life a symbol of the presence of God, and love a symbol of the understanding of God. To those who are able to sense the inner life of things and read into forms even a small part of that great agency which actually ensouls them, the all-sufficiency of Universal Good is all-sufficing.

Symbols are manifesters of a mysterious covenant by which the orderliness and consistency of all natures is decreed. Symbols are indeed the peculiar language of a transcendent agent. Men whose ears are unfitted to hear the profundities of the Torah are permitted to behold the Law graven upon the battlements of space, flashing from the stars, and inscribed upon every leaf and petal. The Law thunders from the rocks, and in mournful cadence may be heard in the cry of the sea. All symbols are things standing for still greater things—the images of a transcendent perfectness, the witnesses of a sufficient truth, the Evangelists of Eternity.

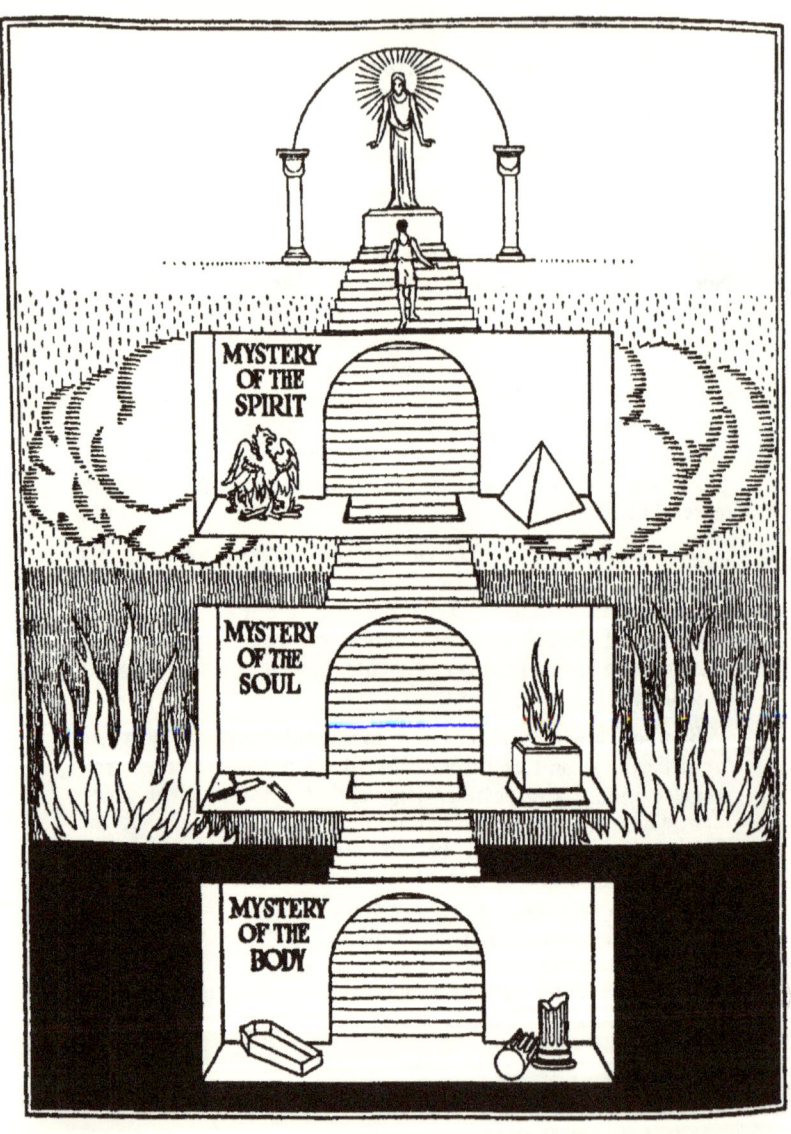

THE CHAMBERS OF THE MYSTERIES

The ancient initiations were given in three chambers which signified the worlds of the Body, the Soul, and the Spirit. After passing successfully through the hazards of the rituals, the neophyte ascended to a vaulted room in which stood the robed figure of the Great Mystery. Thus the secrets of self-mastery were revealed to the candidate.

CHAPTER SIXTEEN

Ancient Mystery Rituals

THE sophisticated pharisees of the 20th century unceasingly give thanks that they have outgrown the fables and rituals of the ancients. The worldly-wise love the evident and are exasperated by that which is not evident. Plutocrat and proletarian alike regard themselves as victimized by that person whose words or actions they do not understand. They love the obvious because it flatters them, and hate the mysterious because it damns their intelligence with faint praise. Riddles are irksome. The modern cry is for facts—facts stripped of their verbal trappings and denuded of nonsense. Yet with facts for their fetish, the modernists are more foolish than their forebears. Decrying superstition, they are most superstitious; rejecting fancies, they are the fanciful product of a fictitious age. The modern world is bored with its own importance; life itself has become a botheration. Having passed the saturation point of realistic culture, satiety is imminent. Suffering from chronic ennui, how can a world ever become interested in anything but itself? Smothered in their self-complacency these all-sufficient ones ask for facts. But what facts are there that fools can understand? How can the helplessly superficial grasp the hopelessly profound, for are not realities reserved for the wise?

For even those interested in philosophy today we often hear the remark, "We have outgrown rituals and symbols. They belong to another age, some previous cycle that has spun its time and long since vanished into the discard." But is it not more than passing strange that we should outgrow all that was beautiful in those worn-out ages and yet hug to ourselves the same vices that they served all too well? We have re-edited and considerably amplified the first books of iniquity, but what of the Book of Beauty and Truth? Why have we torn it from its ancient covers and cast it aside? If we have not outgrown the evils of the past, how can we have outgrown its virtues? How can a man say, "I live in a new age" and then steal more brazenly than the Spartans, intrigue more murderously than the Egyptians, kill more wantonly than the Romans, and oppress more heartlessly than the Brahmans?

Apparently, "ages" do not entirely end, for the dregs of each dying era are dumped into the next to become the common heritage of new civilizations, while the best is all too likely to die or remain obscured, awaiting rediscovery by a philosophic few. There are times when memory is a carrier of carrion, and when committed to writing this carrion becomes history. Not only have civilizations perished, but civilizations have also lived and exemplified some phases of the beautiful. We regard the past as having vanished like a dream. It seems to us unreal, but even as we say "The past is dead," we ourselves die. The modernist cries: "Look to the future!" We follow the direction of his finger and, behold, there is nothing. The future is an unfashioned quantity; it is the highly glorified *now*, the minute stepped up to infinity. The future is a great intangible capacity stuffed full with the same substances of which the past is made. In the last analysis, both *now* and *then* shall pass away. There is, however, a strange philosophic *now* which endures, but the *now* of fools is but an instant slipping into *then*. The past is more kindly than the future; it is rich with memories and redundant with accomplishments. Whereas the future is the abode of the unborn, the past is the dwelling place of the immortals; for when man passes from the little *now* to the great *then*, he either sinks into a kindly obscurity which covers his faults with the mantle of forgetfulness, or his memory grows until men raise altars to do him homage and the ages resound with his name.

The past is the security of the wise—the sure foundation upon which his feet are placed; the present is the slippery footing of the fool, for it passes away even while he stands thereon. We never outgrow the past any more than we outgrow our own childhood, for maturity is something added on. It is the complement, not the contradiction of that which preceded it. Remove the child from the man and he dies; for the child is the beginning, the point of unity from which all the rest springs like the oak from the acorn. The past is the abiding place of tender memories; of wise experiences. It is the fountain of beauty, life, and truth, and although this fountain flows through all the ages to make fertile the distant corners of creation, yet shall it never be greater than its own source.

It is fitting that every man should venerate his tutelaries with some expression of the beautiful. The gods of elder days required no solemn convocation or bloody sacrifice, but rather conjured man to more virtuous living by inclining his soul toward those perfect rhythms which stream continually from the splendor of Abiding Destiny. The gods upon their eternal thrones rejoice not in the groveling mendicant mumbling threadbare litanies, but in the free man rich with the joy of living. Too long have the followers of a jealous and capricious Lord trembled in fear of his displeasure. Too long have men supplicated Deity to spare them yet a little while before the inevitable loosening of his wrath. Too long have men envisioned their Creator as *in*human rather than *super*human. When the sanctuaries ceased to ring with the laughter of a happy human kind, the gods girded up their loins and departed. Too much of solemnity is an oppression of the spirit. He who venerates excessively neither loves nor understands the object of his veneration.

To me, ritualism is essential to philosophy—not the ritualism of a decadent church which had its inception after the decline of Greek aesthetics, but the ritualism of the ancient pagans who served God with joy. Today we serve our faith with sadness, and if all the dwellers in the seven heavens were to perish together the sound of our lament could not be more piteous than those funeral hymns with which we herald the glad tidings of our salvation. Never should we forget the story of the simple-minded jester who, entering the cathedral and having nothing else to offer, performed his repertoire of tricks upon the altar before the statue of the Virgin. When, indignant at the impious act, the priests sought to drive the youth from the church, a miracle happened. The stone figure of the "Mother of God" came to life and bestowed its blessings upon the adoring juggler. The substance of faith is not dignity but sincerity; not formality but naturalness. Ancient religion was devoid of sermonizing. The words of the gods were not made the subjects of ecclesiastical debate. Tiresome clerics did not drown their congregations with a flood of pointless argument. A local exponent of the old-time religion recently offering their prayers and hanging garlands on the hermae chose for his subject the vital question, "Which of the twelve Apostles was the first to drink from the holy cup at the Last Supper." After first intriguing his audience by a few anecdotes concerning his own childhood, the minister analyzed his text from every conceivable, as well as inconceivable angle. At last, running short of time, he postponed his conclusions on this matter of pith and moment until the following Sunday! All the while virtue continues to fail from the earth crime waxes strong, and there are ominous mutterings of new wars.

The priests of the ancient temples were merely the custodians of the treasures bestowed upon the sanctuaries by the wealthy. The temple devotees came when it pleased them, of the illustrious dead. In the presence of the images of the immortals the thoughtful soul sought solitude. Into this inner silence there flowed a mysterious strength—courage to dare, patience to wait, vision to hope, fortitude to die. No discordant choir interrupted the ecstasy of enraptured meditation; no smug-faced deacons doled out the pews. Sanctuary was a place holy and inviolate—a plot of earth separate from worldly concerns where man might go to ponder the realities of life. Here all that was good seemed near, and all that was fearful far removed.

We may brand him an idolater who reverently stands in the presence of a great marble figure carved by the hands of man into the symbol of a formless power. We may say that no mortal sculptor could enliven an image or cut from marble a divinity. But imagine yourself standing within the temple portals. Upon its lofty pedestal before you looms the figure of Olympian Zeus. The face, many times life-sized, is carved from ivory, as are the arms and the sandaled foot that extends beyond the folds of his golden robes. The noble brow is encircled by a wreath of gold and the gilded sandals were pounded from the ornaments of worshippers. In one hand great Zeus holds out the globe of earth, surmounted by the figure of Athena; in the other are his thunderbolts, symbolic of his might. Though you may disbelieve, yet will you be silent; for in the presence of great beauty the soul is stilled. What, then, do men worship; what calls forth their adoration? Is it "the high thundering king" upon his golden throne, or is it that subtle beauty caught in the ringlets of his ivory hair or held as though petrified in each fold of his flowing robe? Where beauty is there is a spirit in the air, and it is this spirit that men worship, and none who worships this spirit can be wholly bad. As a thirsty traveler drinks from the flowing fountain in the oasis, so the thirsty soul drinks life from the beautiful and is renewed by the sheen of a gilded globe or the majesty of a carven face. Remember, it is neither the face nor the stone—it is the something that is caught upon the stone as a sound caught by the breeze, as a ray of light reflected upon the ripples of the sea, or a smile given and returned in anothers eyes. So "High Heaven" in its grandeur is more than an image of stone to a tired and troubled humanity which creeps away from its sorrow to gaze upon a noble brow, or contemplate the quality of a sculptor's skill.

Thus from that which is seemingly not real there issues forth a beautiful reality, and God is never distant from that which is beautiful. Can we blame the ancient pagan if, feeling the force that emanates from a harmonious figure, he declared that a divinity had taken up its abode therein? Is that stone dead which can make strong men weep and give cowards courage to go forth and die? Is that stone dead which can hold the hearts of an entire nation and unite all factions in its presence? Is that stone dead before which the sick are healed of their maladies and the sorrowful are given peace? Is that stone dead which can incline man's mind from the contemplation of earthly interests to the concerns of the spirit? Is that stone dead which can inspire man to cast off his natal ignorance and aspire to the beauty which he senses in a carven face? Nothing that is beautiful is dead; for beauty is life, and wherever beauty exists life is more abundant, and when it departs life flickers out like an expiring candle flame.

Is all this idolatry; in fact, is there such a thing as idolatry? Is not even the fetish a symbol of some standard, some beauty which ennobles life? From the primitive beauty of physical courage men grow to the fuller beauty of integrity, and from integrity still higher to pure aesthetics. *We are all idolaters, not because we worship the lesser in lieu of the greater but because we do not learn to understand what we worship and why we worship.* Analyzing some microscopic creature the scientist is not seeking simply to learn the habits of an order of minutiae; he is seeking knowledge, and the tiny organism is but the instrument by which he gratifies the desire to know. Kneeling before his household shrine the Buddhist does not worship Buddha. The figure before him is but the instrument by which he seeks to know; it is a tangible nature about which, like some auric sheath, is a peculiar atmosphere of beauty. Because of their severity the cold, gray churches of the modern world have failed to catch and hold the spirit of the beautiful. The God of our salvation will not be captured in hard-lined lectern or graceless pulpit. The chill of death is in the air; not the death of the body but the death of the spirit. It may seem sacrilegious to affirm that there should be warmth in the house of God; that men coming to worship should find an edifice as ennobling as the text.

The old cathedrals of Europe hide under their Gothic spans labyrinths of gloomy chambers where in richly-carved sarcophagi lie the princes of church and state sleeping the centuries away. Here also are dismal dungeons where those who offended the laws of their gloomy God awaited death, their only liberator. Above the heads of the illustrious dead still file the solemn processionals of the faith. Still with awful solemnity the celebrant elevates the host, and the sun's rays striking some lightly tinted pane are reflected from the golden implements of the service. Again solemnity, again majesty, again faith muttering over mystic spells!

But instead of man being lifted up into the beauty of God by all this pomp and spectacle, he is caused to cringe with bowed head. Oppressed by the memory of sin, the laity feel rather than see the processional pass by. We say "feel", for they dare not look, the weight of their faith is so heavy upon them. The splendor of God does not raise the worshipper to union with itself, but rather casts him down with the sense of his own insignificance. Whereas the gods of old in gentle tones bade all men come forward and receive their portion of Universal Good, the gods of today, pointing an accusing finger at each cringing sinner, ominously proclaim that if the quality of divine mercy were strained, long ere this the human race would have felt the fires of Tophet.

Nothing is more meaningless than empty ceremonial. The service of forms and letters must pass away, for in themselves they are as ineffectual as the ivory face of Zeus. In the Christian Mysteries it was declared that a spiritual being called the "Angel of the Presence" was invoked by the solemnizing of the mass. Brooding over the congregation, this spirit brought with it the benediction of the Father so that the worshippers should not worship in vain. Is not this Angel the same mysterious power which moved in the adytum of pagan temples; whose proximity was perceptible even to the profane, and whose comings and goings were heralded by tinkling bells? This was the god whose presence was a covenant and whose departure presaged decay. The Angel of the Presence itself is fabricated from the very essences of worship; it is the atmosphere of sanctity which encloses the holy place as within an iridescent bubble. The contents of this bubble are actually breathed in by the assembled multitude whose bodies become charged with a certain ecstasy which defies analysis.

The purpose of ritualism is to create this intangible atmosphere; to incline men's lives to the quest of that inner peace and tranquillity which is temporarily conferred by the celestial visitant. Ritualism fails utterly if it does not induce rhythm in spectator and participant alike. The gods did not rejoice in rituals, but men in whom the higher emotions are latent find in pageantry an opportunity to express the beautiful and thus mingle their lesser lives with the ebb and flow of universal order. Ritualism has no direct appeal to the rational faculties; in fact, the whole subject of religion lies wholly within the province of the emotions. So while in the day of great intellectual achievement religion wanes, in the presence of calamity it waxes strong. Previous to the great earthquake of 1923 the Buddhist faith was not taken seriously by the body of the Japanese people. Even the national shrines wore a dilapidated air, for the empire of the Rising Sun was fast falling under the spell of finance. Then concomitant with disaster came religion. The mourning multitudes again brought offerings to the temples and decked the shrines with flowers. In prosperity man is sufficient for himself, but in adversity he turns to his Creator for strength. Religion is an instinct so deeply implanted within the human soul that it often remains unmanifested until misfortune sweeps away the superficial and bares the inner self.

Thus to the scientist, the intellectualist, and the sophisticate rituals are simply humbug with which a well-fed clergy insure their own expectation of life by themselves eating the offerings, and toasting their benefactors with the sacramental wine. But in the ordeals of the soul of what comfort are stocks and bonds; what consolation can be extracted from the test tube; what condolence can be found in the postmortems of the literati? Trying to make friends out of the printed page and engaging in vicarious romances with their own notions, men of letters live lonely lives. In the great laboratory there is no sound other than the beating of the scholar's heart. Yet there is a rhythm in the air, a slow, measured tempo which inclines the whole deportment to gravity of thought and conduct. As this rhythm infects the nature a great cry issues from the depths of the tormented soul: "There is so much to know and I have such a little while to stay." Overshadowed by towering racks of books—the thoughts of lives unnumbered—the reason is confounded. Thus deprived of faith in the possibility of knowledge, the life that serves the mind recoils in despair before the impossible.

The evangelists of the beautiful summon men to come out of their world of selfishness and thought, and to realize that men can die of excessive mentality, and that thoughts themselves can become the harbingers of great sorrow. "Leave the rhythm of vast enterprise," they cry; "leave behind both your interests and your indifferences and enter into the presence of great beauty." Much thinking is a disease, and idle speculation leads to nothing. Only he who loves the beautiful is wise; only he who serves the beautiful is good; only he who shares the beautiful is happy. Beauty is in the heavens and its power extends throughout all worlds. Beauty is upon the earth, molding all forms into the likeness of God. Beauty is in the human soul, lifting man upward to ever nobler vistas of endeavor. Beauty is that abiding spirit which, hovering over creation, tinctures all being with its ineffable nature. Open your minds, therefore, that beauty may flow into them; open your hearts that beauty may flow out of them.

In one of the uncanonical Gospels it is written that after Jesus and his Apostles had celebrated the Passover together they sang and danced, the Master himself dancing with them on the eve of his betrayal. Pan was regarded by the Greeks as the patron of harmony and rhythm, and his pipes were attuned to the harmony of the spheres. In a choral ode Sophocles addresses Pan as the author and director of the dances of the gods, and also as the author and disposer of the regular motions of the universe, of which these divine dances were symbols. Pan was the aspect of Zeus as lord of the mundane sphere, and according to Athenaeus grave Zeus himself bestowed his favor upon the terpsichorean art. Thus the Gnosian dances sacred to the Demiurgus, and also the Nyssian regarded as peculiar to Bacchus, revealed by their movements the various modes of the all-ruling Principle. One of the Pythagoreans composed a complicated measure by which he was able to interpret, with the aid of gestures, the whole body of Pythagorean lore and thus convey much of its esoteric meaning to the uninitiated. Aristotle classes dancing with the imitative arts, and Lucian calls it "a science of imitation and exhibition which explained the conceptions of the mind, and certified to the organs of sense things naturally beyond their reach." Richard Payne Knight declares dancing to have been part of the ceremony of all mystic rites and that persons of exemplary gravity condescended to cultivate it as a useful and respectable accomplishment. He further notes that dancing, being entirely imitative, was esteemed as honorable as the subject it was intended to express.

In his *Anacalypsis,* Godfrey Higgins advances the theory that the three great elements of primitive ritualism—music, poetry, and the dance—existed before the discovery of writing and were employed in the perpetuation of religious knowledge and historical records. Mr. Higgins deplores the invention of writing, declaring that the decline of pagan virtue was largely due to the wane of the interpretive arts, which were considered unnecessary when more exact methods of perpetuating knowledge were originated. The exploits of all ancient peoples were perpetuated by epic poems. In every community dwelt bards who had committed these lengthy narratives to memory and recited them at feasts and celebrations.

Poetry is the rhythm of words, music the harmony of sounds, and the dance the harmony and rhythm of motion. These higher octaves of ordinary endeavor were reserved for the worship of the gods and to immortalize the deeds of heroes. After the invention of writing, the most important records were either carved into the surface of stone or engraved upon golden plates. Thus deprived of their primal dignity, the interpretive arts became elements of amusement rather than instruction. Men loved the evident then as now, and it was easier to trace a motive in the written word than in some sad harmony or subtle gesture. The ancient poets lamented the decay of their resplendent ceremonials. Ceasing to portray the beautiful in processional and pageantry, the Saturnalia and Bacchanalia degenerated into licentious orgies wherein all that was base and depraved became the theme of interpretive expression. In this state of perversion the fine arts preserved with pomp and show the outward form from which the inner spirit had fled.

Music and the dance were extensively employed in the initiatory rites of the ancient Mysteries. Some of the inner secrets were also perpetuated in archaic meter. Entering upon the path leading to self-liberation, the neophyte found the way beset with rhythms of diverse kinds. Temptation rendered exquisite by a seductive tempo lured him from his austerities. The figures swaying about him in the gloom interpreted the candidate's every thought and feeling. Through the darkness of subterranean crypts resounded the mournful cadences of an infernal music. The rocks re-echoed the doleful sound until it seemed that all creation wept together. The miseries of unrighteous living, the inevitable anguish of uncurbed desire, the hopelessness of irrationality—all these and many other grave realizations were impressed upon the consciousness of the wandering neophyte. When from the dark chamber of earthly horror he passed into the abode of fire, the candidate beheld upon the altar before him a lurid and flickering flame whose eerie light cast vague specters upon the cavern walls. These specters seemed to dance to some fantastic measure ordered by the erratic fire.

Then the music changed. The low monotony gave place to a slight, almost discordant consonance. The tones vibrated with a wild abandon, and invisible fingers strove to tear the human nature from the firm grasp of its will. Dim forms in crimson draperies blended their motions with the gyrations of the altar fire. Bearing in their hands golden platters of grapes and with vine leaves twisted in their hair, these houris of a rhythmic dream besought the candidate to partake of their illusions. Half-frenzied with the exotic harmonies, and holding his hands before his face, the searcher after the greater realities of life staggered from the chamber of desire, seeking escape from the haunting rhythms that sought to hold him to the sphere of sense. Again there was silence and darkness, but even the silence seemed to throb, and with brain still whirling the neophyte pressed on to find himself in another chamber lit with a strange twilight, which apparently coming from nowhere was diffused throughout the whole apartment. About the walls upon stone seats sat a row of grave and pensive figures like senators pondering the problems of the state. The music began again—this time soft and plaintive like a cry from the very depths of the soul. The faces of the silent assemblage were fixed in a melancholy stare as though each man gazed into eternity but saw nothing. The invisible musicians continued their faint and tragic theme which seemed to whisper that all was vanity, that life was a hopeless span, and that all these assembled thinkers thought in vain. The air was sodden with despair; disillusionment filled the cavern like some noxious fume, and in spite of himself the candidate bent his head before its insidious power. Slowly the circle of seated figures began to sway. Without rising they inclined their bodies and heads in unison. The silent but concerted motion breathed a hopeless negation which seemed to say: "There is no use; life is a span of useless suffering, with birth and death the inescapable tragedies of entrance and exit." If only one of these swaying figures would speak! Even though his words were prophetic of naught but ill, it would at least break the terrible tension. But no word was spoken. The disciple felt his courage slowly oozing from him as the chill of despair entered his soul.

Barely able to stand, tormented by the wailing cadence, and half hypnotized by the measured swaying of the old men's heads, the neophyte staggered from the hall of learning back into the dark passageways of the labyrinth. Sobbing and unable to stand, he crawled along the stones, seeking some escape from that cold hopelessness which made all life appear useless and all effort vain. Once out of hearing of the music his courage returned, and recovering his former poise he continued his quest for light. At last he reached the bottom of a flight of steps, and ascending them in the gloom came to two large doors with golden knobs, whereupon a voice bade him open them and enter. As the candidate swung the massive portals wide he was almost blinded by the shaft of light that struck his eyes so long accustomed to somber shadows and gloom. At length his vision cleared and he found himself in a high domed chamber brilliantly illumined by a massive globe of golden light placed in the center of the vaulted ceiling. The dome was supported by twelve pillars of varicolored marble, and the floor was a checkerboard design with alternate blocks of gold and ivory. In the center of this chamber upon a marble base stood the great veiled figure of the Mother of Mysteries, the "Keeper of the Royal Secret." In a circle about the statue knelt four and twenty priests in flowing robes of white, whose inspired faces were turned upward in contemplation and adoration of the Great Mystery. Again the orchestral music began, but this time it was serene, triumphant, victorious. The anthem of praise echoed and re-echoed throughout the vaulted dome, and the four and twenty priests as with but a single voice sang praises to the Seven-Lettered One by whose graciousness the way of light had been established upon the earth. As the victorious mode thundered through the chamber it caused the very walls to quiver. Overwhelmed by the solemnity of the spectacle, the neophyte fell to his knees in adoration of the power that, descending from heaven, had taken up its dwelling in the temple. Then from among the kneeling figures came forth one more glorious than all the rest, upon whose brow was a golden wreath and in whose hand was a great staff with hieroglyphic figures deeply carved into its surface. Gazing into the face of the hierophant, the neophyte could not but ask the question: "Is this great Zeus himself?"

Taking the new initiate by the hand the high priest opened a small door in the pedestal of Ceres' statue, and beckoning the youth to follow him, disappeared into the darkness. The secrets revealed in this inner room it is not lawful to disclose, for they are concerned with the spirit and the end of that long quest which is man's pilgrimage of life. Here the inner meanings of the rituals were revealed; here the purpose of symbol and allegory was made known; here the initiate learned why the great truths of life cannot be imparted by word alone, but must flow through the whole nature, to be sensed as a rhythm in the air, a gesture in the darkness, a power unseen. Here the robes of the Mysteries were conferred. Invested in the outer symbols of an inner power, the new initiate re-entered the great chamber to discover the priests, as though swayed by some mysterious power, encircling the statue with a motion expressive of grace and rhythm. The harmonies pervading the air could not be resisted, and the new initiate found himself a participant in the circumambulations of the sacred rite. He was moving to an exalted tempo and knew that the rhythm which flowed through his body was the same that moves the planets in their orbits and maintains all creation in its appointed place.

The rituals of the Mysteries were first fabricated by the priests in an effort to establish ceremonials which would reveal to the inner perceptions the principle of universal order. These ceremonials, however, gradually assumed an aspect so vast that they became the very backbone of the state. The Mysteries made the gods seem very near to man. Prince and commoner alike feared the retribution of outraged deities and sought to propitiate by word and deed the celestials who were so proximate to them as to lend their presence to the mystic rites. It is difficult for us to conceive of a day when the gods walked with men, for in this generation the divinities have retired before the ridicule of a disbelieving world. But those who have lived in the Orient know what it means to be ever in the presence of the Shining Ones, for in India the immortals still wander the earth in disguise and every mendicant may be Shiva incognito testing the generosity of the pious Brahman. It is sad indeed that human souls should be struck with terror by the proximity of the immortals; that instead of glorying in the nearness of his Creator man should be overcome with foreboding, linking heroes with ill tidings and gods with cataclysms. The guilt that sits heavy on conscience is usually responsible for such uneasiness. Men regard their fellows as fools, and as one mortal to another can satisfactorily explain away their vices. The gods, however, are indefinite quantities with most acute perceptions and accredited with the power of convicting man by his own words. When Nero brutally caused the murder of Agrippina, his own mother, he faced the world unafraid and drowned his small measure of remorse in his cups. But from that day on he dared not join the processionals of the Mysteries or take part in any solemn rite. He feared to approach the gods, for the blood he had shed cried out for vengeance. It is said that upon one occasion when entering the house of a great patrician, Nero beheld a statue of the goddess Ceres. As he looked, the goddess caused her carven face to take on the features of Agrippina. With a hoarse cry Caesar covered his face with a fold of his cape and was carried half senseless from the house.

Pythagoras was accused by his enemies of being theatrical and purposely creating an atmosphere of mystery about his person. Even after the lapse of nearly twenty-five centuries the great sage is still regarded as an impostor simply because he employed dramatic situations for purposes of instruction. Not long ago when discussing with a rather eminent scholar the strange personality of the Samian martyr, the learned doctor exclaimed: "But why did Pythagoras insist upon speaking behind a curtain so that only his feet were visible, when anyone knows that such a procedure is utterly ridiculous? Did he for an instant believe that a few yards of blue silk improved the quality of his thoughts or rendered his erudition more comprehensible to his auditors? All these things were simply a vain show and are enough to convince any educated person that Pythagoras was in reality a philosophic mountebank who dressed up a little knowledge in gilt and tinsel so that it appeared stupendous to a group of gullible followers already convinced that their master was a god. When men really have something to say and are conversant with their subject, they simply and definitely set forth their premises and require no such stage props. The man undoubtedly knew something of mathematics and a little of music. He also had an acquaintance with several other arts, but in all things he was simply a superficial observer dependent for his influence and power upon the magnetism of his own personality and carefully staged miracles."

We early discovered that the so-called learned of today are incapable of appreciating ancient standards of culture; that they are far too brusque to sense or respond to the subtleties employed by the greater exponents of Greek metaphysics. The veil of Pythagoras is a constant reminder of the fact that if the senses are united in the contemplation of externals, the nature is not free for the rational digestion of internals. He who saw Pythagoras could never know Pythagoras, for he was not to be recognized by the outer senses but rather to be realized by the inner perceptions. If those listening to his words had seen the master, they would have believed the words to have been his own and to have issued from mortal mouth. But unable to watch the movements of the man's lips, the words seemingly issued from behind a mystery and could thus be totally dissociated from the personality of the speaker. The human mind skips lightly over what it does not see, and although all who gathered there realized that Pythagoras was speaking the words, the fact that they could not actually see him do this caused them to regard the words almost as unspoken. The veil itself was the symbol of Pythagoras the man, for the human nature is but a drape concealing an inner and most transcendent part.

When men desire to isolate themselves from all external stimuli, they have but to still by the power of the will the action of the outer senses. Close your eyes, and the world of forms disappears; close your ears, and the world of sounds ceases to be. Veil an object and the object itself is no longer there, for the mind then creates and endows as fancy dictates that which the sense perceptions have not dimensionalized. Pythagoras desired his disciples to realize that the words issued not from him but from the Great Mystery which he had penetrated in part. He was but as an oracular vase, a sounding urn, or a tinkling cymbal; his mouth but a vent in which a spirit dwelt. It was this inner and invisible agent that spoke. Hence the words that issued therefrom should be regarded as having their origin not in the man but in the rational soul that is above the limitations of the flesh and superior to the dimensionalizing influence of the external senses. Freed from the hypnosis of a personal idolatry, the disciples might thus receive instruction without learning to love the teacher; might understand without seeking to estimate personality; might come to know the truth and not simply the measure of a man.

Why, then, did he permit them to see his feet below the veil? The symbolism is again evident. Man's whole nature is a mystery of which only the feet are visible, for the physical body which we perceive and regard as the whole of man is really but the pedal extremities of the soul. He who sees but the visible man sees only the feet of a vast superphysical agent whose head is of spiritual gold but whose base is of clay. The feet extending beyond the veil reminded the disciple of Nature —the visible part of God—whereas the rational and illumined parts that dwells behind the veil separating the visible from the invisible may be known only through the products of the reason. He who saw the feet of the master had seen Pythagoras, for Pythagoras himself was but the physical extremity of a resplendent invisible nature. According to an ancient adage, men are called by the names given to their feet. The visible physical man to which we assign various nomenclatures is but an insignificant appendage of a nameless reality which, dwelling behind a veil, may never be known until we have learned to esteem the invisible above the visible and consciousness above form.

After successfully passing the tests of the lesser rites, the Pythagorean neophyte was permitted to step behind the veil and behold the face of the master, for it was presumed that having completed his preparatory instruction the advanced disciple could look upon the inferior nature without mistaking it for the rational power dwelling within and behind it. Pythagoras was not only philosophic; he was also scientific in his use of symbols and rituals. He attained ends which modern education utterly fails to attain, because he employed not dramatic but divine procedures in the accomplishment of spiritual education.

Today the value of an idea is determined by the relative culture and prestige of its author. In antiquity, however, the culture and prestige of a thinker was measured solely by the quality of his ideas. In other words, a man's thoughts were not considered good because he was great; he was considered great because his thoughts were good. The highest authority of the modern world is the modern world itself, and by that criterion the modern world justifies its works. The highest authority of the ancient world was Truth, and antiquity justified its survival by expending its energy in the quest for Truth. No man can learn the truth unless he has the correct rationale of approach. In great measure this attitude is the outgrowth of atmosphere, and atmosphere can sometimes be created by a dramatic flourish. Yet is there not a science of atmospheres? Do we not declare that the color of wallpaper affect our moods? Do we not instinctively feel more optimistic when the sun shines than when it rains? Are we not at one time elated and at another time cast down by environmental trivialities? Does not our entire mental constitution reflect the state of our disposition, and are we not more susceptible to instruction when in one state than in another? Is it not therefore legitimate to increase our efficiency by creating those mental atmospheres which most effectively stimulate and directionalize our rationality? From this point of view a veil of blue silk—though to the superficial an absurdity—might become, when employed by one versed in the profounder aspects of the mind, a definite aid to the student's understanding, and consequently serve a justifiable end.

What has been said of the blue veil applies equally to all forms of ritualism. When rituals are designed and executed by the uninformed they are meaningless and grotesque. When created according to definite philosophic principles and performed with a knowledge of the transcendental arts, these very rites become alive and have resident within their own natures a virtue capable of being transmitted to an assemblage. We have lost the art of ritualism—the science of divine dramatics —yet in the dissemination of philosophic verities it is often necessary to resort to figures and symbols to convey those subtle facts incommunicable by any literal method. The only reason men demand that the statement be direct and simple is that they ignore those elements of life which cannot be stated directly. The Great Arcanum perpetuated through the ages by diverse means depended upon ceremonial and processional for the exposition of certain principles, particularly those concerned with aesthetics. The crassness of our present attitude is largely responsible for the disregard for ritualism that exists in our national life. We do not necessarily refer to the somber rituals of the church, which are all too often depressing and inhibiting, but rather to those racial ceremonies and processionals with which ancient nations were wont to express the composite ideals of an entire nation through exhibitions of grace, rhythm, and beauty.

Niebuhr observes that the ancients never founded their tragedies on real, but on mythical history only. What were the myths? Simply the outer veils of the Mysteries—that part which, though revealed, remained comparatively meaningless until the allegories were unlocked by the philosophic keys. It remained for Christendom to inextricably confuse the issues of mythology and history, causing the former to take on the substance of the latter and thereby lose all semblance to its own true nature. The early Church recognized, however, the peculiar efficacy of the pagan ceremonials as evidenced by the introduction of the Mystery Plays; for on the steps of the cathedrals even during the Middle Ages it was customary to enact episodes from the lives of Jesus and the twelve Apostles.

These pageantries ostensibly were to assist the ignorant in understanding the profundities of the faith. In reality, however, they were perpetuations of the ancient Gnostic practices which the Church fathers outwardly opposed but inwardly accepted.

At this point a subject germane for discussion is the destruction of the pagan Mysteries, or the "death of Great Pan" as it was enigmatically called. The Church affirms that the Gentiles in their frantic eagerness to embrace the new Christian faith deserted, to a man, their heathen altars. Those familiar, however, with the lengthy pleadings and arguments employed by the early Church fathers to convert unbelievers will realize that the accounts of the pagan stampede toward Christianity are more of a rhetorical display than a true statement of the actual facts. As more than one author has observed, the pagan Mysteries actually fell from the combined effect of treachery and profanation. Great Pan, like Caesar, drew his cloak about his face and fell from the thrust of his dearest friend. "Yet Brutus was an honorable man!" He did not slay for personal gain or because he loved Caesar less, but because he loved Rome more. So with the Mysteries. The rending of the Temple veil symbolized the abolition of the Mysteries and the birth of that new dispensation which sought to liberate mankind from bondage to a despotic priescraft by making the way of salvation equally accessible to all men, irrespective of their intellectual, spiritual, or ethical status. Carried away by the blandishments of worthy ideals such as these, Christian zealot persuaded pagan proselyte to commit that most impious crime imaginable—namely, to divulge the secrets of the Mysteries. On the assumption that the end justifies the means, many initiates broke their holy obligations and thus wrought the destruction of those sacred institutions which for uncounted centuries had been the custodians of the secret doctrine. It was but a few hundred years, however, before the Church awoke from its disillusionment. Recognizing that spiritual equality was but a figure of speech, it straightway reversed its position and proceeded to retrench itself behind the very mysteries and rituals of the pagan institutions it had overthrown.

Thus pagandom died to no good end, and the new faith rose upon broken vows and the sincere but misguided efforts of pagan initiates. Upon the desecration of their sanctuaries, the masters of the greater secrets retired therefrom and adopted secret means for the perpetuation of their knowledge. The oaths broken for the glory of God produced no tangible results, for the power of the priestcraft was not destroyed but merely shifted from one organization to another. Through their first spokesman the Christian Church admitted the possession of certain mysteries and spiritual secrets, and these are still preserved in its ritualism and ceremonials. But for lack of certain august mysteries which had not been entrusted to such initiates as might break their vows, the whole body of the inner work is not now and never was in the possession of the Christian Church. For lack of these elements of knowledge, mystagogues could not interpret the symbols which were accepted solely for their apparent virtues, and hence rituals "lost the name of action." So from an outward figure and an unquickened form the science of sacraments and ceremonials was established, the virtues of which Samuel Butler in his *Hudibras* thus describes:

>"With crosses, relics, crucifixes
>Beads, pictures, rosaries and pixes;
>The tools of working out salvation
>By mere mechanic operation."

Upon vain ceremonial and empty rite the antiritualist vents his spleen. All too keenly he senses the superficiality, the tawdriness of outer show, but most of all the absence of the inner spirit. But in common with all extremists, because he does not like a part he would sweep away the whole with imperious gesture. Because he is dissatisfied with the rituals with which he is familiar, he declares the whole science of dramatic instruction to be composed of stuff and nonsense. Estimating things as they should be by the rule of things as they are, the modernist rejects all in the efforts to escape an objectionable fraction. In the ancient Mysteries it was declared that broken oaths induced their own punishment. Religion in the hands of the rabble bears terrible evidence to vows and obligations turned recreant. In time, however, these things will pass away and the beauty now deeply hidden within each deed and thought will again come into its own; for error is mortal, but Truth is immortal, and though crushed to earth shall rise again. For thousands of years the ancients perpetuated by dramatic instruction those secrets of the inner life which formed the substance of every *mythos*. The New Testament of the Christian Church is itself a book of rituals, for it is filled with allegories and parables which inspire by virtue of their dramatic power. Although drama was employed by the priests, it is not essentially a priestly art; for it is an instinct present among even the most primitive types, and serves the innate desire of every creature for self-expression. Though in a certain sense a reproductive or imitative art, it is more than this; for it provides an adequate channel of expression for the surging impulses of the soul.

We must therefore fight to preserve those arts by which the nobler moods of man can be interpreted. Without such means of self-expression the individual is a locked soul whose inhibitions must ultimately canker the whole nature. We might very properly ask ourselves, however, if we can preserve the beauty in ritual and allegory when we have rejected both the religious and ethical systems of which ritualism was the natural expression. Is it possible to live crass and material lives, worshiping our own industrialism while still maintaining the integrity of mystic rites and pageantries? The answer is obviously in the negative, for we cannot serve the God of beauty and the spirit of selfishness at the same time. Man must choose the gods he will serve and abide by his decision. The sorrows of this century are abundant proof of the folly of his choice. Yet ridiculous as it may seem, the day is not far distant when the world, tired of its modern gods, will revert to the pantheons of earlier days. Already a suffering humanity is turning from a god of gloom to seek the god of joy. Caged within the ever-narrowing confines of its commercial endeavor, humankind is seeking to escape and raise again its altars among the hills. The gods of the terminals have grown intolerable; the human soul desires again to fraternize with the rustic spirits and know the carefree life of the faun and satyr.

Great Pan is not wholly dead. Some day he will burst the bonds that chain him in the dark abyss, and returning to his rushes by the stream, will again play glad tunes upon the pastoral pipes. Pan is the patron of the rites and rituals, lord keeper of the dance, and peculiar spirit of the depictive arts. One hundred years ago it was predicted that within a few centuries men would revert to the gods of Plato and Aristotle, and tired of a distant Spirit would rejoice in the proximity of kindlier gods and daemons. We may all look forward with eager anticipation to that nobler day when the gods of philosophy once more shall rule the world; when all will be right in the heavens above and upon the earth beneath. We are weary of our somber codes and dismal doctrines—creeds that hurl men at each other's throats in the frenzy of selfishness and passion. We desire to again make the acquaintance of those laughing spirits that speak from the waterfall and inspire all men to a rational camaraderie. The scientist may scoff, the modernist deride, and the theologian shriek "Blasphemy!" from the pulpit. All these things are merely incidental for it is the soul of man that endures and it is the soul of man that must be satisfied. Mortal institutes rise and fall, but the urge of self-expression never dies because that urge issues from Divinity itself. Men can be ensnared for a little while and their purposes temporarily turned aside. Ultimately, however, they will be themselves, and this being like self involves the expression of the inner motives through the medium of the arts. A new age of beauty is dawning, and a race long servant to its greeds and baser desires is turning toward the contemplation of a nobler purpose and a more exalted destiny.

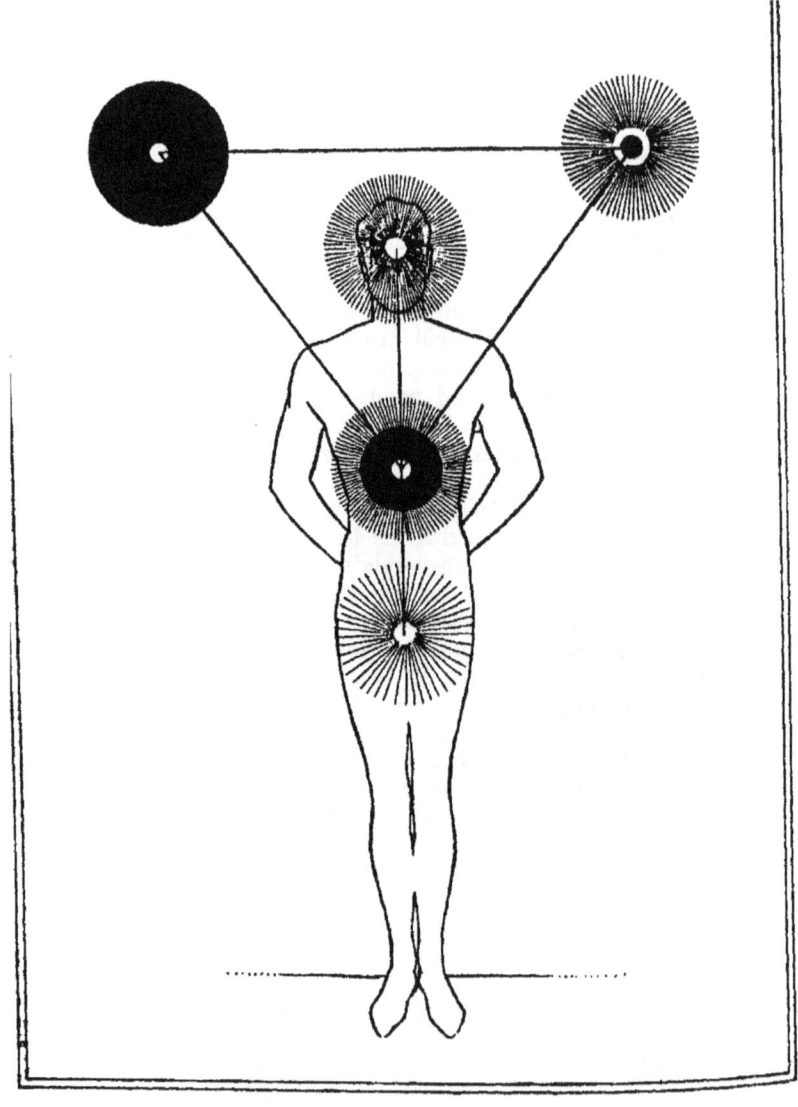

MAN, THE THREEFOLD MYSTERY

In this diagram the divine nature of man is represented by an inverted triangle with its lower point resting in the heart. The spheres of power upon the upper points of the triangle are the *Anthropos*, or Oversoul. From the spirit in the heart come forth two poles, one ascending to become the mind and the other descending to become the generative system.

CHAPTER SEVENTEEN

A Philosophic Consideration of Man

CONSIDERED philosophically, man is the *microcosm*, or little universe—the miniature creation in whose composite nature are epitomized the various orders of life: divine, super mundane, and terrestrial. "Like a fetus," writes H. P. Blavatsky, "he is suspended by all his three spirits, in the matrix of the *macrocosmos*." Humanity, then, is still in an embryonic state and, dwelling within the darkness of the sidereal womb, is suspended from Cause by a threefold umbilical cord—the cable tow of the Freemason and the braided cord of the Brahman initiate. Of the threefold spirit, Paracelsus writes that the first has its seat in the elements, the second in the spirits of the stars, and the third in the divine nature itself. Centuries before, Proclus had defined the triune nature of man as three monads which are one monad—being suspended from unimaginable unity. The first monad is the eternal God; the second, eternity in its own nature; and the third, the paradigm, or pattern, of the universe.

A similar doctrine was promulgated by the ancient Cabalists, whose profound investigation of transubstantial natures revealed that man's superior nature verges toward God, his inferior part toward the earth, and his intermediate part toward the spheres whose radiant energies flow through that intangible atmosphere called the astral light, or *anima mundi*. It should be borne in mind that even body is primarily a spirit, form being merely the objectification of the formless monadic physical principle. Soul is likewise an astral spirit. Hippolytus declared that the Assyrians considered the soul to be a triple unity, "soul" signifying the causal nature—the threefold monad of Proclus.

At this point we may with profit consider a few lines from the famous *Chaldean Oracles*: "The Mind of the Father uttered that all should be divided into three. His will nodded assent, and at once all things were so divided." In response to the decree of the Forth-thinker, "He who governs all things with the Mind of the Eternal," the root division was thus ordered. "In every cosmos there shineth a Triad, of which a Monad is the source." And further, "From this Triad the Father mixed every spirit, arming both mind and soul with triple Might." Issuing from the Paternal Foundation and established in the generations, man thus possesses three moving spirits which collectively are one spirit—the prime mover, the unmoved yet all-moving agent. It is natural, therefore, that each part of man should incline toward its own essential nature, being drawn thereto by a subtle gravity. That spirit which is from God, since it is the most subtle, consequently escapes back into God, "the Thrice-Beyond;" that spirit which is of the soul inclines toward the celestial spheres, since it finds its affinity in the stars of whose substances it is composed; while that spirit which is of the body is drawn downward to mingle its agencies with the dark earth, its common parent. Thus, while these three agencies are combined in the making of man, they still preserve certain individual characteristics, and pursuant to the line of expression indigenous to each seek to move the soul-nature in one direction or another. The *salt* of the alchemists is but the terrestrial nature, the *sulphur* the celestial, and the *mercury* the sidereal. From the blending of these three spirits the Hermetists brought into existence the *philosophers' stone*.

In our analysis of man we first regard him as a threefold being epitomizing in a single nature the whole order of universals. The three powers, or monads, enthroned within his nature become vortices of force around which move respectively the substances of the supreme, the superior, and the inferior spheres. Objectifying environments from their own constitution, these monads surround themselves with spheres of consciousness that have their analogy in the universal planes or worlds. Thus the supreme world outside of man exists within man as the environment of his divine spirit, the superior world in the environment of the soul spirit, and the inferior world in the environment of the body spirit. The three monads are also included within each other. The first includes the second and third; the second is included in the first but includes the third; while the third, including within its nature neither of the others, is included within them both. Hence spirit includes both soul and body; soul includes body, but is included within spirit; and body, being the least of the parts, includes neither spirit nor soul but is included within both. The sphere of man's divine spirit is consequently his heaven world, and his inferior nature exists within this heaven even as the earth floats within the constitution of the sidereal organism. The sphere of the soul is man's human world, where suspended between the superior and the inferior the rational judgment may be inclined by the will to the contemplation of either extreme. The sphere of the body is the inferior world which, analogous to the vast organism of the elements, seeks to swallow up consciousness and hold the innate life within the dark embrace of form. Thus the Universal Man is mirrored in the individual man, in whose parts and members are revealed the laws and processes of cosmic procedure.

The Mysteries instructed man in the nature of his own invisible constitution, revealing to him the structure of the *microcosmos* of which his spirit was the guiding part. They first informed the disciple that the physical organism, devoid of permanence and rationality, and far from being the master of the life, was simply a whimsical gesture, as it were, of the soul. To the initiated, the very death of the body was proof of the immortality of the soul, for it signified that separation in which a stronger nature deserted a weaker. The body and the soul were likened to two runners, the first being subject to fatigue, but the second tireless. For a while they keep abreast of each other. The body, however, having exhausted the vitality that had been loaned to it, soon lagged behind;

but the soul, being tireless because its vitality was inherent, rapidly outdistanced the body which was eventually forced to discontinue the unequal struggle because of exhaustion. Thus, while it is natural for forms to perish, it is also natural for the soul to continue in a vital state for a long period of time. By rational unfoldment it gradually inclines toward spirit, until it finally mingles its own essences with those of immortality.

In Platonism we find the soul continually engendering forms, and after having accomplished the purposes for which the forms were designed casting them aside to redirectionalize its own energies. The Greeks held that both life and death were administered by the soul, declaring that so-called acts of Providence were but the will of the soul for the body which it had fashioned, and of whose destiny it was the arbiter.

In his treatise *On Suicide,* Plotinus describes the difference between natural and violent death thus: "But it is requisite to remain in life, until the whole body is separated from the soul, and when it does not require migration, but is entirely external to the body. After what manner, therefore, is the body separated from the soul? When no longer anything pertaining to the soul is bound in the body? For when this takes place, the body can no longer bind the soul, the harmony of it no longer exists, which the soul possessing, it also possessed. What, then, shall we say, if some one should endeavor to separate the body from the soul? May we not say, that in this case he must employ violence, and that he departs, but the *body* does not depart from him? To which may be added, that he who effects this separation, is not liberated from passion, but is under the influence of some molestation, or pain, or anger. * * * If, also, a fated time is allotted to each individual of the human race, a separation of the body from the soul cannot be prosperous prior to this period, *unless, as we have said, this becomes necessary.*"

In the quotation it is arcanely hinted that under certain conditions the soul—which is, as it were, mixed throughout the substances of the body—is caused to pass out therefrom and hover about the body, proximate to it but not entangled by the physical organism. When the concerns of the soul are liberated from the concerns of the body, the whole nature of the soul inclines away from form, gradually severing its connection therewith until at last having nothing in common with bodies it retires from them into itself. This is in truth the *philosophic death* in which there is not a violent but a gradual segregation of interests. Under normal conditions, the complete separation of the soul from the body is not achieved during a single lifetime, but the soul voluntarily withdraws itself from a decrepit or depleted body because that body is no longer an instrument of rational liberation. Thus in natural death the soul simply casts off a worn-out organism to continue its functions in some newer and more adequate vehicle.

Suicide was considered by the ancients to be a misdirection of power; for whereas natural death is a gesture of the body. In natural death the soul casts off the body, but in suicide the body casts off the soul. Hence such an end is termed violent, for the soul is forcibly ejected from its form without the liberation granted by rational procedure.

In his *Scholia on the Phaedo of Plato*, Olympiodorus declares suicide to be permissible to the wise under five conditions, which specifies the circumstances under which pollution of the divine nature might not be countenanced by the individual. He epitomizes his argument in these words: "Suicide is unlawful, when committed for the sake of the body, but rational when committed for the sake of the soul." Here we have to a certain degree the fundamental tenet of the *samurai*—death before dishonor. Suicide is therefore unjustifiable to escape misfortune and affliction or to evade responsibilities, but a legitimate end when it represents the sacrifice of life for the good of the nation or the service of the gods. Under justifiable suicide the ancients would have classed the deeds of heroes who faced death in the service of the state, as well as the heroism of illustrious men and women of modern times who have willingly given their lives for the cause of science.

Notables among such contemporaneous martyrs are those who have died from experimentation with the X ray and radium.

The first philosophers declared the rational soul to be the spirit's most precious attribute; that it should be reverenced as a god and its dictates never consciously transgressed by will or deed. There is a god within the soul of man; a god which blesses by its approach and curses by its departure. This most exalted spirit quickens the life and renders real the whole purpose of existence. When man serves this inner power it is strengthened, and through the soul, its mediator, approaches the inferior man and lends its glory to terrestrial achievements. Conversely, if the life be ill, the spirit withdraws to the point of greatest isolation, whereupon the soul, overcome by the noxious fumes of materiality, is said to "die." Thus a man may actually be dead in his inner nature while still alive in his outer. After the disintegration of his own soul he becomes a slave to the daemons or spirits residing in the astral light. These agitate his internal parts, causing them to assume the appearance of normal functioning. Such a person, however, is severed from all relations with his divine part. Sorcerers, vampires, and werewolves are thus declared to have lost their souls, being but outer shells from which the inner life has fled or—more correctly—decayed.

Materiality hardens the nature and we frequently hear the expression that this or that person has no soul. This does not mean philosophically, that the soul is necessarily dead, but that the eyes of the soul have been blinded by the concerns of the body. It is not sufficient that man should live physically and exist in the divine sphere as a vortex of reality; it is also necessary that his soul, composed of the astral light, should be caused to verge toward reality and thus impregnate the entire organism with those virtues which are resident in the Seven Spheres. Here a most vital question is introduced, namely: Why should a man be virtuous? According to the materialist, a certain measure of personal integrity is necessary for the success of the physical community life of the race. From the theological outlook, a little virtue coupled with a plentitude of belief is sufficient to preserve the immortal spirit from the pits of hell. Considered from the philosophical point of view, virtues, being resident in the soul, must serve as the bridge across which human consciousness passes to be united with its spiritual cause.

When we elevate the concerns of the body above those of the inner nature we threaten the integrity of our soul-life and thereby endanger our rationality. The *second death* of theology is the death of the soul, at which time the individual's astral-light body is disintegrated back into the *anima mundi*, which is the soul of God. These, then, are the major elements in the occult constitution of man: (1) The *spirit*, which is the eternal foundation and the abiding reality, by virtue of which man is immortal, superior to both beginnings and ends, and eternal in his own heavenly nature; (2) the *soul*, which is the intermediary by which the life in each is mingled with the starry life in all, and the qualities of the sidereal bodies are communicated to each individual, who thus manifests through vices and virtues the states of excess and temperance existent in the sidereal nature; (3) the *body* which, being of the earth earthy, is the outer framework wherein the higher nature is imprisoned as within a cage during the period of its exile in the material universe.

As the constitution of man is suspended from spiritual wholeness by three monads called unities, so in the secret religions of antiquity the orders of the priesthood were patterned from this holy mystery. The temple itself was the human body, and the priests who officiated at the various rites signified the spiritual agencies by which the mortal structure was sustained. In the sacerdotal orders of the pagan Roman Empire, for example, the abiding unity was represented by the *Pontifex Maximus*, the chief of the Pontifical College and supreme monad of the order of spiritual dispensation. This august person was served by three *flamines*, whose duties consisted of lending their sacred presence to the ceremonials of certain gods. Are not these *flamines* the breaths or flames that bear witness to the hidden and unknowable Light dwelling thrice-concealed in their midst? The *flamines* of the first rank were designated the *Flamen Dialis*, the *Flamen Martialis*, and the *Flamen Quirinalis*, and were chosen from the patrician class to signify that they were of the race of heroes. Later the number of *flamines* was increased to fifteen and their order divided into the *Flamen Majores* and the *Flamen Minores*, the first consisting of the holy three and the second of the lesser twelve. The twelve lesser *flamines* are the monads or powers of the twelve Holy Animals which collectively form the physical body of man and which are represented in the almanac by the signs of the zodiac distributed throughout the human body. The *Flamen Majores* in Freemasonry are the three grand masters of the Lodge of Jerusalem who are united together in the service of the Hidden King—the *Pontifex Maximum Universalis*. The *Flamines Minores* have their analogy in the twelve fellow-craftsmen who, venturing forth in parties of three, seek the body of their murdered master. Thus man, the *microcosm*, becomes the pattern after which all the procedures in the inferior universe are ordered and whose parts are combined in a profound and mystical arrangement.

Among the gods of the Cabirian rite were several diminutive figures with curiously distorted bodies, and bearing the marks of advanced age. These monstrosities provoked the ridicule of Cambyses, who could not conceive them objects worthy of veneration. In the Mystery rituals reference is repeatedly made to a strange dwarf equal in size to the human thumb who, dwelling alone in the *sanctum sanctorum*, is never visible to man but hides himself amid the furnishings of the sanctuary. According to Paracelsus, the rational Knower dwells in the auric radiances of the heart, being a flamelike body equal in size to the last joint of a man's thumb. In the Kathopanishads of the Brahmans, it is also written that there is a man, the size of the thumb, who dwells in the ether of the heart and who is called the "Mystery Flame." From these sources is thus established the nature of the Cabirian dwarf whose physical proportions were inconsiderable but who was yet greater than all the universe; for when Krishna in the *Vamuna* avatar assumed a diminutive stature he was yet able to cross the earth in three strides. The Mysteries held the rational part of man to be inconsequential from the standpoint of physical measure, but in its superphysical magnitude great enough to include all existence within its scope. Thus was emphasized the spiritual reality that quality and not bulk is the true measure of size. The little man in the heart rules the great man in the world; for the body structure is like some huge machine whose complexity, while far eclipsing the insignificant proportions of its operator, is powerless without the conscious mind and guiding hand which controls all its parts and functions.

Though the subject of reincarnation has been touched upon elsewhere in this work, it is nevertheless appropriate when considering the relationship of man as a spiritual entity to man as a physical personality, to discuss more at length the bonds which unite the superphysical consciousness to its physical environment. The spiritual agencies conspiring to produce the creature which we designate man are thus described by Plato: "Indeed it is necessary to understand man, denominated according to species, as a being proceeding from the information of many senses, to a perception contracted into one reasoning power." G. R. S. Mead translates the latter part of Plato's statement to read: "and collected into a unit by means of ratiocination." From this definition we are to infer that the objective man is founded in the reaction of the senses and that, after emerging from sensations, man attains stability by organizing these sensations with the aid of his rational nature. If these sense stimulations are not analyzed with respect to cause and mutual relationship, it is impossible for unity to exist within the nature, and for lack of such unity man must continue to exist as a bundle of contradictions held together only by instinct. It has already been stated that man does not actually enter into his immortality until he becomes conscious of that immortality. The instinctive man is consequently not immortal because in his consciousness there is still a vast preponderance of mortal elements. The eternal ebb and flow of cosmic processes contribute instability to the whole temperament and in response to this inconstant action the soul abides in a state of untranquillity. Spirit is the supreme power, and only when through initiation into the mysteries of the spiritual spheres he is moved to unite his soul and body with his spiritual part does man actually achieve immortality. Noble aspirations incline the soul toward the Great King, and only by absorbing his inferior constitution into the substances of this First of Immortals does man actually annihilate the interval between his temporal existence and his eternal endurance.

The problem of metempyschosis was one that profoundly occupied the attention of Platonist, Neo-platonist, and Gnostic alike. The Pythagorean doctrine of transmigration as expounded by Empedocles was admitted to contain an arcane rather than a literal meaning. While apparently accepting the doctrine of the literal transmigration of human souls into the bodies of animals, Plotinus undoubtedly possessed a knowledge of the esoteric interpretation of the doctrine, for nowhere else in his writings does he so freely employ irony and ridicule. Proclus, Chalcidius, and Hermes all maintained that it was unphilosophic to affirm that the human soul could ever return in the body of an animal, for the very will of the gods forever preserves so noble a creature as the soul from such a disgrace. Proclus enters the lists in Plato's defense, setting for himself the task of interpreting Plato's allusions to the return of man in a brutish constitution. Proclus reminds the reader that when in the *Republic* Plato declares that the soul of Thersites assumed the life of an ape, the word *life* (and not *body*) was very explicitly used, thus signifying that the soul assumed the irrational appearance, though not necessarily taking on the physical form of an ape. Again, in the *Phaedrus*, Plato describes the descent of souls into a brutish *life* but nowhere does he state that they assumed brutish *bodies*, for in Platonic philosophy life is not synonymous with form. By all this commentary, Proclus attempts to show that Plato referred solely to the invisible constitution, describing the various changes occurring therein when it is molded by the diversity of human moods. Through living a bestial life man causes his inner nature to assume the appearance of a beast, and is known to the wise not according to the contour of his physical body but according to the visage of his soul. When so completely possessed by animalistic traits that the soul takes on the similitude of a beast, he is classified according to the species of his soul and hence may reasonably be termed an animal.

Pythagoras delved even more deeply into the occult conditions resulting from a depraved life, circulating among a selected group of disciples a conclusion still more profound concerning the condition of the unrighteous dead. He declared that as like attracts like, and man by common impulse verges toward natures most closely resembling his own, it was natural for the virtuous to incline toward God and for the vice-ridden to incline toward the beast. Pythagoras did not intend to liken a bad man to a good animal, but rather employed the animal as a symbol of a nature in which rationality is dormant and the impulsive nature supreme. He stated that under certain circumstances a depraved human soul might attach itself to an animal even as a daemon might attach itself to a man. The human soul did not actually enter into the constitution of the animal but rather verged toward the instinctive nature of the animal in an effort to gratify its own uncurbed desires. Hence an animal may be moved or influenced by a human soul even as Socrates was influenced by his daemon. A certain animal exhibiting almost human intelligence may owe that quality to some human soul that has attached itself to the superphysical nature of that animal.

In ancient theology Hermes was called the *Psychopomp*, "the lord of souls" and shepherd of men, of whom Proclus writes: "Hermes governs the different herds of souls, and disperses the sleep and oblivion with which they are oppressed. He is likewise the supplier of recollections, the end of which is a genuine intellectual apprehension of divine natures." Hermes is, consequently, the divinity presiding over metempsychosis, administering the laws which cause men to return to mortal existence periodically until the generating soul has liberated itself from the idea of form. The "herds of souls" are the life-waves gathered into groups by certain common motives which cause similar nature to incline toward each other. Moving in a circle as it were about the Central Life, these herds are represented in mythology by Ixion bound to the wheel of generation. As the dispenser of sleep and oblivion, Hermes controls the moods by which men are entangled and held to form, or rather released therefrom. It is Hermes also who governs the memories and closes the doors of the past for those as yet not rationally awakened, and therefore unfit to contemplate the record of past actions. He is likewise denominated the supplier of recollections, and in this office is true to his great role of universal instructor. As the god of wisdom, Hermes instructs men by revealing to each individual the record of his own experiences. In the Egyptian myths Hermes is the scribe of the gods, and his writings are traced upon the tables of memory. With a gesture Hermes veils these records from the uninitiated, but reveals them to such as have awakened their inner consciousness.

On the widespread acceptance of the doctrine of metempsychosis among the ancients, Godfrey Higgins in 1836 wrote: "It was held by the Pharisees or Persees, as they ought to be called, among the Jews; and among the Christians by Origen, Chalcidius (if he were a Christian), Synesius, and by the Simonians, Basilidians, Valentiniens, Marcionites, and the Gnostics in general. * * * Thus this doctrine was believed by nearly all the great and good of nearly every religion, and of every nation and age; and though the present race has not the smallest information more than its ancestors on this subject, yet the doctrine has not now a single votary in the Western part of the world."

The theory of reincarnation was frequently employed by ancient historians and philosophers in the interpretation of their fables. Plutarch declares the account of Bacchus being attacked and dismembered by the Titans to be a sacred narrative concerning reincarnation, while Sallust, in *The Gods of the World*, explains the rape of Persephone as an ancient allegory signifying the descent of the soul into birth. Several

Greeks declared themselves to be aware of the previous bodies which their generating soul had precipitated into material existence. Pythagoras discourses at some length on his previous lives, and the description of five of these will be found in my large book on symbolism. Empedocles also remembered when his rational soul had occupied the body of a young girl. The Emperor Julian believed his soul to have manifested in a former life as Alexander the Great, and Proclus, according to Marinus, unhesitatingly declared that his rational nature had achieved its high dignity while in the body of Nicomachus, the Pythagorean. It should be particularly noted that, unlike the present popular concept of reincarnation, *the ancients did not affirm themselves to have been some other person in a previous life, but rather that the rational principle dwelling in them had previously dwelt in other forms.*

Plotinus writes: "It is a universally admitted belief that the soul commits sins, expiates them, undergoes punishment in the invisible world, and passes into new bodies." He might also have added that it was a universally admitted belief that the Mysteries, by assisting the rational soul in its procedures, shortened the number of reincarnations and released the inner nature to return to the felicity of its Father-Star. Here, then, we have the whole purpose of the Mysteries, which existed as institutions of liberation, serving the invisible part of man and surviving only in civilizations where the rational nature was regarded as worthy of culture and education. Plato also affirms that when the soul fails to achieve liberation and willfully follows perversity, it passes into the body of a woman. This enigmatic statement is generally interpreted to signify that the soul takes up its residence in the matrix awaiting rebirth. In the profundities of Platonic philosophy, however, a truth far more recondite was inferred. General Pleasanton discovered that when man degenerates himself through vice of excess, his whole constitution is electrically repolarized and, electrically, he becomes a woman. This does not mean that women are degenerate men, but rather that man in a virtuous state is negative in his vital or etheric body, while woman is positive. When through excessive emphasis of physical propensities and sensibilities man moves his center of consciousness into his physical nature, the latter is rendered positive (and therefore technically feminine), although its manifestations are totally dissimilar to the natural feminine organism which is positive by divine decree. Why do we persist in accusing the ancients of ridiculous fancies when our own generation has proved conclusively the correctness of their deductions? There is but one answer: We have arrived at our findings through what are termed *scientific* means or procedures, and hence are foolish enough to presume that they could not possibly have been discovered in any other way. In reality, philosophy armed only with the instruments of reason has penetrated the rational sphere where science fears to tread, and has left a record of glorious accomplishment in every division of learning.

One other thought before we pass to the consideration of another phase of man's philosophic constitution, namely, the incarnation of deeds and the buildings of bodies composed of actions. Plato has already affirmed that man as a form proceeded from the sensations. It is equally important to bear in mind that all thought, feeling, and action, having their origin in the superphysical nature, descend like monads from their generating sphere, and clothing themselves in appropriate vehicles manifest as entities upon the planes of the inferior universe.

In a symbolical sense insects were regarded by the ancients as the incarnations of human attitudes. Butterflies, for example, were said to be an expression of the beautiful thoughts of men, while evil insects that torment man and beast were the offspring of destructive impulses of the soul. Plagues were attributed to a similar origin; for the bacillus, coccus, and spirillum now the subject of so much scientific disputation were regarded simply as minute organisms enlivened by the various emotions of men.

In the invisible world, therefore, exist manifold orders of life that are actually the mental and emotional progeny of human beings. Paracelsus recognized this fact when he describes the incubus and the succubus—the demons, male and female respectively, fashioned from the stuff of emotional intemperance. Man may yet come to realize that he possesses the power to create living things, and in great measure thus fashion the instruments for his own torment. When Christian theologians substituted hell for the pagan Wheel of Existence, they evidently sensed the import of Plato's intimation that physical existence was the death of the spirit. The material universe, in whose substances our emotions find vehicles of expression and our actions forge weapons to cause us suffering, is indeed a sphere of recompense, a world of retribution, a place of punishment wherein natures perforce must linger until their own innate perversity has been mastered.

In the *Sepher ha Zohar* attributed to Rabbi Simeon ben Jochai it is written: "Wo to the man who says that the Doctrine delivers common stories and daily words! For if this were so, then we also in our time could compose *a Doctrine* in daily words *which would deserve far more praise*. If it delivered usual words then we should only have to follow the lawgivers of the earth, among whom we find far loftier words, to be able to compose a Doctrine. Therefore we must believe that every word of the Doctrine contains in it a loftier sense and a higher MYSTERY. The narratives of the Doctrine are its cloak. Wo to him who takes the covering for the Doctrine itself. The simple look only at the garment, that is, upon the narratives of the Doctrine; more they know not. The instructed (initiated) however see not merely the cloak, but what the cloak covers."

As the written law, thus likened to a garment, conceals within it that unwritten law which is the *first mystery*, so must the body of man be regarded as a vestment within which a most hidden *doctrine* is preserved. Moralizing upon the issues of Scripture, theology fails utterly to comprehend the hidden meaning of the sacred books. It cannot conceive of Scriptures as writings concerned with philosophic anatomy, yet such is necessarily the case; for the regeneration by which man's salvation is wrought must take place within his own constitution. To this mystery Socrates alludes when in the *First Alcibiades* he observes that when the soul enters into herself she will behold all other things. Proclus further adds that when she (the soul) proceeds into her inner recesses and into the adytum of her own nature, she perceives with her eye closed the genus of the gods and the unities of things. The rites and symbols so carefully preserved against the ravages of time and unenlightened ages have been saved for such as can realize that the human body itself is the House of Hidden Places, the Tabernacle of the Most High God, the place of the initiation, the *sanctum sanctorum* where in properly consecrated chambers the deities abide and accept the sacrifices offered up by sensible natures.

Turning inward from the concerns of the outer life, man enters an area dedicated to the immortals. His own interior constitution is holy ground, and here the gods, so distant from his material concerns mingle their personalities with his rational endeavors. Man indeed may be likened to some highly glorified snail carrying his own refuge with him, and in moments of danger retiring into that stronghold which is his real self. The analogies between the house of God in the world and the house of God in the soul, have been very carefully drawn. To those unfamiliar with the concept, the likeness is unsuspected, but the moment the mind ponders the problem the analogy becomes obvious. The secrets of the Mysteries have always been safe from the profane because the average individual applies the principles of ancient philosophy to everything except himself. The modern student of rounds and races, for example, while dividing the whole social order into numberless subdivisions, never applies the principle to the inner part of his own being. The gods are in the heavens and their power is felt to the most distant parts of the earth, yet man has not discovered that, most important of all, they are sitting upon their golden thrones within his own nature. There is a reason why the ancient temples were patterned after the human body and why every ritual finds its correspondence in some function of man's composite constitution. The studious seeker after the keys to the hidden work will do well to take the whole body of symbolism and ritualism and attempt to discover their correspondences in the workings of his own parts and members. Salvation is not alone a matter of theology nor yet a matter of philosophy; it is a matter of science and, of sciences, particularly the concern of biology. Biological salvation is a formidable term, yet it underlies the whole theory of religion, for the redemption of the human race cannot be achieved spiritually until each individual has come to understand the relationship between all his parts and is instructed in the proper manner of combining his forces and resources.

"Man is therefore the quintessence of all the elements," writes Paracelsus, "and a son of the universe or a copy in miniature of its Soul, and everything that exists or takes place in the universe, exists or may take place in the constitution of man. The congeries of forces and essences making up the constitution of what we call *man*, is the same as the congeries of forces and powers that on an infinitely larger scale is called the Universe, and everything in the Universe reflects itself in man, and may come to his consciousness; and this circumstance enables a man who knows himself, to know the Universe, and to perceive not only that which exists invisibly in the Universe, but to foresee and prophesy future events. On this intimate relationship between the Universe and Man depends the harmony by which the Infinite becomes intimately connected with the Finite, the immeasurably great with the small. It is the golden chain of Homer, or the Platonic ring."

Concerning the spiritual agencies which actuate the vast sidereal order we are still comparatively ignorant. In its quest science classifies phenomena but senses few of the motives of which phenomena are but the transitory expression. We recognize an infinite life manifesting through an all-powerful urge which, communicated to universal bodies, hurls them with great violence through the definitionless vistas of space. We sense yet cannot fully comprehend the stupendous agency which orders the infinite diversity of existence. Still it profits us nothing to contemplate this infinite magnificence; for recoiling from the unimaginable the mind is sickened by the awesomeness of cosmic magnitudes. Each new discovery but complicates the issues. Men grow tired of the vain quest for ultimates, and with a certain measure of relief draw their shrouds about them and turn from the whole uncertainty. Life becomes a period of vain searching in which the mind, certain beforehand that it shall not achieve its goal, struggles against its own convictions for a little while. The materialist is not really disappointed when failure rewards his efforts, for down in his very heart he really expected disappointment and would have been genuinely surprised with any other result. The most the uninitiated can hope to accomplish is a certain classification of the problems of the unknown whereby futurity may receive the answerless queries of the past in orderly form.

The astronomer is equiped with the finest instrument that genius of man can produce. Gazing into the starry night through a 40-inch refractor, the pageantry of stars that moves across his field of vision is brought a little nearer, but their mystery is only compounded by their proximity. How can a man, even though long tutored in the science of the heavens, sense the motives of these distant spheres when the very blades of grass outside his observatory door and within the grasp of his hand are a mystery equally unsolvable? If a philosopher should enter that observatory and say to the aged astronomer, "Your quest is in vain; no lens ever ground by mortal hand can discover the souls of the stars," the scientist would answer, "I know that, but how else can I seek? I am born of a race that desires to know and I must search, for only by this vain endeavor can I satisfy that inner urge. Scientists are men of a race apart—a definite mental species; we are eternal questioners, servants to an unfulfillable desire." The philosopher might smile and make reply: "The urge to know is proof of the power to know; for the mind does not seek that which is incomprehensible, but is ever attempting to manifest in its outer functions that knowledge which is inseparable from its inner nature. The knowledge you desire is achievable and you are divided from it only by your method of approach. Imagine that instead of this telescope—the inanimate product of mechanical skill—you possessed a living lens by which the stars could be brought closer to you than your very self. Do you not realize that you yourself are a telescope and that by looking through your own being you can discover the secrets that lurk upon the very boundaries of space? Your own composite nature is a living instrument by whose virtues you partake of the sun, the moon, and the stars; your soul is of the very stuff which lights the stars, and by virtue of these in you and yourself in them their secrets are comprehensible to you. The life that actuates your own parts is a measure of that Universal Life, and the form that renders all these intangible agents perceptible to the outer senses is one with the spirit of form, whether it exists in the earth or in the sky. If you would understand universal mysteries you must realize that only through the living instruments that have united to form your own being are the divisions of cosmic life rendered perceptible. Turn from your telescope which can show you little more than your own unaided eye and will but confuse your already tired brain. Turn to the analysis of your own nature—the manifold parts which unite to form your wholeness—for by learning to know the mystery of your own being you will come to understand the wonders of the All."

Man's only hope of knowing is vested in himself. The creative ingenuity which continually manifests in the development of the arts and sciences discloses, in some measure, man's indwelling Divinity. Though comparatively insignificant, the individual is nevertheless a creature with awareness and the capacity for infinite realization and understanding. While in magnitude he verges toward the inconsequential in potentiality he inclines toward universal immensities. It is irrational, therefore, to judge humanity by the measure of its outward structure. Rather, we must sense through unfolding superphysical faculties the spiritual sufficency of that inward part from which the visible man is suspended. Man is the magnificent atom which baffles estimation and defies analysis. The universe in turn is the magnificent man; one of that race of giants by whose assembly space is rendered populous. Mortals congregate to form communities; these universal beings congregate to form clusters and galaxies of stars. It has been said that men are the shadows of the gods. The simile is most poetic, but man is more than this; for the "shadow" is substantial and to it Divinity has imparted something of itself that the likeness may share the virtues of the original. The life of the aspiring disciple is forever flowing toward his Father-God, that radiant star whose light shines clearly and steadily throughout eternity. Man is forever seeking to escape from his own littleness and return to that greatness which abides in space. The soul springs from a race of giants and yearns for the strength of its progenitors; man's throne is in the heavens and he longs for the day when entering into his own right, he shall seat himself with the immortals.

All this we must remember when, gazing upon the mortal stature, we are led to erroneously conceive man to be a creature of flesh and bone and ignore his reality as a vast being fashioned from the stuff of aspiration. Man may be likened to a walled city standing on the edge of the desert. In the midst of the city is a well, and from it lead the roads which pass through the gates of the city and become the routes for caravans. The walled city finds its analogue in the body, the gates with their dusty trails are the senses, and the well springing up in the midst of the city is the ever-flowing life by which both the community itself and the wandering caravans are nourished and sustained. Man's personality conceals his inner life as effectively as the cold, gray battlements of a fortified town conceal the bustling community that lies behind it. When we see only the physical nature of the individual we behold that which least adequately expresses, and often most misinterprets, the internal qualities. Hence the disciple of the Ancient Wisdom is taught to realize that man is not essentially a personality, but a spirit. His outer parts are not the measure of his inner virtues, but contribute that weakness of the flesh which all too often brings to naught the willingness of the spirit. The body can never know the noble ideals which impel the spirit toward accomplishment. Digestion and assimilation are the concerns of the body; to such homely ends it concerns its endeavors.

Above the provinces of instinct and sensation come the concerns of the rational life. The Greeks gloried in their ability to become rational animals, for man is a rational animal. However, that which is rational and that which is animal are actually two definitely divided natures. Rationality is natural to transubstantial organisms, but is contrary to the moods of matter. Unless the rational part retires from its own body and meditates alone, it cannot escape the chidings of the flesh. Now this separation was accomplished by means of the fourth-dimensional, or qualitative, interval. Seated in the midst of his disciples the ancient philosopher, unheeding the nagging demands of the body that disturb the equilibrium of the rational soul, discoursed at length upon the verities of the intellectual life, regarding his physical vehicle as an organ of expression, a temperament suitable for communication, a structure which focused intellect and thus rendered its findings communicable. The true philosopher maintains the efficiency of his inferior nature not because he is a servant to its dictates, but because his own creative expression is dependent upon the physical nature for concrete organization and tangibility.

Thought is the compensation of the original thinker. In matters of the mind, as in matters of finance, man is paid for what he gives, and owes for what he gets. No creative mind can be underpaid, for thought is its own reward and comes as adequate compensation for rational endeavor. Enriched by his own activities, the philosopher soon becomes fabulously wealthy in that most priceless of all possessions: reason. On the other hand, he who listens to the thoughts of the wise is daily contracting new debts, and the longer he listens the poorer he becomes. This may explain why disciples seldom surpass their masters, unless, as Aristotle, they depart from the master's premises. Men eagerly frequent the assemblages of the wise hoping to pick up the stray bits of knowledge that may fall like crumbs from the banquet table. Those who feed upon the crusts of wisdom, however, become more impoverished even as they eat, and he who listens long enough will eventually become bankrupt from his listening. When the day of payment arrives the unfortunate debtor has nothing with which to pay but his own life. Most of those who now suffer from spiritual and intellectual ailments suffer from the listener's disease. Men who seek masters shall be rewarded by becoming slaves, for it is the free man who speaks and the bondsman who listens. The modern school child is impoverished through the act of remembering, and starts life hopelessly in debt. To a certain extent the great minds of the world have rendered humanity mentally indigent. By being a great philosopher Plato has rendered innumerable other minds unsound, and thus contributed to the ethical delinquency of millions. In a similar sense Christianity is in bankruptcy to its founder, and the Orient will never be able to pay Buddha the interest on its indebtedness.

Instead of stimulating the body of thought the philosopher all too often paralyzes it. The great teachers of the world have ever drawn to themselves a coterie of mental corpses which, like dead planets, take on a semblance of life by reflecting the radiance of the central orb about which they revolve. Followers, to use the words of Shakespeare, "have a lean and hungry look." Though totally unmindful of the fact, they are actually economizing in an effort to liquidate. Disciples owe so much that they dare look no man in the face, but feel duty bound to spend their days and nights hymning their instructors with proper "Glorias." Philosophy today is overwhelmed by a deluge of nondescript *"ites"*. We have the Hegel*ites*, the Bergson*ites*, the Bentham*ites*, the Miller*ites*, the Watson*ites*, *cum multis aliis*. This *-ite* is the significator of approbation and agreement, a fervent so-mote-it-be, as it were, from the "Amen" corner. Individuals incapable of formulating even a notion of their own, frantically search for someone to agree with, thereby entering upon the path of mental deterioration in which the intellect descends from the simple state of not knowing to the actual inability to know. An individual who becomes an *-ite* consequently pleads intellectual bankruptcy and assumes what must ultimately prove to be the odious role of serf.

From all this it becomes evident that thought is its own reward; that no man can actually profit from the labors of others but must work out his own mental salvation with untiring diligence. The purpose of a great mind is to inspire to accomplishment, but this end is usually frustrated by an adoring multitude who cannot preserve inspiration as an indefinite quality but must become letter worshipers by prostrating their own minds before a superior intellect. It has always been a serious question to me whether Jesus ever actually spoke the words: "If ye love me, keep my commandments," for the statement is clearly out of accord with both divine and human reason and reeks to high heaven with the sanctified odor of pious interpolation. Truth personified might well cry out: "Let him who loves me, seek me himself and discover me in his own way, and I will reward him with myself." In an old alchemical figure is depicted an aged alchemist out with a lantern at night following in the footsteps of wisdom, while in another part of the picture is a group of worldly-wise men huddled together exchanging their notions with each other, and totally oblivious to the spirit of Truth but a few feet distant from them. You who would discover the inner mysteries of life, depart from the concepts of the many. Be not followers of strange gods, but seek Reality according to the impulses of your own higher rationality. Become creative thinkers, not simply followers of blind cults. Admit enslavement to no mind; read the words of the wise, but think for yourself. Attend to the conversations of the learned, but let your conclusions be your own. Be not hasty to condemn, but accept only that which you are capable of reasoning through with the aid of that divine power resident within. And finally, remember the words of Buddha: "I will not believe a thing because any man says it, not even if it be the reputed word of God. I will only believe it when to me it is true."

THE PLANETARY ZIGGURAT

The *ziggurats*, or observation towers, of the Chaldeans rise in seven spiral terraces and signify the astral sphere composed of the sidereal agencies of the seven sacred planets. In its ascent to the gods the regenerated soul climbs the spiral pathway, returning to each of the planetary spirits the respective soul qualities they had originally bestowed.

CHAPTER EIGHTEEN

THE LADDER OF THE GODS

WITH his "opened eye" the *Dangma*, or initiated disciple, beholds as a grand staircase the concatenated order of worlds that extends upward from the material darkness, which is the mundane sphere, and disappears into that impenetrable spiritual darkness which is the abiding state of the First Divinity. The midmost portion of this staircase is illumined by the light of reason, but its extremities are rendered incomprehensible by a Stygian gloom. This flight of worlds rests upon earth's lurid base, and the first steps are slimy with the fetid rot of matter. Rising in many levels from this ignoble footing, the stairway of spheres vanishes into the very presence of transcendent Cause, whose blinding radiance, ill-concealed by seven thousand veils, is to man's unordered vision an utter lightlessness. This is the mystic ladder of Jacob's vision upon which the patriarch beheld the angelic choirs. Two great streams of souls move upon this symbolic staircase, one ascending and the other descending, impelled by the rhythm of generation. Virgin spirits, eternal with the fullness of God, emerge from behind the veils that cover The Threefold Darkness above, and swooping downward with birdlike speed are enveloped in the noxious vapors of mortality.

Of this descent Plotinus writes: "And thus the soul, though of divine origin, and proceeding from the regions on high, becomes merged in the dark receptacle of body; and being naturally a posterior god, it descends hither through a certain voluntary inclination, for the sake of power, and of adorning inferior concerns. Hence, if it swiftly flies from hence it will suffer no injury from its revolt, since by this means it receives a knowledge of evil, unfolds its latent powers, and exhibits a variety of operations peculiar to its nature, which by perpetually abiding in an incorporeal habit, and never proceeding into energy, would have been bestowed in vain." Entering the inferior gloom these souls are swallowed up in the living death of the body. This mystery was revealed by the secret rites of the Phrygians, as evidenced by Hippolytus. Hence Heraclites declares that we live the death of the soul and die the life of the soul, thus arcanely intimating that when the rational nature agitates the irrational nature, bestowing upon it the semblance of life, it sacrifices its own life and only regains liberty by retiring from the concerns of the outer organism. Lamenting the "unaccustomed state" in which his soul found itself in form, Empedocles declares that the process of generation causes the living to pass into the dead.

From below mount upward the redeemed, whose natures, increasingly luminous, shine like stars in a Cimmerian night. From the dismal underworld—the abode of vain fears and terrible regrets—moves an endless file, climbing steadily toward God up the steps, or worlds, of its salvation. Thus the illustrious ones who are approaching the summit of their tedious climb, are in the terms of Plato, "raised above all inferior good." Concerning the return of the liberated soul to its virgin nature, H. P. Blavatsky writes: "This is the state which such seers as Plotinus and Apollonius termed the 'Union to the Deity'; which the ancient Yogins called *Isvara*, and the modern call 'Sammaddhi'; but this state is as far above modern clairvoyance as the stars above glow-worms. Plotinus, as is well known, was a clairvoyant-seer during his whole and daily life; and yet, *he had been united to his God* but six times during the sixty-six years of his existence, as he himself confessed to Porphyry." From the foregoing it is evident that the soul for many ages alternately retires from and approaches Divinity, only stabilizing its nature after being completely disentangled from the concerns of the flesh. It is not intended that mortal man should as yet be constant in his power to behold the Perfect Face, but that strengthened by intermittent vision he shall strive with greater temerity to establish the continuity of the spiritual perceptions.

From the many levels, which together form the vast staircase, pour forth lives in quest of forms, and forms in quest of life. From the pits of mortal slime crawl repulsive creatures whose sightless eyes are unresponsive to the light. Slowly, painfully, awkwardly, these half-animate monstrosities obey the deep hidden urge of an imprisoned soul, and grope their way toward truth. From the dark fastnesses of the mist-reeking jungle come forth the slinking horrors whose claws are death and whose bared fangs were fashioned to rend and tear. Then from the broad plains come the patient, sad-eyed, serving brutes, which see and feel but cannot understand. From the dark caves of earth's primal day emerges the dim progenitor of man who, beating his hairy breast with crude, misshapen hands, emitted the first war-cry of his kind. The distant places also give up their savage hordes, for slayer and savior alike are marching on through the ages toward inevitable perfection. Breaking the shackles that bind them to the grindstones of the mighty, the slaves join the great processional, as do the merchants who barter and sell, and the thieves who scheme and steal. From their marble tombs rise up the spirits of the hero dead—the Caesars and the Alexanders—and from their honored crypts come forth prince and potentate bearing orb and scepter, and gathering their ermine robes about them they solemnly climb the stairs of space. Higher upon the great flight are the scientists and the philosophers, who in pensive mood plod the weary way. At the very point where the staircase disappears into the mysterious presence of the Ineffable stand the radiant saviors—the great teachers of humanity—who dimly visible for a moment, pass into the darkness of God. Awesome is the spectacle of this grand march—souls moving toward their Maker; passing from form to form in the endless quest for the formless; approaching ever nearer to that greatness which is the virtue of perfection. Though an infinite diversity confronts the eye, yet the whole mystery may be summed up in three short words: God seeking God.

Philosophy does not give the soul freedom *from* Universal Law. In *The Doctrine of the Mean*, it is written: "The heavenly appointment of life is called nature; an accordance with human nature is called the way; and the regulation of the way is called religion." (From the Confucian ethics as revealed in *The Four Books*.) The power exercised by Buddhism is largely due to the magnificent concept promulgated by it concerning the march of the self to perfection. Oppressed by the irksomeness of their tasks, and rendered hopeless by the ignobility of their station, the *Sudras* of India were victimized by a decadent Brahmanism. Following the letter and not the spirit of Manu's law, the "Holy Born" sedulously avoided contact with inferiors lest the pollution of promiscuous relationships endanger that state of sanctity in which their Brahman souls reposed. That *golden age* had passed when "rich in royal worth and valor, rich in holy Vedic lore," the "Head Born" were the virtuous stewards of the gods. In the *Sita-Swayamvara* of the *Ramayana* is described a noble Brahman king who ruled the righteous city, Ayodhya:

"Like the ancient monarch Manu, father of the human race,
Dasa-ratha ruled his people with a father's loving grace.
Truth and Justice swayed each action and each
    baser motive quelled,
People's Love and Monarch's Duty every thought and
    deed impelled."

A superfluity of laws often proves more detrimental than an insufficiency of laws. In the service of their countless statutes the Brahmans became oppressors of life. Themselves subservient to the cumbersome regulations which they had prescribed for others, the Brahmans also suffered from a plentitude of codes which regulated thought and action until life was reduced to a mere span of forms and conventions. But while the holy Brahman enjoyed a certain uncomfortable security, the Sudra, bereft even of hope, found his lot little better than that of the beast. The gods presumably were too busily engaged in answering the unceasing prayers of the "Twice Born" pious to lend an ear to the supplications of the lowly. To these victims of a misinterpreted caste system Buddhism brought the inspiring doctrine of *freedom in bondage*. While the Sudra could not throw off the metaphorical shackles that bound his physical members, he did free his inner and immortal self from the concepts of limitation and despair. Buddhism revealed the stairway of the immortals, and through this doctrine (which verges on metaphysical evolution) gave hope of ultimate accomplishment to those millions for whom present accomplishment was impossible. Inspired by this new hope, those who previously had cursed their tragic lot sang at their tasks; those who had looked forward to a life of pain smiled through their tears; and those who had faced eternity with fear and trembling were rendered strong by the knowledge of life's purpose. The miseries of the today were forgotten, and men dwelt together in a glorious tomorrow. The lowly uncaste sensed the Brahman within his frame, for to the sinner had been revealed the hidden saint within.

Indra's city vanished from the sky; the gods were dissipated like mist before the dawn of reason; only Self remained—the glorious Universal Self, the One who is in all, the All which is in each. Rising up against their heavenly despots and emancipating themselves from the hierarchies of fears they had worshipped, the Sudras declared themselves free men of the universe. Thus the letter gave place again to the spirit, and human beings faced their own thoughts and actions unafraid. Armed with the tools of the Noble Path, each true believer hewed an appropriate destiny from the eternal substances of being. Recognizing his state to signify that of greatest separateness, the Sudra began to ascend the ladder of diversity, finally raising himself to unity upon its several rungs. True philosophy inspires with the courage to accomplish, and equips with the patience to wait; it reveals not only the end, but also the means to that end. Philosophy is indeed a mystical ladder up which men climb from ignorance to reason. Its rungs are the arts and sciences, and he who ascends the whole of the way finds that its upper extremity rests in the substances of an invisible but most substantial world—the proper abode of the wise. Here are the groves of learning where the sages sit together musing upon consequentials. This is a sphere of peace, for with depth of learning wrangling ceases and "the thoughtful mind to solitude retires." This is indeed the place of the *Isarim*, or blessed souls, of which the Rabbins dreamed and where the *Kedeshim* pondered over the great *Sod;* for it is written in the Proverbs: "And his Sod are for the Isarim."

"Fear not," admonished Pythagoras in *The Golden Verses*, "men come from a heavenly race and are taught by a diviner Nature that which they should accept and that which they should reject." Philo Judaeus describes the allegorical ladder which is raised from earth to heaven, showing its macrocosmic analogies and its application to the microcosm, or man. This ladder, according to Philo, is of the world its astral part and of man the soul; "the foot of which is, as it were, its earthly part—namely, sensation; while its head is, as it were, its heavenly part—the purest mind." Upon this ladder move what Philo terms the *Logi*, which may be interpreted as either the "Words" or, more generally, the "Gods." To these Words or Gods is ascribed a very secret and wonderful meaning. In the chapter on *The Annihilation of the Sense of Diversity* we have already described the spheres of realization, or consciousness, which man causes to manifest out of his own potentialities. The level of integrity upon which the individual functions is his level or sphere of consciousness and each of these levels or spheres, when considered as a whole, is a "God" or "Word" of power moving upon the ladder. Thus Philo declares that when the Logi ascend they draw the ladder, or soul, up with them, which arcanely intimates two things: (1) that the Gods or Words cannot descend other than by the soul, and having once perfected the soul lose contact with the world; (2) that the soul in its ascent absorbs inferior natures into itself so that as it rises there is nothing left beneath it. *The Golden Verses* conclude:

> "Thy mind's reins let reason guide:
> Then stripped of flesh up to free Æther soar,
> A deathless God, Divine, mortal no more."

In his dream Jacob beheld a mysterious ladder with its foot upon the earth and its top extending upward into the divine sphere. In the Mysteries it is declared that seventy-two aeons, or angels, moved upon the ladder. These angels are the seventy-two names or powers that emanate from *Shem-Hammephorash* —the separate and ineffable Deity. Ibn Ezra, writing in the 12th century, states on the authority of Ibn Gebirol that the ladder which Jacob saw in his dream signified the superior, or rational soul, and that the angels of Elohim which ascend and descend thereon are the abstract thoughts of wisdom which attach themselves at the same time, both to a spiritual, or superior subject, and also to the corporeal and inferior. The word which has been rendered "ladder" is *salam*, which means "that which is piled into a heap, raised up or lifted," and it is upon this raised or exalted place that the *Malaki Elohim* moved up and down. We cannot do better than consider the meaning of the word *salam* as here employed. Albert Pike states that in archaic Hebrew there was no word to designate a pyramid. In the word *Jerusalem*, for example, *salem* is generally interpreted to mean "peace" and Melchizedek, the prince of Salem, was called the lord of peace. It might be more accurate, however, to replace the word "peace" with "exalted" or "lifted," in which event Jerusalem could be intrepreted to mean "the city of the ladder." In this connection the fact should not be overlooked that Mohammed on his night journey to heaven, after arriving at Jerusalem on Alborak, beheld a ladder formed of golden rope descending from heaven. The lower end of this ladder rested upon Mount Moriah, and climbing the swaying stair the Prophet of Islam entered into the very presence of the living but many-veiled God.

In the Ancient Wisdom it was also declared that the sacred mountains of the world rose in seven steps or stages (as the Meru of the Hindus), and it was from the high place, or the seventh step, that offerings were made to the Lord whose name is Blessed. Not only did the holy place rise in seven platforms or levels, but upon its topmost level was usually erected a triform symbol of the Divine Nature itself. Thus the seven steps, complemented by this threefold figure, became the mysterious Pythagorean *decad*, or the symbol of the tenfold order of the universe. Jacob's ladder then actually becomes the symbolic mountain or pyramid. Pyramids, wherever found, are symbolic of the axis mountain of the world—the Olympus, Asgard, and Meru of the pagans, and possibly the rock Moriah upon which the temple stood at Jerusalem. In his *Pagan Idolatry*, Faber describes the Mithraic ladder used in the initiatory rites of the Persian Mysteries, which he affirms was in reality a pyramid of seven steps, further declaring that on each step was a door. In the ceremonials, the neophyte climbed the pyramid, passing through the seven doors, and then through similar portals descended on the opposite side. This pyramid was symbolic of both the world and the sidereal system. Nearly all great buildings of antiquity were symbolic of the universe, and according to Cicero the conquering Xerxes destroyed the temples of the Greeks, declaring that the entire world was the proper house of God and that Deity was profaned when man prepared for him a house less dignified than his own solar mansion.

Celsus gives a certain key to the ceremonials of the Mithraic rite, but of these Mysteries comparatively little is known. Having passed successfully through the dangers imposed by his initiators, the candidate was invested with a great cape either embroidered or painted with stars, and with the constellations of the zodiac ornamenting the hem. Like the starry hat of Atys, these star-strewn cloaks signified the soul in its highest and most causal aspect. Thus by the Mysteries a heavenly nature was conferred, and men who formerly dwelt about the earth itself were raised to a heavenly abode and their whole natures invested with celestial raiment. The corporeal body was transmuted by the Mysteries into a celestial body, for men who had previously enveloped themselves in the dark garments of form now put on a more luminous garb resplendent with the heavenly lights. Above the earth are the planets; above the planets are the stars. Uninitiated mortals exist in physical natures limited to the concerns of the earth and are termed material because their rational natures are in servitude to a mortal constitution. Disciples are those who take upon themselves the striped garments of the planets—the cloak of many colors whose shades denote the aspects of the astral soul. When the aspirant has transcended the concerns of the planets and risen through their orbits to liberation, he then assumes the starry clothing of the firmament. Thus the stars are symbols of spirit, the planets of soul, and the elements of body. Herein lies the explanation for the three-runged ladder which unites heaven and earth. The rungs of this ladder are the three mysteries perpetuated in Freemasonry as the Blue Lodge. The lowest round is physical, the second emotional, and the third mental; for it was written in the ancient work: "Our thoughts are from the stars, our emotions from the planets, and our forms from the earth."

Entering the chamber of the Mithraic rites the candidate found himself in a great cavern either formed by natural means or hewn from solid rock by the priests. In the center of the cavern stood a pyramid rising in seven steps, each of its levels painted a different color. In some cases the pyramid was divided into definite platforms; in others a narrow spiral pathway wound from base to summit as in the Chaldean *ziggurats*, or astronomical towers. From the flight of steps leading up the face of the pyramid access to the various planes or levels was had through low gates, each composed of a different metal. The description given by Celsus of these metals is probably a "blind," for the ancients followed a definite system which he has deviated from. Conducted by the hierophant who discoursed to him concerning the mysteries as he progressed, the neophyte ascended the steps of the pyramid, first entering through a silver gate onto the platform of the moon. Beyond was another gate resembling brass, which was that of Mercury, and still farther on a third gate of copper sacred to Venus. The fourth gate was of gold, the fifth of iron, the sixth of tin, and the seventh, and last, of lead. After passing through these gates the neophyte found himself upon a flat square area, and before him a triangular altar upon which burned three fires.

The master of the rite then explained that by this ascent was revealed the felicity of liberated souls—the joyous upward motion of lives toward their sovereign cause; that passing from one plane to another the candidate had recapitulated the after-death process by which his superphysical constitution verged away from matter and inclined itself toward the immaterial foundation which is in the heavens and concealed from the profane by the leaden ramparts of Saturn. In his climb the aspirant had actually stepped from planet to planet, leaving behind him the inferior spheres, finally to approach proximity to that threefold fire—the triform flame of unimaginable being that burns forever and a day upon the glorious altar of Universal Reality. "Learn, O my son," the master continued, "the mystery of the ever-burning fire whose triple wick dipped in an inexhaustible fuel burns with steady luminosity throughout all the Æons. The first flame is Universal Life, the second Universal Light, and the third Universal Motion, and these together are one flame. God is a blinding light and a consuming fire, for his light is eternal reason which renders all things visible and comprehensible. Light the lamp of your own mind upon this altar of Eternal Mind, that the reason which is in all things may call forth the reason that is in you. When the lamp of your reason is lighted, all things become evident; the dark mysteries of life are dissipated and the glow of realization causes all secrets to reveal thmselves and all hidden works to be made manifest. The base of this pyramid is square. It is your body. Its four elements combine to produce the mystic cube called *man*. The seven steps are your senses by which the *within* comes to know the *without* and which the *without* climbs, even as a ladder, to discover the *within*. Consciousness, ascending the ladder of the senses finally brings its message to the inner nature. The threefold flame here is the One, the Beautiful, and the Good, which together are the light of equality, the torch of reason, and the magical fire the magician must carry if he would invoke the dread person of Deity."

Upon the other side of this pyramid the stairs descend into the darkness of the cavern below. The candidate follows his initiator down again into the darkness of the subterranean room. Having passed through the metallic gates and standing once more at the base of the pyramid, the initiator resumes:

"This descent signifies the soul departing from its state of felicity and, after passing downward through the gates of the Seven Spheres taking upon itself the sorrows of birth. In the gloomy cavern of the world uninitiated men and women struggle vainly against the inevitable reactions of their own ignorance. Seeking permanence in an impermanent sphere they suffer without respite and their lot is indeed desperate. But those who by rational procedure have discovered the pyramidal nature of creation and learned to know the order of divine procedure whereby man ascends and descends the steps of destiny—such can no longer be bound to the untranquil sphere, but abiding therein a little while and tolerating its sorrows, prepare themselves for a more auspicious day by inclining their minds to reason.

"By these mysteries, then, is arcanely revealed the order of life and by this pyramid the procedure of life. He who accepts the mystery into himself and ponders its meaning will be rewarded for his industry by the realization of sidereal order. We are ever walking up and down the steps of space—descending either from a more blissful state into one of uncertainty, or ascending from an uncertain state into one of blessed felicity. He who comprehends the wisdom of this divine motion will realize that God is ever drawing lives to himself that they may partake of the fullness of his inspiration, and then casting them from him again that through great need they may learn to value the fullness of that inspiration. From the presence of the Unchanging One there pours ever downward through the substances of the invisible world a host of souls moving inevitably into birth, while from the world of visible and tangible physical things there comes a host of souls pouring into death. Those coming into life descend the ladder, and those coming into death ascend the ladder, for death brings the soul nearer to God than does birth. Through the Mysteries there pours still another stream—that exalted order which ascends the great pyramid to descend no more, who upon reaching the fiery altar upon its summit cast themselves into the eternal flame, and from their own natures feed its eternal hunger."

In his *Chemical Marriage* Christian Rosenkreutz describes the vision of C. R. C. as he slept shackled in the antechamber of the House of Initiation. In his dream C. R. C. beheld the strange sight of a multitude of persons suspended from heaven by cords. In an early Rosicrucian book which I examined some years ago the subject of these "hanging men" was elucidated in detail. The dangling figures are the sophists, those false learners who ever seek to climb to heaven upon their own suppositions. We are all supported by our beliefs, held up as it were by the strength of our premises and the sufficiency of our postulations. Yet in all too many instances how slender and inadequate is the thread of mortal reason to which we trust our weight. Among the Sons of Islam there is an ancient fable to the effect that there shall come forth a prophet who will stretch a hair from the Mount of Olives to the golden gate of Jerusalem, and using it for a bridge will walk across the Valley of Jehoshaphat, or the place of death. The hair, according to the Cabala, is the symbol of the glory of God and the countless diversity of his mercy. Taking this fable in its literal sense, a Mohammedan fanatic wove a rope of human hair and essayed the feat, but was killed.

In the legend of Christian Rosenkreutz it is further stated that an aged man (who represents Cronus, or Time, the justifier of all actions) flew in and out among the hanging sophists. Wearing an hourglass tied to the top of his head and carrying in his hand a pair of sharp shears, the divine iconoclast would fly up behind any of the worldly-wise men who climbed too ambitiously up their swaying ropes and cut away their slender support. Another observation by the author of the *Chemical Marriage* is to the effect that the higher these false learners climbed, the harder and more disastrous was their fall, so that many were dashed to pieces. The more prudent ones, however, realizing the insecurity of their position, remained close to the earth and suffered comparatively little harm when their cords were cut, often alighting uninjured upon their feet.

We all share in common the desire to climb to heaven up the ladder of our own convictions, and believing ourselves to be infallible, we set out to storm the gates of the Eternal. No spectacle is more pathetic than that of the individual who, led to false and dizzy heights by his egotism, has been dashed therefrom into the depths of misery and disillusionment. The more we depend upon the false the more we suffer when that falseness is exposed. The story of the hanging men is evidently concerned with the effort to ridicule those Aristotelian schoolmen whose fallacies were already apparent at the beginning of the 17th century. Elevated above their fellow men by vain assertions, and maintaining themselves by subterfuge and equivocation, these pedants preyed upon the credulity of an illiterate age. But time was finding them out, for science, rising out of this protest against intellectual pettifoggery, furnished Cronus with the shears wherewith to cut down the scholastic befogger of issues. In this allegory heaven is used to signify the sphere of the truly learned, for it was presumed that those whose knowledge was sufficient dwelt in a state of tranquillity far above the abode of ordinary mortals tormented by doubt and rendered impotent by ignorance.

The light of tranquillity, as the followers of Boehme might call it, radiates from the paradisaic sphere of the contented. Humanity moves instinctively toward that tranquil state of the philosophic blest, for we incline toward that person or condition which radiates happiness. This instinct has been shamelessly exploited in the name of religion, but the age of empty promises is closed. Having vainly sought happiness among the dictums of faith and in the company of the so-called holy, the individual is coming to realize that peace lies only within himself. In Dryden's translation of the Aeneid are found several significant copper engravings, one particularly showing a genius cutting the slender thread of life connecting mortal man with his divine origin. A small plate also showing this thread issuing from the crown of the head and disappearing upward into a cloud of divine radiance is to be found in Michael Maier's *Scrutinium Chymicum*.

Various modifications of this idea constituted a favorite theme of the medieval emblem writers, especially such as were in touch with the Rosicrucian activities. This thread rising from the head is the Platonic cord—a fine hypothetical line which unites the personality to its own causal part. According to the Hermetic axiom of analogy, as the spirit and body of man are connected by a thread, so heaven and earth—the spirit and body of the solar man—are united by this swaying ladder which, lowered from above, becomes the way of souls descending into life. Cronus with his reaping scythe is the guardian of this rope, and at his will the line is severed and all the objective nature dissociated from its causal principle. This thread, then, is *Bifrost,* the bridge of the gods, over the immortals—like the Aesir of Scandinavia—crossed before its final severance when returning to their sacred castle. Like the builders of the fated Tower of Babel, the worldly-wise men of C. R. C.'s vision sought to elevate personality above principle and draw the body above its own source; hence their ultimate discomfiture. By attempting to elevate an impermanent nature to a divine state they attempted the impossible and so Death, the master of processes, cut down each one in turn; for that man does not exist who shall be empowered to reach heaven in his physical nature. The cords are the faith and power that sustain the individual during the prime of his life, but like life itself, power is a physical uncertainty, and neither wealth, position, nor physical knowledge can support the soul in that dread extremity which men are pleased to term death.

In his vision of the Apocalypse, the initiate, known to the Christians as St. John the Divine, experienced in his ascent to heaven the spiritual mystery of climbing upward through the seven congregations or churches "which are in Asia," finally coming to the door in the heavenly vault and passing through into the Empyrean to find himself in the presence of the Lord of the Cherubim and the Paschal Lamb. St. John is described as being "in the spirit," a good old Neoplatonic term. From this we are to infer that the Gnostic initiate had learned the mystery of the rope swinging from heaven, for according to tradition he had climbed his way hand over hand in approved nautical fashion. Mohammed, a prudent man of more portly build, overtaxed the meager facilities of a knotted rope and consequently employed (if we are to believe the accounts) a safer and more commodious rope ladder in his ascent. In substance, however, the experiences of the two initiates were practically identical, and though slight differences exist in the terminology of the symbolism, nevertheless the principle involved demonstrates that both men had been initiated—St. John presumably by the Gnostics and Mohammed by the Nestorian Christians. St. John the Divine employed seven great Asiatic cities to symbolize the spiritual knots or ganglia, which placed at intervals along the rope assisted the climber in his difficult task. Mohammed's rope ladder was of golden cords and its rungs presumably were fashioned from the substances of the seven worlds. He was forced, it is said, to stop at each of the seven gates to receive the adoration of the patriarchs, who had apparently waited since their demise for his coming.

There is also an East Indian fable of the goddess Kundalini who, being of an inquisitive mind and seeing a rope hanging from heaven with its lower end concealed in impenetrable gloom, decided to climb down this rope and investigate the unknown darkness below. Having descended the rope for an incalculable period, Kundalini discovered that its lower end rested upon an island that seemed to float in the midst of a great sea of darkness. While exploring this strange island the rope was cut from above, and Kundalini was left floating in the midst of a vast ocean. In terror the goddess ran and hid herself in a cave and refused to come out. In the secret teachings it is revealed that she could be induced to come forth from her asylum only by an aggregation of wise men who with offerings, supplications, and grave discoursings finally persuaded her to leave her gloomy retreat. The goddess Kundalini is the spirit fire that descends the mysterious ladder which is here emblematic of the umbilical cord. When this cord is cut the goddess is left stranded in the underworld. Alarmed, she hides in the great cavern of the sacral plexus, there to remain coiled up as a serpent (as her name implies) until the sage can lure her forth again by holy observances.

Never should we lose sight of the relationship between the processes of the physical body and the universal orders. The umbilical cord is not only the divine ladder in the case of the goddess Kundalini, but is symbolic also of that spiritual cord by which man is ever suspended from his Divine Parent. While man's outer nature is nourished by physical food and drink, his inner nature receives life from the Universal Parent transmitted by means of ethereal cords analogous to the umbilicus.

In the Shinto Mysteries of Japan the luring of an obstinate goddess from her pout was a grave problem. The Goddess of the Sun, Amaterasu O-mikami, had quarreled with the other celestials, and giving vent to her anger hied herself, light and all, into a dark cavern, thus leaving the heavenly world in a condition of deplorable gloom. Realizing that the temperament of the goddess was endangering the whole order of creation, the immortals finally lured her forth by a stratagem which appealed to her vanity. They fashioned a great mirror even as the Titans polished the surface of the universe that Bacchus might see his face therein. Standing this mirror in front of the cavern they made a great ado as though in celebration of some fortuitous circumstance. Chagrined at the thought that the gods could be happy without her, Amaterasu came to the cavern entrance and peered out to discover the cause of their merriment. As she looked she saw her own face, surrounded by a halo of light, reflected in the mirror. Wondering who this radiant person could be and terrified by the possibility that the gods had somewhere discovered a new sun goddess, Amaterasu slowly approached the entrance of the cave, only to see the radiant figure in the mirror also increasing in splendor. At last, overcome by her jealousy she dashed from the cave to discomfit the rival sun goddess, whereupon the other celestials who had gathered above the cavern entrance dropped a net over the irate goddess as she rushed forth, thereby preventing her escape and insuring that the sun should again light the world. Amaterasu and her mirror are household words in every Shinto home, and even the august imperial line regards the sun goddess as its founder, and her mirror is carried in the coronation ceremonials.

The luring of the light out of darkness is an allegory frequently employed by many ancient writers on mysticism. It represents the effort of material man to evoke, by discipline and fetish, that lucid or rational part of himself which for some temperamental reason refuses to make itself known. Offended by the crassness of the outer life, the aesthetic and superphysical attributes of the soul retire into the uttermost recesses of the nature, there to await that more auspicious day when the awakening individual will concern himself with the nobler issues of life. The sages who ponder the problem of enticing the goddess from retirement signify the rational mind, the gods, and the intuitive instincts, while the priest represents the regenerated emotions. All these, holding solemn conclave together, finally lure the rational soul from its dark abode that its radiance may benefit the whole life. The invoking of the soul is possible only to those who have assumed the Great Work and resolved to live with the concerns of the spirit paramount. Through virtue, integrity, and aesthetics the soul life is thus caused to diffuse its power throughout the nature, thereby quickening the parts and rendering the whole more responsive to divine impulse.

From a consideration of these various allegories it becomes evident that the ladder signifies the thread or cord from which the generating soul is suspended from its monadic, or ungenerated part. The God of the philosophic elect is not technically a being, but rather this monad, or universal self. Approach to Deity is consequently, the elevation of the life to unity with its monadic cause. The abode of this monad is the true heaven world, for heaven merely signifies the state of the One divorced from all quality or condition whatsoever and abiding in the felicity of its own nature, without beginning and without end. Thus the ascent of the ladder and the climbing of the knotted cord are both emblematic of man's ceaseless climb toward Self. It is the retirement of life along the lines of its own first emanation—the natural ascent of the wise to wisdom, the virtuous to virtue, the beautiful to beauty, and the good to the enduring state of good. The ladder, then, bridges that mysterious fourth-dimensional interval of quality described in Chapter X; it is the symbolic figure under which are concealed the tedious processes of crossing that vast interval between diversity and unity. The ladder is the bridge of reason, the way of the gods.

The stepped pyramid is significant of man's instinctive urge to build toward Cause, and all action which tends to elevate, ennoble, or perfect may be conceived of as pyramidal, diagrammatically considered. Thus in his discourse to his son on initiation, Hermes declares that the heart was built like a pyramid in that the heart is the seat of aspiration, and aspiration is the universal building power. As the Unknown God dwelt within the deepest recesses of the Great Pyramid, so a mysterious spirit dwells within the heart—man's House of the Hidden Places. The pyramid builders differed from all other architects because of the purpose for which their edifices were constructed. All men are builders—a few in permanent things, the many in impermanent things. St. Paul calls himself a "master builder," by which he intimated that he had been initiated into that body of elect artisans banded together to the erection of *everlasting houses*. The pyramid thus became the symbol of those called together by an inner rationality who, moved by a divine intelligence, heaped up realities that they might form mountains, as it were, up which the aspiring soul could climb in its search for heaven. While many were cutters of stone, hewers of wood, and carriers of water, they were but apprentices of the noble art, not having heard as yet the call that inclines the soul away from temporal accomplishments to the building of those enduring monuments to qualities and convictions.

The mystic Masons, so we are told, built their lodges either upon the mountain tops or deep in the valleys, thus obscurely intimating that the Mysteries, while in their own nature lofty institutions, in the service of mankind descended into the depths of matter to effect the redemption of the human soul. God appeared to the patriarchs as a cloud over some lofty mountain top, and his voice thundered among the summits.

These sacred mountains—hovering places of the Most High—are the sanctified pyramids. These pyramids, in turn, are rationalized natures—the chief accomplishment of the master builders. They are altars set up in the wilderness to signify that integrity has been establised in a sphere to which integrity was once foreign. An ancient fable, in describing the stature of one whom God has thus anointed and lifted up into the assemblage of the illumined, declares that his face shone like the sun, and all the brightness of the stars was in his eyes; the flow of his hair was like the rippling waves of great rivers, and even his breath was as the soft breeze of spring sighing among the trees. Though his body was that of a man, his inner nature was as vast as the world, and his integrity rose like a mighty mountain whose summit is forever hidden by the clouds of meditation. The laughter of this perfected one sounded like the song of the waterfall, yet his sorrow was like the cool of evening among the shelter of the trees. All the beauties of the universe were invoked to define his virtues, and the immensities of space belittled his greatness. It follows that when such an illumined nature heaps together the stones of its accomplishment and forms therefrom the altar of its God—a high and holy place suitable for the reception of the Eternal—the rational soul, invoked by these accomplishments, lends its power to the convocation of perfected faculties. Then, like the awful hierophant of Revelation, the rational self stands in splendid majesty in the midst of the flaming candles.

Thus all natures are symbolic ladders, for by ascending the concatenated orders of his own intelligence man comes proximate to his own rational and enduring part. The allegory of Jack and the beanstalk, which like so many other children's fables has its origin in primitive folklore, well describes the mystery of the ladder. The beanstalk, which in a single night grew up to heaven, reminds one of the fabled mango tree of the elusive Hindu mahatma or the rope thrown into the air which does not fall. The miraculous growth of the magician's plant signifies the culturing of the soul. Every philosopher is a magician, for by the aid of his unfolded intellect he accomplishes that which to the ignorant appears impossible. The rope suspended from nothing, up to which the naked Hindu boy scampers out of sight, teaches a valuable lesson to such as will inquire into its meaning. The question is often asked by the incredulous: "But how can the rope stay there with nothing to hold it?" The magician may answer: "It is well-supported, only you do not see the support." The unenlightened behold the accomplishments of the wise, but the methods by which such ends are attained are incomprehensible. The great truths of life are, like the magician's rope, held in their proper place by an unseen agent. Those unable to pierce the magicians subterfuge have eyes but see not. The millions to whom the concerns of the spirit are of no importance, who though continually surrounded by manifestations of universal intelligence are still oblivious to the whole pageantry—these are the truly blind and their affliction is most grievous.

In the allegory of the beanstalk, Jack is the initiate climbing upward toward perfection. The beanstalk has two significances. First, it is the secret doctrine which may grow up to its fullness in a single night, if that night be regarded as the duration of a soul in the mortal state. The beanstalk is further symbolic of the soul itself, up which consciousness must climb to discover the divine sphere from which it was exiled. It is noteworthy that when Jack reaches the upper world, where one would naturally expect beauty and tranquillity to reign, he finds instead that his newly-discovered sphere is the dwelling place of a fierce ogre who has the distressing proclivity of using strangers to supply the requirements of his menu. This giant is the ancient demiurgus—the lord of the world, the royal autocrat, the vast tyrant who opposes all who would climb out of their materiality. He is selfishness, egotism, lust, and hate. He is the epitome of all physical attachment, and the appetites by which man is inclined toward the corporeal state. He is the giant of form, the hero of little minds, the fetish of the materialist, the god of those who worship through the senses alone, the supreme genius of the physical-minded, the magnificence to which fools bow down. Those who would escape the clutches of this giant must be wise indeed, for they must outwit themselves. In the ancient writings it is said that all will fail except a fortuitous destiny move with them, for skill will not suffice, prayers will be unavailing, and only the graciousness of the gods can insure success.

The subject of *Providence*, or fortuitous destiny, is worthy of amplification at this point. One of the symbolic aphorisms of Pythagoras enjoined the disciple to abstain from the eating of beans. In its literal sense there is seemingly no reason whatsoever for the admonition. Among the Greeks, however, beans were used in gambling and various games of chance, and the esoteric purpose of the admonition was to discharge man's reliance upon auspicious fortune; for he who consigns himself to the vagaries of chance in reality rests his fate upon his own integrity. This point is well made by Mephistopheles in Goethe's *Faust*:

> "How closely linked are Luck and Merit
> Doth never to these fools occur;
> Had they the Philosopher's Stone, I swear it,
> The Stone would lack the Philosopher!"

Man eternally struggles against the littleness that is himself, seeking to increase thereby the virtue of his own destiny. By such effort he frequently is able to maintain a higher footing than would otherwise be his natural right, for effort shall not be left unrewarded. If, however, man ceases his struggle and, doing nothing, trusts to Providence for an auspicious throw, that which is his own will know his face and his reward shall be according to the insufficiency of himself. He who trusts himself to himself is brave indeed! Luck is not what it seems, for it connives with Law to bring about the undoing of the foolish. The bit and bridle which Nemesis carries she slips over the head of the unwary. With blinders she takes away his vision, with checkrein lifts his head so high that he can no longer see the road, and then with loose rein drives him to destruction. But if the gods throw dice they cannot lose, for by reason of their very nature they are predestined to be the victors in every contest. Being as yet imperfect, however man may never relax his vigilance or cease his struggle lest the imperfections which he seeks to outdistance overtake and humiliate him.

What, then, is Providence? It is like flowing into like, a quality reproducing its kind. Providence is not what we desire but what we actually are, and when we open the floodgates of fortune we shall simply be inundated by the torrents of similars—drowned in the substances of ourselves. By confronting destiny with effort we aspire to reach the ideal state of the higher self; but by appealing to fortune we place ourselves in the keeping of an impersonal fate that tortures us with our every defect, and decrees us to abide by the measure of our smallest virtue. Thus only in the truly great is the appeal to fortune to be relied upon; for the rest the law of labor is the only certain way. When it is written that man can suceed only when the gods are auspicious it merely signifies that accomplishment depends upon the perfect mastery of self and the development of all parts, so that the flow of destiny brings to the disciple a propitious end to enterprise. Good fortune is not good to the foolish, nor is evil fortune evil to the wise. The foolish are incapable of benefiting from that which may in its own nature be good; conversely, the wise are incapable of being injured by evil, for understanding renders all things usable. Thus the identical so-called evil serves the philosopher while it undoes the thoughtless.

The theory of evolution as expounded by the ancient sages does not agree with the Darwinian concept that life moves from one form or kind to another, but rather that life continually moves through the various states of itself. For example, plants do not move toward the perfection of man, nor does man incline toward the perfection of daemons. Each of these orders is complete in itself, moving inevitably toward its own perfection in the perfect unfoldment of its own intrinsic characteristics. Growth, then, is that eternal procession of qualities marching to unity with themselves. Man, the personality, approaches Man, the idea, and achieves perfection by unity with his own paradigm. Man reaches completion when he perfectly fills the mold or pattern that exists in the transcendental spheres. Evolution, then, is the fitting of a nature into its own archetype, and its end is attained when no longer any point of difference remains between the object as a transitory body and the object as a permanent idea. By growth we learn to become our essential selves, ordered after the precise image of our own divine prototype.

That growth should be the process whereby man becomes reconciled to his own transcendental being may seem a strange thought, but to those who ponder the mystery, this truth becomes evident. Our path is rendered plain: we are destined by Eternal Providence to become the fullness of ourselves. Inclining to neither side nor departing from our persons, we shall find perfection in the consummation of the destiny for which we were first conceived. The imitator must fail, because departing from self he would assume the virtues of another rather than his own. Each individual is alloted an end peculiar to himself, and through uncounted milleniums moves inevitably toward that archetypal ideal patterned for him prior to his departure from Universal Self in quest of individuality. All creatures of a similar kind share a common origin and destiny. It is the peculiar purpose of men that they should become Man, and united in one nature constitute a complete being—that glorious assemblage of parts possessing three virtues, of which the first is completeness and the other two are the poles of this completeness, namely, rationality and permanence.

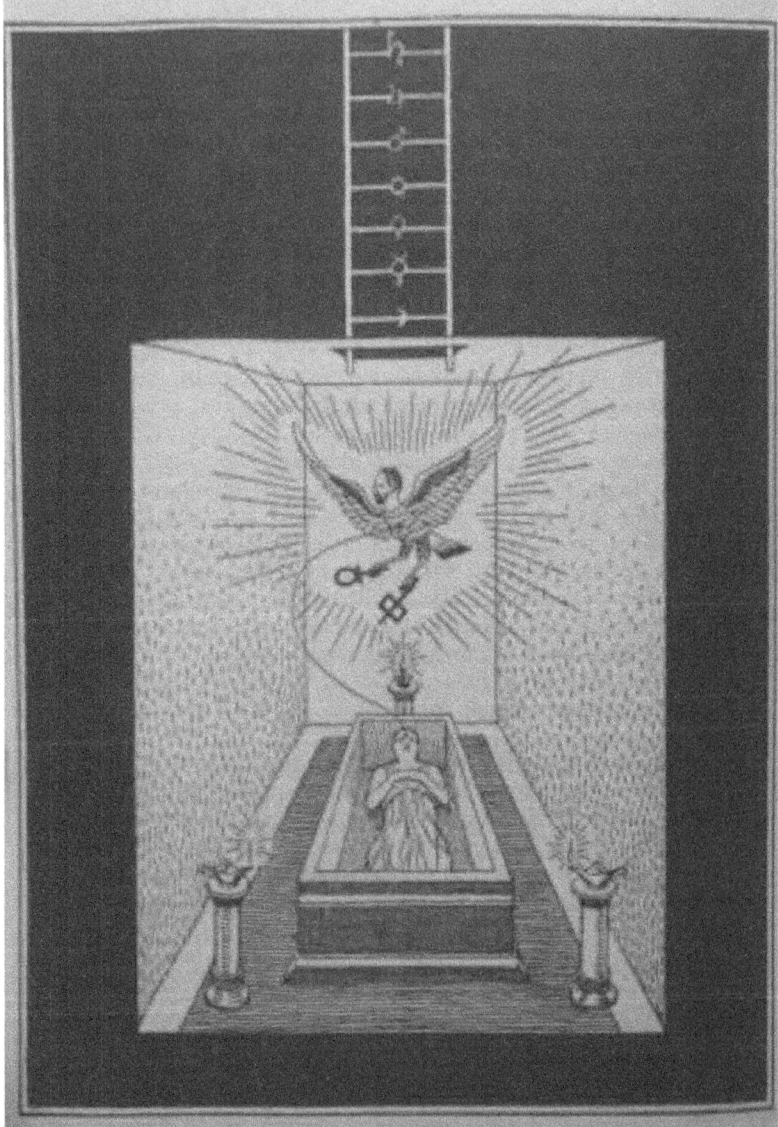

THE BIRD OF THE SOUL

While the body of the candidate lay in the stone sarcophagus, the soul, hovering in the air above it, assumed the form of a bird, and passing upward out of the crypt through the vent or chimney of the planets entered into the presence of the great Osiris, lord of decarnate souls. After remaining three days in the fields of Amenti, the soul returns to its body amidst the rejoicing of the priests.

CHAPTER NINETEEN

ROSICRUCIAN AND MASONIC ORIGINS

FREEMASONRY is a fraternity within a fraternity—an outer organization concealing an inner brotherhood of the elect. Before it is possible to intelligently discuss the origin of the craft it is necessary to establish the existence of these two separate yet interdependent orders, the one visible and the other invisible. The visible society is a splendid camaraderie of "free and accepted" men enjoined to devote themselves to ethical, educational, fraternal, patriotic, and humanitarian concerns. The invisible society is a secret and most august fraternity whose members are dedicated to the service of a mysterious *arcanum arcanorum*. Those brethren who have essayed to write the history of their craft have not included in their disquisitions the story of that truly secret inner society which is to the body Freemasonic what the heart is to the body human. In each generation only a few are accepted into the inner sanctuary of the work, but these are veritable princes of truth, and their sainted names shall be remembered in future ages together with the seers and prophets of the elder world. Though the great initiate-philosophers of Freemasonry can be counted upon one's fingers, yet their power is not to be measured by the achievements of ordinary men. They are dwellers upon the threshold of the innermost, masters of that secret doctrine which forms the invisible foundation of every great theological and rational institution.

The outer history of the Masonic order is one of noble endeavor, altruism, and splendid enterprise; the inner history one of silent conquest, persecution, and heroic martyrdom. The body of Masonry rose from the guilds of workmen who wandered the face of medieval Europe, but the spirit of Masonry walked with God before the universe was spread out or the scroll of the heavens unrolled. The enthusiasm of the young Mason is the effervescence of a pardonable pride. Let him extol the merits of his craft, reciting its steady growth, its fraternal spirit, and its worthy undertakings. Let him boast of splendid buildings and an ever-increasing sphere of influence. These are the tangible evidence of power, and should rightly set a-flutter the heart of the apprentice who does not fully comprehend as yet that great strength which abides in silence, or that unutterable dignity to be sensed only by those who have been "raised" into the contemplation of the inner mystery.

An obstacle well-nigh insurmountable is to convince the Mason that the secrets of his craft are worthy of his profound consideration. As St. Paul (so we are told) kicked against the "pricks" of conversion, so the rank and file of present-day Masons strenuously oppose any effort put forth to interpret Masonic symbols in the light of philosophy. They are seemingly obsessed by the fear that from their ritualism may be extracted a meaning more profound than is actually contained therein. For years it has been a moot question whether Freemasonry is actually a religious organization. "Masonry," writes Pike in the *Legenda* for the Nineteenth Degree, "has and always had a religious creed. It teaches what it deems to be the truth in respect to the nature and attributes of God." The more studious-minded Mason regards the craft as an aggregation of thinkers concerned with the deeper mysteries of life. The all-too prominent younger members of the fraternity, however, if not openly skeptical, are at least indifferent to these weightier issues. The champions of philosophic Masonry, alas, are a weak, small voice which grows weaker and smaller as time goes by. In fact, there are actual *blocs* among the brethren who would divorce Masonry from both philosophy and religion at any and all cost. If, however, we search the writings of eminent Masons, we find a unanimity of viewpoint, namely, that Masonry is a religious and philosophic body. Every effort initiated to elevate Masonic thought to its true position has thus invariably emphasized the metaphysical and ethical aspects of the craft.

But a superficial perusal of available documents will demonstrate that the modern Masonic order is not united respecting the true purpose for its own existence. Nor will this factor of doubt be dispelled until the origin of the craft is established beyond all quibbling. The elements of Masonic history are strangely elusive; there are gaps which apparently cannot be bridged. "Who the early Freemasons really were," states Gould in *A Concise History of Freemasonry*, "and whence they came, may afford a tempting theme for inquiry to the speculative antiquary. But it is enveloped in obscurity, and lies far outside the domain of authentic history." Between modern Freemasonry with its vast body of ancient symbolism, and those original Mysteries which first employed these symbols, there is a dark interval of centuries. To the conservative Masonic historian the deductions of such writers as Higgins, Churchward, Vail, and Waite—though ingenious and fascinating—actually prove nothing. That Masonry is a body of ancient lore is self-evident, but the tangible "link" necessary to convince the recalcitrant brethren that their order is the direct successor of the pagan Mysteries, has unfortunately not been adduced to date. Of such problems as these is composed the "angel" with which the Masonic Jacob must wrestle throughout the night.

It is possible to trace Masonry back a few centuries with comparative ease, but then the thread suddenly vanishes from sight in a maze of secret societies and political enterprises. Dimly silhouetted in the mists that becloud these tangled issues are such figures as Cagliostro, Comte de St.-Germain, and St. Martin, but even the connection between these individuals and the craft has never been clearly defined. The writings of early Masonic history is involved in such obvious hazard as to provoke the widespread conclusion that further search is futile. The average Masonic student is content, therefore, to trace his craft back to the workmen who chipped and chiselled the cathedrals and public buildings of medieval Europe. While such men as Albert Pike have realized this attitude to be ridiculous, it is one thing to declare it insufficient and quite another to prove the fallacy to an adamantine mind. So much has been lost and forgotten, so much ruled in and out by those unfitted for such legislative revision, that the modern rituals do not in every case represent the original rites of the craft. In his *Symbolism*, Pike (who spent a lifetime in the quest for Masonic secrets) declares that few of the original meanings of the symbols are known to the modern order, nearly all the so-called interpretations now given being superficial. Pike confessed that the original meanings of the very symbols he himself was attempting to interpret were irretrievably lost; that even such familiar emblems as the apron and the pillars were locked mysteries, whose "keys" had been thrown away by the uninformed. "The initiated," writes John Fellows, "as well as those without the pale of the order, are equally ignorant of their derivation and import." (See *The Mysteries of Freemasonry*.)

Preston, Gould, Mackey, Oliver, and Pike—in fact, nearly every great historian of Freemasonry—have all admitted the possibility of the modern society being connected, indirectly at least, with the ancient Mysteries, and their descriptions of the modern society are prefaced by excerpts from ancient writings dscriptive of primitive ceremonials. These eminent Masonic scholars have recognized in the legend of Hiram Abiff an adaptation of the Osiris myth; nor do they deny that the major part of the symbolism of the craft is derived from the pagan institutions of antiquity when the gods were venerated in secret places with strange figures and appropriate rituals. Though cognizant of the exalted origin of their order, these historians—either through fear or uncertainty—have failed to drive home the one point necessary to establish the true purpose of Freemasonry: *They did not realize that the Mysteries whose rituals Freemasonry perpetuates were the custodians of a secret philosophy of life of such transcendent nature that it can be entrusted to only an individual tested and proved beyond any*

possibility of human frailty. The secret schools of Greece and Egypt were neither fraternal nor political fundamentally, nor were their ideals similar to those of the modern craft. They were essentially philosophic and religious institutions, and all admitted into them were consecrated to the service of the sovereign good. Modern Freemasons, however, regard their craft as neither primarily philosophic nor religious, but rather as ethical. Strange as it may seem, the majority openly ridicule the very supernatural powers and agencies for which their symbols stand.

The secret doctrine that flows through Freemasonic symbols (and to whose perpetuation the invisible Masonic body is consecrated) has its source in three ancient and exalted orders. The first is the Dionysiac artificers, the second the Roman *collegia,* and the third the Arabian Rosicrucians. The Dionysians were the master builders of the ancient world. Originally founded to design and erect the theaters of Dionysus wherein were enacted the tragic dramas of the rituals, this order was repeatedly elevated by popular acclaim to greater dignity, until at last it was entrusted with the planning and construction of all public edifices concerned with the commonwealth or the worship of the gods and heroes. Hiram, King of Tyre, was the patron of the Dionysians, who flourished in Tyre and Sidon, and Hiram Abiff (if we may believe the sacred account) was himself a grand master of this most noble order of pagan builders. King Solomon in his wisdom accepted the services of this famous craftsman, and thus at the instigation of Hiram, King of Tyre, Hiram Abiff, though himself a member of a different faith, journeyed from his own country to design and supervise the erection of the everlasting house to the true God on Mount Moriah. The tools of the builders' craft were first employed by the Dionysians as symbols under which to conceal the mysteries of the soul and the secrets of human regeneration. The Dionysians also first likened man to a rough *ashlar* which, trued into a finished block through the instrument of reason, could be fitted into the structure of that living and eternal Temple built without the sound of hammer, the voice of workman, or any tool of contention.

The Roman *collegia* was a branch of the Dionysiacs and to it belonged those initiated artisans who fashioned the impressive monuments whose ruins still lend their immortal glory to the Eternal City. In his *Ten Books on Architecture,* Vitruvius, the initiate of the *collegia*, has revealed that which was permissible concerning the secrets of his holy order. Of the inner mysteries, however, he could not write, for these were reserved for such as had donned the leather apron of the craft. In his consideration of the books now available concerning the Mysteries the thoughtful reader should note the following words appearing in a 12th-century volume entitled *Artephil Liber Secretus*: "Is not this an art full of secrets? And believest thou, O fooll that we plainly teach this Secret of Secrets, taking our words according to their literal interpretation?" (See *Sephar H' Debarim*.) Into the stones they trued, the adepts of the *collegia* deeply carved their gnostic symbols. From earliest times the initiated stonecutters marked their perfected works with the secret emblems of their crafts and degrees, that unborn generations might realize that the master builders of the first ages also labored for the same ends sought by men today.

The Mysteries of Egypt and Persia that had found a haven in the Arabian Desert reached Europe by way of the Knights Templars and the Rosicrucians. The Temple of the Rose Cross at Damascus had preserved the secret philosophy of the Rose of Sharon; the Druses of the Lebanon mountains still retain the mysticism of ancient Syria; and the dervishes, as they lean on their carved and crotched sticks, still meditate upon the secret instruction perpetuated from the days of the four caliphs. From the far places of Irak and the hidden retreats of the Sufi mystics, the Ancient Wisdom found its way into Europe. Was Jacques de Molay burned by the Holy Inquisition merely because he wore the red cross of the Templar? What were those secrets to which he was true even in death? Did his companion knights perish with him merely because they had amassed a fortune and exercised an unusual degree of temporal power? To the thoughtless these may constitute ample grounds, but to those who can pierce the film of the specious and the superficial they are assuredly insufficient. It was not the physical power of the Templars, but the knowledge which they had brought with them from the East, that the church feared. The Templars had discovered part of the great arcanum; they had become wise in those mysteries which had been celebrated in Mecca thousands of years before the advent of Mohammed; they had read a few pages from the dread book of the *Anthropos,* and for this knowledge they were doomed to die. What was the black magic of which the Templars were accused? What was Baphomet, the Goat of Mendes, whose mysteries they were declared to have celebrated? All these are questions worthy of thoughtful consideration by every studious Mason.

Truth is eternal. The so-called revelations of truth that come in different religions are actually but a re-emphasis of an ever-existing doctrine. Moses did not originate a new religion for Israel; he simply adapted the Mysteries of Egypt to the needs of Israel. The ark triumphantly borne by the twelve tribes through the wilderness was copied after the Isiac ark, which may still be traced in faint bas-relief upon the ruins of the Temple of Philae. Even the two brooding cherubim over the mercy seat are visible in the Egyptian carving, furnishing indubitable evidence that the secret doctrine of Egypt was the prototype of Israel's mystery religion. In his reformation of Indian philosophy, Buddha likewise did not reject the esotericism of the Brahmins, but rather adapted this esotericism to the needs of the masses in India. The mystic secrets locked within the holy Vedas were disclosed in order that all men, irrespective of caste, might partake of wisdom and share in a common heritage of good. Jesus was a Rabbi of the Jews, a teacher of the holy law who discoursed in the synagogue, interpreting the Torah according to the teachings of his sect. He brought no new message nor were his reformations radical. He merely tore away the veil from the temple in order that not only Pharisee and Sadducee, but also publican and sinner might together behold the glory of an ageless faith.

In his cavern on Mount Hira, Mohammed prayed not for new truths, but for old truths to be restated in their original purity and simplicity in order that men might understand again the primitive religion: God's clear revelation to the first patriarchs. The Mysteries of Islam had been celebrated in the sanctuary of the Kaaba centuries before the holy pilgrimage. The prophet was but the reformer of a decadent pagandom, the smasher of idols, the purifier of defiled Mysteries. The dervishes, who patterned their garments after those of the prophet, still preserve that inner teaching of the elect, and for them the *Axis of the Earth*—the supreme hierophant—visible only to the faith still sits in meditation upon the flat roof of the Kaaba. Neither carpenter nor camel driver, as Abdul Baha might have said, can fashion a world religion from the substances of his own mind. Neither prophet nor savior preached a doctrine which was his own, but in language suitable to his time and race retold that Ancient Wisdom which has been preserved within the Mysteries since the dawning of human consciousness. So with the Masonic Mysteries of today. Each Mason has at hand those lofty principles of universal order upon whose certainties the faiths of mankind have ever been established.

Father C. R. C., the master of the Rosy Cross, was initiated into the great work at Damcar. Later at Fez further information was given him relating to the sorcery of the Arabians. From these wizards of the desert he also secured the sacred book *M*, which is declared to have contained the accumulated knowledge of the world. He translated this volume into Latin for the edification of his order, but only the initiates know the present hidden repository of the Rosicrucian manuscripts, charters, and manifestoes. From the Arabians C. R. C. also learned of the elemental peoples and how, with their aid, it was possible to gain admission to the ethereal world where dwelt the genii and nature spirits. He thus discovered that the magical creatures of the *Arabian Nights Entertainment* actually existed, though invisible to the ordinary mortal. From astrologers living in the desert far from the concourse of the marketplace he was further instructed concerning the mysteries of the stars, the virtues resident in the astral light, the rituals of magic and invocation, the preparation of therapeutic talismans, and the binding of the genii. He became an adept in the gathering of medicinal herbs, the transmutation of metals, and the manufacture of precious gems by artificial means. Even the secret of the elixir of life and the universal panacea were communicated to him. Enriched beyond the dreams of Croesus, the holy master returned to Europe and there established a house of wisdom which he called *Domus Sancti Spiritus*. This house he enveloped in clouds, it is said, so that men could not discover it. What are these "clouds," but the rituals and symbols under which is concealed the great arcanum —that unspeakable mystery which every true Mason must seek if he would become in reality a "Prince of the Royal Secret"?

Paracelsus, the Swiss Hermes, was initiated into the secrets of alchemy in Constantinople and there beheld the consummation of the *magnum opus*. He is consequently entitled to be mentioned among those initiated by the Arabians into the Rosicrucian work. Cagliostro was also initiated by the Arabians, and because of the knowledge he had thus secured incurred the displeasure of the Holy See. From the unprobed depths of Arabian Rosicrucianism issued the illustrious Comte de St.-Germain, over whose Masonic activities the veil of impenetrable mystery still hangs. The exalted body of initiates whom he represented, as well as the mission he came to accomplish, have both been concealed from the members of the craft at large, and are apparent only to those few discerning Masons who sense the supernal philosophic destiny of their fraternity.

The modern Masonic order can be traced back to a period in European history famous for its intrigue both political and sociological. Between the years 1600 and 1800, mysterious agents moved across the face of the Continent. The forerunner of modern thought was beginning to make its appearance, and all Europe was passing through the throes of internal dissension and reconstruction. Democracy was in its infancy, yet its potential power was already being felt. Thrones were beginning to totter. The aristocracy of Europe was like the old man on Sinbad's back; it was becoming more unbearable with every passing day. Although upon the surface national governments were seemingly able to cope with the situation, there was a definite undercurrent of impending change. Out of the masses, long patient under the yoke oppression, were rising up the champions of religious, philosophic, and political liberty. These led the factions of the dissatisfied; people with legitimate grievances against the intolerance of the church and the oppression of the crown. Out of this struggle for expression certain definite ideals materialized which have now come to be considered peculiarly Masonic.

The divine prerogatives of humanity were being crushed out by the three great powers of ignorance, superstition, and fear—ignorance, the power of the mob; superstition, the power of the church, and fear, the power of the despot. Between the thinker and personal liberty loomed the three "ruffians" or personifications of impediment—the torch, the crown, and the tiara. Brute force, kingly power, and ecclesiastical persuasion became the agents of a great oppression, the motive of a deep unrest, the deterrent to all progress. It was unlawful to think, well-nigh fatal to philosophize, rank heresy to doubt. To question the infallibility of the existing order was to invite the persecution of the church and the state. Together they incited the populace, which thereupon played the role of executioner for these arch-enemies of human liberty. Thus the ideal of democracy assumed a definite form during these stormy periods of European history. This democracy was not only a vision, but a retrospection; not only a looking forward, but a gazing backward upon better days and the effort to project those better days into the unborn tomorrow. The ethical, political, and philosophical institutions of antiquity, with their constructive effect upon the whole structure of the state, were noble examples of possible conditions. It became the dream of the oppressed to re-establish a golden age upon the earth; an age in which the thinker could think in safety and the dreamer dream in peace; when the wise should lead and the simple follow, yet all dwell together in fraternity and industry.

During this period several books were in circulation, which to a certain degree registered the pulse of the time. One of these documents—More's *Utopia*—was the picture of a new age when heavenly conditions should prevail upon the earth. This ideal of establishing good in the world savored of blasphemy, for in that day it was assumed that heaven alone could be good. Men did not seek to establish heavenly conditions upon earth, but rather earthly conditions in heaven. According to popular concept, the more the individual suffered the torments of the damned upon earth, the more he would enjoy the blessedness in heaven. Life was a period of chastisement, and earthly happiness an unattainable mirage. More's *Utopia* thus came as a definite blow to autocratic pretensions and attitudes, giving impulse to the material emphasis which was to follow in succeeding centuries.

Another prominent figure of this period was Sir Walter Raleigh, who paid with his life for high treason against the crown. Raleigh was tried, and though the charge was never proved he was executed. Before he went to trial it was known that he must die, and that no defense could save him. His treason against the crown was of a character very different, however, from that which history records. Raleigh was a member of a secret society, or body of men, which was already moving irresistibly forward under the banner of democracy, and for that affiliation he died a felon's death. The actual reason for his death sentence was his refusal to reveal the identity of that great political organization of which he was a member, or his *confreres* who were fighting the dogma of faith and the divine right of kings. On the title page of the first edition of Raleigh's *History of the World*, we accordingly find a mass of intricate emblems framed between two great columns. When the executioner sealed his lips forever, Raleigh's silence, while it added to the discomfiture of his persecutors, assured the safety of his colleagues.

One of the truly great minds of that secret fraternity—in fact, the moving spirit of the whole enterprise—was Sir Francis Bacon, whose prophecy of the coming age forms the theme in his *New Atlantis,* and whose vision of the reformation of knowledge finds expression in the *Novum Organum.* In the engraving at the beginning of the latter volume may be seen the little ship of progressivism sailing out between the pillars of Galenic and Avicennian philosophy venturing forth beyond the imaginary pillars of church and state upon the unknown sea of human liberty. It is significant that Bacon was appointed by the British Crown to protect its interests in the new American Colonies beyond the sea. We find him writing of this new land, dreaming of the day when a new world and a new government of the philosophic elect should be established there, and scheming to consummate that end when the right time came. Upon the title page of the 1640 edition of Bacon's *Advancement of Learning* is a Latin motto to the effect that he was the third great mind since Plato. Bacon was a member of the same group to which Sir Walter Raleigh belonged, but Bacon's position as lord chancellor protected him from Raleigh's fate. Every effort was made, however, to humiliate and discredit him. At last, in the sixty-sixth year of his life, he completed the work which held him in England. He feigned death and passed over into Germany, there to guide the destinies of his philosophic and political fraternity for nearly twenty-five years before his actual demise.

Other notable characters of the period are Montaigne, Ben Jonson, Marlowe, and the great Franz Joseph of Transylvania—the latter one of the most important as well as active figures in all this drama; a man who ceased fighting Austria and retired to a monastery in Transylvania from where he directed the activities of his secret society. One political upheaval followed another. The grand climax culminated in the French Revolution, which was directly precipitated by the attacks upon the person of Alessandro Cagliostro. The "divine" Cagliostro, by far the most picturesque character of the time, has the distinction of being more maligned than any other person of history. Tried by the Inquisition for founding a Masonic lodge in the city of Rome, he was sentenced to die, a sentence later commuted by the Pope to life imprisonment in the old castle of San Leo. Shortly after his incarceration Cagliostro disappeared, and the story was circulated that he had been strangled in an attempt to escape from prison. In reality he was liberated and returned to his masters in the East. But Cagliostro—the idol of France, surnamed "the Father of the Poor," who never received anything from anyone and gave everything to everyone—was most adequately revenged. Though the people little understood this inexhaustible pitcher of bounty which poured forth benefits and never required replenishment, they remembered him in the day of their power.

Cagliostro founded the Egyptian rite of Freemasonry, which received into its mysteries many of the French nobility and was regarded favorably by the most learned minds of Europe. Having established the Egyptian rite, Cagliostro declared himself to be an agent of the order of the Knights Templars, and to have received initiation from them on the Isle of Malta. (See *Morals and Dogma* in which Albert Pike quotes Eliphas Levi on Cagliostro's affiliation with the Templars.) Called upon the carpet by the supreme council of France, it was demanded of Cagliostro that he prove by what authority he had founded a Masonic lodge in Paris, independent of the Grand Orient. Of such surpassing mentality was Cagliostro that the supreme council found it difficult to secure an advocate qualified to discuss with him philosophic Masonry and the ancient Mysteries he claimed to represent. Court de Gebelin —the greatest Egyptologist of his day and an authority on ancient philosophies—was chosen as the outstanding scholar. A time was set and the brethren convened. Attired in an Oriental coat and a pair of violet-colored breeches, Cagliostro was haled before this council of his peers. Court de Gebelin asked three questions and then sat down, admitting himself disqualified to interrogate a man so much his superior in every branch of learning. Cagliostro then took the floor, revealing to the assembled Masons not only his personal qualifications, but prophesying the future of France. He foretold the fall of the French throne, the Reign of Terror, and the fall of the Bastille. At a later time he revealed the dates of the death of Marie Antoinette and the king, and also the advent of Napoleon. Having finished his address he made a spectacular exit, leaving the French Masonic lodge in consternation and utterly incapable of coping with the profundity of his reasoning. Though no longer regarded as a ritual in Freemasonry, the Egyptian rite is available, and all who read it will recognize its author to have been no more a charlatan than was Plato.

Then appears that charming "first American gentleman," Dr. Benjamin Franklin, who together with the Marquis de Lafayette, played an important role in this drama of empires. While in France Dr. Franklin was privileged to receive definite esoteric instruction. It is noteworthy that he was the first in America to reprint Anderson's *Constitutions of the Free-Masons*, which is a most prized work on the subject though its accuracy is disputed.

Through all this stormy period these impressive figures come and go, part of a definite organization of political and religious thought—a functioning body of philosophers represented in Spain by no less an individual than Cervantes, in France by Cagliostro and St.-Germain, in Germany by Gichtel and Andreae, in England by Bacon, More, and Raleigh, and in America by Washington and Franklin. Coincident with the Baconian agitation in England, the *Fama Fraternitatis* and *Confessio Fraternitatis* appeared in Germany, both of these works being contributions to the establishment of a philosophic government upon the earth. One of the outstanding links between the Rosicrucian Mysteries of the Middle Ages and modern Masonry is Elias Ashmole, the historian of the Order of the Garter and the first Englishman to compile the alchemical writings of the English chemists.

The foregoing may seem to be a useless recital of inanities, but its purpose is to impress upon the reader's mind the philosophical and political situation in Europe at the time of the inception of the Masonic order. A philosophic clan, as it were, which had moved across the face of Europe under such names as the "Illuminati" and the "Rosicrucians," had undermined in a subtle manner the entire structure of regal and sacerdotal supremacy. The founders of Freemasonry were all men who were more or less identified with the progressive tendencies of their day. Mystics, philosophers, and alchemists were all bound together with a secret tie, and dedicated to the emancipation of humanity from ignorance and oppression.

In my researches among ancient books and manuscripts I have pieced together a little story of probabilities which has a direct bearing upon the subject. Long before the establishment of Freemasonry as a fraternity, a group of mystics founded in Europe what was called the "Society of Unknown Philosophers." Prominent among the profound thinkers who formed the membership of this society were the alchemists, who were engaged in transmuting the political and religious "base metal" of Europe into ethical and spiritual "gold"; the Cabalists, who as investigators of the superior orders of nature sought to discover a stable foundation for human government; and lastly the astrologers who, from a study of the procession of the heavenly bodies, hoped to find therein the rational archetype for all mundane procedure. Here and there is to be found a character who contacted this society. By some it is believed that both Martin Luther and that great mystic, Philipp Melanchthon, were connected with it. The first edition of the King James Bible, which was edited by Francis Bacon and prepared under Masonic supervision, bears more Mason's marks than the Cathedral of Strasbourg. The same is true respecting the Masonic symbolism found in the first English edition of Flavius Josephus' *The Antiquities of the Jews*.

For some time the Society of Unknown Philosophers moved extraneous to the church. Among the fathers of the church, however, were a great number of scholarly and intelligent men who were keenly interested in philosophy and ethics, prominent among them being the German Jesuit Athanasius Kircher, who is recognized as one of the great scholars of his day.

A Rosicrucian, and also a member of the Society of Unknown Philosophers as revealed by the cryptograms in his writings, Kircher was in harmony with the program of philosophic reconstruction. Since learning was largely limited to churchmen, the body of philosophers soon developed an overwhelming preponderance of ecclesiastics in its membership. The original antiecclesiastical ideals of the society were speedily reduced to an innocuous state, and the organization gradually became an actual auxiliary of the church. A small portion of the membership, however, maintained an aloofness from the literati of the faith, for it represented an unorthodox class—the alchemists, Rosicrucians, Cabalists, and magicians. This latter group accordingly retired from the outer body of the society that had come to be known as the "Order of the Golden and Rose Cross" and whose adepts were elevated to the dignity of Knights of the Golden Stone. Upon the withdrawal of these initiated adepts, a powerful clerical body remained which possessed considerable of the ancient lore but in many instances lacked the "keys" by which this symbolism could be interpreted. As this body continued to increase in temporal power, its philosophical power grew correspondingly less.

The smaller group of adepts that had withdrawn from the order apparently remained inactive, having retired to what they termed the "House of the Holy Spirit," where they were enveloped by certain "mists" impenetrable to the eyes of the profane. Among these reclusive adepts must be included such well-known Rosicrucians as Robert Fludd, Eugenius Philalethes, John Heydon, Michael Maier, and Henri Khunrath. These adepts in their retirement constituted a loosely organized society which, though lacking the solidarity of a definite fraternity, occasionally initiated a candidate and met annually at a specified place. It was the Comte de Chazal, an initiate of this order, who "raised" Dr. Sigismund Bacstrom while the latter was on the Isle of Mauritius. In due time the original members of the order passed on, after first entrusting their secrets to carefully chosen successors. In the meantime a group of men in England, under the leadership of such mystics as Ashmole and

Fludd, had resolved upon repopularizing the ancient learning and reclassifying philosophy in accordance with Bacon's plan for a world encyclopedia. These men had undertaken to reconstruct ancient Platonic and Gnostic mysticism, but were unable to attain their objective for lack of information. Elias Ashmole may have been a member of the European order of Rosicrucians, and as such evidently knew that in various parts of Europe there were isolated individuals who were in possession of the secret doctrine handed down in unbroken line from the ancient Greeks and Egyptians through Boethius, the early Christian Church, and the Arabians.

The efforts of the English group to contact such individuals were evidently successful. Several initiated Rosicrucians were brought from the mainland to England, where they remained for a considerable time designing the symbolism of Freemasonry and incorporating into the rituals of the order the same divine principles and philosophy that had formed the inner doctrine of all great secret societies from the time of the Eleusinia in Greece. In fact, the Eleusinian Mysteries themselves continued in the custody of the Arabians, as attested by the presence of Masonic symbols and figures upon early Mohammedan monuments. The adepts who were brought over from the Continent to sit in council with the English philosophers were initiates of the Arabian rites, and through them the Mysteries were ultimately returned to Christendom. Upon completion of the by-laws of the new fraternity the initiates retired again to Central Europe, leaving a group of disciples to develop the outer organization which was to function as a sort of screen to conceal the activities of the esoteric order.

Such, in brief, is the story which we are able to piece together from the fragmentary bits of evidence available. The whole structure of Freemasonry is founded upon the activities of this secret society of Central European adepts, whom the studious Mason will find to be the definite "link" between the modern craft and the ancient wisdom. The outer body of Masonic philosophy was merely the veil of this cabalistic order whose members were the custodians of the true arcanum. Does this inner and secret brotherhood of initiates still exist independent of the Freemasonic order? Evidence points to the fact that it does, for these august adepts are the actual preservers of those secret operative processes of the Greeks whereby the illumination and completion of the individual is effected. They are the veritable guardians of the "Lost Word" —the Keepers of the Inner Mystery—and the Mason who searches for and discovers them is rewarded beyond all mortal estimation.

In the preface to a book entitled *Long-Livers*, published in 1772, Eugenius Philalethes, the Rosicrucian initiate, thus addresses his Brethren of the Most Ancient and Most Honorable Fraternity of the Free Masons: "Remember that you are the Salt of the Earth, the Light of the World, and the Fire of the Universe. You are living Stones, built upon a Spiritual House, who believe and rely on the chief Lapis Angularis which the refractory and disobedient Builders disallowed. You are called from Darkness to Light; you are a chosen Generation, a royal Priesthood. This makes you, my dear Brethren, fit Companions for the greatest Kings; and no wonder, since the King of Kings hath condescended to make you so to himself, compared to whom the mightiest and most haughty Princess of the Earth are but as worms, and that not so much as we are all Sons of the same one Eternal Father, by whom all Things were made; but inasmuch as we do the Will of his and our Father which is in Heaven. You see now your high Dignity; you see what you are; act accordingly, and show yourselves (what you are) MEN, and walk worthy the high Profession to which you are called. * * * Remember, then, what the great End we all aim at is: Is it not to be happy *here* and *hereafter?* For they both depend on each other. The Seeds of that eternal Peace and Tranquillity and everlasting Repose must be sown in this Life; and he that would glorify and enjoy the Sovereign Good then must learn to do it now, and from contemplating the Creature gradually ascend to adore the Creator."

Of all obstacles to surmount in matters of rationality, the most difficult is that of prejudice. Even the casual observer must realize that the true wealth of Freemasonry lies in its mysticism. The average Masonic scholar is fundamentally opposed to a mystical interpretation of his symbols, for he shares the attitude of the modern mind in its general antipathy toward transcendentalism. A most significant fact, however, is that those Masons who have won signal honors for their contributions to the craft have been transcendentalists almost without exception. It is quite incredible that any initiated Brother, when presented with a copy of *Morals and Dogma* upon the conferment of his fourteenth degree, can read that volume and yet maintain that his order is not identical wth the Mystery schools of the first ages. Much of the writings of Albert Pike are extracted from the books of the French magician, Eliphas Levi, one of the greatest transcendentalists of modern times. Levi was an occultist, a metaphysician, a Platonic philosopher, who by the rituals of magic invoked even the spirit of Apollonius of Tyana, and yet Pike has inserted in his *Morals and Dogma* whole pages, and even chapters, practically verbatim. To Pike the following remarkable tribute was paid by Stirling Kerr, Jr., 33°, Deputy Inspector-General for the District of Columbia upon crowning with laurel the bust of Pike in the House of the Temple: "Pike was an oracle greater than that of Delphi. He was Truth's minister and priest. His victories were those of peace. Long may his memory live in the hearts of the Brethren." Affectionately termed "Albertus Magnus" by his admirers, Pike wrote of Hermetism and alchemy and hinted at the Mysteries of the Temple. Through his zeal and unflagging energy American Freemasonry was raised from comparative obscurity to become the most powerful organization in the land. Though Pike, a transcendental thinker, was the recipient of every honor that the Freemasonic bodies of the world could confer, the modern Mason is loath to admit that transcendentalism has any place in Freemasonry. This is an attitude filled with embarrassment and inconsistency, for whichever way the Mason turns he is confronted by these inescapable issues of philosophy and the Mysteries. Yet withal he dismisses the entire subject as being more or less a survival of primitive superstitions.

The Mason who would discover the *Lost Word* must remember that in the first ages every neophyte was a man of profound learning and unimpeachable character, who for the sake of wisdom and virtue had faced death unafraid and had triumphed over those limitations of the flesh which bind most mortals to the sphere of mediocrity. In those days the rituals were not put on by degree teams who handled candidates as though they were perishable commodities, but by priests deeply versed in the lore of their cults. Not one Freemason out of a thousand could have survived the initiations of the pagan rites, for the tests were given in those strenuous days when men were men and death the reward of failure. The neophyte of the Druid Mysteries was set adrift in a small boat to battle the stormy sea, and unless his knowledge of natural law enabled him to quell the storm as did Jesus upon the Sea of Galilee, he returned no more. In the Egyptian rites of Serapis it was required of the neophyte that he cross an unbridged chasm in the temple floor. In other words, if unable by magic to sustain himself in the air without visible support he fell headlong into a volcanic crevice, there to die of heat and suffocation. In one of the Mithraic rites the candidate seeking admission to the inner sanctuary was required to pass through a closed door by dematerialization. The philosopher who has authenticated the reality of ordeals such as these no longer entertains the popular error that the performance of "miracles" is confined solely to Biblical characters. "Do you still ask," writes Pike, "if it has its secrets and mysteries? It is certain that something in the Ancient Initiations was regarded as of immense value, by such Intellects as Herodotus, Plutarch and Cicero. The magicians of Egypt were able to imitate several of the miracles wrought by Moses; and the Science of the Hierophants of the Mysteries produced effects that to the Initiated seemed mysterious and supernatural." (See *Legenda* for the Twenty-eighth Degree.)

It is self-evident that he who passed successfully through these arduous tests involving both natural and also supernatural hazards was a man apart in his community. Such an initiate was deemed to be more than human, for he had achieved where countless ordinary mortals, having failed, had returned no more. Let us hear the words of Apuleius when admitted into the Temple of Isis, as recorded in *The Metamorphosis, or Golden Ass*: "Then also the priest, all the profane being removed, taking hold of me by the hand, brought me to the penetralia of the temple, clothed in a new linen garment. Perhaps, inquisitive reader, you will very anxiously ask me what was then said and done? I would tell you, if it could be lawfully told; you should know it, if it were lawful for you to hear it. But both ears and the tongue are guilty of rash curiosity. Nevertheless, I will not keep you in suspense with religious desire, nor torment you with long-continued anxiety. Hear, therefore, but believe what is true. *I approached to the confines of death, and having trod on the threshold of Proserpine, I returned from it, being carried through all the elements. At midnight I saw the sun shining with a splendid light; and I manifestly drew near to the Gods beneath, and the Gods above, and proximately adored them.* Behold, I have narrated to you things, of which, though heard, it is nevertheless necessary that you should be ignorant. I will, therefore, only relate that which may be enunciated to the understanding of the profane without a crime."

Kings and princes paid homage to the initiate—the "newborn" man, the favorite of the gods. The initiate had actually entered into the presence of the divine beings. He had "died" and been "raised" again into the radiant sphere of everlasting light. Seekers after wisdom journeyed across great continents to hear his words, and his sayings were treasured with the revelations of oracles. It was esteemed an honor to receive from such a one an inclination of the head, a kindly smile, or a gesture of approbation. Disciples gladly paid with their lives for the master's word of praise, and died of a broken heart at his rebuke. On one occasion Pythagoras became momentarily irritated because of the seeming stupidity of one of his students. The master's displeasure so preyed upon the mind of the humiliated youth that, drawing a knife from the folds of his garment, he committed suicide. So greatly moved was Pythagoras by the incident that never from that time on was he known to lose patience with any of his followers, regardless of the provocation.

With a smile of paternal indulgence the venerable master who senses the true dignity of the mystic tie, should gravely incline the minds of the brethren toward the sublimer issues of the craft. The officer who would serve his lodge most effectively must realize that he is of an order apart from other men; that he is the keeper of an awful secret; that the chair upon which he sits is the seat of immortals; and that if he would be a worthy successor to those master Masons of other ages his thoughts must be measured by the profundity of Pythagoras and the lucidity of Plato. Enthroned in the radiant East, the worshipful master is the "Light" of his lodge—the representative of the gods, one of that long line of hierophants who, through the blending of their rational powers with the reason of the ineffable, have been accepted into the great school. This high priest after an ancient order must realize that those before him are not merely a gathering of properly tested men, but the custodians of an eternal lore, the guardians of a sacred truth, the perpetuators of an ageless wisdom, the consecrated servants of a living God, the wardens of a supreme mystery.

A new day is dawning for Freemasonry. From the insufficiency of theology and the hopelessness of materialism, men are turning to seek the God of philosophy. In this new era wherein the old order of things is breaking down and the individual is rising triumphant above the monotony of the masses, there is much work to be accomplished. The "Temple Builder" is needed as never before. A great reconstruction period is at hand; the debris of a fallen culture must be cleared away; the old footings must be found again that a new Temple significant of a new revelation of law may be raised thereon.

This is the peculiar work of the builder; this is the high duty for which he was called out of the world; this is the noble enterprise for which he was "raised" and given the tools of his craft. By doing his part in the reorganization of society, the workman may earn his "wages" as all good Masons should. A new light is breaking in the East; a more glorious day is at hand. The rule of the philosophic elect—the dream of the ages—will yet be realized and is not far distant. To her loyal sons, Freemasonry sends this clarion call: "Arise ye, the day of labor is at hand; the great work awaits completion, and the days of man's life are few." Like the singing guildsman of bygone days, the craft of the builders marches victoriously down the broad avenues of time. Their song is of labor and glorious endeavor; their anthem is of toil and industry; they rejoice in their noble destiny, for they are builders of cities, the hewers of worlds, the master craftsmen of the universe.

THE PILLARS OF HERCULES

The city of the philosophic elect rises from the highest mountain peak of the earth, and here the gods of the wise dwell together in everlasting felicity. In the foreground are the symbolic pillars of Hercules which appear on the title page of Bacon's *Novum Organum*, and between them runs the path which leads upward from the uncertainties of earth to that perfect order which is established in the sphere of the enlightened.

CHAPTER TWENTY

THE GOAL OF PHILOSOPHY

TODAY is the hope of the world. Here and now we are welding that great chain of tomorrows which extends from the instant to infinity. We live not for ourselves alone but for all futurity. Our accomplishments survive us, for long after we have descended into the earth the orders which we have established shall dominate the activities of men. The world is an ancestral shrine filled with the mortuary tablets of the honored dead. We bow before our illustrious progenitors. We are the substance of their aspirations, the consummation of their dreams, for today is the focal point of time. We are all that has been about to be projected into all that shall be. Each human soul holds eternity in suspension. Recognizing this truth, several modern scientists have formulated the theory that immortality is achieved through a succession of lives—that the father achieves immortality in his son, the son in his progeny, and so on to the end of generation. The torch of life which each expiring personality hands on to another does not go out; it is immortal, but he who bears it must perish by the way. Men are but incidents in the flow of life, yet they have a strange power, for while they cannot cause the vital flame to blaze up from nothingness, they are empowered to snuff it out, and when generations cease the countless ages die together.

To be is to be immortal, for that which has been can never utterly cease. The past hovers in the air like a mirage. Men feel its presence; they breath it in, and enveloped by it live their little now. Upon the surface of their polished mirrors the ancient Magi caught faint visions of forgotten times. Within the next century we shall discover that history is written in the air; that so-called space itself is photographic, preserving as on a sensitized plate the varied activities of created things. Egypt as a physical empire has long since crumbled into dust, but upon each minute particle of the atmosphere the glory of ancient Egypt is preserved for all time. Men speak words, and their words seemingly vanish into nothingness, but in the living substances of the universe these selfsame words are traced in everlasting characters to be read in some distant time by men as yet unborn. Thoughts unuttered are not wholly lost, nor do dreams perish because their dreamer dares not give them speech. Somewhere in the infinite vistas of space, impressed as it were upon the memory of the infinite and sharing together a common immortality, all aspirations, all visions, and all deeds await the day when men with unfolding reason will bind all time into a common now.

In his experiments with plants the late Luther Burbank found substantiation for the scientific concept of immortality through progeny. The *doctrine of natural salvation,* as it is called, was demonstrated to Burbank through phenomena arising from the cross-pollination of plants. For example, Burbank pollinated a variety of plants bearing white flowers with another variety bearing colored flowers, and as a result secured blossoms which were wholly white, some wholly colored, and still others of mixed colors. Taking a white plant from this cross-pollination test, Burbank pollinated it with another white plant, the result being a number of new plants all white. Taking one of the latter, he again pollinated it with white, and the result was again white. This experiment was repeated ten times. In every case the flowers were entirely white, but the eleventh time several blossoms reverted to the original color of the plant, thereby proving that though latent for a considerable period the elements of the first cross-pollination survived to reappear again. The original colored shrub had died long before its activities reappeared among the white blossoms, but Burbank recognized in this phenomena the immortality of the colored flower which was reborn in its own progeny.

To Burbank man was but a human plant, and the great horticulturist solved the philosophic problem of his life by observing the habits of the growing things in his garden. If after the lapse of ten pollinations the identity of a distant progenitor was re-established, was it not reasonable to assume that men are born again to blossom forth in their descendants? Is not immortality the carrying forward of a primitive trace, and is not the urge which we feel within ourselves the voice of some ancestral impulse? For the physical thinker, to whom the invisible universe is simply a vast mechanism, and spirit an unnecessary hypothesis, there can be no immortality other than that which is carried in the seed. How small a germ man springs from, yet how much that germ contains; for in each wriggling sperm is the man with character, personality, and individuality. From so slight a beginning, what great issues come; for in the single tiny germ are contained not only the epitome of all the past, but also all the greatness that is to follow.

The philosopher takes issue with the scientist not as to the accuracy of the conclusion, but rather as to the field to which the conclusion is applied. A fact is a fact, but for the clarification it may often seem half a lie. Recognizing only the physical universe the savant limits all his premises to physical concerns, with the result that his discoveries are rendered of little value by false emphasis. If man were actually a body, physical immortality would be his hope and he would indeed survive in his progeny. But since man is not a physical body the laws controlling the body are powerless over the intangible essence which resides within its innermost parts. Indwelling spirit is not to be measured wholly by its outer form. Body has hands and feet, but spirit has no need of such appendages except when functioning in the physical world. Body has parts and dimensions, but spirit is impartible and dimensionless. Thus, while the laws of physical generation produce the actual phenomena so carefully classified by Burbank, it does not necessarily follow that spirit, which is not material, is dependent upon generation for its survival. It is obvious that spirit depends upon generation for its manifestation in form, but such manifestation is merely a phase in the condition of spirit.

Heredity is limited to the sphere of generation; it is of the accidents and not the essence in man. While men may inherit physical tendencies—even physical attitudes and, under some conditions, physical thoughts—this shell of personality is soulless until he animates it with his own immortal principle and gradually shapes it into an appropriate destiny. Heredity only controls such as are incapable of controlling themselves. Steeped in the vibration of its previous states, the stuff from which bodies are made comes to each incarnating soul. The life into whose vehicles it was formerly incorporated set the minute atoms whirling at a definite speed, and imprinted upon each of them its own purposes and characteristics. The child coming into the world must battle with these strange vibrations, reorganizing the substances of its body into individual vehicles by overcoming the motion of past agencies, and revibrating the electrons according to its own needs. The plant is a victim of circumstances to a far greater extent than is man. To escape its environment the plant must either die or trust to the unlikelihood of some gardener transplanting it to a more ideal habitat. Man, however, if his surroundings be incongenial, may move at will to an environment more propitious to his destiny.

The analogy may be projected into the invisible structures of both plants and men. The evolving plant life is still working through a vehicle too low in its organic quality to respond to the impulses of the inner agent. While man is empowered to resist the impulses of heredity as these incline his physical body in one direction or another, the plant must abide by the dictates of its formal part. The fallibility of the law of heredity has already been proved, and additional evidence of its inaccuracy will be accumulated as evolving man takes more of his destiny into his own hands and relies less upon the elements of chance and environment. As the stars impel yet do not compel, so man's hereditary impulses traced upon the fabric of his atomic nature urge him to follow in the old accustomed way. The self, however, declares otherwise, and one by one the impediments of heredity are overcome by the onward march of consciousness toward perfection.

Whereas science fights to maintain the dignity of form and the supremacy of matter throughout the universe, philosophy would establish the excellence of life and the rulership of all creation by its rational part. If we come to worship matter and elevate the physical universe to first place among the spheres, we can never hope to establish well-being in the nature of men, or fellowship among the nations of the earth. The premise of material supremacy is wholly destructive of the moral sense and reduces ethics to a superstition and aesthetics to an artist's vagaries. All that is beautiful is thus sacrificed in the defense of a premise, and the sovereign good is martyr to a notion. More cruel than Moloch is the God of the materialist, for he would feed whole nations into the maw of greed. To remedy a condition we must discover its cause. Man's boast of a godless age is his undoing, for he who destroys the concept of Deity destroys with it the sufficiency of his own internal nature. In his pride that he is now able to govern the universe unaided, the 20th-century thinker has given the divinities on high Olympus notice to gather up their belongings and depart. The gods have obliged him. Their thrones are empty; they have left for some other sphere where mortals are less vain. But man is still unhappy. His boasted knowledge has brought him doubt, doubt has brought terror, and terror has sapped away his strength. Afraid that his worst conclusions may yet be true, the materialist clings to his little ball of dirt, shuddering in anticipation of that day when he will be hurled therefrom into the abyss he himself has postulated. The heart of the thinker cannot accept the soulless universe that his mind has declared. How strangely fickle is the mind that from pure imaginings fashions a universal order, and then dissatisfied with the fabric it has spun convicts high heaven of manmade inconsistencies!

In his *New Atlantis*, a work unfinished, Sir Francis Bacon recites the virtues of an ideal philosophic empire. This empire, which he calls *Bensalem,* "the sons of peace, or of the ladder," is ruled over by a mysterious institution designated "Solomon's House." This "House" is an order of men united in the quest of universal realities. They are patrons of the arts and sciences, and investigators of nature's lore. The whole story is founded upon Plato's empire of Poseidon—the lost Atlantides, or the Isles of the Sea. One cannot read this account of the perfect state without marveling at the scope of Bacon's vision. Herein is set forth the substance of things hoped for and the prophecy of that which must inevitably come to pass in that time the gods decree to be opportune. Bacon claims America to be the lost Atlantis, adding that the Greeks were mistaken as to the sinking of the ancient continent, which was not actually submerged but rather temporarily inundated by tidal waves and freshets in the mountains. The inhabitants of the valleys were drowned, but the more savage peoples who roamed the tangled highlands escaped. In this manner culture was destroyed, and only savagery left to re-establish the orders of nations. In his *Holy Guide,* John Heydon reprints the *New Atlantis* as an alchemical allegory, definitely connecting the book with the Rosicrucian Mysteries and, through inference, with the symbols of Freemasonry. The discriminating Mason can hardly ignore the obvious fact that "Solomon's House" as described by Bacon is the temple of universal wisdom and education. Nor can he overlook "the several degrees of ascent, whereby men did climb up to the same, as if it had been a *scala coeli.*" In its philosophy the *New Atlantis* sets forth an ideal government of the earth. It foretells that day when in the midst of men there shall rise up a vast institution composed of the philosophic elect—an order of illumined men banded together for the purpose of investigating the laws of life and the mysteries of the universe. In this labor will be employed the ancient disciplines reconstructed and restated by Bacon in the *Novum Organum.*

Fate decrees that empires must fall and states vanish from the earth, for, erected upon and maintained by selfishness, these shall ultimately be destroyed by the internal dissension generated through selfishness. The age of boundaries is closing, and we are approaching a nobler era when nations shall be no more; when the lines of race and caste shall be wiped out; when the whole earth shall be under one order, one government, one administrative body. As Asgard rose amid the fertile plains of earth and as the Aesir guided the destinies of mortal creatures from their lofty thrones upon the snow-capped peaks, so upon the earth there shall arise a noble institution destined to lead humanity toward the condition of knowledge. A great city shall be established like the Holy City of ancient fable, which shall be the capitol of the world, the seat of all power, the hub of world administration. Here an exalted legislative body shall be convened which will mete out the justice of the wise and guide the unfoldment of the indigent many. From the seats of their authority the various heads of human undertaking will direct the destinies of all enterprise. Being in agreement with each other, these enlightened executives will move in accordance with the principles of harmony and compatibility. No longer will the various divisions of society oppress each other, for when all the parts work toward a common end the excellence of one over another is without consequence.

The time has not yet arrived when the average man is strong enough or wise enough to rule himself. Even when unfolding destiny greatly magnifies the accomplishments of the many, there will not come a day when the wisdom of the mass will be equal to the wisdom of its wisest few. As men's minds increase in capacity and establish newer and nobler codes of ethics and morals, there will still be the exceptional intellect that by divine Providence excels, and by virtue of such excellence demonstrates its fitness for honor and responsibility. By an exceptional intellect we do not mean an individual who through scheme or subterfuge steals glory from the impotent. Such thieves of prestige have a special substratum reserved for them in the realm of retribution. We refer to those illumined philosophers and mystics who, marching ahead of the body of the race, are the only ones actually fitted to directionalize human activities. Never will peace reign upon the earth until we are ruled by the fit; until he who possesses vision is permitted to see for the blind; until he who senses greatness is permitted to interpret its issues for those who are unresponsive to magnitudes. Men are truly free only when, governed by the wise, they are inclined gently toward the perfection of their own natures. Men are truly great only when, admitting the supremacy of the wise, they offer both life and chattel to the service of integrity.

Plato dreamed of that glorious day when the wranglings and contentions of mankind would cease; when people would turn from their petty tyranny to unite in a common destiny; when the needs of the many would be removed from exploitation by the few. He dreams in vain, however, who envisions a government *of* the people or *by* the people; but he is a seer indeed who can formulate the concept of a rational government *for* the people. That man is happy who can trust his lord; that state is fortunate whose prince is a philosopher. Humanity turns toward wisdom when the fruits of wisdom are apparent to it. Having once beheld the rewards of integrity, all men will move joyously toward that state of concord wherein dwell the wise, conserving their resources and fulfilling the destiny of rational souls. We must learn that wisdom is neither book-learning nor empty pedantry. The sham studiousness of the sophists was facetiously termed "eyeglass believing" by the medieval mystics.

Our present educational system would be fundamentally opposed to this philosophic program, because the school is the servant of utility and our standards of utility are lamentably insufficient. We teach men to bargain, barter, and connive; we are unsparing of both time and money in our effort to fit them into a "system" obviously impractical. Centuries must pass before the body of society will be sufficiently sickened of the vanities it supports to be inclined toward integrity. Eventually the day of awakening must come, for man cannot suffer indefinitely, and the saturation point of human endurance must sometime reach its limit. The unnecessary burden which we carry and have borne through uncounted ages will then be cast aside, and turning to truth we shall find liberation.

Polemics is not necessarily the abode of the wise, nor is much hairsplitting to be confused with erudition. The elevation of a man to high position does not *ipso facto* improve the quality of his nature or increase his capacity to receive. True elevation is opportunity, but the innate characteristics of the one promoted must determine the use to be made of that opportunity. To remove politicians from power and replace them with scientists or philosophers trained according to our present concepts would not necessarily solve our problem. The sages of Plato's vision are the truly wise—men initiated into the disciplines of the soul and deeply versed in the mysteries of life. In the senates of the philosophic elect, blocs of biologists would not combine to frustrate the legislation of the physicists, nor would astronomers hold out on technicalities against the geometricians. Savants would neither give a little of this for a little of that, nor arbitrate away the rights of men to prolong an ephemeral political prestige. Where the learned differ, it is evident there is no learning. In that city of the wise all the arts and sciences will complement each other, and the disciples of every branch of learning will mutually venerate each other's knowledge. Competition will cease, and co-operation will be reinstated as the true life of trade. The bartering of interests, the misappropriation of power, the malfeasance of office—all these are crimes possible only in a nonphilosophic age where the blind who follow are unable to discern the fallacies of the blind who lead.

For thousands of years a devotee to the fetish of competition, man has devastated that Edenic garden over which the Lord designed him to be the keeper. A poor gardener he has made! He has torn up all the flowering plants which lend beauty to the spot, that in their place he might grow weeds for a little profit. The highest expression of wisdom on the part of the many involves, first, appreciation for the still greater wisdom of the few, and secondly, the high-minded-ness to waive the rights of personal privilege that thereby the greatest good to the greatest number may be achieved.

Death is the invariable product of ignorance, but life is prolonged in conformity with intelligence. Heedless of our own destiny, in the vain struggle for possessions we often perish for lack of wisdom even as we reach out to grasp the substance of our desires. The plains of earth are broad, the resources of earth are incalculable, and on this globe there is ample to satisfy the needs of all. Through commerce and industry, through legitimate intercourse and exchange, and with reasonable effort man can enjoy those necessities which contribute to his well-being. Acceptance of the false principle of diversity, however, has been man's undoing, for the existence of contiguous states or nations has been the excuse for their exploitation.

Boundary lines were originally set up that they might later become diplomatic technicalities, for it was presupposed that an invading horde should some day sweep them away. Nations consequently prey upon nations according to their presumptions of necessity. Strong peoples absorb weaker peoples into themselves, thereby depriving some of that which is necessary that others may have more than enough. Oppression by the invader and retaliatory wars by the oppressed are the inevitable products of such encroachments. Fighting for what he conceives to be his inherent rights, the patriot is a martyr to vain standards and hopeless issues. He opposes ignorance with ignorance, and thus the sorrows of the ages are compounded. Man destroys man that man may live; life lives by killing; freedom is achieved by intolerance; and, if we are to believe the pronouncements of the foolish, peace is preserved by the sword. Where, may we ask, is the beginning or the end of this vicious circle which survives by destroying and also destroys by surviving?

Occasionally we find an individual of such innate perversity that he will actually cheat himself in material things. In matters pertaining to the spirit, however, dishonesty is quite the common order. In our foragings we generally descend

Assyrian-like upon the stranger, still reasoning with primitive caveman logic that that which is not already our own is legitimate prey. With the abolishment of political states and the unification of all peoples into one great nation, the misunderstanding directly due to national jealously and competition would be outlawed; for what people would be so foolish as to raise an army for the conquest of that which is already part of itself and co-operating for the sovereign good? Such a national attitude, when once established, would constitute a powerful moral deterrent to individual conduct. So far-reaching is the influence of our environment that in a comparatively short time the spirit of competition, as applied to individual concerns, would be broken, and men would build into the common pattern of public weal instead of striving to acquire a passing supremacy over the bodies of the dead. To be a wholesale killer is no longer the hallmark of greatness, for no strength is stronger than that which, withholding the hand, prevents violence; no courage more courageous than that which, facing the problems of each passing day, fights the battles of peace.

Upon first thought it may be difficult to visualize a world ruled by philosophy instead of politics. What is politics, however, but the philosophy of government? Is it not universal law applied to the government of men, and should not the one who is made a ruler over others be conversant also with those sidereal forces by which the order of creation is maintained? If a knowledge of cosmogony and universal law were a prerequisite to rulership, how many of our present governors would occupy their official chairs? Yet, for the regulation of human affairs, what pattern is more sublime than the harmony of the celestial spheres or the innate orderliness of crystal formation? *The science of mundane government has failed because it has ceased to be a science of government and has become a science of personal interests.* What is responsible for this perversion and misdirection of executive power? Simply the elevation of the unfit. We recall the words of that satirist who, philosophizing upon the effects of the French Revolution, declared that the reign of terror had taken the affairs of the state out of the hands of a despotic few and transferred them into the keeping of the unqualified many. Let us never forget the words of that great Jewish statesman, Disraeli, who said: "The world is weary of statesmen whom democracy has degraded into politicians." The theory of democracy is one of the noblest yet conceived by man. It is the aristocratic gesture of the proletarian. It fails, however, because at no time can man be more than himself; for man's government—like his God—perforce must be but a highly magnified reflection of himself. The true seat of government is in the home. In his *Apophthegms of Kings and Grand Commanders*, Plutarch describes a reformer who was discussing with Lycurgus the setting up of a democracy in Sparta. "Pray," retorted the Spartan lawgiver, "do you first set up a democracy in your own house?" Governments obviously cannot succeed where men fail, for we are the makers of government and our statutes unsparingly reflect both the depth and the shallowness of our own individual selves.

When the citizen is told to appoint a representative, he generally takes the advice too literally. If the leader resembles too faithfully his constituency he is unable to point out to his following any course of action which they could not have discovered by their own efforts. Hence, the interval of rationality should intervene between the governed and the governor. When this interval of superiority is insufficient, our vices and not our virtues become the rulers of the state. "Democracy," writes Lowell in the *Bigelow Papers*, "gives every man a right to be his own oppressor." Each faction of the people mistakenly assumes that its primal need is a representative who will interpret its whims and further its own particular ends at the expense of all other groups. Philosophy, however, corrects this attitude, declaring that the popular need is a virtuous mind strong enough to incline the populace toward a greater good. The spokesman of the masses seldom says anything, for the voice of the masses is the incoherent babble of many voices in which no single voice is intelligible. The political philosopher should be an idealist, not a realist. Not content with preserving things in their present state, he should desire to elevate them to the state of the ideal. Government is the science of leadership, the philosophy of administration, the art of reconciling the apparently irreconcilable viewpoints of the many. Of all the sciences, government demands the greatest measure of integrity. A position requiring a superlative quality of integrity and involving the widest sphere of influence should, by every rule of logic, be reserved for the wisest and best fitted. Only that man who is above personal interest is a safe politician, for the citizenry suffers when so-called public servants are the servants of their own desires.

Only when the world is ruled by its best balanced intellects can we expect it to be well-ruled. We have never had a sufficient number of illumined leaders to permit the smaller nations a proper and adequate form of government. Only by combining into a single people and choosing the wisest of men—regardless of race or creed—to directionalize the activities of the human race, can we approach that philosophic empire which Bacon, profoundly versed in the theory of government, advanced as the true solution of empire. When inferior intellects are chosen to administer governmental destinies, dissension is inevitable in the state. The true philosopher is the born ruler of men. Though now considered impractical because he lives in a world divorced from personal interest, in reality the philosopher dwells in the sphere of things-as-they-ought-to-be. Contemplating, as he does, the eternal verities of the universe, he is peculiarly fitted to ponder the affairs of government; for from such contemplation of eternal verities he has come to realize that if any institution is to endure it must be patterned after the enduring qualities of the universe. By incorporating universal truths into the social structure the philosopher effects the stabilization of society. The true ends of philosophy are not realized in the spinning of vain theories or fourth-dimensional woolgathering. Philosophy is the pondering of problems, the quest for solutions, the effort to organize life so that by conforming his life to the dictates of rationality man may come to enjoy the maximum of peace, efficiency, and individual completeness.

As each age comes into manifestation it brings with it a definite philosophic revelation designed to solve the problems peculiar to that age. These revelations are *keynotes of thought*, and by their aid we bridge the ethical intervals between generations. Racial systems of culture now dead are remembered chiefly for the words of power which they passed on to the civilizations that succeeded them. Through the tangled mystery of time we have wound our way, achieving according to the measure of our understanding. In philosophic history certain outstanding individuals have come to be regarded as the epitome of vast orders of learning. We regard these individualities as the formers and reformers of doctrines and orders of life. Thus, all the elements of Hindu Brahmanism are gathered into one colossal personality—Manu, the giver of the law. As the embodiment of Egyptian culture, Hermes founded the mysteries of statecraft, giving to the world the doctrines of universal order and procedure. In ancient Greece the half mythical Orpheus established the cult of beauty, teaching men the gospel of rhythm. Then to Asia came the strong voice of Buddha, calling men to the way of renunciation and the noble eightfold path. Again in Greece, while pondering the science of numbers, Pythagoras revealed God to the world as the Great Geometrician, bidding men enter upon the mathematical life. Then Socrates, the immortal proletarian, affirmed the necessary to be the greatest good, giving men the gospel of justice. In China, Confucius, the unapotheosized saint and utilitarian of the Celestial Empire, expounded the worship of the imminent and the service of the now. In Syria, Jesus, the Rabbi of the Essenes, preached the gospel of friendship, seeking to unite the diverse interests of mankind in the fellowship of the spirit. To Arabia, Mohammed, "the desired of all nations," holding high the sword of Islam, brought the philosophy of retribution and a righteous destiny. Modern religious and philosophic concepts thus comprise an intricate eclecticism, combining the reconcilable elements of these and various other revelations. The faith we live by is woven from many threads. We are the sons of the prophets of elder days, and half-heartedly we strive to keep the varied array of their commandments.

But, behold, the dawn of a new era is at hand! Humanity has elevated itself in temporal things far above all previous states of power. National strength has become so dominating as to require a code more ample, a revelation more specific. Ascendancy brings with it great responsibility, and the ethical structure of society must be rendered stable if integrity is to be preserved amid the temptations of pre-eminence. Never before has the lawgiver been faced with a problem involving humanity as a whole. Previous revelations have been addressed, for the most part, to single nations or "chosen peoples". The prophet of those days brought that which was necessary for the survival of his own clan and the well-being of that particular order of which he himself was a part. Thus, while each of these messages contains elements of truth that are imperishable, they are not wholly suitable to present needs. *For this age we must have a doctrine of synthesis, a code actuated and dominated by the spirit of unification.* The supreme need is to blend the diverse interests of men into a common purpose. The philosophy of this age must reveal the interdependence of the Chinaman and the Turk, the white man and the black, the great and the small. In other words, we have need of a common denominator, a fundamental premise upon which all will be agreed; for if we are to establish the government of the philosophic elect it must be erected upon the foundation of mutual understanding. Today we have one set of laws for men who live in the valleys, and another for those who dwell upon the hills. The diversified interests of a great populace require many representatives to interpret those needs at the seats of government; for the tiller of the soil is a stranger to the captain of industry, and the financier in the environment of his money world little senses those broad impulses animating the souls of poets and philosophers.

Humanity has grown to be so strong that it is now dangerous to allow its parts to remain disunited. No longer can we maintain our position of isolated individualism without endangering the rights of all men. The old truth that man cannot live by himself alone is still true. The ever-increasing strength of the individual confers upon him an ever-increasing capacity to injure, and unless the desire to hurt ceases within his own soul he is capable of infinite destructiveness. The same is true of nations on a grander scale. War has revealed the destructive potentialities resident in aggregations of people. Communities apparently benign and harmless can be metamorphosed over night into a death-dealing mechanism which, justifying its destructiveness, like the Macedonian phalanx from which it was derived can move across the face of the virgin earth and leave nothing but shattered hopes and smoldering ruins in its wake. This power to injure, inherent in human nature and now scientifically organized and trained to wreak the fullest measure of evil, is an impending menace against which the race must protect itself. The social structure is infected with the hereditary taint of war, and none is so wise that he can predict at just what point the plague will break out next. In such emergencies laws are impotent, preachments in vain, and moralizings futile; for intoxicated with the lust for power men will turn against all that they formerly held dear, and in the name of patriotism march ruthlessly to their own ultimate destruction. When they have loosed the dogs of war, men study Napoleon, not Socrates. When the blood-letting is over and men have turned from the gory altar of Ares, they seek solace not in Caesar's memoirs but in the words of Jesus or Buddha. But man's forethought always comes behind, for he keeps the power of devastation in his own name and invokes Deity only during the reconstruction periods. After the plenitude of destruction has been wrought, a repentant people like naughty children turn to their Eternal Parent for sympathy.

In those more placid moments when our emotions are at rest and the stagnant pools of our desires are left unstirred, we are indeed a noble race, striving for a heavenly crown! But when greed stirs up our bile we revert to a most barbarous and primitive type, eagerly trading our equity in a state of future bliss for a few square leagues of more substantial earth. From all of which it is apparent that as yet no spiritual revelation has come sufficiently strong to successfully withstand the inherent weakness of the flesh. The rewards promised for virtue are so distant and ephemeral that they do not tempt mere sordid men as do the instantaneous compensations which are apparently the rewards of perversion. Centuries must yet pass before the human soul will be sufficiently liberated from the involvements of the material nature to dominate and directionalize the activities of its objective nature. We have come to a day of intensive classifications, of vast industries and corporations, of factional organizations. Each individual is ambitiously striving to become a specialist in some department of the arts, sciences, or professions of living. Each one's goal is to attain a position of familiarity with his subject which will enable him to "corner" the field and exploit it to his own aggrandizement. It consequently follows that when men simply use each other as means to further their own selfish ends there must result an ever-decreasing bond of understanding between them, for their selfishness and divergence of interest inevitably segregates and eventually results in utter isolation. Like rays of light pouring from a radiant center, humanity today is traveling at an incalculable rate towards diversity, limited only by its innate capacity to diverge.

A new keynote must consequently be struck, a new word of power sounded, a new message brought which will warn men that in this mad dash toward diversity lies annihilation; that this senseless separateness of interests must ultimately result in a confusion of tongues and the obliteration of all effort. The highest message of yesterday was the message of friendship—an effort to unite men in a common cause. But friendship has proved insufficient as a remedy, for friendship is capable of perversion. The undeveloped man is a natural abuser of privileges and a perverter of issues. Friendship has become the chosen institution of rogues, and thus the power of evil has been strengthened; for when thugs fraternize the entire social order is at hazard. It has been demonstrated that the powers of evil, unable to lean upon the Infinite which was presumably against them, have developed the pernicious habit of depending upon themselves and each other, with the result that virtue is a disorganized and vice a well-regulated institution.

Friendship has failed, first, because men could not understand it and hence degraded it to a tool of interest; secondly, because to the average individual it is an artificial relation established in an effort to create a condition which did not naturally exist. Men have mouthed the word until it has become obnoxious and synonymous with the vagaries of a decadent faith. As yet we have not reached that point in our spiritual unfoldment where universal friendship is apparent to us. When you tell a man that friendship exists in nature and that God has decreed his creations to live together in amicable relations, he may point to the jungle law where every animal lurks behind a bush ready to devour the passerby. Or he may ask you to explain the earthquake or the storm, and the host of natural agencies which conceal their affinity for each other so successfully that only a theologian can hope to discover them.

The new message is the *gospel of identity*. It is not an effort to unite lives in a common interest, but a recognition of the fact that all forms are but manifestations of one indivisible agent. According to this concept there are no longer two who can be friends, but rather one that cannot be divided and in whom the sense of diversity is an illusion of form and not a reality of spirit. No longer must we conceive of that type of friendship in which several parts fraternize, and all too often patronize, but rather that indissoluble unity which is fundamental throughout the universe. To the wise, however, this is not one life working against another, but the parts of one life moving upon each other. Cataclysms possibly evidence a magnified form of those same inconsistencies which man manifests when he deliberately injures some part of his own body for the gratificaton of a whim. The *gospel of identity* is not one that can be thundered from the pulpits, preached from the housetops or harangued in the marketplace. It is something that must come to be realized, that must be felt within the nature itself. It is that fundamental unity of each with all; that power which discovers all things within the Self and the Self within all things. The gospel of tomorrow will be a gospel of one being. No longer will a million universes or billions of half-formed creatures struggle out the destiny of worms; no longer will there be a seemingly endless, crawling, seething mass of minute lives, for out of his Tushito heaven has come the Lord of Tomorrow, the Sovereign of Eternity, whose doctrine is that of *identity*. The star and the gnat will be united, suspended as it were from a single monad—one in essence, though several in aspect. No longer will there be the great and the small, but one spirit moving inevitably toward itself. No longer will there be a great order of evolving lives, but rather one ideating whole; an expression moving from itself outward to the inclusion of all.

Today we live in an involuting civilization, a civilization of separateness, a world dedicated to the concept of struggling with the parts of itself, a world obsessed with the illusion that the self has parts. We must overcome the belief that Self can rise up against its own nature, or that spirit is fragmentary; for that one man should compete with another is as senseless as that the fingers should fight the hands to which they are attached, or dissent from each other as to their individual supremacy. From the condition of primitive isolation man has raised himself through successive revelations to a limited capacity to understand the issues of life. A few broad-minded, far-seeing individuals have recognized the fundamental equality of life, and have issued an emancipation proclamation declaring all creatures by right of their divine origin to be entitled to a place in the sun. From equality it is but a logical step to identity. So the enlightened man who has been elevated to that point where, when he meets another man, he says, "You are my friend," will tomorrow meet that same man and say, "You are myself." No longer will complicated codes be necessary to administer human affairs when each man's interest becomes the interest of all the rest and each man's needs the needs of all. Laws are largely established to govern relationships, but when all relationships are done away with, laws will pass with them; for the one is always itself, and the intervals for which theoretical relationships are remedial agencies cannot exist in a united body.

An intellectual concept of the *gospel of identity* is not sufficient. In fact, intellectualism is the trap by which most minds are ensnared. A fact is not established by the intellect, but by a deeper power which we like to term *realization*. Hence the truth of identity is demonstrated by the realization of identity. Never will we have true equality until we realize that equality is based upon identity, for that which is Self is equal to Self, and upon the appreciation of this fact democracy is established. Democracy is not the condescending, patronizing attitude of the politician, nor is it the system whereby a hundred million folk of uncertain mind are empowered to elect one from their number as their leader. Democracy is the realization of the unity of life, and this realization shatters forever the competitive standard of civilization which is based upon the erroneous assumption that one part of life can survive without or at the expense of another. Competition was founded upon the dualistic theory—an ancient anthropomorphism in which two spirits wage an endless fight for supremacy. So wherever two individuals, institutions, or nations conceive a separate origin or a separate destiny, we have the boast that one will be holier than the other. As long as we conceive of separateness in origin and ultimate there will be grounds for competition, and upon the basis of competition is erected the whole structure of human sorrow.

We have an age, therefore, in which the parts struggle with each other, a world that thinks it has accomplished greatly when it picks its right pocket to fill its left pocket. Diversity is simply the manifestation of those potentialities that are ever within the substance of unity. The universe is simply the objectification of a single causal agent. This does not imply that all things are alike, but rather that while they may differ in nonessentials (as, for example, external composition), they are composed of the same agencies and essences. The *gospel of identity* includes the theory of difference, not difference from the standpoint of inequality but from the standpoint of condition. The philosopher does not infer that a gnat is a star, but that in their essential natures each is the manifestation of a common life, and that whatever may occur to one is registered in the single life principle that agitates them both. We have a civilization in which each part is attempting to include the whole within itself. Man as an individual dreams of the day when he can dominate men as a mass, failing to realize that such dominance is in appearance only, and that the individual can never be more than he is—one of the many. Through consciousness he may elevate himself to the point where he and the many are one, but having achieved this exalted goal he ceases to be himself and becomes the many—thinking in the terms of the many and serving the ends of the many. The *gospel of identity* shows man his true greatness; namely, that he possesses the power to interpret the whole and can actually come to realize his kinship with all. Through such realization he achieves philosophic liberation. He who escapes from the littleness which is his not-self, into the vastness which is his real Self, achieves greatly and serves the sovereign good.

There is but one cure for selfishness; namely, to realize that nothing can be added to us and nothing taken from us—that we are what we are and have what we have. We may temporarily possess a certain measure of opulence, but unless it is our own it will depart from us again. Yet in departing it is not gone, for that which is the possession of any one is ultimately the possession of all. What use, then, can there be for selfishness when he who believes that he takes from another really takes from himself? And why should not a man be generous when that which he gives to another he gives to himself? In philosophy there is consequently neither giver nor receiver, in that the gift, the giver, and the receiver are one. The spirit in man is not merely a life enclosed within a frame. Man is really a frame enclosed within a spirit. The thing in you that says "I am" is identical with the thing in me that says "I am." Then why should we not unite in common purpose? Why should we struggle for a little outer glory and battle with shadows in the service of our greeds? If he so desires, each individual by receding into his own divine nature may discover within himself the divine nature of all creatures. He may even become every other creature, for that part of himself which is real is every other creature.

In the annihilation of the sense of separateness we annihilate both life and death, for when we identify ourselves with the one life moving through all things how can we end? As long as there is life we are that life; as long as a single star twinkles in the heavens we are that star; as long as a single blade of grass grows we are that blade of grass. We are not of the same race as those hands and feet which we have so long identified with ourselves; we are not that driveling creature, clutching at power—that mad thing of destruction which tears and rends in childish rage and harbors revenge within its heart. When we have recognized the universality of spirit we are one with the very fabric of life, and are no longer tortured with fears and premonitons. In our folly we have tried to be petty despots and establish empires of our own. We have desired the gold braid and tinsel of princes, and are peevish when someone takes away our principality. Let us turn from our petty despotism to behold that greater glory which is our natural right; for we are citizens of eternity; we are that very life that in the beginning moved upon the face of the deep; we are that shining power that walked in the garden with the Lord; we are the seraphim and the cherubim and the choirs of the ineffable. We are not gods—we are God exiled for a little while into the forgetfulness of ourselves, yet soon to awaken to the full measure of our splendor.

O slumbering life, awake from your dreams of manyness and soar into the free air of concord. Turn from the wheels that you have set spinning in the building of an ephemeral empire. Depart from the unsubstantialness which you have come to love too well, and lift your eyes to the contemplation of a nobler state. You have given so much for a little power. You have become so weary in your fruitless quest of gain. The world asks so much for the little it can give, and that semblance of happiness which oppression has given you is so shallow and devoid of peace. Philosophy summons you to a greater calling, a more noble profession, a more excellent destiny. The sages of old would welcome you into the brotherhood of the elect, into the true ranks of the immortals where life flows on in broad full sweep throughout all eternity. Leave the half-built world which crumbles even as you raise its structures, for the Great Mother already has shaken countless civilizations from off her back. The very dust beneath our feet cries out with desire unfulfilled, for it is the powdered substance of ambition. Only in truth is there sufficiency, only in reality is there power. The unity of life is man's great truth upon which foundation he may build the empire of his soul. He is rich who is rich in truth; he is poor who is poor in truth. All else is of little moment. We are immortal, and that our soul tomorrow may be in peace let us rebuild our civilization. Let us establish our government of realities, our commonwealth of the wise. We as citizens of today are also the citizens of tomorrow. We are the life that shall throb in the communities yet to come; we are the voice that shall speak in the senates of an unborn day. To that great life which is our true Self, to that tomorrow which to us must ever be the now, let us dedicate our inner selves and the achievements of our external natures.

INDEX

	PAGE
Absolute (See also SPACE)	
Absolute, absorption into	93
Absolute, analogy of to sleep and death	35
Absolute, definition of by affirmation and negation	255
Absolute, generation of gods and worlds out of	34
Absolute impossible to define	1
Absolute only definable from negative point of view	5
Absolute related to Time by Orphics	220
Absolute symbolized by blank sheet of paper	1
Actions, building of bodies from	398
Activity postulated as a fundamental attribute of Being	25
Activity the distinguishing property of spirit	12
Adam the monad of mankind	220
Addition, philosophically always 1, or wholeness	247
Adversary, Eternal, symbolized by form	74-75
Aesthetics (See also Beauty)	
Aesthetics a philosophical discipline	166 - 173 - 181
Aesthetics a stimulus to rationality	322
Aesthetics considered indispensable by Pythagoreans to acquisition of knowledge	320
Aesthetics indispensable to true interpretation of arts and sciences	325
Aesthetics, mysteries of Intermediate Sphere revealed by	123
Aesthetics, secret of Greek supremacy in	172
Aesthetics reduced to vagary by premise of supremacy of matter	461
Aesthetics, the basis of	169
Aether and Chaos the first manifestations of primordial activity	220
Affirmation, employment of to define Absolute	255
Affirmation, futility of	104 - 143
Affirmation philosophically unsound	268
Ages, method of calculating time by	228
AIN SOPH equivalent to Absolute	5
AIN SOPH symbolic of the nature of God	32
Air the symbol of rationality	285
Airs, the two principles of generation in Chinese cosmogony	233
Alchemists, activities of in political and religious reformation of mediaeval Europe	447

INDEX

	PAGE
Allegories, why interpretations concerning were circulated by the Mysteries	347
Alphabet of Wisdom is symbolism	9
Amaterasu Omikami, symbolism of in Shinto Mysteries	424
Ambrosia, symbolism of	198
America identified with lost Atlantis by Bacon	462
Analogy, employment of in interpreting symbolism	354
Analogy, law of, importance of	35
Andreae one of the early champions of the ideals of democracy	446
Animal soul the basis of Freud's sex psychology	342
Anthropomorphic God swayed by caprice	152
Anthropos identical with the Archetypal Man	295
Anthropos the non-incarnating part of Divinity	17
Appreciation a fundamental factor in acquisition of wisdom	332
Appreciation, redeeming properties of	166
Apuleius' account of his initiation into the Temple of Isis	453
Ark of Israel a copy of Isaic ark in Temple of Philae	439
Art, true end of	172
Arts, decline of with invention of writing	370
Asceticism a fundamental tenet of early Christianity	145
Ashmole, Elias, one of the outstanding links between the Mysteries and modern Masonry	446
Ashmole, Elias, Rosicrucian affiliations of	449
Aspiration symbolized by upright pyramid	282
Astral light, illusions of	19
Astrologers, activities of in political and religious reformation of medieval Europe	447
Astronomy, analogy of to the circle of fundamental symbolic triad	123
Astronomy, esoteric principles of confused with exoteric by Greeks	245
Astronomy, knowledge of a requisite for admission to Pythagorean school	122
Astronomy, magnitude of Reality established by	126
Atheism, philosophic, the basis of Greek philosophy	218
Atlantis identified with America by Bacon	462
Atomic theory the outgrowth of monadology	245
Atoms, *quality of wholeness* common to	240
Atoms the archetypal unities of wholeness	245
Atonement, vicarious, based upon precedency of love over law	151
Atonement, vicarious, doctrine of the most vicious of all superstitions	149
Atonement, vicarious, evils of doctrine of	149
Atonement, vicarious, source of in pagan philosophy	154
Attitudes, mental, creation of by mental environment	378
Auric egg isolates man from universe	286

	PAGE
Austerity a fundamental tenet of early Christianity	146
Austerity, futility of to liberate the soul	265
Autocracy as exemplified in the government of the human organism	176
Autocracy, expression of in national life	177
Bacchus the last of the heavenly line	223
Bacon (Sir Francis) the organizer of democratic ideals in mediaeval Europe	444
Bacon (Sir Francis) the third great mind since Plato	444
Bacon's (Sir Francis) *Novum Organum Scientiarum* a vision of reformation of knowledge	444
Bacon's (Sir Francis) vision of ideal philosophic empire	461
Bacstrom (Dr. Sigismund), Rosicrucian affiliations of	448
Beans, arcane meaning of Pythagoras' injunction against	429
Beanstalk, symbolism of	428
Beautiful, the, a fitting element of veneration	363
Beautiful the distinguishing attribute of all the Savior-Gods	74
Beautiful, the, part of the great Platonic triad	75
Beauty (See also Aesthetics)	
Beauty a natural attribute of spiritual nature	181
Beauty contributes greatness and endurance to civilization	190
Beauty, cult of represented by Orpheus	470
Beauty, definition of	74
Beauty, ennobling influence of	369
Beauty, redeeming power of	74, 165
Beauty, dependency of upon virtue and utility	174
Beauty, evolution of dependent upon power of observation and sense of proportion	170
Beauty, order of, according to Plotinus	179
Beauty, spirit of worship	365
Beauty, standards of vary with evolutionary status of races and individuals	169
Beauty, steps taken by Greeks to perpetuate ideals of	188
Beauty the molding factor in racial and national life	175
Beauty the deadly enemy of every excess	191
Beauty the predominant factor in ceremonial	365
Bees, symbolism of	197
Being, activity postulated as a fundamental attribute of	25
Being one of seven grand divisions of existence, according to Neoplatonists	219
Belief as a factor in salvation	162
Belief, effectiveness of emphasized by St. Paul	155
Belief, stimulation of rational soul through	163
Bias as a philosophical factor	130, 133

INDEX 483

PAGE

Bible, Mason's marks in King James edition 447
Biological salvation, significance of 401
Birth, first, meaning of 88
Birth, lower universe ruled by 20
Birth, second, meaning of 88, 90,
Birth, why considered illusionary 203
Blavatsky's statement concerning return of libreated soul 410
Boar incarnation of Brahma 228
Bodhisattvas, images of representatives of the ways of perfection . . 99, 113
Bodies, building of from actions 399
Body one of seven grand divisions of existence, according
    to Neoplatonists 219
Body one of three major elements in occult constitution of man 391
Body primarily a spirit 386
Body symbolized by the elements 417
Body, trinity of 14
Brahma, boar incarnation of 228
Brahma, day of, method of calculating 228
Brahma the creative aspect of Brahmanic triad 225
Brahmin theology, analogies in Orphic theology 225
Brahminism, elements of embodied in Manu 470
Buddha, image of representative of perfection 98
Buddha, way of renunciation taught by 470
Burbank's experiments with cross-pollination of plants 459

Cabalists, activities of in political and religious reformation of
    medieval Europe 447
Cabirian Rite, rational Knower represented by
    diminutive figure in .... 392 - 444
Cagliostro, connection of with Freemasonry .... 435 - 441
Cagliostro founder of Egyptian Rite of Freemasonry 444
Cagliostro one of early champions of ideals of democracy 446
Cancer the gate of physical birth 198
Caprice characteristics of the anthropomorphic God 152
Capricorn the gate of physical death 198
Caricature, difference between and symbolism 338
Carp an emblem of the soul 69
Carp, ceremony of flying in Japan 69
Cause, First (See also SPACE) ....
Cause, First, neither positive nor negative 25
Cause, First, power in absolute suspension 25
Cause synonymous with Unity 245
Cavern, symbolism of gates into and out of 198
Caves ancient symbols of the world 196

	PAGE
Caves, significance of initiation in	196
Ceremonial, beauty the predominant factor in	365
Ceremonialism, purpose of to create atmosphere of sanctity	368
Ceremonials of Mysteries first fabricated to reveal principles of universal order	374
Cervantes one of early champions of ideals of democracy	449
Change, fallacy of growth by change	344
Change the law of matter	248
Chaos and aether the first manifestations of primordial activity	220
Chaos, significance of in Chinese cosmogony	233
Character, how determined	77
Character not to be remodeled through despotism of will	265
Character regenerated through reformation of impulse	266
Chazal, Comte de, Rosicrucian affiliations of	448
Chinese system of cosmogony	233
Christ (Christos) numerical value of	161
Christ the personification of qualities of the rational soul	161
Christianity, austerity a fundamental tenet of the early church	145
Christianity eclectic in its philosophy	147
Christianity, pagan source of its doctrines	147
Christianity, strength of in conquest of death	199
Christianity, theory of redemption unique	145
Christendom, survival of	149
Circle symbolic of end	5
Circle symbolic of government by people	83
Circle symbolic of hell	11
Circle symbolic of science	8
Circle symbolic of universal force	6
Civilization, greatness and endurance of conferred by beauty	191
Civilization, influence of environment upon	190
Civilization, internal weakness of structure of	183
Classic of Change, exposition of Chinese cosmogony in	230
Clothing the outgrowth of desire for ornamentation	171
Cold symbolic of circumference of sphere of Being	80
Cold symbolic of stupefying effect of form	79
Collegia a branch of the Dionysians	437
Collegia one of the sources of secret doctrine of Freemasonry	437
Compensation, Law of (See Karma)	
Competition founded upon dualistic theory of separateness in origin and ultimate	476
Competition outlawed by unification of all peoples	467
Completion, individual, the realization of identity with the archetypal pattern	431
Complexity as an element of beauty	171

INDEX 485

	PAGE
Concentration a prerequisite of knowledge	128
Concentration, definition of	136
Concentration, environment most suitable for	139
Confucius, worship of the imminent expounded by	470
Conscience identified by Plato with natal daemon	290
Conscience, source of in the soul	300
Consciousness, difference of in gods and man	276
Consciousness, diffussion of throughout illusionary universe	102
Consciousness distinguished from emotion	65
Consciousness distinguished from intellect	65 - 70
Consciousness, Eastern and Western viewpoints contrasted	97
Consciousness, esoteric significance of	97
Consciousness, evolution of, how measured	253
Consciousness, extension of represented by Ptolemaic system of astronomy	102 - 105
Consciousness, extensions and modes of represented by idols	98
Consciousness, indivisibility of	86
Consciousness, planes of form order of the gods	97
Consciousness, projection of the goal of human effort	92
Consciousness, recognition of in lower kingdoms	112
Consciousness, refinement of vehicles of	51
Consciousness, states of represented by hand postures	100
Consciousness, tendency of to expand	51
Consciousness the union with Self	64
Consciousness, three states of	207
Consciousness, universal, symbolized by dot	6
Consistency a factor in true growth	344
Continuity a factor in true growth	344
Contraction the natural tendency of matter	50
Conversion, true, meaning of	104
Co-operation the true life of trade	465
Cosmic Egg formed by action of Aether upon Chaos	220
Cosmogonies, pagan and Christian contrasted	230
Cosmogony, parallels between Brahmin and Chinese systems of	233
Cosmogony, parallels between Greek and Chinese systems of	233
Creation, Chinese concept of	233
Creation, duration of, according to Brahmins	228
Creation is motion away from self	4
Creation, Orphic concept of	220
Creation, pagan and Christian concepts contrasted	230
Creation, Vedic concept of	224
Creations, duration of measured by Kalpas	234
Crime, esoteric significance of related to consciousness	98
Crime the outgrowth of environment	188

486   LECTURES ON ANCIENT PHILOSOPHY

	PAGE
Cronus, establishment of Material Universe by	223
Cronus, rebellion of against Heaven	223
Cronus, symbolism of in initiation of C. R. C.	420
Cupid, allegory of sets forth mystery of the soul	302
Cupid, dual nature of love symbolized by	308
Cycle of Necessity, meaning of	199
Cycle of Necessity, release from	204
Cyclops identified with natal daemon	292
Daemon, essential, identical with Father-Star	292
Daemon, essential, relation of to heroes	292
Daemon, natal, identified with conscience	296
Daemon, natal, identified with Cyclops	292
Daemon, natal, identified with self-will	292
Daemon, natal, is consciousness born of experience	295
Daemon, natal, of the individual	290
Daemon, natal, represented by spirit of the six	291
Daemon, natal, synonymous with instinct	289
Daemon, natal, the blossoming of soul qualities	290
Daemons analogous to the elemental spirits	293
Daemons, distinction between natal and essential	292
Daemons, philosophy of an outgrowth of veneration for rationality universally manifest	292
Daemons, production of through combinations of forces, substances or circumstances	293
Dancing an important element in ancient ritualism	370
Dancing, decline of with invention of writing	370
Dancing employed in initiatory rites of the Mysteries	371
Dancing the harmony and rhythm of motion	370
Death, analogy of to Absolute	35
Death and life administered by the soul	388
Death, concept of annihilation through gospel of identity	478
Death, conquest of the power of Buddhism and Christianity	199
Death, difference between natural and violent, according to Plotinus	388
Death, effect of upon life and form	194
Death, natural, that in which soul casts off body	388
Death, philosophic, meaning of	88 - 90
Death, philosophic, complete severance of soul from its bodies	389
Death, second, the death of the soul	391
Death, why considered illusionary	203
Decad symbolic of tenfold order of the universe	415
Decay, lower universe ruled by	20
Deductive reasoning, purpose of to establish consciousness at point of equilibrium	274
Degeneracy the outgrowth of environment	188
Deity (See also God)	

	PAGE
Deity envisioned as *in*human rather than *super*human	363
Deity, procession of deified natures from, according to doctrine of unities	217
Deity, Supreme, of philosophy the Principle of principles	218
Demigods the instructors of humanity	57
Demigods not personalities	59
Demiurgus, elevation of to chief place among the gods	158
Demiurgus likened to ogre in allegory of Jack in the beanstalk	428
Demiurgus, primitive concept of as part God, part demon	158
Demiurgus related to Pwan-koo	234
Demiurgus the Lord of Form	21
Democracy a realization of the unity of life	476
Democracy, fallacy of	464
Democracy, genesis of ideals of in Europe	442
Democracy, ideals of related to Masonic order	442
Democracy one of the noblest theories conceived by man	468
Denial philosophically unsound	268
Descent of soul into the sphere of generation	409
Destiny ordered by Providence	429
Development, individual, how measured	89
Dialectics, refining effect of upon rational faculties	322
Dionysiac artificers one of the sources of the secret doctrines of Freemasonry	437
Dionysians, building of all ancient public buildings entrusted to	437
Dionysians the builders of Solomon's Temple	437
Discrimination a prerequisite of knowledge	128
Discrimination, attributes of	138
Discrimination equilibrates mental faculties	136
Discrimination, function of	132 - 136
Discrimination the faculty by which things are organized in value sequence	132
Discrimination, three form of	132
Discrimination to be applied with impersonal attitude	134
Diversity a property of Numbers	249
Diversity, illusion of dispelled only by realization	105 - 118
Diversity, illusions of called Maya	6
Diversity of manifestation not due to separate spiritual agencies	103
Diversity, recognition of principle of man's undoing	466
Diversity synonymous with effect	245
Divine qualities transmitted to inferior natures through sympathy and participation	281
Divinity, capacity for the Universal Savior in man	167
Divinity, similars exemplified by	286
Division, philosophic, the quotient always 1, or wholeness	244

	PAGE
Dot, line, and circle the supreme of primary symbols	4
Dot representative of self	4
Dot representative of the One in Platonic philosophy	73
Dot represents spirit in man	6
Dot symbolic of cause	5
Dot symbolic of government by state	83
Dot symbolic of heaven	11
Dot symbolic of philosophy	7
Dot symbolic of universal consciousness	6
Dot the symbol of the ALL considered as the One	2
Dramatic situations employed by Pythagoras for purposes of instruction	375
Dream symbols of Freud, analysis of	342
Duad likened to science	260
Dying-god mythos, esoteric interpretation of	63
Dying-god mythos, exoteric interpretation of	61
Dying-god the motif of many allegories	62
Earth born of Night and Phanes in Orphic theology	222
Earth called the Great Mother in Chinese cosmogony	233
Earth, Chinese concept of creation of	233
Earth, illusionary existence of	200
Earth, pagan and Christian concepts contrasted	230
Earth related to the phenomenon of Kant	223
Earth symbolized by the line	11
Earth the plane of the material nature of God	11
Eclecticism characteristic of modern religions	470
Eclecticism contributory to shallowness of thought	346
Education, ancient and modern systems contrasted	327
Education, enslavement of the intellect by	329
Education, modern, abortive effects of	323
Education, modern, deficiency of	327
Education, modern, interpretation a preponderant factor in	325
Education, Pope's excoriation of	329
Education, present-day, why inadequate	332
Education, spiritual, Hermes' elucidation of	332
Education, symbolism the perfect medium of	339 - 341
Education the discipline of appreciation	332
Education, true office of the drawing out of inner potentialities	334
Education, utilitarian standard of	464
Educator, true, must be an idealist	325
Effect synonymous with diversity	244
Egg, Orphic, formed by action of aether upon Chaos	221
Ego, incarnating, represented by Jupiter	17
Egyptian Rite of Freemasonry founded by Cagliostro	445

	PAGE
"Electric head," depiction of in Samothracian Mysteries	321
Electricity, employment of in Greek Mysteries	321
Electrum, remedial properties of	356
Elemental spirits analogous to daemons	293
Elements symbols of body	417
Emanationism (See also Monads)	
Emanationism, principle of unfolded in Orphic theogony	218
Emanationism the basic doctrine of Greek theology	217
Emanationism the vital doctrine of the Gnostics	218
Emerson's definition of the Oversoul	294
Emotion distinguished from consciousness	65
Emotion symbolized by water	19
Emotions, building of bodies from	398
Emptiness, philosophical concept of	39
Environment, creation of mental attitudes by	378
Environment, effect of upon crime and degeneracy	188
Environment, effect of upon man and the plant contrasted	460
Environment, how determined	50
Environment, influence of upon civilization	189
Environment, influence of	338 - 341
Equilibrium, application of philosophic principle to consciousness	257
Equilibrium, principle of exploited in Judo	258
Equilibrium represents the perfection of endurance	257
Esoteric knowledge a knowledge of inherent nature of knowledge	314 - 316
Esoteric knowledge limited to issues of philosophy and religion	314
Esoteric knowledge relates to that which is unknowable in terms of mortal intellect	316
Ethics, corruption of responsible for decadence of pagandom	326
Ethics indispensable to true interpretation of arts and sciences	325
Ethics reduced to a superstition by premise of supremacy of matter	461
Evil, intrinsic nature of	255
Evolution, definition of	78
Evolution is activity inward toward self	4
Evolution of the soul out of sphere of generation	411
Evolution the fitting of each nature into its own archetype	431
Evolution the inclination of the rational soul toward unity	268
Exactness a prerequisite of philosophy of salvation	123
Existence, seven grand divisions of, according to Neoplatonism	219
Excess, beauty the deadly enemy of	191
Exoteric knowledge includes all knowledge discoverable to the physical mind	316
Exoteric knowledge the knowledge of particulars	314
Expansion the natural tendency of spirit	51

	PAGE
Faith as a factor in salvation	162
Faith, stimulation of rational soul through	164
Fall of man the descent of soul into Cycle of Necessity	207
Familiar (See Daemon)	
Fates the personification of the three hypothetical intervals of Time	247
Father, Great, synonymous with Heaven in Chinese Cosmogony	233
Father-Star identical with essential daemon	292
Feeling, sublimation of effected by music	323
Feminine, why considered predominant attribute of Deity	31
Fire the symbol of the threefold God	49
Flail symbolic of authority of Demiurgus	82
Flame, analogy of threefold constitution to the Trinity	49
Flamen Majores analogous to three Grand Masters of Lodge of Jerusalem	392
Flamen Minores analogous to twelve Holy Animals which form physical body of man	392
Flamines analogous to three monads of spiritual wholeness	392
Fludd, Robert, Rosicrucian affiliations of	440
Force, universal, symbolized by circle	4
Form (See also Matter)	
Form an inferior life inhibiting a superior life	75
Form and life, manner of association of	194
Form called Shiva	75
Form called Typhon	75
Form, characteristics of	194
Form considered necessary by science for conveyance of thoughts	318
Form, definition of	75
Form, inertia the characteristic attribute of	76
Form, life restored to perfect wholeness through destruction of	248
Form, manifestation of a phase in condition of spirit	460
Form not limited to physical bodies	74
Form not synonymous with matter	7
Form one of the illusions of diversity	6
Form, permanence of contrasted with space	39
Form, quality of measured by quantity of monadic parts	262
Form, ramifications of	75
Form, stupefying effect of symbolized by cold	79
Form symbolized by skeleton	75
Form termed the Eternal Adversary	74 - 75
Form the effect of consciousness working upon matter	7
Form the graveyard of consciousness	75
Form the objectification of the formless monadic physical principle	385
Forms related to numbers by the Pythagoreans	259

INDEX

	PAGE
Forms the sense of wholeness superimposed upon parts by the rational soul	262
Fortune, element of in destiny	429
Fourth Dimension, relation of to the qualitative interval	250
Franklin, Benjamin, one of the early champions of the ideals of democracy	447
Franz Joseph of Transylvania one of the early champions of the ideals of democracy	444
Freedom the goal of all life	51
Freemasonry, admissions of historians regarding connection with ancient Mysteries	436
Freemasonry a fraternity within a fraternity	433
Freemasonry a religious and philosophic body	434
Freemasonry, body of rose from mediaeval guilds of workmen	433 - 435
Freemasonry, Egyptian Rite of founded by Cagliostro	445
Freemasonry, Elias Ashmole an outstanding link between the Mysteries and	446
Freemasonry founded in a period of political and sociological intrigue	441
Freemasonry, historical elements strangely elusive	435
Freemasonry, modern ritualis of not representative of original rites	435
Freemasonry, original meanings of symbols now lost	436
Freemasonry, presence of transcendentalism in	451
Freemasonry regarded as ethical rather than philosophic or religious	437
Freemasonry, source of the secret doctrine in	437
Freemasonry, symbolism of designed by Rosicrucian adepts from Central Europe	449
Freemasonry the custodian of the secret doctrine of the Mysteries	440
Freemasonry, transcendentalism of Albert Pike	451
Freemasonry, wealth of lies in its mysticism	451
French Revolution the climax of political unrest in Europe	444
Freud, analysis of sex psychology of	342
Friendship, gospel of taught by Jesus	470
Friendship, Pythagoras' definition of	108
Friendship the highest message of yesterday	473
Friendship, why insufficient as an ethical code	474
Fuh-he (See also Pwan-koo)	
Fuh-he related to Noah	237
Gall, symbolism of	197
Generals, reasoning from to particulars the master key to rational cognizance	269
Generals, true knowledge founded upon	269
Generation, descent of the soul into sphere of	409
Generation, heredity limited to sphere of	460

492   LECTURES ON ANCIENT PHILOSOPHY

	PAGE
Generation the law of the body	208
Genius the product of study of symbolism	341
Gichtel one of the early champions of the ideals of democracy	446
God, androgynal nature of	30
God, anthropomorphic, swayed by caprice	153
God, importance of man's concept of	37
God, nature of compared to a focal point by mystics	33
God, nature of symbolized by AIN SOPH	32
God neither masculine nor feminine	30
God, primitive concept of as part God, part demon	158
God revealed as the Great Geometrician by Pythagoras	470
God the first-born of Absolute Self	28
Gods, analysis of natures of essential to understanding of human nature	278
Gods, arcane meaning of the "birthdays" of	280
Gods are cosmic planes or modes of realization	97
Gods are differentiated phases of Universal Consciousness	97
Gods are principles rather than personalities	256
Gods, divine qualities of transmitted to inferior natures through sympathy and participation	281
Gods do not partake of attribute of personality	278
Gods, emanation of from nature of simple Unity	218
Gods, genesis of	34
Gods, how different from man	276 - 287
Gods, incarnation of in man	98
Gods legion in number	279
Gods, mundane, constitution of	304
Gods, nature of	278
Gods not independent forces but Monads	40
Gods, omnipresence and omniscience of	284
Gods, omnipresence of the rational foundation of universal religion	279
Gods, racial, fallacy of	279
Gods, rationality the measure of proximity to	280
Gods, relative order determined by proximity to First Cause	40
Gods symbolic of individualized states of consciousness within nature of Absolute Being	26
Gods symbolic representations of states of relative dependency	43
Gods the phases of cosmic activity	28
Gods those beings in whom knowledge is relatively perfect	56
Gold the alchemical symbol for rational soul	87
Gold the alchemical symbol for Spirit or Self	87
Good, definition of	74
Good, intrinsic nature of	255
Good, the, part of the great Platonic triad	73

	PAGE
Government by philosophy instead of politics	467
Government by the philosophic elect the ideal of the future	464 - 469
Government *of* or *by* the people a vain dream	464
Government, true seat of in the home	468
Grace the redeeming virtue in man	161
Grace, two shades of meaning of	161
Greek philosophy of monotheistic foundation	218
Growth, continuity and consistency factors of	344
Growth, fallacy of growth by change	344
Growth, lower universe ruled by	20
Growth, philosophic, how attained	268
Growth synonymous with increasing inclusiveness	107
Growth the effort of life to objectify its perfection	53
Growth the process whereby man is reconciled to his own trasncendental being	431
Growth the struggle to control environment	51
Guardian spirits (See Daemons)	
Habit the hypothetical urge of SPACE	37
Hades (See also Underworld)	
Hades an environment resulting from crystallization	20
Hand postures significant of states of consciousness	100
Harmony, absence of in human organism	176
Heaven born of Night and Phanes in Orphic theology	222
Heaven called the Great Father in Chinese cosmogony	233
Heaven, Chinese concept of creation of	233
Heaven, illusionary existence of	200
Heaven, location of in Orphic theology	222
Heaven, pagan and Christian concepts contrasted	230
Heaven related to the noumenon of Kant	223
Heaven symbolized by the dot	11
Heaven the plane of spiritual nature of God	11
Heaven, Viking concept of	200
Hell, derivation of word	80
Hell, illusionary existence of	200
Hell symbolized by the circle	11
Heredity, fallacy of	188
Heredity limited to physical tendencies	460
Heredity limited to sphere of generation	460
Heredity only controls those incapable of controlling themselves	460
Hermes, mysteries of statecraft founded by	470
Hermes the lord of souls	395
Hermes the universal instructor	396
Hero a vassal of the gods	291

	PAGE
Hero one devoted to contemplation of the eternal	291
Heydon, John, Rosicrucian affiliations of	448
History and mythology inextricably confused by Christianity	379
Homage of inferior natures for superior natures	281
Honesty, mental, the ideal of philosophy	128
Honey, symbolism of	197
Hope, Maitreya the consciousness of	101
Human nature to be understood through analysis of natures of the gods	278
Humanity, dissimilars exemplified by	286
Hydromancy employed by Pythagoras for divination	357
Idealism contrasted with realism	182
Idealism, office of according to Dr. Durant	187
Idealism indispensable to true interpretation of arts and sciences	326
Idealism the emphasis of life upon its spiritual part	77
Idealism the true interpreter and educator	326
Identity, intellectual concept and gospel of not sufficient	476
Identity, gospel of, the new message	475
Idolatry, pagan attitude toward	366
Idolatry, prevalence of	365
Idolatry the inability to differentiate between symbol and abstract principle	23
Idols signify extensions and modes of consciousness	98
Illusion signified by the duad, or the 2	249
Images signify extension and modes of consciousness	98
Immortality, conscious, attainable through philosophy alone	199
Immortality, meaning of	277
Immortality, physical, the goal of science	186
Immortality the union of soul and body with spirit	394
Immortality, theory of through a succession of lives	457
Immortality, what it consists of	204
Impulse should be reformed, not inhibited	266
Incarnation, definition of	206
Incarnation, number of earth lives in	206
Incarnation of deeds in appropriate vehicles	398
Incarnation of gods in man, meaning of	99
Incubus and succubus the progeny of emotional intemperance	399
Individualism, danger of in rational processes	271
Individualism, isolated, danger of	472
Individualism the outgrowth of principle of separateness	286
Individuality a potentiality in the germ	459
Individuality as a factor in Oriental and Occidental philosophy	150
Individuality, creation of by the spiritual causal nature	89
Individuality, dissolution of	205

	PAGE
Individuality nonexistent in realm of consciousness	86
Inductive reasoning declared by Socrates to be instrument of philosophy	265
Inductive reasoning, liberation of rationality through	266
Inductive reasoning, mental reactions caused by	275
Inductive reasoning, purpose of	274
Inertia the characteristic attribute of form	12 - 76
Inferiority complex, definition of	134
Inferiority-inferiority complex, definition of	134
Inferiority-superiority complex, definition of	134
Inhibition, futility of to liberate the soul	265
Initiation in caverns, significance of	196
Initiation of Apuleius in Temple of Isis	453
Initiation, severity of ordeals in pagan rites	452
Initiatory rites, dancing and music employed in	369
Initiative, how destroyed by form	79
Inspiration symbolized by inverted pyramid	282
Instinct the urge of irrational natures to act in a rational manner	293
Intellect distinguished from consciousness	64 - 70
Intellect likened to the monad	260
Intellect one of seven grand divisions of existence, according to Neoplatonists	219
Intelligence, recognition of in lower kingdoms	112
Intelligence the mediatory element between spirit and matter	54
Intelligence the highest manifestation of matter	18
Intelligence, universal, symbolized by line	6
Interest as a philosophical factor	130
Interest stimulated by the study of philosophy	340
Interest the directing factor in observation	130
Interpretation a preponderant factor in modern education	325
Intuition, source of in the soul	300
Inventory of assets and liabilities—mental, emotional, and physical	135
Involution, definition of	78
Involution is activity outward from self	4
Involution of the soul into sphere of generation	409 - 410
Involution the inclination of the rational soul toward diversity	268
Irony declared by Socrates to be instrument of philosophy	265
Irony, liberation of rationality through	266
Ishtar, descent of symbolic of "fall" of the soul	305
Ishtar, meaning of the allegory of	77
Jack and the beanstalk, symbolism of allegory of	428
Jam-pa (Se Maitreya)	
Jehova the Lord of Form	81
Jesus, gospel of friendship taught by	470

	PAGE
Jizo, the god of little children	100
Jonson (Ben), one of the early champions of ideals of democracy	444
Judo, principle of equilibrium exploited in	258
Jujutsu, principle of equilibrium exploited in	258
Jupiter, analogy of in individual life	16 - 17
Jupiter, significance of as lord of the sun	15
Jupiter the Lord of Form	81
Jupiter, trinity of	14
Justice, gospel of enunciated by Socrates	470
Justice, material universe controlled by	81
Justice why blindfolded	133
Kalpa, calculation of time by	228 - 235
Karma, Law of	212
"Keyhole" philosophers, arcane significance of	357
Kheen the active principle in Chinese cosmogony	233
Khunrath, Henry, Rosicrucian affiliations of	448
Khwan the receptive principle in Chinese cosmogony	233
Khwan, trigrams of in Chinese cosmogony	233
Knights Templars, Mysteries of Egypt and Persia brought to Europe by	438
Knower, rational, represented in Cabirian Rite by diminutive figure	392
Knowledge (See also Wisdom)	
Knowledge, absolute, incomprehensible to the physical (irrational) mind	340
Knowledge, arcane method employed by Mysteries to communicate	317 - 321
Knowledge, attainability of through correct method of approach	403
Knowledge considered by Pythagoras unattainable without aesthetics	320
Knowledge differentiated from understanding	104
Knowledge, division of into science, philosophy and theology	118
Knowledge, esoteric, a knowledge of inherent nature of knowledge	314 - 317
Knowledge, esoteric, limited to issues of philosophy and religion	314
Knowledge essential to right living	193
Knowledge, exoteric, the knowledge of particulars	314
Knowledge founded upon generals, not particulars	269
Knowledge, four states of, according to Pythagoras	260
Knowledge, hope of vested in man's knowledge of self	403
Knowledge not the common property of all	315
Knowledge, phases of represented by science, theology, and philosophy	9
Knowledge, sciences the practical phases of	314
Knowledge, struggle for identical with struggle for survvial	348

INDEX 497

	PAGE
Knowledge the outgrowth of intellectual comprehension	66
Kundalini, symbolism of	423
Kwan-Yin (Kwannon), the Goddess of Mercy	99
Ladder, Jacob's a symbolic mountain or pyramid	416
Ladder symbolic of bridge of reason	426
Ladder symbolic of descent of soul into sphere of generation	409
Ladder symbolic of thread of the generating soul	425
Ladder, symbolism of ascent of	425
Lafayette, Marquis de, one of early champions of ideals of democracy	446
Language of initiates called Senzar	10
Language, unspoken, of philosophy	320
Law, divine, the keynote of the Causal Universe	153
Law, material universe controlled by	81
Law of analogy, importance of	35
Law of periodicity the habit of SPACE	36
Law of spirit governs Causal Universe	154
Law the keynote of the Inferior Universe	154
Laws of Nature govern Inferior Universe	154
Liberation attained through projection of consciousness	91
Liberation, philosophic, achieved through realization of kinship with all	477
Life a symbol of presence of God	359
Life and death administered by the soul, according to the Greeks	388
Life and form, manner of association of	194
Life, characteristics of	194
Life, concept of annihilated through gospel of identity	478
Life, generation of	277
Life one of seven grand division of existence, according to Neoplatonists	219
Light the symbol of manifesting spirit	49
Line symbolic of earth	11
Line symbolic of government by church	83
Line symbolic of means	5
Line symbolic of universal intelligence	7
Literalist an inveterate profaner of the beautiful	350
Logic the first step toward realization	121
Love a greater riddle than life	151
Love a symbol of understanding of God	259
Love defined by Plato as the longing of diversity for unity	209
Love, duality of nature as symbolized by Cupid	309
Love, human, definition of	211
Love, stimulation of rational soul through	163
Love the keynote of the Intermediate Sphere	154

	PAGE
Love the law of the soul	208
Love the synchronizing urge of the sphere of mediation	154
Luck, element of in destiny	429
Maier, Michael, Rosicrucian affiliations of	449
Maimonides' statement regarding secret import of the Scriptures	351
Maitreya the Buddhist Messiah	101
Maitreya the consciousness of hope	101
Maitreya the consciousness of noble destiny	101
Man, analogy between and the universe	401
Man not essentially a personality but a spirit	405
Man, objective, founded in reaction of the senses	393 - 398
Man the quintessence of all the elements	401
Manu, elements of Hindu Brahmanism embodied in	470
Manus the First Men of each root race	236
Marlowe one of the early champions of ideals of democracy	444
Marriage of the gods, significance of	210
Masculine, why considered predominant attribute of Deity	31
Masonry (See Freemasonry)	
Mason's marks in King James edition of Bible	447
Material sciences, mental and spiritual value of	122
Materialism the emphasis of life upon its material part	77
Mathematics, analogy of to the dot of the fundamental symbolic triad	123
Mathematics, Divine, concerned with order and arrangement of corporeal bodies	245
Mathematics, esoteric principles of confused with exoteric by Greeks	245
Mathematics, exactness the characteristic of	123
Mathematics, knowledge of a requisite for admission to Pythagorean school	122
Mathematics, mysteries of causal sphere revealed by	123
Mathematics, Proclus' encomium to science of	254
Mathematics, study of a stimu'us to rationality	322
Mathematics, sympathetic bond with rational soul	258
Mathematics the science of magnitudes and multitudes	241
Mathematics the symbol of the procedure of Being	124
Mathematics, why a divine science	241
Matter (See also Form)	
Matter, contraction the natural tendency of	50
Matter, eternal duration of	232
Matter, intelligence the highest manifestation of	18
Matter not synonymous with form	7
Matter synonymous with Absolute	232
Matter the negative manifestation of SPACE	2
Matter the Supreme God of Chinese theogony	233

	PAGE
Maya, significance of in connection with birth of Savior-Gods	6
Maya the illusions of diversity	6
Medallions, therapeutic powers of	355
Meditation, necessity for principle of	55
Memory, past, governed by Hermes	396
Mental faculties equilibrated by discrimination	136
Mental reactions caused by inductive reasoning	274
Mercury of the alchemists the sidereal nature of man	386
Metempsychosis, arcane meaning of Pythagorean doctrine of	394
Metempsychosis, erroneous concept of	205
Microcosm, man philosophically likened to the	385
Mind likened to two-faced Roman god Janus	18
Mind, mortal and immortal phases of	18
Mind, physical (irrational), incapable of comprehending absolute knowledge	340
Mind the martyred Savior-God	63
Mind, trinity of	14
Mohammed, philosophy of retribution and righteous destiny brought by	470
Molay, Jacques de, burning of by Holy Inquisition	438
Monad (See also Emanationism)	
Monad likened to intellect	260
Monads (See also Unities and Emanationism)	
Monads, doctrines of in procession of deified natures from Deity	217
Monads, three, constituting triune nature of man	385
Monadology the basic doctrine of Greek theology	217
Monotheism, fundamental nature of	26
Monotheism manifested in Greek philosophy through complex polytheism	218
Monotheistic foundation of Greek philosophy	218
Montaigne one of the early champions of the ideals of democracy	444
Moral sense destroyed through premise of supremacy of matter	461
More one of the early champions of the ideals of democracy	446
More's *Utopia* a picture of a new age to be	443
Mother, Great, synonymous with Earth in Chinese cosmogony	233
Motion and Number of kindred nature	242
Motive, right, the unifying power of the human faculties	178
Motives, search for promoted by study of symbolism	340
Mountains, sacred, symbolism of	416 - 426
Multiplication, philosophic, the product cannot exceed 1, or wholeness	244
Music ameliorates the austerity of number	125
Music, analogy of to the line of the fundamental symbolic triad	123
Music an important element in ancient ritualism	371

	PAGE
Music, decline of with invention of writing	370
Music employed in initiatory rites of the Mysteries	371
Music, esoteric principles of confused with exoteric by Greeks	245
Music, knowledge of a requisite for admission to Pythagorean school	122
Music, mysteries of Intermediate Sphere revealed by	123
Music, Real and ideal blended in	125
Music, sublimation of feeling effected by	323
Music reveals the moods of the Causal Nature	125
Music the harmony of sounds	370
Music the stimulus of lofty emotional reactions	125
Mudras significant of states of consciousness	100
Mysteries, abolition of symbolized by rending the Temple veil	380
Mysteries, arcane methods of communicating knowledge of to neophyte	317 - 321
Mysteries, connection with admitted by historians of Freemasonry	436
Mysteries, fall of from treachery and profanation	380
Mysteries not fraternal or political fundamentally	437
Mysteries, perpetuation of the secret doctrine of world religions	440
Mysteries, twofold phase of wisdom of	314 - 315
Mystery Plays a perpetuation of ancient Gnostic practices	380
Mythology and history inextricably confused by Christianity	379
Myths the outer veils of the Mysteries	379
Naiades, symbolism of	196
National exploitation the outcome of recognition of false principle of diversity	466
National jealousy outlawed by unification of all peoples	467
Nature one of seven grand divisions of existence, according to Neoplatonists	219
Necessity, Cycle of, meaning of	199
Necessity, Cycle of, release from	204
Nectar, symbolism of	198
Negation, employment of to define Absolute	255
Neophyte, severity of ordeals undergone in initiation into pagan rites	452
Neoplatonism based upon revelations of Orpheus and erudition of Plato	217
Neoplatonism, seven grand divisions of existence according to	219
Neptune, symbolism of	16
Neptune the lord of the inferior world	18
Nerves the impulse carriers of consciousness	52
Nerves the link between consciousness and environment	52
New Atlantis, Bacon's a prophecy of the coming age	444
Nirvana, absorption into	93
Nirvana, achievement of	103 - 115 - 116

	PAGE
Nirvana represents ultimate annihilation of every interval of quality	252
Noumenon related to Heaven	223
Number and Motion of kindred nature	242
Number identified by Pythagoreans with Unity	242
Number the monads from which numbers are suspended	242
Number, why considered synonymous with God	242
Numbers, diversity a property of	249
Numbers fractional parts and not multiples of the 1, according to philosophy	244
Numbers, Numerative Soul gives form and subsistence to	261
Numbers related to forms by the Pythagoreans	259
Numbers, revelation of doctrine of perfections by	256
Numbers the diversified elements suspended from monad of Number	242
Numerative Soul gives form and subsistence to numbers	261
Nymphs, symbolism of	196
Observation a prerequisite of knowledge	128
Observation directionalized by interest	130
Observation, function of	131
Observation, generalizing effect of	130
Observation the ability to see *through* things	129
Olive, symbolism of	198
One said to be Unity established in place	243
One the capstone of pyramid of numbers	73
One of the first manifestation of principle of Number	243
One, the, part of the great Platonic triad	73
One, Plato's concept of the	73
One, the, represented by dot	73
One, the, the highest definable state	73
Opinion likened to triad	260
Oracle, meaning of	57
Oracles, explanation of phenomenon of	357
Originality the product of study of symbolism	341
Orpheus, gospel of beauty taught by	470
Orphic Egg, formed by action of Aether upon Chaos	221
Orphic theology, analogies in Brahmanism	226
Orphic theology, origin of in Vedic writings	224
Oversoul (See also Daemon)	
Oversoul, Emerson's definition of	294
Pagan philosophy, idealism of	148
Pagan source of Christian doctrines	148
Pain, mission of	80
Paracelsus, initiation of by the Arabians	441

	PAGE
Participation a medium by which divine qualities are transmitted to inferior natures	281
Particulars, danger of reasoning from to generals	269
Particulars, overemphasis of responsible for present confusion of science	269
Patriotism essentially national egotism	109
Pedantism, Pope's excoriation of	329
Perfection represented by image of Buddha	99
Perfection the only real freedom	51
Perfection, ways or disciplines of represented by images of Bodhisattvas	99, 113
Perfections, doctrine of, as revealed by numbers	256
Periodicity, law of, the habit of SPACE	36
Permanence the law of spirit	248
Personal idolatry, measures adopted by Pythagoras to avoid	376
Personality a potentiality in the germ	459
Personality, creation of by the spiritual causal nature	89
Personality nonexistent in realm of consciousness	86 - 87
Personality not an attribute of the gods	278 - 279
Personality of God responsible for divine caprice	152
Personality of Pythagoras concealed by veil	376
Personality, survival of throughout period of incarnation	206
Phallic import of symbolism	342
Phanes, birth of from the Cosmic Egg	221
Phenomenon related to Earth	223
Philalethes, Eugenius, letter of addressed to his Masonic Brethren	450
Philalethes, Eugenius, Rosicrucian affiliations of	448
Philosopher the idealist	469
Philosophers' Stone symbolic of liberation	88
Philosophers' Stone the blending of the threefold spirit of man	386
Philosophic atheism the basis of Greek philosophy	218
Philosophic death the complete severance of all connection between the soul and its bodies	389
Philosophy, Christian, eclectic nature of	147
Philosophy, conscious immortality conferred by	199
Philosophy contrasted with theology	9
Philosophy, essential nature of unchangeable	8
Philosophy, goal of to establish supremacy of life and rule of creation through reason	461
Philosophy, interest stimulated by study of	340
Philosophy never free from involvements of mind	8
Philosophy one of the divisions of knowledge	118
Philosophy, pagan, idealism of	148
Philosophy, seeming austerity of	126

	PAGE
Philosophy, stimulation of rational soul through	163
Philosophy, symbolism the language of	339
Philosophy symbolized by dot	7
Philosophy the closest approach to Reality	8
Philosophy the mental bodies of knowledge	9
Philosophy the source of the camaraderie of the spirit	127
Physical immortality the goal of science	186
Physical life begins where matter dominates spirit	11
Physical nature the vehicle by which rational nature renders its findings communicable	405
Pike, Albert, contribution of to Freemasonry	451
Place, concept of common to theology	279 - 283
Place, concept of relatively unimportant in philosophy	283
Place one of the illusions of diversity	6
Planets symbols of soul	417
Platitude philosophically unsound	268
Plato theology of summarized by Thomas Taylor	217
Plato's definition of wisdom	287
Pleasanton, discovery by of repolarization of man through vice or excess	397
Plotinus' statement regarding descent of soul into sphere of generation	409
Pluto the regent of death	20
Poetry an important element in ancient ritualism	370
Poetry, decline of with invention of writing	370
Poetry the rhythm of words	370
Polarity, principle of symbolized by two pyramids	283
Politics the philosophy of government	467
Polytheism a veneration for causal agencies	27
Polytheism, philosophic aspect of	27
Polytheism the personnel of cosmic government	26
Polytheism the outgrowth of a fundamental monotheism	26
Pontifex Maximus, analogous to the hidden and unknowable Light	391
Pope's excoriation of pedantism	329
Prejudice as a philosophical factor	130 - 134
Pressure of environment, how determined	50
Priesthood, orders of patterned after the human body	391
Principle of Principles one of seven grand divisions of existence, according to Neoplatonism	219
Principle of Principles, procession of deified natures from	217
Principle of Principles the Supreme Deity of philosophy	218
Principle, universality of	283
Priority, determination of	41
Proclus' encomium to science of mathematics	254

	PAGE
Providence, acts of the will of the soul for the body	388
Providence, meaning of	429
Psyche, allegory of sets forth mystery of soul	302
Ptolemaic system of astronomy, esoteric meaning of	102-104
Pwan-koo related to Adam	237
Pwan-koo related to the Demiurgus	234
Pwan-koo the Monad of human generation	236
Pyramid, inverted, the symbol of inspiration	282
Pyramid symbolic of axis mountain of the world	416-426
Pyramid the symbol of aspiration	426
Pyramid the symbol of rationalized natures	427
Pyramid, upright, the symbol of aspiration	282
Pyramid, use of in Mithraic rites	416
Pyramids, principle of polarity symbolized by	283
Pyrolatry one of the oldest forms of religious expression	49
Pythagoras, employment of dramatics by, for purposes of instruction	375
Pythagoras, measures adopted by to prevent personal idolatry	376
Quality interval the barrier between the divine and inferior natures	286
Quality, interval of, relation of fourth dimension	251
Quality, method of measuring	253
Quality of thought the measure of man's status in cosmos	56
Ra, derivation of the word	16
Racial spirit, birth of	110
Raleigh (Sir Walter) one of the early champions of the ideals of democracy	443
Raleigh, execution for high treason	443
Rational cognizance, establishment of mind in unities the masterkey to	269
Rational Knower represented by diminutive figure in Cabirian Rite	392
Rational nature dependent upon physical vehicles to render its findings communicable	405
Rational processes, danger of individualism in	271
Rational soul, Christ personification of qualities of	160
Rational soul, germ of stimulated in three ways	163
Rational soul, Greek concept of	162
Rational soul, sympathetic bond with mathematics	258
Rational soul the most precious attribute of spirit	390
Rationality, arts and sciences a definite stimulus to sensitivity of	322
Rationality, awakening of the subject of ancient allegory	425
Rationality, liberation of through irony and induction	266
Rationality, stimulation of by environment	378
Rationality symbolized by air	285
Rationality the first step towards realization	121

	PAGE
Rationality the measure of proximity to the gods	280
Rationality, veneration for universality of productive of philosophy of daemons	292
Rationalized natures symbolized by pyramid	427
Realism contrasted with idealism	182
Realism, office of, according to Dr. Durant	187
Reality dependent upon permanence	5
Reality most closely approached by philosophy	8
Reality signified by the monad, or the 1	249
Reality, unaging quality of	248
Realization contrasted with affirmation	104
Realization dependent upon philosophic disciplines	121
Realization, diagrammatic unfoldment of	106
Realization, meaning of	105 - 118
Realization, powers conferred by	104
Realization the measure of individual magnitude	105
Realization, two paths of	105
Reason symbolized by ladder	426
Reason the law of the intellect	208
Reasoning *a posteriori* characteristics of modern thought	272
Reasoning *a priori* characteristic of ancient Mysteries	272
Reasoning, deductive, purpose of to establish consciousness at point of equilibrium	274
Reasoning, inductive, purpose of	274
Redemption, Christian theory of unique	145
Redemption the awakening of divine potentialities in man through aspiration	167
Redemption, three major doctrines of	150
Refinement of rationality effected through aesthetics	323
Reincarnation, descent of soul into birth signified by	396
Reincarnation, meaning of	89
Reincarnations, number of shortened by Mysteries	397
Relationships, illusion of dispelled by discrimination	137
Relativity, theory of	250
Religion, universal, omnipresence of the gods the rational foundation of	279
Religions, world, perpetuate the secret doctrine of the Mysteries	440
Renunciation taught by Buddha	470
Resurrection, real import of	207
Retribution, philosophy of brought by Mohammed	470
Retrospection, mental reactions caused by	275
Revelation, spiritual, none sufficiently strong to withstand weakness of the flesh	473
Revelations the keynotes of philosophic thought	470

	PAGE
Rhythm, divine, the salient point of Taoism	125
Right motive the unifying power of the human faculties	178
Ritualism a channel of self-expression	382
Ritualism an emotional expression	368
Ritualism essential to philosophy	363
Ritualism, purpose of to create atmosphere of sanctity	368
Ritualism the science of divine dramatics	379
Ritualism, unpopularity of	361
Rituals of Mysteries first fabricated to reveal principles of universal order	374
Rituals rendered ineffective through inability to interpret their symbolism	381
Rituals, scientific use of by Pythagoras in spiritual education	377
Rosencreutz, Christian, initiation of into the Great Work	440
Rosencreutz, Christian, vision of the "hanging" men in House of Initiation	420
Rosicrucians, Mysteries of Egypt and Persia brought to Europe by	438
Rosicrucians one of the sources of the secret doctrine of Freemasonry	437 - 449
Rudra (See Shiva)	
St. Germain, Comte de, connection of with Freemasonry	435 - 441
St. Germain one of the early champions of the ideals of democracy	446
St. Martin, connection of with Freemasonry	435
Salt of the alchemists the terrestrial nature of man	386
Salvation, biological, significance of	401
Salvation, Christian theory of unique	145
Salvation, exactness a prerequisite of philosophy of	123
Salvation, natural, doctrine of	458
Salvation, origin of word	11
Salvation the escape of the eternal Knower from sheath of materiality	160
Salvation, three major doctrines of	150
Savior-Gods always born out of Maya	6
Savior-Gods, why termed *Beautiful*	74
Savior, Universal, description of	167
Science likened to duad	260
Science, objective phenomena the province of	314
Science one of the divisions of knowledge	118
Science, present confusion in due to overemphasis of particulars	270
Science symbolized by circle	8
Science the physical body of knowledge	9
Sciences, material, mental and spiritual value of	122
Sciences the practical phases of knowledge	313

INDEX

	PAGE
Scriptures, literal absurdities of transmuted into allegorical realities by symbolism	352
Scriptures, Maimonides' statement regarding secret import of	351
Scriptures writing concerned with philosophic anatomy	399
Sculpture, refining effect of upon rational faculties	322
Self (individual) represented by dot	4
Self, level of determined by quality of realization	102
Self synonymous with SPACE	2
Self, unaging quality of the	248
Selfishness annihilated through gospel of identity	477
Selfishness the disintegrating element in empire	463
Sense likened to tetrad	260
Senzar the language of the initiates	10
Service, stimulation of rational soul through	163
Sex in an undivided state in spirit	210
Sex psychology of Freud analyzed	342
Sex, twofold expression of in man	211
Shang-te, Chinese anthropomorphic deity	233
Shepherd's crook symbolic of authority of Demiurgus	82
Shinto Mysteries, symbolism of Goddess of the Sun in	424
Shiva symbolic of form	75
Shiva the destroying aspect of Brahmanic triad	225
Shrine, meaning of	58
Simplicity the characteristic of Cause	295
Simplicity the chief prerequisite of beauty	171
Six, natal daemon represented by spirit of the	291
Skeleton the symbol of form	75
Sky Emperor, Chinese anthropomorphic deity	233
Sleep, analogy of to Absolute	35
Society of Unknown Philosophers, activities of in political and religious reformation of Europe	447
Society of Unknown Philosophers, domination of by ecclesiasticism	448
Socrates, gospel of justice enunciated by	470
Solomon's Temple built by Dionysians	437
Sophists, C. R. C.'s vision of in House of Initiation	420
Sorcerer a person severed from all relations with its divine part through death of the soul	390
Soul, absorption of man's bodies into	299
Soul, age of, how measured	253
Soul an astral spirit	385
Soul, animal, the basis of Freud's sex psychology	342
Soul, arcane meaning of Pythagorean doctrine of transmigration of	394
Soul, awakening of attributes of symbolized in ancient allegory	425

	PAGE
Soul, death of, the second death	391
Soul, descent of, cryptic statements of Heraclites and Empedocles regarding	410
Soul, descent of into sphere of generation	410
Soul, descent of symbolized by ladder	409
Soul, descent of through orbits of the divine planets	305
Soul, evolution of	411
Soul, indivisibility of	86
Soul, intrinsic nature of	298
Soul, involution of	310
Soul, irrational definition of	61
Soul, irrational, related to Yin of Chinese	234
Soul, liberated, Blavatsky's statement concerning return of	410
Soul, liberation of through contemplation of intellect	304
Soul, meaning of so-called "fall" of	304
Soul, misdirected homage to	306
Soul, mystery of set forth in allegory of Cupid and Psyche	302
Soul, number of earth lives in incarnation of	206
Soul, Numerative, gives form and subsistence to numbers	261
Soul occupies place midway between life and form	298
Soul one of seven grand divisions of existence, according to Neoplatonists	219
Soul one of the three major elements in occult constitution of man	391
Soul, Platonically defined as "the first of bodies"	196
Soul, rational, Christ personification of qualities of	161
Soul, rational, definition of	61
Soul, rational, germ of stimulated in three ways	163
Soul, rational, Greek concept of	162
Soul, rational, related to Yang of Chinese	234
Soul, rational, sympathetic bond with mathematics	258
Soul, rational, the most precious attribute of the spirit	390
Soul symbolized as two creatures	300
Soul symbolized by the beanstalk	428
Soul symbolized by the planets	416
Soul the individualized source of bodily life	196
Soul the source of intuition and conscience	300
Souls, Hermes the divinity presiding over destinies of	395
Souls, why termed *Naiades* or *Nymphs*	196
SPACE (See also Absolute; Cause, First)	
SPACE, habit the hypothetical urge of	36
SPACE, permanence of contrasted with form	40
SPACE symbolized by blank sheet of paper	1-2
SPACE synonymous with Self	2
SPACE the origin and destiny of all things	1-2

	PAGE
SPACE unfathomable by human intellect	25
Spirit dependent upon generation for manifestation in form	460
Spirit, expansion the natural tendency of	50
Spirit (individualized) represented by dot	6
Spirit, indivisibility of	86
Spirit of man divided into divine, soul, and body natures	387
Spirit, soul, and body the major elements in occult constitution of man	391
Spirit symbolized by the stars	417
Spirit the causal nature permeating all life	86
Spirit the first limitation of Self	3
Spirit the level of Self determined by quality of realization	102
Spirit the positive manifestation of SPACE	2
Spirit, trinity of	14
Spirit, trinity of in man	386
Spirituality, germ of awakened in three ways	162
Staff, Anubis-headed, symbolic of authority of Demiurgus	82
Stars, figures of used to ornament cloaks of candidates	416
Stars symbols of spirit	417
Stone, Philosophers', the blending of the threefold spirit of man	376
Substraction, philosophic, the remainder always 1, or wholeness	244
Succubus and incubus the progeny of emotional intemperance	399
Sudras emancipated from limitation by Buddhism	412
Sudras, victimization of by Brahmins	412
Suffering, mission of	80
Suicide considered a misdirection of power by the ancients	389
Suicide permissible under five conditions, according to the Greeks	389
Suicide the death in which body casts off the soul	389
Sulphur of the alchemists the celestial nature of man	386
Sun, astronomical symbol of	15
Sun, phases of represented by Jupiter, Neptune, and Pluto	14
Superiority-superiority complex, definition of	134
Supermen the instructors of humanity	59
Survival, struggle for identical with struggle for knowledge	348
Symbolism a divine language	358
Symbolism, arcana of ancient philosophy preserved inviolate by	347
Symbolism, difference between and caricature	338
Symbolism, figures of reflect the celestial will	358
Symbolism, literal absurdities of Scriptures transmuted into allegorical realities by	352
Symbolism occupies middle ground between knowledge and ignorance	355
Symbolism of ritualism rendered ineffective through lack of interpretation	381

	PAGE
Symbolism, phallic import of	342
Symbolism, study of productive of originality and genius	341
Symbolism, study of promotes search for hidden motives	340
Symbolism, the ancient Alphabet of Wisdom	9
Symbolism the language of philosophy	339
Symbolism the perfect medium of education	339 - 341
Symbolism, triangular foundation of	354
Symbolism, unpopularity of	361
Symbolism, value of in education	339 - 341
Symbols are forms designed to portray abstract qualities	337
Symbols, dream, of Freud analyzed	342
Symbols employed by Phrygian Dactyls because of their therapeutic powers	355
Symbols, oracular forms	357
Symbols, scientific use of by Pythagoras in spiritual education	377
Symbols, significance of simple and compound	337
Symbols, variety of interpretations explained	343
Symbols, why interpretations concerning were circulated by the Mysteries	347
Sympathy a medium by which divine qualities are transmitted to inferior natures	281
Synthesis the supreme need of modern philosophy	471
Talismans, therapeutic powers of	355
Talking images, explanation of phenomena of	356
Taoism, divine rhythm the chief doctrine of	125
Technique, place of in art	172
Telepathy employed in Mysteries to communicate knowledge to neophyte	317 - 321
Templars, Knights, Mysteries of Egypt and Persia brought to Europe by	438
Templars, Knights, reason for persecution of by the church	438
Tetractys, symbolism of	260
Tetrad likened to sense	260
Tetrad, why declared to be the symbol of God	260
Theologies, pagan and Christian contrasted	230
Theology a servant to concept of place	283
Theology contrasted with philosophy	8
Theology, Greek, doctrine of unities the basic doctrine of	218
Theology of Plato summarized by Thomas Taylor	217
Theology one of the divisions of knowledge	118
Theology the emotional body of knowledge	9
Theory of relativity	250
Therapeutic powers of symbols	355

	Page
Thinking, right, consists in keeping mentally upon plane of greatest inclusiveness	272
Thought, body of paralyzed rather than stimulated by the philosopher	406
Thought, conveyance of through forms considered necessary by science	318
Thought, shallowness of due to eclecticism	345
Thought the compensation of rational endeavor	405
Tien the Supreme God of Chinese theogony	233
Time as a factor in religious place	283 - 284
Time, calculation of by Kalpas	228 - 234
Time considered as the Absolute by the Orphics	220
Time, illusion of	247
Time, immortals unaffected by	280
Time one of the illusions of diversity	6
Time, relation of to the fourth dimension	249
Time restores life to perfect wholeness by destroying form	248
Time symbolic of relationship between abiding principles and nonabiding personalities	280
Time the acid test of permanence	247
Time the measure of parts or divisions	248
Time, three hypothetical intervals of	246
Totem analogous to natal daemon of the Greeks	289
Transcendentalism, antipathy of modern mind to	451
Transcendentalism of Albert Pike	451
Transcendentalism, presence of in Freemasonry	451
Transmigration, arcane meaning of Pythagorean doctrine of	394
Triad likened to opinion	260
Triads, relationship of the true basis of philosophic procedure	142
Triangular foundation of all existence	53
Trinity, first, of SPACE, and Matter	2
Trinity of dot, line, and circle of both universal and individual application	20
Trinity of Father, Power and Mind	12
Trinity of Zeus	14
Truth, revelations of a re-emphasis of an ever-existing doctrine	439
Truth the way of God in *all* things	242
Truth the way of God in *particular* things	243
Typhon symbolic of form	75
Ultimates only definable in terms of negation	25
Understanding differentiated from knowledge	104
Understanding the one true light of universe	83
Understanding the outgrowth of consciousness	66
Underworld the realm of form	76

	PAGE
Unities (See also Monads)	
Unities, establishment of mind in the masterkey to rational cognizance	269
Unities the basic doctrine of Greek theology	217
Unity identified with Number by the Pythagoreans	242
Unity of life, recognition of true democracy	476
Unity, realization of the basis of philosophic growth	268
Unity synonymous with Cause	245
Universal Savior, description of	167
Universal Self, diffusion of throughout illusionary universe	103
Universe, pagan and Christian concepts contrasted	230
Urns of prophecy, explanation of phenomenon	356
Utility, dependency of upon beauty and virtue	173
Utopia (More's) a picture of a new age	443
Vampire a person severed from all relations with its divine part through death of the soul	390
Veil, Temple, rending of symbolic of abolition of the Mysteries	380
Veneration to be shown through some expression of the beautiful	363
Venus, twofold phase of	307
Vicarious atonement based upon precedency of love over law	151
Vicarious atonement, doctrine of the most vicious of all superstitions	148
Vicarious atonement, evils of doctrine of	149
Vicarious atonement, source of in pagan philosophy	153
Virtue, dependency of upon beauty and utility	173
Virtue the bridge over which consciousness passes to union with spiritual cause	391
Vishnu the preserving aspect of Brahmanic triad	225
War a hereditary taint in the social structure	472
Washington one of the early champions of the ideals of democracy	446
Water symbolic of emotion	19
Web, symbolism of spinning of	197
Werewolf a person severed from all relations with its divine part through death of the soul	390
Wholeness, all-pervading and permanent quality of	248
Wholeness an archetypal quality	246
Wholeness an attribute of Deity	246
Wholeness, archetypal quality of shared by forms	246
Wisdom, Plato's definition of	313
Wisdom the source of all sciences	313
Works, ineffectiveness of emphasized by St. Paul	155
Works, stimulation of rational soul through	163
World, age and duration of, according to Brahmins	228
World a symbol of permanence of God	359

	PAGE
Worlds, genesis of	34
Worship, pagan concept of	366
Worship, the spirit of beauty essence of	365
Worship to be shown through some expression of the beautiful	363
Writing, invention of, the cause of decline of interpretive arts	370
Yang related to the rational soul of Greeks	234
Yang the subtle Air of spirit	234
Yih King, exposition of Chinese cosmogony in	230
Yin related to the irrational souls of Greeks	234
Yin the coarse Air of matter	234
Yugas, method of calculating time by	228 - 234
Zeus, establishment of physical universe by	223
Zeus the Lord of Form	81
Zeus, trinity of	14

ABOUT THE AUTHOR

Manly P. Hall (1901–1990), widely regarded as a sage and teacher steeped in the wisdom of antiquity, was one of the leading esoteric scholars of the twentieth century. His many books include the masterpiece of symbolic philosophy, *The Secret Teachings of All Ages*. In 1934, he founded the Philosophical Research Society, which continues his educational mission today.

An independent scholar, Hall always emphasized the practical aspects of philosophy and religion as they apply to daily living. He restated for modern man those spiritual and ethical doctrines that have given humanity its noblest ideals and most adequate codes of conduct. Believing that philosophy is a working tool to help the individual in building a solid foundation for his dreams and purposes, Hall steadfastly sought recognition of the belief that world civilization can be perfected only when human beings meet on a common ground of intelligence, cooperation, and worthy purpose.

The Philosophical Research Society (www.prs.org) is a nonprofit organization dedicated to assisting thoughtful persons to live more graciously and constructively in a confused and troubled world. The Society is entirely free from educational, political, or ecclesiastical control. Dedicated to an idealistic approach to the solution of human problems, the Society's program stresses the need for the integration of religion, philosophy, and the science of psychology into one system of instruction. The goal of this instruction is to enable the individual to develop a mature philosophy of life, to recognize his proper responsibilities and opportunities, and to understand and appreciate his place in the unfolding universal pattern.

Manly P. Hall's legacy also includes the nation's premier educational institution dedicated solely to the wisdom traditions and leading-edge consciousness studies. **The University of Philosophical Research** (www.uprs.edu) in Los Angeles offers state-approved master's degree programs in consciousness studies and transformational psychology.

www.ingramcontent.com/pod-product-compliance
Lightning Source LLC
Chambersburg PA
CBHW022111080426
42734CB00006B/86